Lecture Notes in Computer Science 15754

Founding Editors

Gerhard Goos
Juris Hartmanis

Editorial Board Members

Elisa Bertino, *Purdue University, West Lafayette, IN, USA*
Wen Gao, *Peking University, Beijing, China*
Bernhard Steffen , *TU Dortmund University, Dortmund, Germany*
Moti Yung , *Columbia University, New York, NY, USA*

The series Lecture Notes in Computer Science (LNCS), including its subseries Lecture Notes in Artificial Intelligence (LNAI) and Lecture Notes in Bioinformatics (LNBI), has established itself as a medium for the publication of new developments in computer science and information technology research, teaching, and education.

LNCS enjoys close cooperation with the computer science R & D community, the series counts many renowned academics among its volume editors and paper authors, and collaborates with prestigious societies. Its mission is to serve this international community by providing an invaluable service, mainly focused on the publication of conference and workshop proceedings and postproceedings. LNCS commenced publication in 1973.

Bernhard Haslhofer · Java Xu · Friedhelm Victor ·
Massimo Bartoletti · Andrea Bracciali ·
Kanta Matsuura · Jarek Nabrzyski ·
Vero Estrada-Galiñanes · Claudio Tessone ·
Jurlind Budurushi · Karola Marky
Editors

Financial Cryptography and Data Security

FC 2025 International Workshops

CoDecFin, FinTeAchin, VOTING
Miyakojima, Japan, April 18, 2025
Revised Selected Papers, Part II

Editors
Bernhard Haslhofer
Complexity Science Hub
Vienna, Austria

Friedhelm Victor
TRM Labs
San Francisco, CA, USA

Andrea Bracciali
Università di Torino
Turin, Italy

Jarek Nabrzyski
University of Notre Dame
Notre Dame, IN, USA

Claudio Tessone
University of Zurich
Zurich, Switzerland

Karola Marky
Ruhr-Universität Bochum
Bochum, Germany

Java Xu
University College London
London, UK

Massimo Bartoletti
Università degli Studi di Cagliari
Cagliari, Italy

Kanta Matsuura
The University of Tokyo
Tokyo, Japan

Vero Estrada-Galiñanes
Neuchâtel, Switzerland

Jurlind Budurushi
University of Karlsruhe
Karlsruhe, Germany

ISSN 0302-9743　　　　　ISSN 1611-3349　(electronic)
Lecture Notes in Computer Science
ISBN 978-3-032-00494-9　　ISBN 978-3-032-00495-6　(eBook)
https://doi.org/10.1007/978-3-032-00495-6

© International Financial Cryptography Association 2026

This work is subject to copyright. All rights are solely and exclusively licensed by the Publisher, whether the whole or part of the material is concerned, specifically the rights of translation, reprinting, reuse of illustrations, recitation, broadcasting, reproduction on microfilms or in any other physical way, and transmission or information storage and retrieval, electronic adaptation, computer software, or by similar or dissimilar methodology now known or hereafter developed.
The use of general descriptive names, registered names, trademarks, service marks, etc. in this publication does not imply, even in the absence of a specific statement, that such names are exempt from the relevant protective laws and regulations and therefore free for general use.
The publisher, the authors and the editors are safe to assume that the advice and information in this book are believed to be true and accurate at the date of publication. Neither the publisher nor the authors or the editors give a warranty, expressed or implied, with respect to the material contained herein or for any errors or omissions that may have been made. The publisher remains neutral with regard to jurisdictional claims in published maps and institutional affiliations.

This Springer imprint is published by the registered company Springer Nature Switzerland AG
The registered company address is: Gewerbestrasse 11, 6330 Cham, Switzerland

If disposing of this product, please recycle the paper.

Preface of CoDecFin 2025

These proceedings collect the papers accepted at the Sixth Workshop on Coordination of Decentralized Finance (CoDecFin 2025 - http://fc25.ifca.ai/codecfin/) associated to the Financial Cryptography and Data Security 2025 international conference (FC25). This year was the fourth opportunity to have an in-person workshop after the pandemic, and it was brilliant to have the opportunity to meet colleagues in person and exchange ideas with them during the conference and the workshop. Nonetheless, we were able to offer technical support to speakers/authors that could not yet travel to Miyakojima and allow them to join their sessions on-line.

The main purpose of the series of Workshop on Coordination of Decentralized Finance (CoDecFin) is to discuss multi-disciplinary issues regarding technologies and operations of decentralized finance based on permissionless blockchain.

From an academic point of view, security and privacy protection are some of the leading research streams. The Financial Cryptography conference discusses these research challenges. On the other hand, other stakeholders than cryptographers and blockchain engineers have different interests in these characteristics of blockchain technology. For example, regulators face difficulty in tracing transactions in terms of anti-money laundering (AML) against privacy-enhancing crypto-assets. Another example is consumer protection in the case of cyberattacks on crypto-asset custodians. Blockchain business entities sometimes start their business before maturing technology, but the technology and operations are not transparent to regulators and consumers. The main problem is a lack of communication among stakeholders of the decentralized finance ecosystem. The G20 discussed the issue of insufficient communication among stakeholders in 2019. It concluded that there is an essential need to have a multi-stakeholder discussion among engineers, regulators, business entities, and operators based on the neutrality of academia.

The CoDecFin workshop was initiated in 2020 to facilitate such multi-stakeholder discussion in a neutral academic environment. The goals of CoDecFin are to have a common understanding of technology and regulatory goals and to discuss essential issues of blockchain technology with all stakeholders mentioned above. It was especially a fantastic series of academic workshops because we could involve regulators and engineers in the discussion at the venue of the Financial Cryptography Conference.

This year, we had four sessions: (1) Protocol design, (2) Assets, applications, and risks, (3) Joint keynote session with WTSC 2025, and (4) Interactive workshop session on Crypto-Agility and PQC migration for Blockchain.

This year's edition of CoDecFin received ten submissions by about thirty authors. Given the high quality of the submissions, nine papers were accepted after an average of two double-blind peer reviews each. Thanks to the generous effort by the PC, each paper received constructive feedback of review comments. Revised papers after the discussion at the workshop are collected in the present volume. CoDecFin also hosted, jointly with the 9th Workshop on Trusted Smart Contracts (WTSC25), a joint keynote session.

CoDecFin25's chair and program committee members would like to thank everyone for their usual effort and valuable contributions: authors, reviewers, and participants, as well as the support by the IFCA and FC25 committees.

June 2025

Kanta Matsuura
Jarek Nabrzyski

CoDecFin 2025 Organization

Program Committee Members

Julien Bringer	Kallistech, France
Feng Chen	University of British Columbia, Canada
Joaquin Garcia-Alfaro	Télécom SudParis, France
Byron Gibson	Stanford University, USA
Steven Nam	CodeX Stanford Blockchain Group, USA
Michele Benedetto Neitz	Golden Gate University, USA
Roman Danziger Pavlov	SafeStead Inc., Canada
Robert Schwentker	DLT Education and BSafe.network, USA
Yonatan Sompolinsky	Hebrew University of Jerusalem, DAGlabs, Israel
Ryosuke Ushida	JFSA, Japan
Robert Wardrop	University of Cambridge Judge Business School, UK
Aaron Wright	Cardozo Law School, USA
Anton Yemelyanov	Base58 Association, Canada

General Chair

Shin'ichiro Matsuo	Virginia Tech/Georgetown University, USA

FinTeAchIn 2025

First International Workshop on the Role of Education in FinTech and Innovation

Preface

These proceedings collect the papers accepted at the First International Workshop on the Role of Education in Fintech and Innovation (FinTeAchIn 2025 - https://fc25.ifca.ai/finteachin), associated with the Financial Cryptography and Data Security 2025 international conference (FC25). FinTeAchIn 2025 was hosted on the idyllic island of Miyakojima, Okinawa, Japan.

The FinTeAchIn 2025 Workshop explored the role of education in emerging financial technologies and innovation. The aim was to better understand ongoing and potential disruptive changes, along with the challenges that must be addressed to realize the full range of anticipated and potential benefits—such as greater financial inclusion, faster and more secure transactions, and reduced operational costs—while accounting for risks and concerns around security, privacy, and regulation.

The workshop aimed to foster a multidisciplinary environment where educators, researchers, and industry practitioners could discuss open challenges, examine solutions, and contribute actionable insights. Topics of interest included responsible FinTech innovation, individual and organizational adoption, AI in FinTech, curriculum development, multi-generational literacy, and strategies for enhancing public understanding and trust. We were particularly interested in how education can drive safe and responsible adoption of FinTech, improve digital competencies, and bridge generational and socio-economic gaps in financial literacy.

The multidisciplinary Programme Committee of this first edition of FinTeAchIn comprised members from companies, universities, and research institutions from several countries worldwide. The association with FC25 provided an appropriate context for running our workshop during the morning of April 18, 2025.

The first part of the workshop's program included two invited talks. The first, "**Decentralized Finance:** Impact on Financial Services and Required DeFi Literacy in 2034" was presented as work-in-progress by a respected pracademic (practitioner-academic) of the fintech community, Daniel Liebau. The second invited speaker, Sandy Oh, presented the book "**Decentralized Autonomous Organizations:** How Finance Can Interact With Blockchain-based DAOs" co-authored by Daniel Liebau and herself. We also hosted a **fireside chat** with Johnatan Messias, a research scientist from MPI-SWS, who shared insights from his experience conducting research in both industry and academia, including recent outcomes related to airdrops, incentives, and DAOs.

The second part of the workshop included two peer-reviewed articles and a hands-on activity facilitated by Derek Ariss. The 55-minute session was designed to create a collaborative space for participants with the following goals:

1. Discussing fintech education with peers
2. Identifying challenges and research opportunities for FinTeAchIn
3. Connecting with others interested in fintech education
4. Forming a working group to help shape the future of fintech learning

This year, FinTeAchIn received five articles for double-blind review by our Program Committee. Articles received an average of four reviews to provide constructive feedback. Following thoughtful deliberation, two papers were accepted in the program and included in these proceedings. Each accepted paper was assigned a shepherd.

The accepted papers address key challenges in designing effective blockchain loyalty programs and central topics in the design of a curriculum for open finance.

We would like to thank all members of our Program Committee for their efforts.

FinTeAchIn 2025 was supported by Covenant Holdings, our "backing guard" financial sponsor, and our in-kind sponsors Innoventiem and the UZH Blockchain Center.

FinTeAchIn's chairs would like to thank everyone involved in the making of this first workshop: authors, program committee members, reviewers, participants, our generous sponsors, and, last but not least, the support by IFCA and the FC25 committees. Special thanks to Ray Hirschfeld and Kazue Sako for their excellent coordination and support for our workshop's specific needs.

May 2025

Claudio Tessone
Vero Estrada-Galiñanes

FinTeAchIn 2025 Organization

Program Committee

Agostino Capponi	Columbia University, USA
Co-Pierre Georg	Frankfurt School of Finance and Management, Germany
Maurice Herlihy	Brown University, USA
Leander Jehl	University of Stavanger, Norway
William Knottenbelt	Imperial College London, UK
Jiasun Li	George Mason University, USA
Sheng-Nan Li	University of Zurich, Switzerland
Daniel Liebau	Singapore Management University, Singapore
Patrick McCorry	Arbitrum Foundation, UK
Hein Meling	University of Stavanger, Norway
Johnnatan Messias	Max Planck Institute for Software Systems (MPI-SWS), Germany
Sergio Rajsbaum	National Autonomous University of Mexico (UNAM), Mexico
Stefanie Roos	RPTU Kaiserslautern-Landau, Germany
Fabian Schär	University of Basel, Switzerland
Tanushree Sharma	Pennsylvania State University, USA
Markos Zachariadis	University of Manchester, UK
Kyrie Zhixuan Zhou	University of Illinois Urbana-Champaign, USA

VOTING 2025 Preface

These proceedings collect the papers accepted (http://fc25.ifca.ai/voting/) at the 10th Workshop on Advances in Secure Electronic Voting (Voting 2025), associated with the Financial Cryptography and Data Security 2025 conference (FC 2025). The Voting workshop was held on April 18, 2025.

This year's workshop received 15 submissions, of which 8 were accepted for publication. Thanks to the generous efforts of the Program Committee, each submission received two double-blind reviews, providing constructive feedback to authors, followed by Program Committee discussion where appropriate. We are grateful to our Program Committee for their time and effort.

We express our sincere gratitude to all those who submitted their work, the Program Committee for their careful work, and all those who participated in the workshop. We are grateful to Ray Hirschfeld and IFCA for organizing the event logistics and to the FC chairs and steering committee for their continued support for the Voting workshop.

May 2025

Jurlind Budurushi
Karola Marky

Voting 2024 Organization

Program Chairs

Jurlind Budurushi	Baden-Württemberg Cooperative State University Karlsruhe, Germany
Oksana Kulyk	IT University of Copenhagen, Denmark

Program Committee

Roberto Araujo	Universidade Federal do Pará, Brazil
Josh Benaloh	Microsoft Research, USA
Matthew Bernhard	University of Michigan, USA
Jurlind Budurushi	Baden-Württemberg Cooperative State University Karlsruhe, Germany
Jeremy Clark	Concordia University, Canada
Costantin Catalin Dragan	University of Surrey, UK
Aleksander Essex	Western University, Canada
Tamara Finogina	Polytechnic University of Catalonia, Spain
Kristian Gjøsteen	Norwegian University of Science and Technology, Norway
Rolf Haenni	Bern University of Applied Sciences, Switzerland
Thomas Heines	Queensland University of Technology, Ustralia
Oksana Kulyk	IT University of Copenhagen, Denmark
Johannes Müller	University of Luxembourg, Luxembourg
Olivier Pereira	UCLouvain, Belgium
Daniel Rausch	University of Stuttgart, Germany
Peter Rønne	University of Luxembourg, Luxembourg
Peter Y. A. Ryan	University of Luxembourg, Luxembourg
Carsten Schürmann	IT University of Copenhagen, Denmark
Philip Stark	University of California, Berkeley, USA
Vanessa Teague	Thinking Cybersecurity, Australia

Contents – Part II

Optimizing Liveness for Blockchain-Based Sealed-Bid Auctions
in Rational Settings 1
    Maozhou Huang, Xiangyu Su, Mario Larangeira, and Keisuke Tanaka

Blockchain-Based Carbon Footprint Management 29
    Umut Pekel and Oğuz Yayla

An Analysis of Financial Stability Risk Propagation Through Leveraged
Staking Activities 50
    *Takaya Sugino, Benjamin Kraner, James Angel, Shin'ichiro Matsuo,
    and Rohil Paruchuri*

SCOOP: CoSt-effective COngestiOn Attacks in Payment Channel
Networks 69
    Mohammed Ababneh, Kartick Kolachala, and Roopa Vishwanathan

Universal Blockchain Assets 84
    Owen Vaughan

Private Electronic Payments with Self-custody and Zero-Knowledge
Verified Reissuance 100
    Daniele Friolo, Geoffrey Goodell, D. R. Toliver, and Hazem Danny Nakib

Rayls: A Novel Design for CBDCs 122
    Mario Yaksetig and Jiayu Xu

Hybrid Stabilization Protocol for Cross-Chain Digital Assets Using
Adaptor Signatures and AI-Driven Arbitrage 138
    Shengwei You, Andrey Kuehlkamp, and Jarek Nabrzyski

Intmax2: A ZK-Rollup with Minimal Onchain Data and Computation
Costs Featuring Decentralized Aggregators 162
    *Erik Rybakken, Leona Hioki, Mario Yaksetig, Denisa Diaconescu,
    František Silváši, and Julian Sutherland*

Quest Love: A First Look at Blockchain Loyalty Programs 196
    Joseph Al-Chami and Jeremy Clark

SoK: Designing a Curriculum for Open Finance 212
    Daniel Broby and Eduardo T. Valencia Jr.

3+ Seat Risk-Limiting Audits for Single Transferable Vote Elections 226
  Michelle Blom, Alexander Ek, Peter J. Stuckey, Vanessa Teague, and Damjan Vukcevic

Doing More with Less: Mismatch-Based Risk-Limiting Audits 241
  Alexander Ek, Michelle Blom, Philip B. Stark, Peter J. Stuckey, Vanessa J. Teague, and Damjan Vukcevic

Voting Without Self-voting 256
  Peter B. Rønne

Anamorphic Voting: Ballot Freedom Against Dishonest Authorities 266
  Rosario Giustolisi, Mohammadamin Rakeei, and Gabriele Lenzini

E2Easy: a Simple Lattice-Based in-Person End-to-End Voting Scheme 281
  Eduardo L. Cominetti, Marcos A. Simplicio, Diego F. Aranha, Paulo Matias, and Roberto Araújo

Security Analysis of the Australian Capital Territory's eVACS 2020/2024 Paperless Direct Recording Electronic Voting System 297
  Chris Culnane, Andrew Conway, Vanessa Teague, and Ty Wilson-Brown

opn.vote: A Publicly Verifiable Blockchain-Based eVoting System 306
  Felix Maduakor, Thi Van Thao Doan, and Joerg Mitzlaff

Enhancing Helios for Elections at Qatar University 309
  Jurlind Budurushi, Khalid Abdallah, Farhan Al Sadi, Hosam Zarouk, Abdelwahab Almasri, and Armstrong Nhlabatsi

Author Index 313

Contents – Part I

On the Lifecycle of a Lightning Network Payment Channel 1
   Florian Grötschla, Lioba Heimbach, Severin Richner, and Roger Wattenhofer

The Writing Is on the Wall: Analyzing the Boom of Inscriptions and Its Impact on EVM-Compatible Blockchains 17
   Johnnatan Messias, Krzysztof Gogol, Maria Inés Silva, and Benjamin Livshits

Price Oracle Accuracy Across Blockchains: A Measurement and Analysis 32
   Robin Gansäuer, Hichem Ben Aoun, Jan Droll, and Hannes Hartenstein

A Public Dataset For the ZKsync Rollup 47
   Maria Inês Silva, Johnnatan Messias, and Benjamin Livshits

Early Observations of Based Rollups: A Case Study of Taiko 63
   Jan Gorzny, Phillip Kemper, and Martin Derka

What Drives Liquidity on Decentralized Exchanges? Evidence from the Uniswap Protocol 78
   Brian Zhu, Dingyue Liu, Xin Wan, Gordon Liao, Ciamac Moallemi, and Brad Bachu

Liquidity Fragmentation or Optimization? Analyzing Automated Market Makers Across Ethereum and Rollups 94
   Krzysztof M. Gogol, Manvir Schneider, Claudio J. Tessone, and Benjamin Livshits

Quantifying Price Improvement in Order Flow Auctions 111
   Brad Bachu, Xin Wan, and Ciamac C. Moallemi

Short Paper: Atomic Execution is Not Enough for Arbitrage Profit Extraction in Shared Sequencers 127
   Maria Inês Silva and Benjamin Livshits

Revisiting Bitcoin's Merkle Tree Security: Practical Implications and an Attack on Core Chain 137
   Yogev Bar-On

A Quantitative Notion of Economic Security for Smart Contract
Compositions 147
    Emily Priyadarshini and Massimo Bartoletti

Hollow Victory: How Malicious Proposers Exploit Validator Incentives
in Optimistic Rollup Dispute Games 164
    Suhyeon Lee

A Formalization of Signum's Consensus 180
    Fausto Spoto

Monero's Decentralized P2P Exchanges: Functionality, Adoption,
and Privacy Risks 200
    Yannik Kopyciok, Friedhelm Victor, and Stefan Schmid

Toward a Secure Tokenized Green Credit Management System: Case
Study of WREGIS 216
    Mahmudun Nabi and Reihaneh Safavi-Naini

Parallel Execution Fee Mechanisms 245
    Abdoulaye Ndiaye

SoK: Modelling Data Storage and Availability 263
    Carlo Brunetta and Massimiliano Sala

Author Index 281

Optimizing Liveness for Blockchain-Based Sealed-Bid Auctions in Rational Settings

Maozhou Huang[1], Xiangyu Su[2(✉)], Mario Larangeira[2,3], and Keisuke Tanaka[2]

[1] Department of Mathematics, New Uzbekistan University, 1 Movarounnahr street, Tashkent, Uzbekistan
mz.huang@newuu.uz
[2] Department of Mathematical and Computing Sciences, School of Computing, Institute of Science Tokyo, 2-12-1 W8-55 Ooookayama, Meguro City, Tokyo, Japan
{su.x.4029,rebello.m.f72a}@m.isct.ac.jp, keisuke@comp.isct.ac.jp
[3] Input Output, Global, Singapore, Singapore
mario.larangeira@iohk.io

Abstract. Blockchain-based auction markets offer stronger fairness and transparency compared to their centralized counterparts. Deposits and sealed bid formats are usually applied to enhance security and privacy. However, to our best knowledge, the formal treatment of deposit-enabled sealed-bid auctions remains lacking in the cryptographic literature. To address this gap, we first propose a decentralized anonymous deposited-bidding (DADB) scheme, providing formal syntax and security definitions. Unlike existing approaches that rely on smart contracts, our construction utilizes a mainchain-sidechain structure that is also compatible with the Extended UTXO (EUTXO) Model. Based on Algorand (SOSP '17), this design further allows us to customize the sidechain by integrating a novel block qualification mechanism into block selection. Consequently, we prove, from a game-theoretical perspective, that our design optimizes liveness latency for rational users who want to join the auction, even without explicit incentives (e.g., fees) for including bids. Finally, we analyze the cost of our protocol and demonstrate the potential performance degradation without our block qualification mechanism using implementation results.

Keywords: Deposit-Enabled Sealed-Bid Auctions · Blockchain-Based Auctions · Algorand-Style Consensus Protocol · Rational Analysis

1 Introduction

Auction markets have been a long-standing topic in applied economics. Decentralization enhances their fairness and transparency by eliminating the requirement for trusted auctioneers while ensuring security through the persistence and liveness of consensus protocols. Blockchain, as an embodiment of these protocols [4], is ideal for securely recording and verifying auction outcomes.

However, the direct application of blockchain to auction markets suffers from the maximal extractable value (MEV) activities. Specifically, miners can manipulate the order of bid inclusion (similar to transactions in traditional cryptocurrency blockchains) to maximize their profit (see [45, Section 2.2.2] for a precise definition). As demonstrated in [38], sealed-bid auctions address this issue by concealing both bid contents and bidder information, preventing miners from learning bids' intent. Moreover, most existing implementations of blockchain-based sealed-bid auctions [15, 21, 23, 28, 36–38, 40, 44, 46, 49] rely on the Ethereum-type smart contracts [47], and some further assume a trusted execution environment (TEE) [22, 35]. These assumptions may increase execution costs in real life as fees for including such smart contracts are much higher than those for including normal transactions [32], even the extended UTXO (EUTXO)-type ones [11].

In contrast, this work takes a more fundamental approach, building directly on the consensus layer by using a committee-based Algorand-style blockchain. This enables us to incorporate a novel block qualification mechanism into block selection, which optimizes *how* liveness is achieved. Specifically, we show our enhancements to the Algorand protocol [14] preserve its original security and, additionally, allow us to reduce liveness latency when rational users operate the protocol, even without fees for including bids.

1.1 Our Approach and Contributions

To realize blockchain-based sealed-bid auctions, we develop two building blocks, which may be of independent interest.

Decentralized Anonymous Deposited-Bidding Scheme. For auction markets, a reasonable requirement for bidders is an appropriate amount of deposits before participation. This ensures bidders' compliance with the bidding process[1]. Moreover, for blockchain-based auctions, deposits are separated from bids to conceal bidders' information (hence to prevent MEV activities).

Despite this separation (*i.e.*, a deposit-enabled sealed-bid auction) has been considered in [38], we notice that, to the best of our knowledge, there is no formalization. Following the spirit of Zerocoin [39] and decentralized anonymous credential [26] frameworks, we formalize the deposit-enabled sealed-bid auction into a decentralized anonymous deposited-bidding (DADB) scheme, providing its syntax and security (see Sect. 3.1). As for the security: *Anonymity* requires that no adversary can infer the owner or the intent (e.g., the bidding price) of a given bid, even when given the corresponding deposit embedded in an anonymous set; and *one-more bidding unforgeability* requires that no adversary can issue a bid without possessing an associated deposit transaction.

Our construction leverages a *mainchain-sidechain* structure, unlike [38], in which Ethereum-type smart contracts are utilized to oversee the state of deposits and bids. The deposit mechanism can be implemented solely on the mainchain

---

[1] As noted in [16, Footnote 2], an auction with deposits that mismatch the value of bids may suffer from severe defaults.

under the EUTXO Model [1,11], which offers more simplicity and lower execution cost. Assuming a secure ledger (*i.e.*, with persistence and liveness) as the mainchain, we give a generic DADB construction based on a CCA-secure timed commitment scheme [31] and signatures of knowledge [13]. The timed feature is used to automatically open bids, hence revoking the anonymity so that the results of bid allocation are publicly known. For this, we provide a timed variant of anonymity to highlight the difference due to our revocation approach. The security is proven in Lemma 2.

Algorand-Style Sidechain Protocol. The mainchain-sidechain structure further enables us to customize the consensus mechanism on the sidechain to establish an agreement on the common set of sealed bids among all users. Our starting point is the Algorand protocol [14]. Based on one-more bidding unforgeability, we adapt their stake-based committee selection to our deposit setting and propose a novel block qualification mechanism (Sect. 3.2).

Our block qualification mechanism introduces a threshold $\mathfrak{h} \in (0,1]$. In an honest user's view, for y being the number of bids in the candidate block with the maximum number of bids among her received candidate blocks, only candidate blocks with $\geq \mathfrak{h} \cdot y$ bids are admitted into her block selection. The user then selects a block based on a value derived from the hash of each admitted candidate block (see Algorithm 2 for details). Note that: if each honest user simply selects the block with the maximum number of bids, many candidate blocks proposed by honest users may have zero chance of being selected. For instance, the adversary can withhold bids from certain honest users, preventing them from formulating blocks with enough bids. To further mitigate this, when an honest user counts bids in a received candidate block, she only counts those already known to her (the intersection in Eq. 3.1), *i.e.*, those in her mempool. This restriction implies that the malicious users "have to propagate" their bids.

By assuming the honest majority of deposits, *i.e.*, $> 2/3$ of deposit transactions, are submitted to the mainchain by honest users, we prove in Theorem 1 (Sect. 4.1) that our modifications do not compromise the security of the original Algorand protocol [14]. On the other hand, our modification plays a critical role in the game theoretical analysis. In Sect. 4.2, we define a game that simulates the candidate block proposal phase of our sidechain protocol. Due to anonymity, users have no incentive to prevent a bid from being included in the blockchain. Hence, in this game, we may replace honest users with rational ones whose utility is derived solely from having their bids recorded on the block. An explicit attacker strategy in the game is presented in [29]. It replicates the worst outcomes given by the adversary, and thereby validates that our game accurately simulates the block selection process. Our block qualification mechanism enables us to show that the honest behavior (*i.e.*, including all bids in candidate blocks) constitutes an equilibrium, even without incentives such as fees for including bids (Theorem 2).

Finally, we analyze the cost for getting bids recorded in the Aucrand protocol and show the advantage of our protocol in cost control. We also present experimental results demonstrating the potential performance degradation caused by the selfish behavior of rational users without our block qualification mechanism (Sect. 5).

Our Contributions. In summary, they are threefold: (1) a formally defined DADB scheme and its generic construction; (2) a novel block qualification mechanism for Algorand-style protocols; (3) a blockchain-based sealed-bid auction protocol, named Aucrand[2], which is built upon the previous two primitives.

1.2 Related Works

A comparison with blockchain-based sealed-bid auction protocols is given below (Table 1).

Table 1. Comparison with related works.

Works	Techniques	Focus of Analysis
[15,28,36,37,44,46,49]	SC & Secure blockchain	SC-based privacy and security
[22,35]	SC & TEE	TEE-based security
[21,23]	SC	SC programming
[40]	SC & State channel	SC-based dispute resolution
[38]	SC	Economical analysis
This work	EUTXO-based structure & Block qualification	DADB provable security; Consensus when honest/rational

Moreover, we review several committee-based consensus protocols that influenced our design, *e.g.*, Algorand [14], Ouroboros [18,33], and others [17,41,42,48]. These protocols employ a small, randomly selected committee to make decisions, enhancing scalability and efficiency compared to traditional models [34]. Ouroboros, a Nakamoto-style blockchain [4] with longer finality times, introduced a probabilistic, stake-based committee selection mechanism using verifiable random functions. This mechanism was later refined in the Byzantine agreement-based Algorand [14]. By adapting Algorand's construction to our deposit setting, we inherit the resilience against adaptive corruption from its frequent committee selection and the rapid finality from the Byzantine agreement.

However, these protocols fall short in addressing rational analysis, which incorporates incentives to enable protocols with greater efficiency in more realistic settings [3,24]. Our approach bridges this gap by modifying Algorand's block proposal and selection, complemented by a rigorous game-theoretic analysis. Consequently, we show that our modifications can effectively mitigate negative impacts of rational behavior, maintaining protocol performance and security.

---

[2] Our design is versatile enough to support various auction models, *e.g.*, double auctions and frequent batch auctions [7].

2 Preliminaries

Notations. This paper uses κ for the security parameter. For any integer $a \leq b$, let $[a\mathrel{..}b] := \{a, a+1, \ldots, b\}$; and any integer $n > 0$, let $[n] := [1\mathrel{..}n]$ and $[n]_0 := [0\mathrel{..}n]$. $a \leftarrow \mathsf{Alg}$ denotes that a is assigned the output of the algorithm Alg on fresh randomness. Denote a collision-free hash function by $H\colon \{0,1\}^* \to \{0,1\}^\kappa$.

Protocol Execution Model. We adopt the standard Interactive Turing Machines (ITM) model [10], in which a protocol refers to algorithms for a set of nodes (users) to interact with each other. Regarding the adversary model, for security analysis in Sect. 4.1, we consider that all corrupted users are controlled by a *rushing* Byzantine adversary $\mathcal{A}$ who can read inputs and set outputs for these users. For game-theoretic analysis in Sect. 4.2, all users are modeled to be rational in a pre-defined game. Their behaviors are described by strategy sets and utility functions. Our additional protocol settings are as follows.

- Time and network: Round-based execution that is further divided into steps; All users' clocks proceed at the same speed, and the local computation is instant; A semi-synchronous network with two known delay upper bounds: λ for short messages; Λ for full blocks;
- Participation and corruption: A constrained permissionless setting: Permissionless so that anybody can submit deposit transactions; and Permissioned for the sidechain protocol, *i.e.*, only users who have deposited can issue bids; The adversary can corrupt honest users adaptively at any time.

Building Blocks. Cryptographic primitives below are treated as black-boxes.

- A digital signature scheme $\mathsf{DS} := (\mathsf{KGen}, \mathsf{Sign}, \mathsf{SigVrfy})$ satisfying correctness and EUF-CMA [27];
- A non-interactive timed commitment (NITC) scheme $\mathsf{TC} := (\mathsf{PGen}, \mathsf{Com}, \mathsf{OpenVrfy}, \mathsf{FOpen})$, in which commitments can be forced opened after time t_{fo}. An NITC should satisfy correctness, CCA-hiding and CCA-binding [31]. The formal syntax and definitions can be found in Appendix A;
- A zero-knowledge proofs of knowledge (ZKPoK) protocol that satisfies completeness, (perfect) zero-knowledge, and knowledge-soundness [19].

Briefly, we denote the key pair of user i by (sk_i, pk_i). Additionally, we consider the ephemeral keys model from [14], which supports forward security [5,30], to achieve resilience against adaptive corruption. The ephemeral key pair in round r and step s is denoted by $(sk_i^{r,s}, pk_i^{r,s})$. Let $sig_i(m)$ ($esig_i(m)$) be the (ephemeral) signature on message m. We write $SIG_i(m) := (m, sig_i(m))$ and $ESIG_i(m) := (m, esig_i(m))$ for the message-signature pair in the rest of this paper.

For ZKPoK, we consider the protocols tailored to proofs of set membership and range proofs [8]. We refer to the non-interactive proofs, obtained by Fiat-Shamir heuristic [20], as signatures of knowledge as given in [13]. We adopt the notations from [9]. For the commit algorithm Com of any commitment scheme and a value x, let NIZKPoK $\{(c,r) : (c,\cdot) \leftarrow \text{Com}(x;r) \land c \in C\}$ denote a set membership proof that proves the knowledge of witness r s.t. $(c,\cdot) \leftarrow \text{Com}(x;r) \land c \in C$. We denote the signature of knowledge on message m w.r.t. this relation by SoK$[m]\{(c,r) : (c,\cdot) \leftarrow \text{Com}(x;r) \land c \in C\}$. Moreover, for a range proof concerning $[a,b]$ where $a,b \in \mathbb{R}$, we denote the proof of x s.t. $(c,\cdot) \leftarrow \text{Com}(x) \land x \in [a,b]$ by NIZKPoK $\{(x) : (c,\cdot) \leftarrow \text{Com}(x) \land x \in [a,b]\}$.

A Secure Public Ledger. To simplify the design of our mainchain-sidechain structure, we assume a secure public ledger protocol $(\Pi_M, \mathcal{L})$ to be our "mainchain" for recording deposit transactions. We consider it to satisfy 0-persistence and u-liveness. This can be achieved by truncating the last k blocks from any k-persistent and (k,u)-live ledger protocol (with formal definitions available in [25]). For readability, we omit Π_M and use $\mathcal{L}$ to refer to both the protocol and the ledger. Let $\mathcal{L}[-1]$ denote the head (*i.e.*, the latest block) of $\mathcal{L}$.

3 Our Aucrand Protocol

To avoid payment defaults, we require users to submit deposit transactions to the mainchain to participate in the auction market. Each deposit transaction recorded on the mainchain allows its owner to issue exactly one bid in the sidechain protocol. All bids should be sealed for privacy guarantees, and hence to mitigate the MEV activities. Our modified Algorand-style sidechain protocol is then executed to achieve consensus on the sealed bids for all honest users, represented by the resulting blockchain. An application of a timed commitment scheme to seal bids (hence, revealing bids and revoking the anonymity in a timely manner) enables that allocation results can be determined *automatically* based on the revealed bids and the predefined auction model.

This section presents our main contribution: the Aucrand protocol. It includes a decentralized anonymous deposited-bidding (DADB) scheme and a novel sidechain protocol based on Algorand.

3.1 Formal Treatment and Generic Construction of DADB

A DADB scheme consists of algorithms (Setup, Deposit, dVrfy, Bidding, bVrfy).

- Setup(1^κ) takes as input the security parameter κ and outputs a public parameter pp *s.t.* $d \in$ pp where d is the amount of deposit for one bid;
- Deposit(pp, i) takes as input pp and a user index i. It outputs a deposit transaction d_i and a trapdoor td_i;
- dVrfy(pp, i, d_i) outputs 1 if d_i is valid; or 0 otherwise;
- Bidding(pp, P, d, td, D) takes as input pp, a bidding string $P \in \{0,1\}^*$, a deposit transaction d and its trapdoor td, and a set of deposits D. It outputs a sealed bid b $:= (c_P, S, \pi)$ where c_P is the sealed bidding string; S and π are the serial number and proof indicating d $\in D$;

- bVrfy(pp, b, D) outputs 1 if b is valid, *i.e.*, c_P is valid concerning P, and (S, π) is valid concerning D; or 0 otherwise.

Note that each bid should be associated with exactly one deposit transaction. Hence, we require S to be a unique value released during the issuance of a bid, designed to prevent any user from consuming the same deposit transaction twice.

DADB Security Definitions. We formally define the correctness, anonymity (with a timed variant), and one-more bidding unforgeability for DADB.

Intuitively, correctness means that any output from Deposit passes dVrfy, and any bid from Bidding corresponding to a valid deposit transaction passes bVrfy.

Definition 1 (Correctness). *A DADB scheme is perfectly correct if the following properties hold for any $\kappa > 0$, any user i, and $(d_i, td_i) \leftarrow$ Deposit(pp, i).*

- *Deposit transaction verifies, i.e.,* dVrfy(pp, i, d_i) = 1.
- *For any* b $\leftarrow$ Bidding(pp, P, d, td, D') *s.t.* d $\in D'$, *it verifies that* bVrfy(pp, b, D') = 1. *Moreover, for any $D \supseteq D'$, we have* bVrfy(pp, b, D) = 1.

In the anonymity game, the PPT adversary $\mathcal{A}$ is provided with two honestly generated deposit transactions d_0, d_1. It is then allowed to choose an arbitrary anonymous set D and specify the bidding strings P_0, P_1 for the respective deposit transactions. The challenger prepares a bit $b \xleftarrow{\$} \{0, 1\}$ and issues a sealed bid b_b from the corresponding deposit transaction (based on d_b and P_b). $\mathcal{A}$ is said to win the anonymity game if it outputs $b' = b$. By this game, the anonymity (resp. T-timed anonymity) ensures that any PPT adversary (resp. any PPT adversary whose run time is upper bounded by T) cannot link any given bid to its originating deposit transaction, even knowing the bidding price.

Definition 2 (Anonymity and Timed Anonymity).

- *A DADB scheme satisfies anonymity if for any PPT adversary $\mathcal{A} = (\mathcal{A}_1, \mathcal{A}_2)$, given an index $i \in \{0, 1\}$, the following probability is* negl(κ) *for any $\kappa > 0$ and $(d_i, td_i) \leftarrow$ Deposit(pp, i).*

$$\left| \Pr \left[b' = b \;\middle|\; \begin{array}{l} (P_0, P_1, D, \text{st}) \leftarrow \mathcal{A}_1(d_0, d_1); \\ b \xleftarrow{\$} \{0, 1\}; \\ b_b \leftarrow \text{Bidding}(pp, P_b, d_b, td_b, D \cup \{d_0, d_1\}); \\ b' \leftarrow \mathcal{A}_2(b_b, \text{st}) \end{array} \right. \right] - \frac{1}{2} \right|$$

- *Moreover, we say a DADB scheme satisfies T-timed anonymity if for any anonymity adversary $\mathcal{A}$ above whose run time is upper bounded by T, the probability above is* negl(κ) *for any $\kappa > 0$ and $(d_i, td_i) \leftarrow$ Deposit(pp, i). Here, $T = T_1 + T_2$ and $\mathcal{A} = (\mathcal{A}_1, \mathcal{A}_2)$ such that (1) the run time of $\mathcal{A}_1$ is upper bounded by T_1; and (2) the run time of $\mathcal{A}_2$ is upper bounded by T_2.*

On the other hand, in the one-more bidding-unforgeability game, the adversary $\mathcal{A}$ is provided with $n \leq \mathsf{poly}(\kappa)$ deposit transactions $\{\mathsf{d}_i\}_{i\in[n]}$. It can query, for $q \leq \mathsf{poly}(\kappa)$ time, to a bidding oracle $\mathcal{O}_{\mathsf{Bidding}}$ that helps issue bids corresponding to the given deposit transactions, with a query being dropped if the queried deposit transaction is not in $\{\mathsf{d}_i\}_{i\in[n]}$. To win the game, $\mathcal{A}$ must output $m \geq 1$ deposit transactions $\{\mathsf{d}'_j\}_{j\in[m]}$ and $m+1$ sealed bids $\{\mathsf{b}'_i\}_{i\in[m+1]}$ that satisfy the following conditions.

- All output bids should be valid concerning a set containing $\{\mathsf{d}_i\}_{i\in[n]} \cup \{\mathsf{d}'_j\}_{j\in[m]}$ (this set is denoted D' below);
- No output bid is previously queried to $\mathcal{O}_{\mathsf{Bidding}}$;
- All serial numbers in the output bids should be distinct.

By this game, one-more bidding-unforgeability ensures that the adversary cannot issue more bids than deposit transactions that it possesses.

Definition 3 (One-More Bidding-Unforgeability). *A DADB scheme satisfies one-more bidding unforgeability if for any PPT adversary $\mathcal{A}$ that is given $n \leq \mathsf{poly}(\kappa)$ deposit transactions d_i from $(\mathsf{d}_i, \cdot) \leftarrow \mathsf{Deposit}(\mathsf{pp}, i)$. $\mathcal{A}$ can query, up to $q \leq \mathsf{poly}(\kappa)$ times, to a bidding oracle $\mathcal{O}_{\mathsf{Bidding}}(\cdot, \cdot, \cdot)$. The oracle works as follows: when queried (d_j, P_j, D) where the set D contains $\{\mathsf{d}_i\}_{i\in[n]}$,*

- *returns $\perp$ if $\mathsf{d}_j \notin \{\mathsf{d}_i\}_{i\in[n]}$;*
- *otherwise, returns $\mathsf{b} \leftarrow \mathsf{Bidding}(\mathsf{pp}, P_j, \mathsf{d}_j, \mathsf{td}_j, D)$ to $\mathcal{A}$ and records the pair of a sealed bidding string and a serial number (c_{P_j}, S_j) to a queried set Q.*

The following probability is $\mathsf{negl}(\kappa)$ for any $\kappa > 0$.

$$\Pr\left[\begin{array}{l} \forall \mathsf{b}' \in \{\mathsf{b}'_i\}_{i\in[m+1]}, \{\mathsf{d}_i\}_{i\in[n]} \cup \{\mathsf{d}'_j\}_{j\in[m]} \subseteq D': \\ \mathsf{bVrfy}(\mathsf{pp}, \mathsf{b}', D') = 1 \wedge \\ \forall i \in [m+1],\ \text{parse } \mathsf{b}'_i = (c'_{P_i}, S'_i, \cdot): \\ (c'_{P_i}, S'_i) \notin \mathsf{Q} \wedge S'_i \text{ is unique for each } \mathsf{b}'_i \end{array} \middle| \begin{array}{l} (\{\mathsf{d}'_j\}_{j\in[m]}, \{\mathsf{b}'_i\}_{i\in[m+1]}) \\ \leftarrow \mathcal{A}^{\mathcal{O}_{\mathsf{Bidding}}}(\{\mathsf{d}_i\}_{i\in[n]}) \end{array}\right]$$

A Generic Construction. We present our generic DADB construction based on the mainchain-sidechain structure. On the mainchain $\mathcal{L}$, each user i with a key pair (sk_i, pk_i) from DS is uniquely identified by her public key pk_i. A participant holding multiple key pairs is regarded as multiple users. However, the total amount of deposit transactions that a participant can submit is upper bounded by the total amount of currency she possesses on the ledger $\mathcal{L}$.

For simplicity, we instantiate the bidding string in DADB syntax to be a normalized bidding price: $P \in [-1, 0) \cup (0, 1]$, where the sign of P indicates the direction of bids, i.e., $P > 0$ for buy bids, $P < 0$ for sell bids, and the actual bidding price is $|P|$. For each bid, a user is required to make a constant amount of deposit $d > 1$ on $\mathcal{L}$ by submitting a transaction that embeds a commitment of a unique serial number. Users can submit deposit transactions within a time interval. This interval is counted by the number of blocks on $\mathcal{L}$, named by a deposit epoch, and indexed by $e \geq 0$.

Our DADB construction is performed for each epoch and starts with pp ← Setup(1^κ). It can be instantiated either by a trusted party [39]; or through a negotiation-based approach [12]. Setup runs TC.PGen(1^κ) and setup algorithms for ZKPoK protocols as subroutines. pp includes ($\mathcal{L}, e, d$) and two forced-opening parameters t_1, t_2 for NITC schemes in Deposit and Bidding, respectively.

A Deposit Epoch. Let TC be an NITC scheme. In deposit epoch $e \geq 0$ on $\mathcal{L}$, a user i with (sk_i, pk_i) performs (Deposit, dVrfy, ReadL).

- Deposit(e, d, sk_i) samples a serial number and a randomness with $S, r \xleftarrow{\$} \{0,1\}^\kappa$. It outputs a deposit transaction $\mathsf{d}_i = SIG_i(e, d, c)$ to $\mathcal{L}$, where $(c, \cdot) \leftarrow \mathsf{TC.Com}(S; r)$ is the commitment w.r.t. (S, r) that can be forced opened via TC.FOpen after time t_1;
- dVrfy(e, d, pk_j, d_j) parses $\mathsf{d}_j = SIG_j(e', d', c)$. It outputs 1 if $e' = e \wedge d' = d \wedge \mathsf{SigVrfy}(pk_j, \mathsf{d}_j) = 1$; or 0 otherwise;
- ReadL($\mathcal{L}, e$) is only executed after the liveness[a] delay u of $\mathcal{L}$ following the end of the deposit epoch e. Let PK^e denote the set of all public keys on $\mathcal{L}$ in epoch e. ReadL outputs:
  - For each $j \in PK^e$, the set of valid deposit transactions issued by j: $D_j^e := \{\mathsf{d}_j \mid \mathsf{dVrfy}(e, d, pk_j, \mathsf{d}_j) = 1\}$;
  - The set $C^e := \left\{ c \in \mathsf{d} \,\middle|\, \mathsf{d} \in \bigcup_{j \in PK^e} D_j^e \right\}$ of all committed serial numbers[b].

---

[a] For completeness, we provide the interface for reading the ledger in addition to our DADB syntax. Moreover, the liveness of $\mathcal{L}$ guarantees that any d outputted to $\mathcal{L}$ will be recorded after this delay.
[b] Due to the one-to-one correspondence between a deposit transaction and a committed serial number, we will focus on using C^e in the following of this paper for better explicitness.

Note that d serves only as a data structure for recording deposits. It must be completed according to the accounting model of $\mathcal{L}$, e.g., the Extended UTXO [1,11] or the account model [47]. We deliberately consider *signed* deposit transactions to align with the transaction format of UXTO models, contrasting with the unsigned deposit payloads proposed in the smart contract-based [38].

In parallel to a deposit epoch, a user can issue bids w.r.t. deposit transactions submitted by herself. Each bid is sealed in the sense that: (1) the price P is committed with an NITC scheme while guaranteed by an NIZKPoK range proof π_P showing $|P| \in (0, 1]$; (2) the bid is decoupled from its corresponding deposit transaction (also the user's public key) using an SoK scheme. Even if a user only knows a subset $C' \subseteq C^e$ when issuing bids, she can still hide her deposit transactions by proving, in a zero-knowledge manner, that she knows the randomness s.t. the committed serial number lies in C'. The bidding process:

> **Bidding Process.** Let TC be an NITC scheme. To issue and verify bids, a user performs (Bidding, bVrfy) as follows.
>
> - Bidding(P, S, r, C') takes as input a bidding price P, a serial number S, a randomness r, and a set of committed serial numbers $C' \subseteq C^e$ chosen by the user. It outputs a sealed bid $\mathsf{b} := (c_P, \pi_P, S, \pi_{\mathsf{SoK}})$ where:
>   - $(c_P, \cdot) \leftarrow \mathsf{TC.Com}(P)$ is the commitment of P and can be forced opened via TC.FOpen after time t_2;
>   - $\pi_P = \mathsf{NIZKPoK}\{(P) : (c_P, \cdot) \leftarrow \mathsf{TC.Com}(P) \wedge |P| \in (0,1]\}$ is a range proof showing $|P| \in (0,1]$ w.r.t. c_P;
>   - $\pi_{\mathsf{SoK}} = \mathsf{SoK}[(c_P, \pi_P)]\{(c, r) : (c, \cdot) \leftarrow \mathsf{TC.Com}(S; r) \wedge c \in C'\}$ is a signature of knowledge on (c_P, π_P) where $C' \subseteq C^e$.
> - bVrfy(b, C') takes as input a sealed bid $\mathsf{b} = (c_P, \pi_P, S, \pi_{\mathsf{SoK}})$ and a set of committed serial numbers C'. It outputs 1 if π_P is a valid proof of c_P indicating $|P| \in (0,1]$, and π_{SoK} is a valid signature of knowledge on (c_P, π_P) indicating that the commitment of S is in C'; or 0 otherwise. Specifically, we have bVrfy$(\mathsf{b}, C^e) = 1$ if $\exists C' \subseteq C^e$ s.t. bVrfy$(\mathsf{b}, C') = 1$.

Remark 1 (The necessity of timed anonymity). The timed commitment reveals the recipient and transfer amount (hence revoking anonymity) automatically so that users can allocate their bids. This feature is explicitly captured by the upper bound T of the anonymity adversary's run time (Definition 2). While methods like multiparty computation may achieve this without compromising anonymity, our timed approach offers the advantages of being transparent and low-cost.

By assuming $t_2 \geq t_1$, we conclude with the following lemma, whose proof can be found in [29].

Lemma 2. *Assuming a secure signature* DS *and a secure public ledger* $\mathcal{L}$, *our construction satisfies the following properties.*

- *Correctness (Definition 1);*
- t_1-*timed anonymity (Definition 2) if the NITC scheme* TC *is CCA-hiding and the signature of knowledge is at least computationally zero-knowledge;*
- *One-more bidding-unforgeability (Definition 3) if the NITC scheme* TC *is CCA-binding, the signature of knowledge is at least computationally zero-knowledge and is knowledge-sound.*

Finally, we remark that: (1) a non-timed commitment, e.g., [43], enables our construction to satisfy anonymity without time constraints; (2) in Aucrand, we may configure the time constraints t_1, t_2 to be large enough so that its anonymity preservers until sealed bids are securely recorded on the sidechain. Thereafter, we use the term "anonymity" instead of its timed variant.

3.2 The Sidechain Protocol

Based on the deposit transactions recorded on the mainchain $\mathcal{L}$, users seek to agree on a common set of sealed bids to determine bid allocation results. Unlike existing smart contract-based solutions, we design a dedicated sidechain for the consensus of sealed bids. The sidechain is based on an Algorand-style (*i.e.*, Byzantine agreement) protocol [14] with modified block proposal and selection. Algorithm specifications can be found in Appendix B.

For simplicity, the following considers a fixed epoch e and omits it in upper indices, *i.e.*, we use PK, D_i, and C to denote respectively PK^e, D_i^e, and C^e.

Initialization. When a deposit epoch is completely finished, *i.e.*, $(\{D_i\}_{i \in PK}, C) \leftarrow \mathsf{ReadL}(\mathcal{L}, e)$ is known to all users after the liveness delay of $\mathcal{L}$, users initialize the sidechain protocol with an empty blockchain $\mathcal{C} = \emptyset$ at round index $r = 0$ and step index $s = 1$. Let pp be the parameter consisting of the tuple $(\lambda, \Lambda, \mathcal{L}, e, d, \{D_i\}_{i \in PK}, C)$, and[5]

- $\mathfrak{h} \in [0, 1)$, the threshold for qualifying candidate blocks. See Eq. 3.1;
- L, analyzed in Sect. 4.1, is the lower bound for the number of serial numbers in candidate blocks so that the block qualification mechanism is activated;
- $p^{r,s}$ is the fraction whose denominator is $|C|$, and the numerator is the expected number of votes for committee members[6] in round $r \geq 0$ step $s \geq 1$;
- t_H denotes the number of votes needed to certify a block.

We parameterize the protocol with pp and denote it by $(\Pi^{\mathsf{pp}}, \mathcal{C} = \emptyset)$. Thereafter, pp is in the input of all algorithms and will be omitted for simplicity.

Moreover, when specified with a round index $r \geq 0$, $\mathcal{C}^r := B^0 || \cdots || B^r$ denotes the blockchain by the end of round r, where $B^{r'}$ is the selected block of round r' for all $r' \in [r]_0$. The user who generates round r's selected block is called the leader of round r, denoted by ℓ^r. The seed of round r is used to determine the committee selection for the next round and is computed by $Q^r = H(SIG_{\ell^r}(Q^{r-1}), r)$, or $Q^r = H(Q^{r-1}, r)$ if the leader selection fails. We allow $r = -1$, and put $\mathcal{C}^{-1} = B^{-1} := \mathcal{L}[-1]$ and $Q^{-1} := H(\mathcal{L}[-1])$.

Thereafter, by leader selection, we mean the block selection (we use the former to align with "committee selection" and "potential leader").

Definition 3. *A candidate block generated by user i in round $r \geq 0$ of the sidechain protocol $(\Pi^{\mathsf{pp}}, \mathcal{C}^{r-1})$ is defined as $B_i^r := (r, H(B^{r-1}), SIG_i(Q^{r-1}), \mathsf{B}_i^r)$,*

where B_i^r is a set of bids collected by i. If the leader selection fails in round r, $B^r = B_\epsilon^r := (r, H(B^{r-1}), Q^{r-1}, \emptyset)$; otherwise, $B^r = B_{\ell^r}^r$ for the leader ℓ^r.

---

[5] We can configure Λ for each round r s.t. it is lower bounded by the number of serial numbers in C but not in the bids on $\mathcal{C}^{r-2}$ ($\mathcal{C}^{r-2}$ is known to all users).
[6] A deposit transaction becomes one vote in committee selection with probability $p^{r,s}$.

Committee Selection. Our committee selection adapts the stake-based mechanism [14, Section 6] to the set of deposits $\bigcup_{i \in PK} D_i$. Given pp, a user i is selected with a weight proportional to $a_i := |D_i|$. Briefly:

- $\sigma_i^{r,s} := SIG_i(r, s, Q^{r-1})$, i's round r step s credential for committee selection;
- $\mathsf{GetVotes}(p^{r,s}, a_i, \sigma_i^{r,s})$ outputs the number of i's votes (Algorithm 1);
- $\mathsf{GetMinHash}(a_i, \sigma_i^{r,1})$ essentially outputs the "minimum hash" (Algorithm 2);
- Let $SV^{r,s}$ denote the set of committees in round $r \geq 0$ step $s \geq 1$. Moreover, (1) $i \in SV^{r,s}$ if and only if $\mathsf{GetVotes}(p^{r,s}, a_i, \sigma_i^{r,s}) > 0$. Particularly, we call users in $SV^{r,1}$ *potential leaders*, and those in $SV^{r,s}$ for $s > 1$ *verifiers*. (2) i's power as a committee member is proportional to the number of her votes.

Step-by-Step Execution. This section presents the step 1 and 2 in the sidechain protocol Π^{pp}, in which we make significant modifications to the original Algorand. For completeness, the remaining steps are provided in [29].

In any round $r \geq 0$, each user i starts her (own) round r as soon as she is sure about B^{r-1}, i.e., gets $CERT^{r-1}$ consisting of Q^{r-1} and $\geq t_H$ signatures on the same $H(B^{r-1})$ from the same step (see step 5 in [29])[7].

Step 1: Block Proposal. Each user i starts her step 1 as soon as she starts round r. She waits[a] time $t_1 := \Lambda$ and performs as follows then.

1. i gets her mempool MP_i^r by collecting bids b from the network[b] s.t.: (1) $\mathsf{bVrfy}(\mathsf{b}, C) = 1$; and (2) $\nexists \mathsf{b}' \in \mathsf{MP}_i^r \cup \left(\bigcup_{r' \in [r-1]_0} B^{r'}\right)$ satisfying $\mathsf{b}' \neq \mathsf{b}$ and the serial number S in both b and b';
2. i runs $\mathsf{GetVotes}(p^{r,1}, a_i, \sigma_i^{r,1}) = x$. She ends her step 1 if $x = 0$ (i.e., $i \notin SV^{r,1}$); Otherwise, she performs as follows[c].
   i sets $\mathsf{B}_i^r = \mathsf{MP}_i^r$, computes her candidate block $B_i^r = (r, H(B^{r-1}), SIG_i(Q^{r-1}), \mathsf{B}_i^r)$, prepares $m_i^{r,1} := (B_i^r, esig_i(H(B_i^r)), \sigma_i^{r,1})$ with her ephemeral key pair $(sk_i^{r,1}, pk_i^{r,1})$, destroys $sk_i^{r,1}$, and propagates $m_i^{r,1}$.

---

[a] The waiting period ensures that the user can receive B^{r-1}. Moreover, we propose an alternative configuration in [29] that eliminates this waiting procedure, provided we admit that a serial number appears at most twice.
[b] Some of these bids may come from candidate blocks in previous rounds.
[c] Unlike Algorand [14], each user in $SV^{r,1}$ propagates the entire candidate block, as our leader selection requires the qualification of candidate blocks.

We prepare $\mathsf{VrfyMsg}$ (Algorithm 3) for users to verify the validity of messages. Specially for step 1, the algorithm also verifies candidate blocks, e.g., each bid

---

[7] Some user may not know the full block B^{r-1} even she knows $CERT^{r-1}$ which is a short message.

in the input candidate block should be valid and not duplicated concerning its serial number. Let $M_i^{r,s}$ denote the set of all *valid* messages collected by user i from $SV^{r,s}$. That is, $\mathsf{VrfyMsg}(p^{r,s}, a_j, \mathcal{C}^{r-1}, m_j^{r,s}) = 1$ for any $m_j^{r,s} \in M_i^{r,s}$.

For each user i, the leader selection takes as input her mempool MP_i^r and the valid message set $M_i^{r,1}$ collected by her. We outline $\mathsf{SelectL}(\mathsf{MP}_i^r, M_i^{r,1})$ algorithm for this purpose, which is specified in Algorithm 4.

On a high level, the algorithm first extracts all serial numbers from MP_i^r to a set of serial numbers, denoted by SP_i^r. By one-more bidding-unforgeability, we consider SP_i^r instead of MP_i^r. Hence, the adversary cannot take advantage by issuing multiple bids under the same serial number. Next, from the candidate block B_j^r embedded in each message $m_j^{r,1} \in M_i^{r,1}$, it extracts all serial numbers to a set of serial numbers, denoted by S_j^r. It sets $V_i := \{\mathsf{S}_j^r \mid m_j^{r,1} \in M_i^{r,1}\}$,

$$y := \max_{\mathsf{S}_j^r \in V_i}\{|\mathsf{S}_j^r \cap \mathsf{SP}_i^r|\}, \quad W_i := \begin{cases} \{j \mid |\mathsf{S}_j^r \cap \mathsf{SP}_i^r| \geq \mathfrak{h}y, \mathsf{S}_j^r \in V_i\} & y \geq L; \\ \{j \mid \mathsf{S}_j^r \in V_i\} & y < L. \end{cases} \quad (3.1)$$

See Remark 7 for the use of the intersection defining y. $\mathsf{SelectL}$ outputs the leader in the view of i as $\ell \leftarrow \arg\min_{j \in W_i} \mathsf{GetMinHash}(a_j, \sigma_j^{r,1})$.

Step 2: Leader Selection. In any round $r \geq 0$, each user i starts her step 2 as soon as she finishes her step 1. The user waits time $\lambda + \Lambda$ in step 2. Hence, the total waiting time is $t_2 := \lambda + 2\Lambda$. She performs as follows *after* the waiting period.

1. i collects $M_i^{r,1}$. If $M_i^{r,1} = \emptyset$, she sets $v_i := \perp$; Otherwise, she selects $\ell := \mathsf{SelectL}(\mathsf{MP}_i^r, M_i^{r,1})$ and sets $v_i := (H(B_\ell^r), \ell)$;
2. i runs $\mathsf{GetVotes}(p^{r,2}, a_i, \sigma_i^{r,2}) = x$. She stops and propagates nothing if $x = 0$ (i.e., $i \notin SV^{r,2}$); Otherwise, she prepares[a] a message $m_i^{r,2} := (ESIG_i(v_i), \sigma_i^{r,2}, SIG_\ell(Q^{r-1}))$ with her ephemeral key pair $(sk_i^{r,2}, pk_i^{r,2})$, destroys $sk_i^{r,2}$, and propagates $m_i^{r,2}$.

---

[a] $SIG_\ell(Q^{r-1})$ is included in $m_i^{r,2}$ to propagate the seed in her view.

Remark 4. Our Aucrand protocol finishes with immutably recorded sealed bids that can be revealed automatically. The transfer of goods and currency, and the potential dispute resolution, can be achieved by the "claim-or-refund" functionality [6]. This functionality can be constructed without using smart contracts [2]. Designing such a mechanism tailored to Aucrand remains future work.

4 Security Analysis for Aucrand

In this section, we first show that Aucrand is secure under certain assumptions (cf. those in [14, Section 5.2]). Then, we define a strategic game simulating Aucrand step 1 and work out its equilibrium. Retain the notations in Sect. 3.2.

4.1 Security Against the Byzantine Adversary

We first model a user to be either honest or corrupted. The corrupted ones (named malicious users) are controlled by a Byzantine adversary. We make the honest majority of deposit (HMD) assumption, *i.e.*, the fraction of the deposit transactions submitted by honest users (in each round of the sidechain protocol) is *always* $> 2/3$ (although there might be corruption). By the one-more bidding-unforgeability property (Lemma 2), HMD is equivalent to the honest majority of serial number (HMS) assumption, *i.e.*, the fraction of serial numbers corresponding to deposit transactions submitted by the honest users is always $> 2/3$. We list notations and assumptions below (cf. those in [14, Section 5]):

- h is a number s.t. the fraction of the deposit transactions submitted by honest users is always $> h$;
- $HSV^{r,s}$ and $MSV^{r,s}$ denotes respectively the subset of $SV^{r,s}$ of honest verifiers and malicious verifiers. $|HSV^{r,s}|$ and $|MSV^{r,s}|$ denote respectively the number of votes from verifiers in $HSV^{r,s}$ and $MSV^{r,s}$: for $x_i := \mathsf{GetVotes}(p^{r,s}, a_i, \sigma_i^{r,s})$, $|HSV^{r,s}| := \sum_{i \in HSV^{r,s}} x_i$ and $|MSV^{r,s}| := \sum_{i \in MSV^{r,s}} x_i$;
- The numbers $p^{r,s}$ and t_H are chosen so that we have the following inequality with overwhelming probability

$$|HSV^{r,s}|/2 + |MSV^{r,s}| < t_H < |HSV^{r,s}|; \tag{4.1}$$

- T^{r+1} denotes the time when the first honest user is sure about B^r *i.e.*, got $CERT^r$. I^r denotes the interval $[T^r, T^r + \lambda]$;
- ℓ denote the r-leader who, if exists[12], is the unique user s.t. the value $(H(B_\ell^r), \ell)$ gets $\geq t_H$ votes from $HSV^{r,2}$. This uniqueness follows from that no other value gets $\geq t_H$ votes from $SV^{r,2}$ (by Lemma 5(1) below).

Lemma 5 (Proven in [29]).

(1) (cf. [14, Lemma 5.7]) Assume that[13] all honest users are sure about the same B^{r-1}. Let v denote the value in the message signed by verifiers in $SV^{r,s}$. If there is a value v getting $\geq t_H$ votes from verifiers in $SV^{r,s}$, then there exists no other value $v' \neq v$ s.t. v' and v have the same length and v' gets $\geq t_H$ votes from verifiers in $SV^{r,s}$;

(2) Assume that all honest users are sure about the same B^{r-1} in the time interval I^r and the same B^{r-2}. Any honest user i receive the block B^{r-1} before collecting her mempool MP_i^r of round r.

Qualification in the Leader Selection. Admit that all honest users are sure about the same B^{r-1}. For a verifier $i \in HSV^{r,2}$, given the set W_i in Eq. 3.1, the leader in her view is the user in W_i who has the minimal hash. For an

---
[12] Even if no r-leader exists, the block may be nonempty and the leader for round r may exist, *i.e.*, $B^r \neq B_\epsilon^r$.
[13] This assumption is the induction hypothesis for proving Theorem 1.

honest potential leader $i' \in HSV^{r,1}$, we know $\mathsf{S}_{i'}^r = \mathsf{SP}_{i'}^r$. However, HMS does not necessarily imply that $\mathsf{SP}_{i'}^r$ is large enough[14] so that it may happen that $i' \notin W_i$. In the leader selection of round r, one of the following cases happens:

- (bad case) $\exists\, i \in HSV^{r,2}$ and $\exists\, i' \in HSV^{r,1}$ s.t. $i' \notin W_i$;
- (good case) otherwise.

We propose basic properties concerning two cases (see [29] for proofs).

Proposition 6. *(1) If the good case happens and some honest potential leader ℓ has the minimal hash, then ℓ is the r-leader;*
(2) Put $\mathsf{SP}_H^r := \bigcup_{i \in HSV^{r,2}} \mathsf{SP}_i^r$. If $\geq \mathfrak{h}$ of serial numbers in SP_H^r belong to $\mathsf{SP}_{i'}^r$ for any verifier $i' \in HSV^{r,1} \cup HSV^{r,2}$, then the good case happens;
(3) Admit $\mathfrak{h} = 2/3$. Assume that[15] all honest users are sure about the same $B^{r'-1}$ in $\Gamma^{r'}$ for $r' \in [r, r+5]$. If $L \geq |C| \cdot 5\%$, where C denotes the set of all serial numbers, then the bad case can not consecutively happen[16] for $r' \in [r..r+5]$.

Remark 7. (1) Due to HMS, the good case could be easily realized if all honest users issue their bids before the round 0 of the side chain;
(2) By the inverse of Proposition 6(2), to let the bad case happen, some malicious users have to send a large enough number of their bids to a part of honest users so that $< \mathfrak{h}$ of serial numbers in SP_H^r belong to $\mathsf{SP}_{i'}^r$ for some verifier $i' \in HSV^{r,1} \cup HSV^{r,2}$. We use this to show Proposition 6(3);
(3) The occurrence of the bad case does not necessarily imply that the leader is malicious. We may assume that the adversary intends to let some malicious user's candidate block get $\geq t_H$ votes from $SV^{r,2}$, because for otherwise, no honest user in step $s \geq 3$ regards a malicious user as the leader. Then, by the intersection in Eq. 3.1, the malicious users need to compete with the hash values of $> 1/2$ of honest potential leaders.

The Main Theorem. We propose the main theorem for the security of Aucrand with HMD, whose proof is postponed to [29]. This theorem is similar to that of [14, Theorem 1] in Algorand. In fact, HMD plays a similar role as the honest majority of money assumption in [14].

Theorem 1. *The following properties hold with overwhelming probability for each round $r \geq 0$:*

(1) (a) All honest users agree on the same block B^r;

---

[14] In fact, if malicious users do not send their bids to i' before honest users collect their mempools, then $\mathsf{SP}_{i'}^r$ may be too small so that the candidate block of i' gets disqualified by honest users who have received malicious users' bids.
[15] By Theorem 1, this assumption is fulfilled in our setting.
[16] Admit a slightly lower $\mathfrak{h}$, e.g., $\mathfrak{h} = 1/2$. If $L \geq |C| \cdot 1.1\%$, then the bad case can not consecutively happen for $r' \in [r..r+5]$..

(b) All honest users receive the block B^{r-1} before waiting time Λ ends in round r step 1 so that each bid b in B^r satisfies $\mathsf{bVrfy}(\mathsf{b}, C) = 1$ and that any b' in the chain C^r with $\mathsf{b}' \neq \mathsf{b}$ corresponds to a serial number different from that of b.

(c) Let z denote the number of bids issued by honest users that are not in the chain. If $z \geq L$ and B^r is nonempty, then B^r contains at least $\mathfrak{h}z$ bids.

(2) If r-leader ℓ exists, then the following holds.
  - The leader is ℓ and generates $B^r = B_\ell^r$. All honest users are sure about B^r in the time interval I^{r+1} and $T^{r+1} \leq T^r + 5\lambda + 2\Lambda$;
  - The block B^r is nonempty. If ℓ is honest, then the set of bids in B^r consists of all bids in ℓ's mempool MP_ℓ^r.

(3) If r-leader does not exist, then all honest users are sure about B^r in the time interval I^{r+1}. Moreover, one of the following two cases happens.
  - If every verifier $i \in HSV^{r,4}$ has $g_i \leq 1$, then the Aucrand round r finishes in step 6 with an empty block and $T^{r+1} \leq T^r + 8\lambda + 2\Lambda$.
  - Otherwise, i.e., some verifier $i \in HSV^{r,4}$ has $g_i = 2$, then Aucrand round r finishes before step $6 + 3 \cdot L^r$ and $T^{r+1} \leq T^r + (6L^r + 8)\lambda + 2\Lambda$, given that $6 + 3 \cdot L^r$ is smaller than the maximal number of steps allowed by the protocol designer. Here L^r denotes the random variable representing the number of Bernoulli's trials needed to see a 1.

(4) Assume the good case happens in rounds $r - 1$ and r. The probability of some honest user becoming r-leader is $\geq h^2(1 + h - h^2)$.

4.2 Security in Rational Settings

When the context is clear, we put $H^s := HSV^{r,s}$ and $M^s := MSV^{r,s}$ for $s \geq 2$.

An Strategic Game. The goal is to define a game to simulate Aucrand step 1. On a high level, we replace honest potential leaders with those rational users who want to join the auction.

Recall that we assume a network with bounded delay and the adversary being rushing, i.e., can see all candidate blocks of potential leaders beforehand. Hence, it is reasonable to treat the Aucrand step 1 as an extensive game with perfect information. For simplicity, we only present a strategic game below. One may regard it as the strategic form of an extensive game given in [29, Section 4.2].

Definition 8 (*r-Election as a strategy game*). *The strategic game r-election is the tuple $\left(SV^{r,1}, (S_i)_{i \in SV^{r,1}}, (u_i)_{i \in SV^{r,1}}\right)$ defined as follow:*

(1) The set of players $SV^{r,1}$ consists of potential leaders of Aucrand round r. A player is said to be an r-candidate if she is an honest user before waiting time Λ ends in round r. Let I denote the set of r-candidates. Put $J := SV^{r,1} \setminus I$. A player $j \in J$ is called an r-villain;

(2) For each r-candidate $i \in I$, her strategy set S_i is the set $\mathcal{MP}_i^r$ of all subsets of MP_i^r. Let $j \in J$ be an r-villain. Let A_j denote the set consisting of functions $f_j : PK \setminus \{j\} \to \mathcal{MP}_j^r$. We may regard that $\exists\, i, i' \in PK$ with $i \neq i'$ such that

$f_j(i) \neq f_j(i')$, which indicates that j intentionally send different candidate blocks to different r-candidates. The j's strategy set S_j consists of functions $s_j : \prod_{i \in I} S_i \to A_j$;
(3) Regard $s_i \in S_i$ as the candidate block propagated by the r-candidate i. Given $(s_i)_{i \in I}$, for $j \in J$ and $s_j \in S_j$, put $f_j := s_j((s_i)_{i \in I})$ and regard $f_j(i')$ as the candidate block that j sends to the user $i' \in PK \setminus \{j\}$. Following Eq. 3.1, each verifier i'' in H^2 can select a leader according to the received candidate blocks.
- If an r-candidate $\hat{i}$ is the leader whose candidate block gets $\geq t_H$ votes from verifiers in H^2 (we name $\hat{i}$ the r-leader[17]), we put $u_i = n_i$ and $u_j = -|s_{\hat{i}}|$ for $i \in I$ and $j \in J$, where n_i denotes the number of bids issued by i that are included in the candidate block of $\hat{i}$;
- Otherwise, put $u_i = -\tau$ for $i \in I$ and $u_j = 0$ for $j \in J$, where $\tau > 0$ reflects[18] the time cost caused by empty blocks.

The rationale of u_i: By anonymity (Lemma 2), bids' information is hidden. For an r-candidate, once there are some bids in the pool, her allocation result depends on the price of her bids and whether or not these bids are recorded on the block. Moreover, the r-candidate's time cost for obtaining this result increases if there are more empty blocks. So, within one epoch, in her view: (1) whether a bid *not* issued by her is recorded on the chain does not affect her allocation result; (2) she earns nothing if her bids are not recorded; (3) the relative time cost of empty blocks should give her a negative utility. Therefore, she is better off letting her own bids in the chain and avoiding the empty block case.

The rationale of u_j: (1) By the utility function, r-villains' goal is to prevent that some r-candidate becomes the r-leader; (2) As r-villains have the same utility, we may regard that they are controlled by one player, denoted r-*Villain*. In particular, her strategy set is

$$(s_j)_{j \in J} : \prod_{i \in I} S_i \to \prod_{j \in J} A_j \qquad (4.2)$$

and r-Villain's utility is u_j for any $j \in J$.

Remark 9. By the equality $u_i = -\tau$, even if all of an r-candidate's bids are recorded on the chain, she is better off avoiding the empty block case.

Remark 10 (r-Villain behaves like adversary). Admit: (1) The r-villains are controlled by the adversary in round r step $s \geq 2$; (2) If not corrupted, r-candidates behave the same as honest users after round r step 1. We show (see [29, Section 4.2]) that the strategies of the r-villains may lead to the same consequences as those caused by the adversary (cf. Theorem 1(3)) if Aucrand step 1 is replaced with the r-election. This means that we make virtually no assumption about r-villains' behavior. Hence, we regard r-villains to behave the same as malicious users and the r-Villain to resemble the Byzantine adversary.

---

[17] The r-leader here is compatible with the one defined in Sect. 4.1. We restrict to the case where an r-leader is an r-candidate (cf. utility function of an r-villain).

[18] $\tau > 0$ is a relative value for the time cost, which is the difference between the time cost of empty blocks and that of the case where an r-leader exists.

On Equilibrium of the r-Election Game. We work out an equilibrium under certain assumptions. For a player $k \in SV^{r,1}$, put $-k := SV^{r,1} \setminus \{k\}$. Retain the notations in Definition 8. We admit, w.l.o.g.[19], $\mathsf{SP}^r_j = \mathsf{SP}^r_H := \bigcup_{i \in H^2} \mathsf{SP}^r_i$ for any $j \in J$. For $i \in I$ and $j \in J$, the inclusion $\mathsf{SP}^r_i \subseteq \mathsf{SP}^r_j$ holds as honest users propagate their bids.

Consider a strategy profile $(s^*_k) = (s^*_k)_{k \in SV^{r,1}} \in \prod_{k \in SV^{r,1}} S_k$ defined below.

- Each r-candidate $i \in I$ behaves the same as an honest user, $i.e.$, $s^*_i = \mathsf{MP}^r_i$;
- For an r-villain $j \in J$, consider a constant function s^*_j on $\prod_{i \in I} S_i$ s.t.

$$s^*_j : PK \setminus \{j\} \to \mathcal{MP}^r_j, \quad s^*_j(i) = \begin{cases} \mathsf{MP}^r_j & i \in H^2_+; \\ \emptyset & i \in H^2_-, \end{cases}$$

where $H^2_+ \subsetneq H^2$ consists of players $i \in H^2$ s.t. $|H^2_+| = a$ for $|H^2| - t_H < a < t_H$ and $H^2_- := H^2 \setminus H^2_+$ hold. Here $|H^2_+|$ is calculated as in Sect. 4.1.

Theorem 2. *Assume that $\geq \mathfrak{h}$ of series numbers in SP^r_H belong to SP^r_i for any $i \in I \cup H^2$ and $\mathfrak{h} \cdot |\mathsf{SP}^r_H| \geq L$. Then the profile (s^*_k) is an equilibrium for the r-election. Moreover, this profile is an equilibrium even if we regard all r-villains as one player – the r-Villain.*

The assumption of this theorem has appeared in Proposition 6(2). By Proposition 6(3) (see also Remark 7(2)), the adversary can not take advantage of the negation of this assumption consecutively, $i.e.$, it can not let the bad case happen consecutively. In this theorem, when regarding all r-villains as the r-Villain, the utility function is referred to the one defined in Eq. 4.2. The proof of this theorem is postponed to [29].

Remark 11. We sketch partial results concerning this theorem's enhancements below (see [29] for details):

(1) For an r-candidate i, the strategy MP^r_i is a best response to any strategy of $-i$ if there exists another r-candidate chooses a strategy containing MP^r_i;[20]
(2) For $i \in I$, any strategy $s_i \subsetneq \mathsf{MP}^r_i$ is not a best response to certain $-i$'s strategy;
(3) Regard all r-villains as one player. Given certain behavior of the adversary before the r-election, the strategy profile (s^*_k) is not a subgame equilibrium.

Let h be a number such that $\geq h$ fraction of deposit transactions are issued by honest users (hence candidates) in any round. Theorem 1(4) implies

Corollary 12. *Assume that the setting and the equilibrium in the theorem hold for rounds $r' \in [r-1..r+k]$, $k \geq 1$. Then if a serial number S belongs to SP^r_i for all r-candidates i, then the probability for a bid corresponding to S included in the chain $\mathcal{C}^{r+k}$ is at least $1 - (1-p_h)^k$ with $p_h = h^2(1 + h - h^2)$.*

---

[19] This assumption is natural. Indeed, it implies $\mathsf{SP}^r_j = \mathsf{SP}^r_{j'}$ for any $j, j' \in J$, which is compatible with that the r-Villain controls r-villains (Eq. 4.2). Moreover, by Eq. 3.1, for an r-villain j, the case $\mathsf{SP}^r_j \supset \mathsf{SP}^r_H$ and the case $\mathsf{SP}^r_j = \mathsf{SP}^r_H$ are equivalent.

[20] We tried to remove the condition "$\geq \mathfrak{h}$ of serial numbers in SP^r_H belong to SP^r_i for any $i \in I \cup H^2$" to get a stronger result. This is difficult, but we give a partial result.

Remark 13 (Fee-less liveness). The liveness of blockchain protocols [25] briefly means that transactions known by all honest users are eventually inserted into the chain before a certain amount of delay. The corollary may read: without explicit reward, *e.g.*, fees for including bids, the bids known by all rational users who want to join the auction are eventually inserted into the sidechain before a certain amount of delay under certain conditions.

5 Cost Analysis and Implementation

This section briefly presents: (1) a cost analysis to show that bids in Aucrand cost less than those in smart contracts-based protocols; (2) an implementation to exhibit the potential harm caused by selfish behavior *without* block qualification.

Cost Analysis. We analyze the cost of an honest (rational) user spent on each bid due to transaction fees and MEV[21]. As anonymity ensures MEV prevention [38], and our Aucrand inherits anonymity from DADB (Lemma 2), it suffices to analyze transaction fees. Optimistically, once the equilibrium in Theorem 2 is achieved, then no transaction fee is required on the sidechain. As for mainchain, a ledger supporting Ethereum-type smart contracts will generally incur a higher operation cost than EUTXO-type ledgers. Moreover, even if Ethereum is chosen as the mainchain, the cost of a typical bid is solely the transaction fee for the corresponding deposit transaction in the optimistic case. Our fee is $112,800$ gas by the data in [38, Table 1], but $629,300$ gas is needed for a bid in *loc. cit.*

Implementation. We implement the sidechain protocol *without* our block qualification mechanism[22]. Concrete setup and more analysis are detailed in [29]. For any round index $r \geq 0$, recall that B^r denotes the set of bids in a block B^r. Here, we consider the following metrics, parameterized by r:

1. Inclusion rate: $IR = |\mathsf{B}^r|/(\#\text{bids issued in round } r)$. Values of $IR > 1$ occur when users include bids from previous rounds, leading to larger blocks;
2. Mempool size: $MS = \sum_{r' \in [r]_0}(\#\text{bids issued in round } r) - \sum_{r' \in [r]_0}|\mathsf{B}^{r'}|$. A positive MS indicates there are unprocessed bids not recorded on the blockchain.

In Fig. 1, the frequency and scale of events where $IR > 1$ and $MS > 0$ increases along with the fraction of selfish rational users. An exception arises when the fraction reaches 1, where each block only consists of the leader's bids; MS increases due to the accumulation of unprocessed bids in the mempool.

---

[21] As the mechanism for the transfer of goods and currency is undetermined (cf. Remark 4), we leave analyzing the related cost as future work.
[22] See https://anonymous.4open.science/r/aucrand.

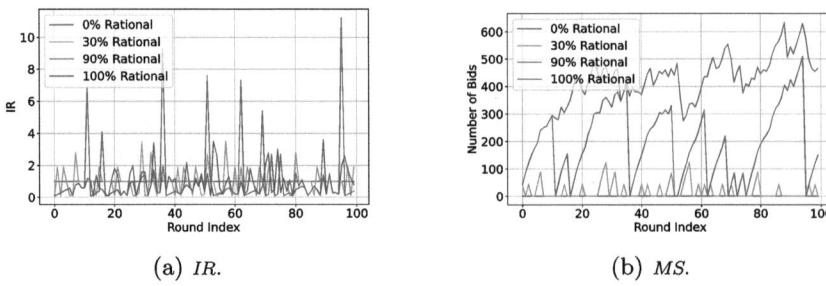

Fig. 1. Experiment results.

6 Conclusion

In this work, we propose Aucrand, a novel blockchain-based sealed-bid auction protocol. Our contributions include the formalization of a decentralized anonymous deposited-bidding (DADB) scheme and the development of an Algorand-style sidechain. By integrating a novel block qualification mechanism into the consensus process, we first prove that our protocol maintains Algorand's original security guarantees. Regarding rational users, our implementation results show that their behavior can lead to performance degradation. However, through game-theoretical analysis, we demonstrate that our block qualification mechanism can incentivize honest behavior, effectively mitigating such degradation, even *without* relying on explicit incentives.

A Formal Definitions for Timed Commitments

Following the formalization in [31], a t_{fo}-NITC scheme consists of a tuple of algorithms TC := (PGen, Com, OpenVrfy, FOpen):

- PGen(1^κ) takes as input the security parameter κ and outputs a common reference string crs;
- Com(crs, m) takes as input a string crs and a message m. It outputs a commitment c and an open o;
- OpenVrfy(crs, c, m, o) takes as input a string crs , a commitment c, a message m, and an open o. It outputs 1 (accept) or 0 (reject);
- FOpen(crs, c) takes as input a string crs and a commitment c. After time *at least* t_{fo}, it outputs m or $\bot$.

The security of NITC is enhanced to the CCA-model, in which the adversary is given access to a forced-opening oracle $\mathcal{O}_{\mathsf{FOpen}}(\mathsf{crs}, \cdot)$. Formally, the correctness, CCA-hiding, and CCA-binding are defined as follows.

Definition 4 (Correctness). *An NITC is correct if the following property holds for any $\kappa > 0$, $\mathsf{crs} \leftarrow \mathsf{PGen}(1^\kappa)$, and any m.*

$$\Pr\left[\begin{array}{l}\mathsf{OpenVrfy}(c,m,o) = 1 \wedge \\ \mathsf{FOpen}(c) = m\end{array}\,\middle|\,(c,o) \leftarrow \mathsf{Com}(m)\right] = 1$$

Definition 5 (CCA-Hiding). *An NITC is (T_1, T_2)-CCA-hiding if for any PPT adversary $\mathcal{A} = (\mathcal{A}_1, \mathcal{A}_2)$ s.t. $\mathcal{A}_1$ can query a forced-opening oracle $\mathcal{O}_{\mathsf{FOpen}}(\mathsf{crs}, \cdot)$ for at most $T_1(\kappa)$ times, and $\mathcal{A}_2$ can query $\mathcal{O}_{\mathsf{FOpen}}(\mathsf{crs}, \cdot)$ for at most $T_2(\kappa)$ times without querying the challenged c, the following probability is $\mathsf{negl}(\kappa)$ for any $\kappa > 0$ and $\mathsf{crs} \leftarrow \mathsf{PGen}(1^\kappa)$.*

$$\left|\Pr\left[b' = b \,\middle|\, \begin{array}{l}(m_0, m_1, \mathsf{st}) \leftarrow \mathcal{A}_1^{\mathcal{O}_{\mathsf{FOpen}}}(\mathsf{crs}); \\ b \xleftarrow{\$} \{0,1\}; \\ (c, \cdot) \leftarrow \mathsf{Com}(m_b); \\ b' \leftarrow \mathcal{A}_2^{\mathcal{O}_{\mathsf{FOpen}}}(c, \mathsf{st})\end{array}\right] - \frac{1}{2}\right|$$

Definition 6 (CCA-binding). *An NITC is T-CCA-binding if for any PPT adversary $\mathcal{A}$ that can query a forced-opening oracle $\mathcal{O}_{\mathsf{FOpen}}(\mathsf{crs}, \cdot)$ for at most T times, the following probability is $\mathsf{negl}(\kappa)$ for any $\kappa > 0$ and $\mathsf{crs} \leftarrow \mathsf{PGen}(1^\kappa)$.*

$$\Pr\left[\begin{array}{l}(c, m, o, m', o') \\ \leftarrow \mathcal{A}^{\mathcal{O}_{\mathsf{FOpen}}}(\mathsf{crs})\end{array}\,\middle|\,\begin{array}{l}(m \neq m' \wedge \mathsf{OpenVrfy}(c, m, o) = 1 \wedge \\ \mathsf{OpenVrfy}(c, m', o') = 1) \vee \\ (\mathsf{OpenVrfy}(c, m, o) = 1 \wedge \mathsf{FOpen}(c) \neq m)\end{array}\right]$$

B Algorithm Specifications

Committee Selection. Given the hash function $H(\cdot)$, we denote the string of "0." concatenated with the hash value by $.H(\cdot) := (0.H(\cdot))_2$. Let pp be the aforementioned parameter. On a high level, our committee selection is realized by applying the stake-based mechanism [14, Section 6] to the set of deposits $\bigcup_{i \in PK^e} D_i^e$ so that a user i is selected with a weight proportional to $|D_i^e|$. Following notations in loc. cit., the set of committees in round $r \geq 0$ step $s \geq 1$ is denoted by $SV^{r,s}$. Particularly, we call users in $SV^{r,1}$ potential leaders, and those in $SV^{r,s}$ for $s > 1$ verifiers.

Let $a_i := |D_i|$ be the number of deposit transactions issued by user i in epoch e. To realize the committee selection, we propose two helper algorithms GetVotes and GetMinHash (Algorithm 1 and 2). In the algorithms, each user i essentially "gets a hash value as a lottery ticket" for each deposit transaction in D_i so that i has a_i hash values in each committee selection. In Algorithm 1, a deposit transaction becomes a vote if and only if the corresponding hash is small enough, which happens with probability $p^{r,s}$. In Algorithm 2, the minimal hash value among a_i hash values of a user's deposit transaction is obtained.

We abstract two helper algorithms below. For each user i, her committee credential of round r step s is $\sigma_i^{r,s} := SIG_i(r, s, Q^{r-1})$.

- GetVotes($p^{r,s}, a_i, \sigma_i^{r,s}$) outputs the number of i's votes so that (1) i is a committee member if and only if GetVotes($p^{r,s}, a_i, \sigma_i^{r,s}$) > 0 and (2) i's power as a committee member is proportional to the number of her votes.
- GetMinHash($a_i, \sigma_i^{r,1}$) essentially outputs the "minimum hash" value $w.r.t.$ $\sigma_i^{r,s}$.

Message Verification and Leader Selection. VrfyMsg is specified in Algorithm 3 and SelectL in Algorithm 4.

Algorithm 1: GetVotes outputs the number of copies of i in $SV^{r,s}$.

1 **function** GetVotes($p^{r,s}, a_i, \sigma_i^{r,s}$) ;
2 Compute $y = .H(\sigma_i^{r,s})$;
  // Denote with $p := p^{r,s}$ in the following.
3 **for** $x \in [a_i]_0$ **do**
4 $\quad$ Compute $p_x = \binom{a_i}{x} p^x (1-p)^{a_i - x}$;
5 $\quad$ **if** $y \in [0, p_0]$ **then**
6 $\quad\quad$ Return 0 ;
7 $\quad$ **else**
8 $\quad\quad$ **if** $y \in \left(\sum_{x' < x} p_{i,x'}, \sum_{x' \leq x} p_{i,x'} \right]$ **then**
9 $\quad\quad\quad$ Return x ;
10 $\quad\quad$ end
11 $\quad$ end
12 end

Algorithm 2: GetMinHash outputs the "minimum hash" $w.r.t.$ $\sigma_i^{r,s}$.

1 **function** GetMinHash($a_i, \sigma_i^{r,1}$) ;
2 **if** GetVotes($p^{r,1}, a_i, \sigma_i^{r,1}$) $= 0$ **then**
3 $\quad$ Return 0 ;
4 end
5 Compute $y = .H(\sigma_i^{r,s})$;
6 **for** $x \in [2^\kappa]_0$ **do**
7 $\quad$ Compute $p_{i,x} = \left(\frac{2^\kappa - x + 1}{2^\kappa + 1} \right)^{a_i} - \left(\frac{2^\kappa - x}{2^\kappa + 1} \right)^{a_i}$;
8 $\quad$ **if** $y \in [0, p_0]$ **then**
9 $\quad\quad$ Return 0 ;
10 $\quad$ **else**
11 $\quad\quad$ **if** $y \in \left(\sum_{x' < x} p_{i,x'}, \sum_{x' \leq x} p_{i,x'} \right]$ **then**
12 $\quad\quad\quad$ Return x ;
13 $\quad\quad$ end
14 $\quad$ end
15 end

Algorithm 3: VrfyMsg verifies messages of step $s \geq 1$.

1 **function** VrfyMsg$(p^{r,s}, a_i, \mathcal{C}^{r-1}, m_i^{r,s})$;
2   Parse $\sigma_i^{r,s} \in m_i^{r,s}$;
3   **if** SigVrfy$(pk_i, \sigma_i^{r,s}) = 0 \lor$ GetVotes$(p^{r,s}, a_i, \sigma_i^{r,s}) = 0$ **then**
4 | Return 0 ;
5   **end**
6   **if** $s = 2$ **then**
7 | Parse $m_i^{r,2} = (ESIG_i(v_i), \sigma_i^{r,2}, SIG_\ell(Q^{r-1}))$;
8 | **if** SigVrfy$(pk_i^{r,2}, ESIG_i(v_i)) = 0 \land$ SigVrfy$(pk_\ell, SIG_\ell(Q^{r-1})) = 0$ **then**
9 | Return 0 ;
10 | **end**
11   **else if** $s = 3$ **then**
12 | Parse $m_i^{r,3} = (ESIG_i(v_i), \sigma_i^{r,3})$;
13 | **if** SigVrfy$(pk_i^{r,3}, ESIG_i(v_i)) = 0$ **then**
14 | Return 0 ;
15 | **end**
16   **else if** $s > 4 \land s \in \mathbb{N}$ **then**
17 | Parse $m_i^{r,s} = (ESIG_i(b_i), ESIG_i(v_i), \sigma_i^{r,s})$;
18 | **if** SigVrfy$(pk_i^{r,s}, ESIG_i(b_i)) = 0 \lor$ SigVrfy$(pk_i^{r,s}, ESIG_i(v_i)) = 0$ **then**
19 | Return 0 ;
20 | **end**
21   **else if** $s = 1$ **then**
22 | Parse $m_i^{r,1} = (B_i^r, esig_i(H(B_i^r)), \sigma_i^{r,1})$;
23 | **if** SigVrfy$(pk_i^{r,1}, H(B_i^r), esig_i(H(B_i^r))) = 0$ **then**
24 | Return 0 ;
25 | **end**
26 | Parse $\mathcal{C}^{r-1} = B^0||\ldots||B^{r-1}$ and $\mathsf{B}^{r'} \in B^{r'}$ for all $r' \in [r-1]_0$;
27 | Parse $B_i^r = (r_i, H_i, SIG_i(Q_i^{r-1}), \mathsf{B}_i^r)$;
28 | **if** $r_i \neq r \lor H_i \neq H(B^{r-1}) \lor Q_i^{r-1} \neq H(SIG_{\ell^{r-1}}(Q^{r-2}), r)$
              $\lor$ SigVrfy$(pk_i, SIG_i(Q_i^{r-1})) = 0$ **then**
29 | Return 0 ;
30 | **end**
31 | **for** $\mathsf{b} \in \mathsf{B}_i^r$ **do**
32 | **if** bVrfy$(\mathsf{b}, C) = 0$ **then**
33 | Return 0 ;
34 | **else**
35 | Parse $\mathsf{b} = (c_P, \pi_P, S, \pi_{\mathsf{SoK}})$;
36 | **if** $\exists \mathsf{b}' \in \mathsf{B}_i^r \cup (\bigcup_{r' \in [r-1]_0} \mathsf{B}^{r'})$ s.t. $S \in \mathsf{b}' \land \mathsf{b}' \neq \mathsf{b}$ **then**
37 | Return 0 ;
38 | **end**
39 | **end**
40 | **end**
41   **else**
42 | Return 0 ;
43   **end**
44   Return 1 ;

Algorithm 4: SelectL outputs the selected leader index of round r.

1 **function** SelectL($\mathsf{MP}_i^r, M_i^{r,1}$) ;
   // Extract the set of serial numbers from the mempool.
2 $\mathsf{SP}_i^r = \emptyset$;
3 **for** $b \in \mathsf{MP}_i^r$ **do**
4   Parse $b = (c_P, \pi_P, S, \pi_{\mathsf{SoK}})$;
5     $\mathsf{SP}_j^r = \mathsf{SP}_j^r \cup \{S\}$;
6 **end**
   // Extract the set of serial numbers from each candidate block.
7 $V = \emptyset$;
8 **for** $m_j^{r,1} \in M_i^{r,1}$ **do**
9   Parse $m_j^{r,1} = (B_j^r, esig_j(H(B_j^r)), \sigma_j^{r,1})$ with
10     $B_j^r = (r, H(B^{r-1}), SIG_j(Q^{r-1}), \mathsf{B}_j^r)$;
11     $\mathsf{S}_j^r = \emptyset$;
12   **for** $b \in \mathsf{B}_j^r$ **do**
13   Parse $b = (c_P, \pi_P, S, \pi_{\mathsf{SoK}})$;
14         $\mathsf{S}_j^r = \mathsf{S}_j^r \cup \{S\}$;
15   **end**
16     $V = V \cup \{\mathsf{S}_j^r\}$;
17 **end**
18 Compute $y = \max_{\mathsf{S}_j^r \in V}(|\mathsf{S}_j^r \cap \mathsf{SP}_i^r|)$;
   // Leader selection with block qualification.
19 $W = \emptyset$;
20 **if** $y \geq L$ **then**
21   **for** $\mathsf{S}_j^r \in V$ **do**
22   **if** $|\mathsf{S}_j^r \cap \mathsf{SP}_i^r| \geq \mathfrak{h}y$ **then**
23             $W = W \cup \{j\}$;
24   **end**
25   **end**
26 **else**
27     $W = \{j \mid \mathsf{S}_j^r \in V\}$
28 **end**
29 **Return** $\arg\min_{j \in W} \mathsf{GetMinHash}(a_j, \sigma_j^{r,1})$;

References

1. Atzei, N., Bartoletti, M., Lande, S., Zunino, R.: A formal model of bitcoin transactions. In: Meiklejohn, S., Sako, K. (eds.) FC 2018. LNCS, vol. 10957, pp. 541–560. Springer, Heidelberg (2018). https://doi.org/10.1007/978-3-662-58387-6_29
2. Aumayr, L., et al.: Generalized channels from limited blockchain scripts and adaptor signatures. In: Tibouchi, M., Wang, H. (eds.) ASIACRYPT 2021. LNCS, vol. 13091, pp. 635–664. Springer, Cham (2021). https://doi.org/10.1007/978-3-030-92075-3_22

3. Badertscher, C., Garay, J., Maurer, U., Tschudi, D., Zikas, V.: But why does it work? A rational protocol design treatment of bitcoin. In: Nielsen, J.B., Rijmen, V. (eds.) EUROCRYPT 2018. LNCS, vol. 10821, pp. 34–65. Springer, Cham (2018). https://doi.org/10.1007/978-3-319-78375-8_2
4. Barbulescu, R., Gaudry, P., Kleinjung, T.: The tower number field sieve. In: Iwata, T., Cheon, J.H. (eds.) ASIACRYPT 2015. LNCS, vol. 9453, pp. 31–55. Springer, Heidelberg (2015). https://doi.org/10.1007/978-3-662-48800-3_2
5. Bellare, M., Miner, S.K.: A forward-secure digital signature scheme. In: Wiener, M. (ed.) CRYPTO 1999. LNCS, vol. 1666, pp. 431–448. Springer, Heidelberg (1999). https://doi.org/10.1007/3-540-48405-1_28
6. Bentov, I., Kumaresan, R.: How to use bitcoin to design fair protocols. In: Garay, J.A., Gennaro, R. (eds.) CRYPTO 2014. LNCS, vol. 8617, pp. 421–439. Springer, Heidelberg (2014). https://doi.org/10.1007/978-3-662-44381-1_24
7. Budish, E., Cramton, P., Shim, J.: The high-frequency trading arms race: frequent batch auctions as a market design response. Q. J. Econ. **130**(4), 1547–1621 (2015). https://doi.org/10.1093/qje/qjv027
8. Camenisch, J., Chaabouni, R., Shelat, A.: Efficient protocols for set membership and range proofs. In: Pieprzyk, J. (ed.) ASIACRYPT 2008. LNCS, vol. 5350, pp. 234–252. Springer, Heidelberg (2008). https://doi.org/10.1007/978-3-540-89255-7_15
9. Camenisch, J., Stadler, M.: Efficient group signature schemes for large groups. In: Kaliski, B.S. (ed.) CRYPTO 1997. LNCS, vol. 1294, pp. 410–424. Springer, Heidelberg (1997). https://doi.org/10.1007/BFb0052252
10. Canetti, R.: Universally composable security: a new paradigm for cryptographic protocols. In: 42nd FOCS, pp. 136–145. IEEE Computer Society Press (2001). https://doi.org/10.1109/SFCS.2001.959888
11. Chakravarty, M.M.T., Chapman, J., MacKenzie, K., Melkonian, O., Peyton Jones, M., Wadler, P.: The extended UTXO model. In: Bernhard, M., et al. (eds.) FC 2020. LNCS, vol. 12063, pp. 525–539. Springer, Cham (2020). https://doi.org/10.1007/978-3-030-54455-3_37
12. Chakravarty, M.M.T., et al.: Hydra: fast isomorphic state channels. Cryptology ePrint Archive, Report 2020/299 (2020). https://eprint.iacr.org/2020/299
13. Chase, M., Lysyanskaya, A.: On signatures of knowledge. In: Dwork, C. (ed.) CRYPTO 2006. LNCS, vol. 4117, pp. 78–96. Springer, Heidelberg (2006). https://doi.org/10.1007/11818175_5
14. Chen, J., Micali, S.: Algorand: a secure and efficient distributed ledger. Theor. Comput. Sci. **777**, 155–183 (2019). https://doi.org/10.1016/J.TCS.2019.02.001
15. Constantinides, T., Cartlidge, J.: Block auction: a general blockchain protocol for privacy-preserving and verifiable periodic double auctions. In: Xiang, Y., Wang, Z., Wang, H., Niemi, V. (eds.) 2021 IEEE Blockchain 2021, Melbourne, Australia, 6–8 December 2021, pp. 513–520. IEEE (2021). https://doi.org/10.1109/BLOCKCHAIN53845.2021.00078
16. Cramton, P.C.: Money out of thin air: the nationwide narrowband pcs auction. J. Econ. Manag. Strat. **4**(2), 267–343 (1995). https://doi.org/10.1111/j.1430-9134.1995.00267.x. https://onlinelibrary.wiley.com/doi/abs/10.1111/j.1430-9134.1995.00267.x
17. Daian, P., Pass, R., Shi, E.: **Snow White**: robustly reconfigurable consensus and applications to provably secure proof of stake. In: Goldberg, I., Moore, T. (eds.) FC 2019. LNCS, vol. 11598, pp. 23–41. Springer, Cham (2019). https://doi.org/10.1007/978-3-030-32101-7_2

18. David, B., Gaži, P., Kiayias, A., Russell, A.: Ouroboros praos: an adaptively-secure, semi-synchronous proof-of-stake blockchain. In: Nielsen, J.B., Rijmen, V. (eds.) EUROCRYPT 2018. LNCS, vol. 10821, pp. 66–98. Springer, Cham (2018). https://doi.org/10.1007/978-3-319-78375-8_3
19. Feige, U., Shamir, A.: Zero knowledge proofs of knowledge in two rounds. In: Brassard, G. (ed.) CRYPTO 1989. LNCS, vol. 435, pp. 526–544. Springer, New York (1990). https://doi.org/10.1007/0-387-34805-0_46
20. Fiat, A., Shamir, A.: How to prove yourself: practical solutions to identification and signature problems. In: Odlyzko, A.M. (ed.) CRYPTO 1986. LNCS, vol. 263, pp. 186–194. Springer, Heidelberg (1987). https://doi.org/10.1007/3-540-47721-7_12
21. Galal, H.S., Youssef, A.M.: Verifiable sealed-bid auction on the ethereum blockchain. In: Zohar, A., et al. (eds.) FC 2018. LNCS, vol. 10958, pp. 265–278. Springer, Heidelberg (2019). https://doi.org/10.1007/978-3-662-58820-8_18
22. Galal, H.S., Youssef, A.M.: Trustee: full privacy preserving vickrey auction on top of ethereum. In: Bracciali, A., Clark, J., Pintore, F., Rønne, P.B., Sala, M. (eds.) FC 2019. LNCS, vol. 11599, pp. 190–207. Springer, Cham (2020). https://doi.org/10.1007/978-3-030-43725-1_14
23. Galal, H.S., Youssef, A.M.: Publicly verifiable and secrecy preserving periodic auctions. In: Bernhard, M., et al. (eds.) FC 2021. LNCS, vol. 12676, pp. 348–363. Springer, Heidelberg (2021). https://doi.org/10.1007/978-3-662-63958-0_29
24. Garay, J.A., Katz, J., Maurer, U., Tackmann, B., Zikas, V.: Rational protocol design: cryptography against incentive-driven adversaries. In: 54th FOCS, pp. 648–657. IEEE Computer Society Press (2013). https://doi.org/10.1109/FOCS.2013.75
25. Garay, J., Kiayias, A., Leonardos, N.: The bitcoin backbone protocol: analysis and applications. In: Oswald, E., Fischlin, M. (eds.) EUROCRYPT 2015. LNCS, vol. 9057, pp. 281–310. Springer, Heidelberg (2015). https://doi.org/10.1007/978-3-662-46803-6_10
26. Garman, C., Green, M., Miers, I.: Decentralized anonymous credentials. In: NDSS 2014. The Internet Society (2014)
27. Goldwasser, S., Micali, S., Rivest, R.L.: A digital signature scheme secure against adaptive chosen-message attacks. SIAM J. Comput. **17**(2), 281–308 (1988)
28. Górski, T., Bednarski, J.: Modeling of smart contracts in blockchain solution for renewable energy grid. In: Moreno-Díaz, R., Pichler, F., Quesada-Arencibia, A. (eds.) EUROCAST 2019. LNCS, vol. 12013, pp. 507–514. Springer, Cham (2020). https://doi.org/10.1007/978-3-030-45093-9_61
29. Huang, M., Su, X., Larangeira, M., Tanaka, K.: Optimizing liveness for blockchain-based sealed-bid auctions in rational settings. IACR Cryptol. ePrint Arch. 1643 (2024). https://eprint.iacr.org/2024/1643
30. Itkis, G., Reyzin, L.: Forward-secure signatures with optimal signing and verifying. In: Kilian, J. (ed.) CRYPTO 2001. LNCS, vol. 2139, pp. 332–354. Springer, Heidelberg (2001). https://doi.org/10.1007/3-540-44647-8_20
31. Katz, J., Loss, J., Xu, J.: On the security of time-lock puzzles and timed commitments. In: Pass, R., Pietrzak, K. (eds.) TCC 2020. LNCS, vol. 12552, pp. 390–413. Springer, Cham (2020). https://doi.org/10.1007/978-3-030-64381-2_14
32. Khyathi, D.: Ethereum gas fees are sky high: Here are some social media reactions (2023). https://www.nasdaq.com/articles/ethereum-gas-fees-are-sky-high:-here-are-some-social-media-reactions
33. Kiayias, A., Russell, A., David, B., Oliynykov, R.: Ouroboros: a provably secure proof-of-stake blockchain protocol. In: Katz, J., Shacham, H. (eds.) CRYPTO 2017. LNCS, vol. 10401, pp. 357–388. Springer, Cham (2017). https://doi.org/10.1007/978-3-319-63688-7_12

34. Lamport, L., Shostak, R., Pease, M.: The byzantine generals problem. ACM Trans. Program. Lang. Syst. 382–401 (1982). https://www.microsoft.com/en-us/research/publication/byzantine-generals-problem/
35. Liu, B., Yang, Y., Wang, R., Hong, Y.: Poster: privacy preserving divisible double auction with A hybridized tee-blockchain system. In: 41st IEEE ICDCS 2021, Washington DC, USA, 7–10 July 2021, pp. 1144–1145. IEEE (2021). https://doi.org/10.1109/ICDCS51616.2021.00128
36. Liu, L., Du, M., Ma, X.: Blockchain-based fair and secure electronic double auction protocol. IEEE Intell. Syst. **35**(3), 31–40 (2020). https://doi.org/10.1109/MIS.2020.2977896
37. Ma, X., Xu, D., Wolter, K.: Blockchain-enabled feedback-based combinatorial double auction for cloud markets. Future Gener. Comput. Syst. **127**, 225–239 (2022). https://doi.org/10.1016/J.FUTURE.2021.09.009
38. McMenamin, C., Daza, V., Fitzi, M., O'Donoghue, P.: Fairtradex: a decentralised exchange preventing value extraction. In: Proceedings of the 2022 ACM CCS Workshop on Decentralized Finance and Security, DeFi'22, pp. 39–46. Association for Computing Machinery, New York (2022). https://doi.org/10.1145/3560832.3563439
39. Miers, I., Garman, C., Green, M., Rubin, A.D.: Zerocoin: anonymous distributed E-cash from bitcoin. In: 2013 IEEE Symposium on Security and Privacy, pp. 397–411. IEEE Computer Society Press (2013). https://doi.org/10.1109/SP.2013.34
40. Nguyen, T.D.T., Thai, M.T.: A blockchain-based iterative double auction protocol using multiparty state channels. CoRR (2020). https://arxiv.org/abs/2007.08595
41. Pass, R., Shi, E.: The sleepy model of consensus. In: Takagi, T., Peyrin, T. (eds.) ASIACRYPT 2017. LNCS, vol. 10625, pp. 380–409. Springer, Cham (2017). https://doi.org/10.1007/978-3-319-70697-9_14
42. Pass, R., Shi, E.: Thunderella: blockchains with optimistic instant confirmation. In: Nielsen, J.B., Rijmen, V. (eds.) EUROCRYPT 2018. LNCS, vol. 10821, pp. 3–33. Springer, Cham (2018). https://doi.org/10.1007/978-3-319-78375-8_1
43. Pedersen, T.P.: Non-interactive and information-theoretic secure verifiable secret sharing. In: Feigenbaum, J. (ed.) CRYPTO 1991. LNCS, vol. 576, pp. 129–140. Springer, Heidelberg (1992). https://doi.org/10.1007/3-540-46766-1_9
44. Thakur, S., Breslin, J.G., Malik, S.: Privacy-preserving energy trade using double auction in blockchain offline channels. In: Prieto, J., Martínez, F.L.B., Ferretti, S., Guardeño, D.A., Nevado-Batalla, P.T. (eds.) 4th IEEE BLOCKCHAIN 2022, L'Aquila, Italy, 13–15 July 2022. Lecture Notes in Networks and Systems, vol. 595, pp. 289–302. Springer, Heidelberg (2022). https://doi.org/10.1007/978-3-031-21229-1_27
45. Weintraub, B., Torres, C.F., Nita-Rotaru, C., State, R.: A flash(bot) in the pan: measuring maximal extractable value in private pools. In: Proceedings of the 22nd ACM Internet Measurement Conference, IMC '22, pp. 458–471. Association for Computing Machinery, New York (2022). https://doi.org/10.1145/3517745.3561448
46. Wongsamerchue, T., Leelasantitham, A.: An electronic double auction of prepaid electricity trading using blockchain technology. J. Mobile Multimedia **18**(6), 1829–1850 (2022). https://doi.org/10.13052/JMM1550-4646.18616
47. Wood, G., et al.: Ethereum: a secure decentralised generalised transaction ledger. Ethereum Proj. Yellow Pap. **151**(2014), 1–32 (2014)

48. Yin, M., Malkhi, D., Reiter, M.K., Golan-Gueta, G., Abraham, I.: HotStuff: BFT consensus with linearity and responsiveness. In: Robinson, P., Ellen, F. (eds.) 38th ACM PODC, pp. 347–356. ACM (2019). https://doi.org/10.1145/3293611.3331591
49. Zhang, S., Miao, P., Wang, B., Dong, B.: A privacy protection scheme of microgrid direct electricity transaction based on consortium blockchain and continuous double auction. IEEE Access **7**, 151746–151753 (2019). https://doi.org/10.1109/ACCESS.2019.2946794

Blockchain-Based Carbon Footprint Management

Umut Pekel[✉] and Oğuz Yayla

Institute of Applied Mathematics, Middle East Technical University, Ankara, Türkiye
{umut.pekel,oguz}@metu.edu.tr

Abstract. This paper introduces a novel approach to managing carbon footprints using blockchain technology to integrate these footprints intrinsically into the attributes of products, akin to their price. In contrast to conventional methods that treat carbon footprints as distinct, tradeable units, our model incorporates them directly into the product life cycle, thus maintaining the connection between environmental impact and product consumption. By closely examining blockchain's functionality, this study illustrates how it can improve transparency and security in transactions while influencing market dynamics by making carbon accountability an integral part of product ownership. This method may aid in establishing a more sustainable economic model by better incorporating environmental costs into transactions, potentially fostering progress in environmental finance and sustainability initiatives.

Keywords: Blockchain · CO_2 · Blockchain Technology · CO_2 Emissions · Carbon Footprint Management · Carbon Credits · Environmental Sustainability · Tokenization · Token Economy · Tokenization of Assets · Utility Tokens · Multiple Attribute System · Smart Contracts for Data Sharing

1 Introduction and Background

1.1 Motivation

Currently, the economic system operates primarily on the basis of the monetary price alone. In contrast, it is conceivable to tokenize each attribute of a product, including its price, and embed these attributes distinctly within the product's characteristics, which can then be administered through blockchain technology. In particular, the carbon footprint emerges as a crucial attribute suitable for tokenization and embedding, underscoring its prominence in contemporary environmental discourse. Recognizing carbon credits as essential to environmental sustainability, this document addresses the pressing challenge of integrating carbon accountability into routine economic operations by redefining carbon credits as both additional and embedded intrinsic attributes of products and services, similar to, but distinct from, their pricing. Using blockchain technology, this innovative strategy not only challenges conventional views on environmental accountability but also harmonizes sustainability with economic activities. Traditionally, carbon has been treated as an independent commodity, disconnected from its product of origin, and exchanged independently throughout its life cycle. This perspective commodifies carbon as an asset that can be purchased and monetized, overlooking the necessity to influence consumer behavior or production processes directly. By embedding carbon within the product's attributes itself—similar to its price—this paper advocates for a paradigm shift. Blockchain technology has the potential to improve transparency, traceability, and equitable accountability, potentially influencing economic and environmental paradigms. Unlike existing models, this approach incorporates carbon credits directly as product attributes, thereby revamping both the economic and environmental paradigms.

The contributions of this paper are delineated in four principal areas. First, reconceptualization of carbon credits as distinct intrinsic attributes of products and services, establishing a direct association between carbon accountability and product value, thus fundamentally reshaping existing economic and environmental paradigms. Secondly, the proposition of a blockchain-based architecture that guarantees transparency, confidentiality, and tamper-resistant record keeping, thus addressing the limitations inherent in traditional systems. In addition, smart contracts are utilized for data sharing, offering a practical and effective alternative to conventional cryptographic methods of data exchange. Finally, the evaluation of the suitability of existing blockchain platforms for the deployment of this system explains the strengths and limitations of various technologies, thus providing a foundation for selecting solutions that align with a multi-attribute economic system. Specifically, the proposed blockchain-based architecture incorporates features such as smart contracts for automation and tokenization for integration.

A multi-user, privacy-preserving tamper-proof database is essential for data governance and audit trails. The key role of blockchains in ensuring tamper-proof operations and privacy is highlighted in [1]. It supports data sharing with multiple users, as noted in [2]. Blockchain technology provides tamper-proof data management, transparent governance, and privacy mechanisms, confirmed by [1,2]. The search for encrypted records is crucial, as shown in [3]. The multistage processes of blockchain databases add versatility and complexity, as discussed in [4]. This combination significantly advances database technology, meeting modern data governance needs. The secure and decentralized nature of blockchain supports a viable economic model for tracking carbon credits in products and services.

1.2 Background

Our model [12] assigns both the price and tokenized carbon footprint to the products, challenging traditional economic paradigms that historically have lacked the capacity to manage multiple attributes per product. Blockchain technology addresses this limitation by facilitating the integration and tracking of numerous attributes, thereby presenting a transformative potential for conventional economic systems. We contend that carbon accountability should be considered as fundamental as pricing in fostering conscientious consumption. Existing strategies perceive carbon credits as mere tradable commodities, thereby detaching them from their origins and contributing to a superficial market that inadequately modifies behavioral or production norms. This often disproportionately burdens those with fewer financial resources, exacerbating inequalities. Our model incorporates carbon accountability as a core attribute, aiming to promote sustainability as an important value, moving beyond its commodification. This approach fosters an equitable economic framework in which carbon costs are equitably distributed, thus promoting sustainable practices. The integration of environmental considerations with economic practices is pivotal in ensuring that the true ecological costs are accurately represented, thus cultivating a market that is informed and responsible. Blockchain can be used to improve transparency and accountability by integrating carbon credits as fundamental attributes, with the aim of better aligning environmental stewardship with market behavior. This initiative aims to support more sustainable consumption and align with ethical standards, contributing to the development of a more just and sustainable economic framework.

1.3 Related Work

The article by Kalaiselvan et al. [7] introduces a blockchain-based system to transform carbon credit markets by addressing inefficiencies such as overcrediting and high costs. It proposes a decentralized marketplace to improve transparency, reduce expenses, and improve collaboration among stakeholders. The platform provides a secure and accessible environment for trading carbon credits, using a decentralized ledger to ensure transaction transparency and prevent fraud. Smart contracts automate processes, lowering costs, and supporting stakeholder collaboration. The integration of blockchain is intended to streamline trading, improve regulatory compliance, and promote sustainable practices. The initiative emphasizes a strong governance structure that involves diverse stakeholders for collective decision making, aligning with global efforts to reduce greenhouse gas emissions. It aims to serve as a model for future carbon trading platforms through technological innovation. The research by Jawalkar et al. [8] proposes a blockchain framework to tokenize and securely transfer carbon credits, in order to improve accessibility and market efficiency. Addresses issues in traditional carbon credit systems—such as fragmentation, lack of transparency, high costs, and overcrediting—by establishing a Carbon Credit Ecosystem. This system uses smart contracts to improve market consistency, liquidity, and transparency, with key features such as fair token distribution and an automated market maker for efficient trading. The project seeks to reduce fraud and errors through secure digitalization, promoting inclusivity, transparency, and efficiency in carbon trading and other systems to combat climate change. Implementation relies on smart contracts and blockchain for task automation, transaction transparency and security, and verification of emission reduction. The study by Zhang et al. [9] explores how blockchain technology can enhance traceability in low carbon supply chains using evolutionary game theory. It highlights the broader potential of blockchain beyond carbon credits, particularly in managing carbon emissions within supply chains. The research focuses on the influence of government policies and stakeholder relationships, employing mathematical modeling and MATLAB simulations to identify optimal blockchain adoption strategies for manufacturers, suppliers, and governments. Key findings suggest that manufacturers and suppliers should manage blockchain costs while collaborating on eco-friendly certifications. Local governments are encouraged to foster stakeholder participation through reward and punishment systems. In general, blockchain has been shown to improve transparency and accuracy in tracking carbon footprints while reducing costs, with collaborative strategies and governmental support crucial to successful technology adoption. The article by Swinkels [10] examines the role of blockchain in carbon credit trading, focusing on tokenization, pricing, and market dynamics. It highlights the efficiency improvements blockchain provides, using the ACX platform as a case study, which tokenized 3.8 million tons of CO_2e, with 2.8 million burned and 1 million available for trading by the end of 2022. Swinkels reports a turnover of USD 21.2 million in the secondary market during 2021–2022, indicating limited liquidity and pricing alignment with similar projects. The study illustrates blockchain's ability to reduce costs and enhance transparency in the carbon credit market, concluding that blockchain can significantly improve transaction processes and has wider potential in environmental finance, suggesting further exploration of its global market impact. The paper by Akiladevi et al. [11] presents a strategy using multichain blockchain technology for tokenization of energy assets, emphasizing environmental sustainability. Examines the role of blockchain in improving carbon credit markets and energy asset management through a secure decentralized ledger that improves transparency, trust, and reduces fraud. By tokenizing assets as digital tokens, the method facilitates easier trading and management, encouraging investment in renewable energy projects. Blockchain resistance to tampering, automation capabilities, and cost efficiency contribute to reducing carbon footprints and support sustainable energy development. The paper concludes by highlighting the transformative potential of multi-chain blockchain in energy management and suggests further research to address technical issues.

As corroborated by the reviewed studies, the prevalent methodology in carbon management frequently entails disassociating a product's carbon footprint from the product itself, considering it as a tradable commodity. In contrast, the approach delineated herein incorporates the carbon footprint as an integral characteristic of the products, analogous to their pricing. This paradigm establishes a direct correlation between emissions responsibility and product consumption, thereby ensuring that environmental responsibility cannot be transferred or alleviated through the acquisition of credits. Such a framework effectively deters the perpetuation of unsustainable operations by economically advantaged entities, while simultaneously addressing the disproportionate adversities encountered by less affluent individuals who contribute minimally to global emissions. By embedding the carbon footprint within the fundamental attributes of products, this model cultivates authentic sustainability and endorses equitable environmental responsibility across all socioeconomic strata.

2 Challenges in Data Management Approaches

Traditional databases lack transparency, tamper-proof security, and scalability, but the blockchain addresses these issues through decentralized architecture, ensuring data integrity and smooth integration of records such as carbon credits. The current data infrastructure is characterized by the widespread utilization of centralized database systems by organizations. These systems are conducive to facilitating audits; however, they hinder cross-industry enhancement due to data siloing, especially within complex logistics and supply chains. Centralized databases, while effective in optimizing data management processes, frequently contribute to an increased carbon footprint. The current auditing methodologies employed by government and centralized systems, which utilize central servers, necessitate a re-evaluation to improve environmental sustainability. Analogous Applications across Industries: Homogeneous database systems that span various sectors present both environmental challenges and opportunities in terms of the management of carbon footprints. Decentralized Data Management: Isolated databases hinder collaboration and optimization in logistics and supply chains, increasing carbon footprints through inefficiencies. Isolated systems hinder efficiency and sustainability, complicating carbon footprint reduction efforts across industries.

2.1 Existing Systems for Data Collection

The Point of Sale (POS) system, as shown in Fig. 1 is essential for modern business operations and streamlined retail transactions. Invoicing: Records transactions to ensure sales transparency and accuracy, helping businesses and customers understand purchases. Stock/Inventory Management: Manage product stock, improve restocking efficiency, minimize waste, and improve operations. Customer Loyalty Programs: POS programs also handle customer rewards and promotions, promoting retention and lasting engagement. (as demonstrated in Fig. 2)

Transaction data collection at critical checkpoints is managed by a Data Acquisition System in devices like 'Cash Registers' or 'POS Terminals'. These checkpoints efficiently capture transactional data, which is a key part of the data lifecycle. Data Preservation Methods: Transaction records are stored in plain text within protected memory, or in sealed memory chips such as EEPROMs to ensure accessibility and integrity, or encrypted for critical audits to secure sensitive information. Navigating Data Management Challenges: Organizations balance data security, privacy, and collaboration in data management. Enhancing multi-user capabilities and governance structures transforms data infrastructure. Cryptographic protocols such as "Public Key Encryption with Keyword Search" simplify database use and sharing by managing data access permissions more effectively, as noted in [5].

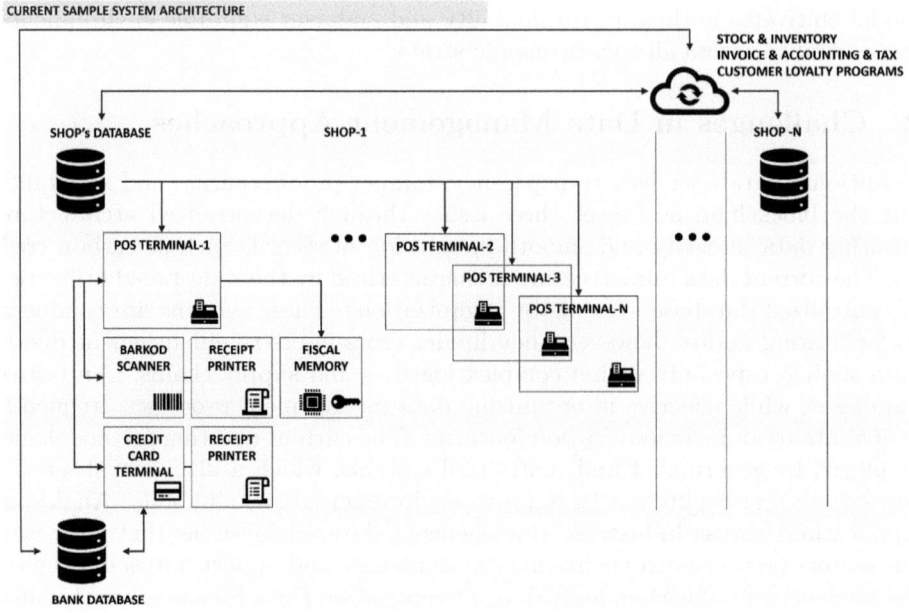

Fig. 1. Current Sample System Architecture

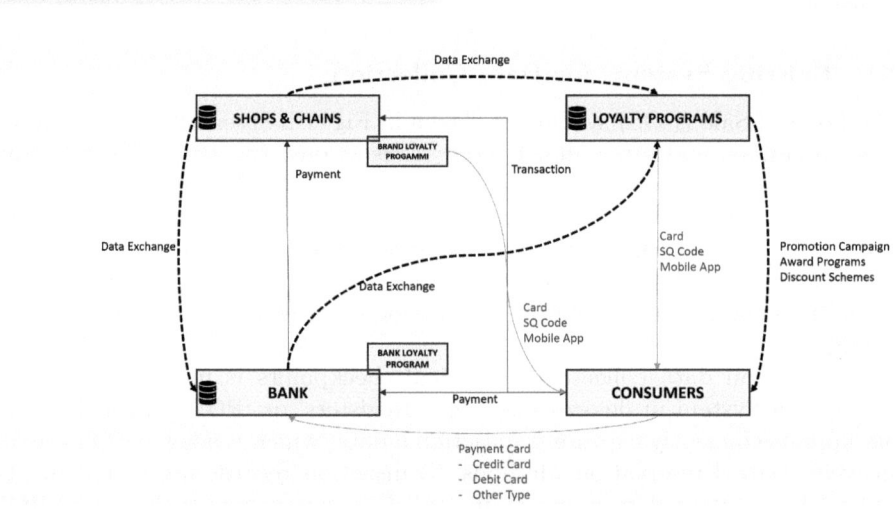

Fig. 2. Current Framework in General

2.2 What is Missing in Current Systems

In spite of progress in digital infrastructure, present systems possess significant deficiencies impacting efficiency, security, and privacy. These challenges are predominantly: firstly, challenges in data sharing, which arise from incompatible formats and platforms. Secondly, there are common database management difficulties, where maintaining data integrity and security during database management is strenuous. In addition, there exists the problem of data silos, which obstruct efficient utilization and integration. Furthermore, designing systems for multiple users introduces complications, as these systems must navigate access permission issues, striking a balance between accessibility and security. Lastly, privacy concerns in the management of sensitive records, particularly those related to healthcare, require a high degree of confidentiality. Recognizing these concerns underscores the necessity for blockchain technology to provide decentralized, secure, and transparent data management. To address this, an approach involves the implementation of end-to-end encryption, which ensures that each transaction within the database is safeguarded, maintaining the security of data from its creation to its ultimate destination. This encryption is pivotal in protecting sensitive information against unauthorized access and potential security breaches. Another approach emphasizes efficient keyword search over encrypted data; this crucial feature allows conducting efficient keyword searches on encrypted information, thus resolving the typical trade-off between data security and usability and enabling users to query encrypted data without privacy compromise. The research carried out by Jiang et al. [6] supports the feasibility of this solution, demonstrating how blockchain technology can be used effectively to create a secure and privacy-preserving database. Their findings highlight the potential for blockchain-based systems to revolutionize data management practices, particularly when it comes to addressing privacy and security concerns.

2.3 The Need for Blockchain

Blockchain databases, by employing cryptographic methods and encryption, offer a novel approach to data management that can improve the tracking of carbon footprints and potentially enhance security, transparency, and overall efficiency. Firstly, blockchain implementation makes tokenization feasible. Secondly, blockchain ensures exceptional immutability and security, with cryptographic chaining fostering tamper-evident records that uphold data integrity and provide a verifiable history. In addition, innovative record sharing is facilitated through searchable attribute-based encryption (ABE), allowing data owners to encrypt records with attributes, allowing authorized entities to access precise and secure data while preserving privacy. Furthermore, the blockchain fosters decentralized trust by eliminating central authorities and using consensus-driven validations for democratic and transparent data management. Furthermore, smart contracts within blockchain systems automate complex processes and transactions based on predefined rules, thereby reducing the reliance on intermediaries. Finally, the shared blockchain database supports multi-stakeholder collaboration, leading to optimized operations, improved data sharing, and reduced redundancies. In summary, blockchain databases advance data management by offering solutions for immutability, record sharing, decentralized governance, and automation, thus establishing a secure, transparent, and efficient digital infrastructure for data storage, sharing, and use across various industries.

2.4 Blockchain-Based Database for Environmental and Carbon Footprint Management

In addition to tokenization, implementing a blockchain-based database for environmental management improves data handling by allowing multi-party transaction recording. This advancement allows data sharing, improves integrity, and usability without the need for replication. The primary benefits include the following: Firstly, *No Replication of Data* eliminates the redundancy found in traditional systems, ensuring that data are singular and authoritative. This process reduces inconsistencies, streamlining management for both efficiency and versatility. Secondly, *Versatility for Other Purposes* means that while it is primarily used for environmental data, it can be extended to various applications, such as marketing and delivery optimization, transforming consolidated data into actionable insights. Moreover, *Multi-Stakeholder and Sector-Wide Optimization* is achieved through its user-friendly design that fosters collaboration among stakeholders, optimizing operations both at the organizational level and across sectors. In addition, *Data Exchange Between Industry Layers* is facilitated by blockchain, which enables smooth data transfer between industry layers, creating a more integrated and responsive business ecosystem.

The blockchain-based database enhances carbon footprint management through its robust security and transparency features. It offers a secure, efficient framework for handling carbon data, ensuring data integrity and confidentiality via cryptography. To begin with, secure transaction management involves encrypting transactions to safeguard environmental data against unauthorized access. Next, the system allows effective data management and querying without jeopardizing integrity. Moreover, integrating smart contracts automates transactions, streamlining operations, and boosting efficiency and transparency.

3 Methodology

Enhancing the carbon footprint tracking system with additional features improves the accuracy of the data and its integration into existing processes. Embedding data collection and carbon credit payment terminals in retail stores, similar to POS terminals, and using blockchain technology can transform transaction methods. This not only simplifies carbon credit payments, but also ensures transparency, such as credit card transactions. Blockchain integration offers immutability, transparency, and trust, ensuring carbon data and transactions are secure and reliable, fostering trust among consumers and businesses.

3.1 Use-Case Scenario

Consider a consumer who purchases a product from a retailer that participates in the blockchain-based carbon credit system. Each product is tagged with its carbon footprint, which is verified and recorded on the blockchain. During purchase, the system automatically deducts associated carbon credits from the consumer's balance and logs the transaction immutably on the blockchainas as shown in Fig. 3. For example, a smartphone with a carbon footprint of 50 kg CO2e requires 50 carbon credits. When the consumer completes the purchase, the system deducts 50 credits from their account and updates the blockchain ledger, ensuring transparency and accountability. This process not only provides consumers with clear visibility into the environmental impact of their purchases but also incentivizes manufacturers to adopt sustainable practices by making carbon emissions a tangible cost of production.

3.2 Proposed System Architecture

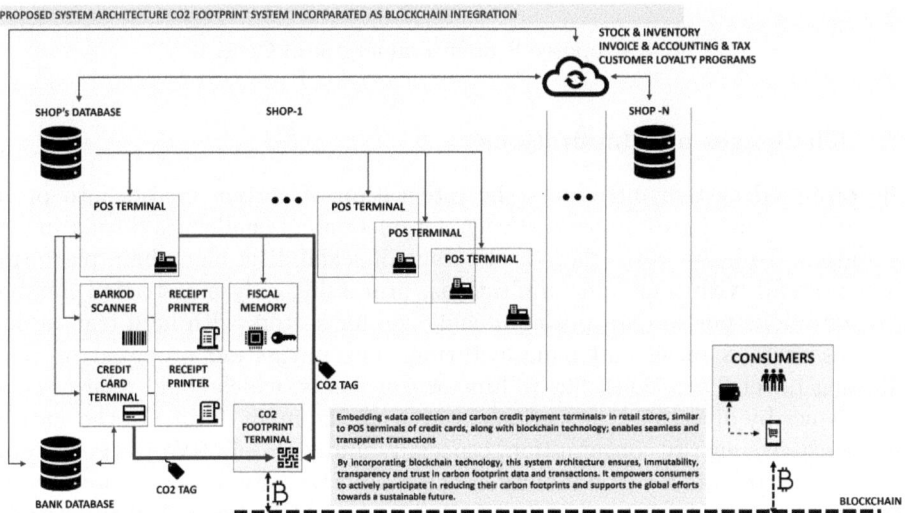

Fig. 3. Proposed System Architecture Co2 Footprint System Incorparated As Blockchain Integration. (The large 'B' symbol with vertical stripes in this figure is inspired by the Bitcoin logo but is used here to represent cryptocurrencies or blockchain tokens in a general sense, rather than specifically Bitcoin.)

The blockchain-based carbon credits system ensures transparency and accountability by integrating them into the lifecycle of products (Fig. 4). Key features include smart contracts for secure transactions and a decentralized ledger to track carbon footprints across supply chains. Scalability is enhanced through side chains or Layer-2 solutions *(where possible)*, reducing costs and increasing speed. Tokens represent carbon emissions, facilitating exchanges and environmental actions, while smart contracts manage these transactions. This framework provides a decentralized, immutable, and transparent integration of carbon credit management into global supply chains.

PROPOSED SYSTEM FRAMEWORK IN GENERAL

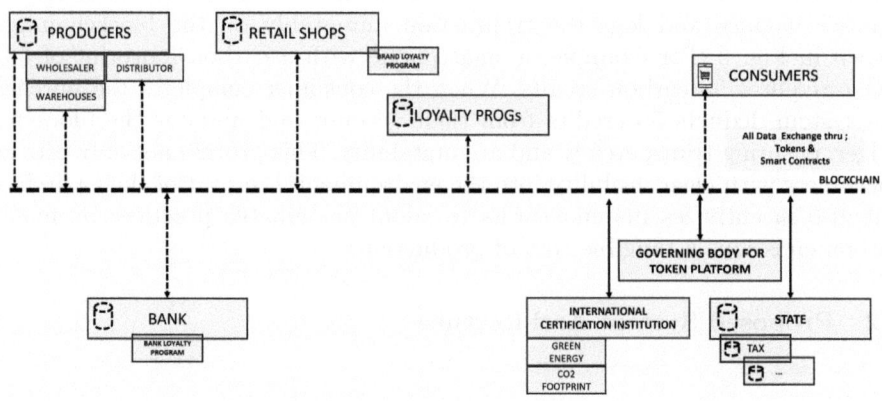

Fig. 4. Proposed System Framework in General

3.3 Challenges and Limitations

The proposed system introduces the integration of carbon credits into products and services in an innovative way, yet encounters challenges during implementation. To begin with, there is the issue of scalability; blockchain platforms often contend with scalability limitations, processing only a restricted number of transactions per second, posing a challenge for sectors with high transaction volumes such as retail and manufacturing. The mitigation proposed involves adopting Layer-2 solutions, like rollups or sidechains, which could relieve scalability issues by diverting transactions away from the main chain. On the subject of blockchain's energy consumption, especially under Proof-of-Work (PoW) protocols, this presents a sustainability concern, and transitioning to more energy-efficient models such as Proof-of-Stake (PoS) is not without complexity. As a mitigation strategy, it is suggested to promote the adoption of PoS-based blockchains or private blockchain configurations that require less energy. Blockchain systems can also be cost prohibitive in terms of infrastructure and maintenance for small and medium enterprises (SMEs). Therefore, a proposed mitigation is financial assistance or subsidies from governments or NGOs, designed to defray these costs for SMEs, thus fostering broader adoption.

Additionally, data privacy and security lead to concerns: while blockchain ensures the immutability of data, it poses risks to the privacy of sensitive data, such as proprietary carbon footprint calculations. Incorporating searchable encryption (SE) and zero-knowledge proofs adds to the complexity. Instead of relying on traditional techniques, we could adopt privacy-preserving technologies, like homomorphic encryption, enabling interaction with blockchain-based databases via smart contracts; this approach is more straightforward, demands less computational power, and facilitates economical data-sharing transactions.

SE allows secure queries of encrypted carbon data, safeguarding privacy, which is essential for manufacturers. Despite SE's advantages in data privacy, its implementation on large databases can result in computational complexity. Traditional SE involves cryptographic operations that are resource-intensive and inefficient for large-scale systems; however, the more straightforward and efficient SE solution of blockchain differs. The blockchain retains encrypted data that engages with smart contracts, thereby avoiding direct data exposure. Smart contract systems possess different identifiers across blockchains, being referred to as "smart contracts" in Ethereum. A blockchain-based carbon credit system stores encrypted emissions data securely, enabling users to verify carbon footprints via smart contracts without revealing data, hence ensuring privacy and efficiency. This approach reduces encryption/decryption costs and incorporates economic dimensions, as users compensate for query transactions using tokens or cryptocurrency, guaranteeing transparency and fairness. Regulators are provided with privileged encrypted data access for audit functions, maintaining compliance. This model exploits blockchain and smart contracts to simplify SE, enhance privacy, support transparency, drive efficiency, and sustain economic viability.

Moreover, there are regulation and standardization issues: the global adoption of blockchain-based carbon credit systems encounters regulatory challenges due to disparate environmental policies and data governance standards from country to country. Mitigation proposed includes collaboration with international organizations to establish standardized frameworks for carbon credit accounting and blockchain interoperability. Finally, user adoption issues arise: resistance from stakeholders and a lack of technical expertise, including among manufacturers and consumers, may disrupt the system's adoption. A proposed mitigation for this involves educational campaigns and the development of user-friendly interfaces to foster acceptance of the proposed system.

4 Details of System Structure and Roles of Main Stakeholders

For effective management, stakeholder roles such as producers, consumers, governing bodies, and environmental organizations must be defined. The system manages carbon footprints through smart contracts and blockchain tokens, serving as an immutable ledger for carbon transactions. Users can monitor their carbon footprint and token balance through digital wallets. The system rewards eco-friendly actions such as reforestation and support of renewable energy with tokens. Blockchain ensures reliability and transparency, fostering sustainable consumer participation. Users earn tokens for verified green activities, such as tree planting and recycling. Validators, like environmental organizations, verify these activities and distribute rewards, promoting sustainable behaviors. Carbon tracking and offset use blockchain for accurate transaction records, giving users transparency in their carbon use and tokens, enhancing sustainability responsibility. The system links producers and consumers with smart contracts and tokens, ensuring secure exchanges and promoting sustainable practices. Here is the list of main stakeholders with brief role descriptions and functions.

1. Producers The system relies on producers to establish the carbon footprint of the product according to the guidelines of the International Certification Institute (ICI). Assesses the use of green energy in the sources, manufacturing, packaging, and distribution to provide precise environmental impact data. Manufacturers calculate carbon footprints using the ICI criteria, focusing on integrating green energy in the extraction, manufacturing, packaging, and distribution of raw materials.

2. International Certification Institution The International Certification Institute (ICI) establishes standards for carbon footprints, devises guidelines for their computation, and provides blockchain-based tokens to measure carbon emissions. Firstly, ICI defines and standardizes carbon footprints. Secondly, it develops guidelines and methodologies for their calculation. In addition, factors such as production methods, materials, energy consumption, and transportation are taken into account. Then, ICI issues carbon footprint tokens, followed by generating and securely storing these tokens on a transparent blockchain platform.

3. The State The proposed framework employs blockchain technology to incentivize environmentally sustainable behaviors by issuing carbon tokens that are authenticated by environmental organizations. In addition, the system facilitates carbon tracking and fosters sustainability education.

4. The Governing Body The regulatory authority enhances the operational capacity of the carbon footprint token ecosystem by overseeing token issuance aligned with carbon emissions, ensuring a consistent supply, and modifying conversion rates to prevent inflation. By partnering with carbon offset initiatives, it aids in emissions reduction, while blockchain technology provides security and transparency in transactions. Additionally, it fosters awareness through educational programs and collaborates with regulators to uphold the system's integrity. The main functions include: firstly, token issuance; secondly, regulating token supply and distribution; next, adjusting the token conversion rate; furthermore, overseeing token redemption and offset; in addition, ensuring token utility and rewards; also, managing token burning; moreover, facilitating carbon credit trading; besides, maintaining transparency and auditing; additionally, advancing education and awareness; and finally, ensuring regulatory compliance.

5. Consumers In the proposed framework, consumers play an essential role, as their choices in buying and participating in environmental practices heavily influence the success of carbon footprint management. Within this system, consumers play a key role in financial and purchasing transactions. When a product is bought, consumers pay not only the item's price but also the related carbon footprint cost through a digital wallet or payment platform linked to a blockchain network. This setup automatically deducts the necessary carbon footprint tokens from the consumer's wallet, thus aiding in the tracking and reduction of carbon emissions. To elaborate on these processes, First, environmental activities are verified, after which token rewards are distributed. Following this, the redemption and offset of carbon credits take place. In addition to this, consumers are involved in purchasing and payment activities. Furthermore, the carbon footprints of products are calculated. Alongside these, tracking and offset of carbon footprints is conducted. As a result, carbon footprint tokens are created. Finally, the blockchain platform is implemented.

6. Retail stores Retail stores serve as essential intermediaries, embedding carbon credit transactions within everyday consumer engagements, and encouraging eco-friendly practices. They employ systems similar to POS to collect data and assess the carbon footprint for each transaction. Carbon credit payment systems allow customers to use digital wallets for carbon offset activities. Stores engage consumers in recognized activities such as tree planting and recycling, which are certified by environmental organizations that distribute tokens and promote stewardship. Using blockchain technology, product costs and carbon footprints are calculated simultaneously, ensuring secure and transparent record-keeping. Retailers provide real-time reporting, enhancing system comprehension and enabling stakeholders to produce comprehensive reports, thereby increasing accountability and raising environmental awareness. Initially, data collection and the calculation of the carbon footprint are carried out. Following this, carbon credit payment terminals are utilized. Subsequently, environmental activities are validated, and token rewards are distributed. Then, consumer purchases and payments take place. The blockchain integration is then used for secure record-keeping. Finally, reporting and transparency are ensured.

5 Suitable Blockchains

The selection of a blockchain platform for applications related to carbon footprint tracking and offset is crucial to determine the efficiency, security, and scalability of the system. To achieve interoperability and global-level scalability for the carbon footprint application, a fungible Utility Token on a public blockchain is necessary. Different blockchains come with varying features, and it is important to carefully match these attributes with the project's specific needs. In the following, we present a concise overview of several notable blockchain options and considerations for their applicability in carbon footprint management. Among the diverse range of blockchain platforms that could be effectively harnessed to manage carbon footprints, Ethereum stands out as a notable option. Ethereum's transition to a Proof-of-Stake (PoS) consensus mechanism aligns well with global sustainability goals by reducing energy consumption. However, the platform is challenged by substantial transaction fees, which may hinder broad adoption. In contrast, Hyperledger Fabric's permissioned architecture facilitates data confidentiality, rendering it a compelling choice for enterprises seeking secure blockchain applications. The prospective development of hybrid models might effectively synergize these strengths, offering improvements in scalability and privacy without sacrificing energy efficiency. Initially considered is Ethereum, followed by Hyperledger Fabric. Beyond these, other suitable candidates include Algorand, Polkadot, Tezos, and Avalanche. Additional viable alternatives are Cardano, Stellar, and EOS, as well as emerging blockchains like Hedera Hashgraph, Neo, Vechain, Nano, and Solana. Each of these platforms has unique features that make them potentially favorable for certain elements of applications aimed at tracking and offset of carbon footprint, depending on specific project requirements such as transaction speed, scalability, energy efficiency, and compliance with regulatory standards.

In the rapidly changing realm of blockchain technology, Ethereum is noteworthy due to its established ecosystem and strong smart contract capabilities. However, challenges such as scalability and transaction fees during high-demand periods must be carefully evaluated. With the shift to Proof of Stake (PoS), Ethereum considerably decreases its energy consumption, which aligns with environmental objectives; nevertheless, its transaction throughput, ranging from 15 to 30 TPS, can restrict scalability in large-scale systems.

Hyperledger Fabric, particularly suited for enterprise applications, prioritizes privacy and scalability through its permissioned network and modular consensus protocols. Although appropriate for permissioned settings, it may pose a more intricate setup challenge compared to public blockchains. Additionally, Hyperledger Fabric may not be the best fit for interstate or global-level applications.

Algorand is celebrated for its high throughput and rapid transaction completion, utilizing a pure proof-of-stake model for enhanced energy efficiency. However, its relative novelty within the blockchain sector and the evolving ecosystem support are aspects worth considering.

Polkadot emphasizes interoperability and the provision of specialized functionality in parachains, offering scalability and customization; however, its complexity and the need for a well-defined ecosystem could influence the ease of adoption.

Tezos, featuring on-chain governance and formal verification, improves security and allows stakeholders to participate in protocol upgrades. However, its ecosystem might not be as comprehensive as those of more established platforms.

Avalanche, distinguished by its subsecond finality, provides a highly scalable platform with an innovative consensus mechanism. Its approach to achieve decentralization and high throughput differentiates it, making it ideal for applications demanding rigorous performance requirements.

5.1 Blockchain Implementation Analysis

To assess the operational costs related to the issuance of sample tokens, which is essential to evaluate the economic viability of blockchain applications in environmental sustainability projects, two examples are provided herein.

Operational Costs Analysis for ERC-20 Token Issuance

```
1 // Solidity smart contract for ERC-20 based Carbon Token
    issuance
```

```
2  pragma solidity ^0.8.0;
3  import "@openzeppelin/contracts/token/ERC20/ERC20.sol";
4
5  contract CarbonToken is ERC20 {
6      address public administrator;
7
8      constructor() ERC20("CarbonToken", "CTN") {
9          administrator = msg.sender;   // Set the
              administrator as the contract deployer
10     }
11
12     // Function to issue new tokens
13     function issueTokens(address to, uint amount) public {
14         require(msg.sender == administrator, "Only the
              administrator can issue tokens.");
15         _mint(to, amount);}}
```

Transaction Cost in ETH = $55{,}000 \times 30$ gwei = $1{,}650{,}000$ gwei = 0.00165 ETH,
Transaction Cost in USD = 0.00165 ETH $\times 2073.56 = \approx 3.42$ USD.

This cost analysis indicates that each token-issuance transaction incurs a fee of approximately \$3.42 USD based on the current ETH/USD value of 2,073.56USD on March 25, 2025. It is important to note that while the cost per transaction might be manageable, the cumulative cost for multiple transactions can become significant, suggesting that Ethereum's current gas fee structure may impact the scalability of deploying such a system for large-scale environmental projects. Deployment costs are beyond our current scope of analysis, but are acknowledged as a critical factor in the overall budget. It is worth mentioning that Layer 2 solutions have the potential to significantly reduce these costs. However, a detailed analysis of Layer 2 solutions falls outside the scope of this paper. The Layer 2 ecosystem is continuously evolving, with ongoing research, improvements, and the development of alternative solutions aimed at enhancing scalability and reducing transaction fees on the Ethereum network.

Operational Costs Analysis for Algorand Standard Assets Token Issuance

```
1  // Algorand smart contract for ASA based Carbon Credit
       issuance
2  # Python code to demonstrate creating an ASA on Algorand
3  from algosdk import algod
4  from algosdk.future.transaction import AssetConfigTxn
5  from algosdk.v2client import algod
6  # Connect to an Algorand node
7  algod_address = "https://testnet-algorand.api.purestake.io
       /ps2"
8  algod_token = "YourApiKey"
```

```
 9  headers = {
10      "X-API-Key": algod_token ,}
11  algod_client = algod.AlgodClient(algod_token ,
        algod_address , headers)
12  # Account setup (ensure the account is funded and holds
        enough Algos for fees)
13  params = algod_client.suggested_params()
14  # Define the ASA parameters
15  asset_name = "CarbonCredit"
16  unit_name = "CCU"
17  total_supply = 1000000
18  decimals = 0
19  # Create the ASA
20  txn = AssetConfigTxn(
21      sender=creator_address ,
22      sp=params ,
23      total=total_supply ,
24      default_frozen=False ,
25      unit_name=unit_name ,
26      asset_name=asset_name ,
27      manager=creator_address ,
28      reserve=creator_address ,
29      freeze=creator_address ,
30      clawback=creator_address ,
31      url="http://example.com",
32      decimals=decimals)
```

ASA Creation Txn Cost (Algo) $= 0.001$ Algo,

ASA Creation Txn Cost (USD) $= 0.001$ Algo $\times$ 0.2056 USD $= 0.0002056$ USD.

This cost analysis shows that creating an ASA incurs a transaction fee of approximately 0.0002056USD, based on the current Algo/USD value of 0.20506USD on March 25, 2025. However, this calculation only includes the Algorand blockchain transaction fee. PureStake API fees, which vary based on the plan and number of API calls, are not included in this analysis. Algorand's fixed transaction fee structure significantly reduces transaction costs compared to networks with variable gas fees, such as Ethereum. This lower cost structure improves the feasibility of deploying Algorand-based systems for large-scale environmental projects without the burden of high cumulative transaction costs. Deployment costs (e.g., smart contract deployment, server costs, and development costs), although not covered here, are crucial for complete budgeting and planning.

On the whole, we offer a comparative analysis among the chosen blockchains. The tables provided present a comparison of blockchain platforms, emphasizing their appropriateness for carbon credit management applications.

Table 1. General Properties of Selected Blockchain Platforms

Blockchain	Type	Consensus	Smart Contracts	Interoperability	Governance	Energy Efficiency
Ethereum	Public	PoW to PoS	Yes	Limited	Decentralized	Moderate
Hyperledger Fabric	Permissioned	Pluggable	Chaincode	Limited	Configurable	Depends on Setup
Algorand	Public	Pure PoS	Yes	Limited	On-chain Voting	High
Polkadot	Heterogeneous	Nominated PoS	Yes	Yes	Referenda	Depends on Parachains
Tezos	Liquid PoS	LPos	Yes	Yes	On-chain Governance	High
Avalanche	Permissioned/Public	Avalanche	Yes	Yes	On-chain Governance	High

Table 2. Txn Speed, Finality, and Txn Cost for Selected Blockchains

Blockchain	Transaction Speed	Finality	Transaction Cost
Ethereum	Moderate (15–45 seconds)	Probabilistic Finality	Variable, influenced by network congestion
Hyperledger Fabric	High (within seconds)	Depends on consensus algorithm	Low, suitable for enterprise solutions
Algorand	Very High (5 s)	Fast and Irreversible	Low, scalable and energy-efficient
Polkadot	High (within seconds)	Depends on relay chain and parachain consensus	Variable, influenced by relay chain and parachain mechanisms
Tezos	Moderate to High (15–30 seconds)	Depends on consensus	Adjustable through governance, generally moderate
Avalanche	Very High (few seconds)	Fast and Irreversible	Low, scalable and energy-efficient

6 Discussion

6.1 Implications of Findings

The study suggests that blockchain has the potential to play a significant role in redefining carbon credits, moving them from primarily tradeable commodities to more essential product attributes. This change challenges traditional economics by making a product's environmental impact a key market factor. Blockchain enhances transaction transparency and security, helping consumers make environmentally sustainable choices. By embedding carbon credits into product lifecycles, it merges ecological responsibility with economic activity, rewarding sustainability in markets. This method could affect ecological impact assessments and play a role in incremental changes in worldwide economic frameworks and consumer habits. Additionally, it could drive worldwide regulatory and corporate shifts, rethinking carbon credits' role in sustainability.

6.2 Comparison with Traditional Methods

Traditional carbon credit management treats credits as separate, tradeable assets, often disconnecting them from actual environmental impacts, leading to inefficiencies. Conversely, a blockchain-based approach integrates carbon credits into product lifecycles, making carbon footprints a core part of product value and enhancing transparency. Blockchain's decentralization has the potential to reduce the role of intermediaries, which may help in reducing corruption and improving the reliability of carbon credit tracking. Smart contracts automate and record transactions, boosting compliance and accountability. This approach aligns with environmental goals, creating a transparent market that discourages manipulation and encourages sustainability, significantly improving over traditional methods and offering a framework for global environmental governance transformation.

7 Conclusion

This article discusses the need for a blockchain-based database in carbon footprint tracking and management. With carbon footprint being a fundamental product attribute, similar to price, it can be effectively managed using blockchain tools rather than traditional data silos. Future product attributes will likely require management through token economics and blockchain systems. "If scalability and regulatory challenges are addressed, the proposed system has the potential to significantly improve global carbon footprint management.

7.1 Summary of Key Findings

The main discoveries of this study highlight the transformative capacity of blockchain technology in not only increasing the transparency and security of carbon credit transactions but also embedding these credits into the core structure of product and service lifecycles, thereby significantly modifying market dynamics. Firstly, Tokenization and Intrinsic Integration of Carbon Credits: The study illustrates that embedding carbon credits as integral attributes of products ensures a clear connection between a product's environmental impact and its market value. This integration enhances transparency and compels stakeholders to prioritize sustainability, effectively connecting economic activities with environmental impact. Secondly, Enhanced Transparency and Trust: Due to its inherent nature, blockchain technology provides an unprecedented level of transparency and traceability in transactions. This visibility is crucial in building trust among consumers and regulators by offering an unchangeable record of carbon emissions and credits, thus supporting more informed decision-making and improving regulatory compliance. In addition, Decentralization of Carbon Credit Management: The decentralization intrinsic to blockchain technology challenges the traditional carbon credit markets, which have historically been plagued by inefficiencies and vulnerability to manipulation. By removing intermediaries, blockchain technology decreases administrative costs and the potential for fraud, resulting in a more efficient and fair carbon credit market. Furthermore, Automation through Smart Contracts: Smart contracts automate multiple aspects of carbon credit transactions, including issuance, transfer, and retirement, thus simplifying compliance, reducing transaction costs, and minimizing human error. This automation ensures that environmental goals are seamlessly integrated into business processes, enhancing operational efficiency and adherence to sustainability standards. The findings indicate that blockchain technology possesses the capacity to markedly advance the management of carbon credits, thereby contributing substantially to the progression of global sustainability objectives. The study lays a strong foundation for further investigation into how these technologies can be improved and broadened to promote a sustainable economic framework that aligns with conservation efforts globally. Through an examination of various blockchain architectures, including *Ethereum, Hyperledger Fabric, Algorand, Polkadot, Tezos, and Avalanche*, this study explains the potential of these platforms in addressing one of the complex challenges of environmental sustainability. Firstly, Ethereum's Important Role and Constraints: Ethereum stands out in the realm of decentralized applications by offering smart contract features essential for creating secure and transparent carbon management systems. However, its scalability challenges and the unpredictable nature of transaction costs underline the need for continuous technological improvements to enhance its effectiveness in extensive applications. In addition, Ethereum displays a paradox in these contexts. The platform has shifted towards becoming a value storage for market participants rather than resolving practical issues, consequently causing increasing prices and transaction expenses. Therefore, in the short term, Ethereum might not be an efficient tool for solving real-world issues. Secondly, Hyperledger Fabric's Enterprise-Level Solutions: The permissioned blockchain framework of Hyperledger Fabric provides a tailor-made solution for state-specific carbon management, focusing on data privacy and scalability. This platform's modular design offers a versatile approach, especially fitting for complex organizational systems that require strict data oversight. Nonetheless, there is still a need for a worldwide solution. Hyperledger Fabric reduces data silos and supports comparisons at the corporate level but only up to the individual state scale, which falls short. Additionally, Algorand's Efficiency and Scalability: Algorand's pure proof-of-stake method is distinguished by its high processing capability and quick transaction finality, presenting an energy-efficient option for monitoring carbon footprints. Yet, the long-term adoption and community backing remain unpredictable. Moreover, Polkadot and Tezos - Specialized Innovations: Polkadot's focus on interoperability and Tezos's on-chain governance give blockchain applications distinctive perspectives on an international level. These platforms provide specialized functions that can boost collaborative efforts and community-focused endeavors in managing carbon footprints. Although Polkadot seems to be a feasible choice, it still faces fluctuations in transaction costs. In addition, Avalanche's Advanced Consensus Protocol: The Avalanche platform, with its cutting-edge consensus process, provides a promising solution for high throughput and swift finality needs in carbon footprint tracking. Its recent introduction to the market indicates the potential for significant impact, although its developing ecosystem should be considered. Among various blockchains, Avalanche appears to be the most suitable candidate for such an application. To conclude, a globally governed system with extremely high finality and very low transaction costs will be essential.

7.2 Future Research Directions

Future research endeavors should firstly emphasize tackling the scalability and adaptability challenges of blockchain architectures to facilitate their widespread adoption across various industrial sectors. Secondly, it is crucial to explore the integration of advanced artificial intelligence (AI) and machine learning (ML) algorithms with blockchain technology to enhance the prediction and optimization of the carbon footprints of products and services. Firstly, concerning the scalability of blockchain systems, there is a need for additional research to increase their ability to efficiently handle the extensive transaction data generated by global carbon credit markets. Such efforts might involve the development of new consensus algorithms or alterations to existing ones to boost transaction throughput without sacrificing security or decentralization. Secondly, regarding regulatory frameworks and standardization, it is important to establish comprehensive frameworks accommodating the decentralized nature and global reach of blockchain. Research should also aim to create standardized protocols for carbon credit verification and transfer to ensure consistency and interoperability across borders. In addition, investigating the potential of blockchain to facilitate the trading and distribution of renewable energy credits, alongside carbon credits, could significantly impact both markets. Studies may examine how blockchain could integrate these systems to establish a unified platform that encourages sustainable development. Furthermore, the application of AI and ML techniques for analyzing blockchain data can provide a deeper understanding of consumption patterns and assist in predicting future trends in carbon emissions. Such endeavors would refine carbon management strategies and improve predictive accuracy regarding environmental impacts. Additionally, examining the human and organizational behavior associated with adopting blockchain technology for carbon credit management can shed light on the barriers and facilitators related to its adoption. Research might focus on psychological, cultural, and institutional factors influencing the acceptance and utilization of blockchain systems within various industries. Finally, conducting longitudinal studies to evaluate the long-term environmental, economic, and social impacts of carbon credit systems integrated with blockchain is essential. Such studies can quantify the tangible benefits and potential issues of these systems over time, thereby providing a more comprehensive understanding of their sustainability. These research directions aim to refine technological applications and comprehend the effect of blockchain on social norms and environmental policies, which can contribute to the development of robust, transparent, and efficient systems for managing global resources and promoting sustainable development.

A Appendix

A.1 Terminology

(1) Carbon Footprint. Refers to the total greenhouse gas emissions associated with a product or process, typically expressed in terms of carbon dioxide equivalents (CO2e). **(2) Carbon Credits.** Tradable units that represent a specific amount of carbon dioxide or equivalent greenhouse gas that has been reduced, avoided, or offset. Carbon credits are obtained through tokenization of carbon footprints. **(3) Tokenization.** The process of representing assets, data, or rights as digital tokens on a blockchain, allowing secure and efficient management.

References

1. Bogdanov, D., Jõemets, M., Siim, S., Vaht, M.: How the estonian tax and customs board evaluated a tax fraud detection system based on secure multi-party computation. In: Financial Cryptography and Data Security, vol. FC2015, pp. 227–234 (2015)
2. Niu, S., Chen, L., Wang, J., Yu, F.: Electronic health record sharing scheme with searchable attribute-based encryption on blockchain. IEEE Access **8**, 7195–7204 (2019)
3. Hu, S., Cai, C., Wang, Q., Wang, C., Luo, X., Ren, K.: Searching an encrypted cloud meets blockchain: A decentralized, reliable and fair realization. In: IEEE INFOCOM 2018, IEEE Conference on Computer Communications, pp. 792–800 (2018)
4. Søgaard, J.S.: A blockchain-enabled platform for VAT settlement. Int. J. Account. Inf. Syst. **40**, 100–502 (2021)
5. Boneh, D., Di Crescenzo, G., Ostrovsky, R., Persiano, G.: Public key encryption with keyword search. In: International Conference on the Theory and Applications of Cryptographic Techniques, pp. 506–522 (2004)
6. Jiang, S., Cao, J., McCann, J. A., Yang, Y., Liu, Y., Wang, X., Deng, Y.: Privacy-preserving and efficient multi-keyword search over encrypted data on blockchain. In: I2019 IEEE International Conference on Blockchain (Blockchain), pp. 405–410 (2019)
7. Kalaiselvan, S., Venkatesh, J., Kumar, A.: Blockchain powered carbon credit marketplace. In: 2024 10th International Conference on Communication and Signal Processing (ICCSP), pp. 582–585. IEEE (2024). https://doi.org/10.1109/ICCSP60870.2024.10543794
8. Jawalkar, S., Shende, R., Selokar, R., Sendre, S.: Carbon credit transfer system using blockchain. In: Third International Conference on Intelligent Techniques in Control, Optimization and Signal Processing (INCOS), pp. 1–6 (2024). https://doi.org/10.1109/INCOS59338.2024.10527749
9. Zhang, C., Xu, Y., Zheng, Y.: Blockchain traceability adoption in low-carbon supply chains: an evolutionary game analysis. Sustainability **16**(5) (2024). https://doi.org/10.3390/su16051817
10. Swinkels, L.: Trading carbon credit tokens on the blockchain. Int. Rev. Econ. Finance **91**, pp. 720–733 (2024). https://doi.org/10.1016/j.iref.2024.01.012
11. Akiladevi, R., Sardha, S., Shruthi, R.: Tokenization of energy assets: a multichain blockchain approach. In: 5th International Conference on Mobile Computing and Sustainable Informatics (ICMCSI), pp. 702–709 (2024). https://doi.org/10.1109/ICMCSI61536.2024.00110
12. Pekel, U., Yayla, O.: Carbon footprint traction system incorporated as blockchain. Cryptol. ePrint Arch. Paper 2024/1863 (2024)

An Analysis of Financial Stability Risk Propagation Through Leveraged Staking Activities

Takaya Sugino[1], Benjamin Kraner[2], James Angel[1], Shin'ichiro Matsuo[1], and Rohil Paruchuri[1(✉)]

[1] Georgetown University, Washington, USA
{ts1433,angelj,sm3377}@georgetown.edu, rohilparuchuri@gmail.com
[2] University of Zurich, Zurich, Switzerland
benjamin.kraner@uzh.ch

Abstract. This study investigates financial stability risks associated with leveraged staking activities in decentralized finance (DeFi) systems, particularly focusing on liquid staking, restaking, and liquid restaking. Market participants can have opportunities to maximize their staking rewards while engaging in additional leveraged staking activities, but leveraged staking activities introduce vulnerabilities akin to those observed in traditional finance. In addition, such activities introduce vulnerabilities unique in DeFi, leading unprecedented financial stability risks to propagate within financial systems.

This paper identifies and categorizes vulnerabilities within protocols that offer opportunities for such leveraged staking activities. It examines how risks propagate through interconnected DeFi systems using historical cases, including the Terra/Luna and FTX collapses. The analysis culminates in a generalized framework illustrating how risks propagate through vulnerabilities when a shock occurs. The study underscores the need for quantitative risk assessment based on the framework, prioritization of critical risks, and risk mitigation approaches to enhance resilience in DeFi systems.

Keywords: Staking · Liquid Staking · Restaking · Liquid Restaking · Ethereum · Lido · Renzo · EigenLayer

1 Introduction

In Ethereum [1] and other Proof of Stake (PoS) [2] blockchains, entities responsible for verifying blocks and transactions must deposit native tokens, a process known as staking [3]. The allocation of validation tasks is proportional to the amount staked. To increase the number of participants in staking, thereby enhancing decentralization and security, these blockchains offer staking rewards in the form of transaction fees or other incentives. However, when staking, one's native tokens are locked in a staking pool, leading to a loss of opportunities for yield farming through liquidity provision in other DeFi protocols [4]. Consequently, leveraged staking activities such as liquid staking [5], restaking [6], and liquid restaking [7] have emerged within the ecosystem. These activities allow users to earn staking rewards while simultaneously participating in additional yield farming opportunities [8].

While these protocols, driven by the demand for additional returns, have attracted a significant number of users, they also pose potential financial stability risks within the decentralized finance (DeFi) system as the market expands [9]. Although there is no instance where these activities have triggered a systemic financial crisis, there are several cases where risks have already manifested [10–13]. While the impact on traditional finance remains limited, identifying and addressing the financial stability risks associated with the use of these mechanisms is a meaningful endeavor, especially considering the potential for long-term market expansion.

1.1 Background

In these activities designed to obtain additional yield farming opportunities, newly issued derivative tokens backed by staked native tokens, such as liquid staking tokens and liquid restaking tokens, are used [5,7]. The financial stability risks associated with the use of these derivative products can be somewhat analogous to those observed in traditional finance.

At the same time, DeFi poses unique financial stability risks. For instance, restaking, which gained attention following the launch of EigenLayer [6] in 2023, could concentrate governance power among specific participants in protocols that claim to be decentralized. [9]. This concentration could undermine the soundness and fairness of governance of the protocols. Such governance vulnerabilities could amplify other vulnerabilities, such as asset value declines and liquidity crises, potentially leading to a financial crisis. Analyzing these new types of vulnerabilities will significantly contribute to this work.

1.2 Our Contribution

In the following subsection, this paper explains the mechanisms of the leveraged staking models. Section 2 analyzes the market dynamics of these models. Subsequently, Sect. 3 delineates the structural elements critical for identifying the vulnerabilities associated with each model. This structure analysis examines key aspects, including what actions are being trusted, for what purposes, and how rewards are distributed for these actions. In Sect. 4, a comprehensive classification of vulnerabilities contributing to financial stability risks is proposed, leveraging the framework employed by the Financial Stability Board (FSB) for analyzing such risks. The section then explores how potential shocks may propagate within the decentralized finance (DeFi) systems.

While concerns regarding financial stability risks associated with these leveraged staking models have been suggested in several studies [9,14–16], this paper is the first to propose a generalized framework for risk propagation mechanisms associated with the leveraged staking models. Despite growing regulatory attention, including from the FSB, on systemic financial risks in DeFi with potential spillover effects on traditional finance, the analysis of financial stability risks specifically tied to these leveraged staking models remains underdeveloped. As the DeFi market continues to expand, research in this area is expected to become essential for both regulators and industry stakeholders. Moreover, the proposed framework will serve as a valuable tool for further academic studies.

1.3 Terminology

This subsection provides an explanation of the mechanisms behind liquid staking, restaking, and liquid restaking, which allow Ethereum validators to maximize staking rewards in exchange for contributing to the security and functionality of the broader ecosystem, as claimed by service providers or protocol developers. It also defines the specialized terminology that is used in subsequent sections to ensure clarity in the discussion. This paper consistently focuses on Ethereum in its discussions, assuming no consideration of other chains. Appendix A introduces a more detailed structure analysis of each leveraged staking model.

Staking: Staking refers to the process by which participants in the Ethereum network commit a fixed amount of ETH to the network to support its operations, such as validating transactions and securing the chain. In the Ethereum network, participants lock their ETH in an official deposit contract and, in return, earn staking rewards. These rewards are typically distributed in the form of newly issued ETH (inflationary rewards) and a share of the transaction fees collected from users of the network. However, participants also take on the risk of getting slashed, losing part of their staked funds in cases of deliberate misbehavior or protocol violations. [1]

Validator: A validator is a participant in the Ethereum network who is responsible for proposing and attesting to new blocks as part of the consensus mechanism. By locking their ETH into the official deposit contract, a validator commits to the network's security and integrity, and, in return, earns staking rewards in ETH as a percentage of the funds they have staked. Becoming an official full validator requires staking 32 ETH. However, for participants who wish to earn rewards with a smaller stake, some validators offer a service that pools funds from multiple participants. These validators stake the combined funds on behalf of the participants and distribute some of the staking rewards to the participants (hereinafter referred to as pooled staking). Centralized organizations, such as staking service providers or custodians, facilitate pooled staking by matching validators (hereinafter referred to as delegated validators) with participants (hereinafter referred to pooled stakers) who wish to stake their funds and managing the staking process on their behalf. [1,17]

Liquid Staking: Liquid staking can be considered a specific form of pooled staking, but it has a key distinguishing feature: participants (hereinafter referred to liquid stakers) delegate their ETH to professional validators through a Liquid

Staking Protocol (LSP) and, in return, receive derivative tokens known as Liquid Staking Tokens (LSTs). [5] These LSTs are issued by the protocol and reflect the staked ETH along with the staking rewards it accrues. Unlike traditional pooled staking, where participants simply receive periodic payouts of staking rewards, liquid staking allows participants to hold and use LSTs while their ETH remains locked in the deposit contract. These tokens are liquid, meaning they can be traded on the secondary market, used as collateral for loans, or employed in other DeFi protocols such as liquidity mining. The process of redeeming LSTs is typically managed through smart contracts. Upon redemption, participants exchange their LSTs for ETH along with any accrued staking rewards.

Gogol et al. (2024) [18] propose a taxonomy of liquid staking protocols based on key attributes, including token models, LSP Deligated Validator (DV) selection methods, LSP DV visibility, network architecture, and governance structures. The distribution of staking rewards to LST holders varies depending on the token model implemented by the protocol. In the 1) rebasing token model, staking rewards are distributed directly to holders in the form of additional LSTs, which are automatically deposited into their wallets. In contrast, the 2) reward-bearing token model reflects the value of staking rewards in the price of the LST itself, meaning that the rewards are embedded in the increasing value of the token held by the participants rather than distributed as additional tokens. For simplicity, this paper focuses on the reward-bearing token model in its analysis.

Restaking: Actively Validated Services (AVSs) are critical components of the broader Ethereum ecosystem that rely on Ethereum validators to perform specialized tasks distinct from basic transaction validation and block production on the Ethereum network. Examples of AVSs include Oracles [19], Data Availability Layers [20], and Layer 2 Scaling Solutions [21]. These services require decentralized operations supported by their own set of validators (hereinafter referred to as AVS-specific validators). For instance, in the case of ZK-Rollups [22], AVS-specific validators must submit off-chain transaction batches and cryptographic proofs of transaction validity to the Ethereum network.

To ensure economic security, protocol operators often issue their own ERC-20 tokens and require their own set of validators to deposit these tokens as collateral. This collateral can be slashed in cases of rule violations or malicious behavior. Those validators are incentivized through fees denominated in these tokens as compensation for their work. However, attracting sufficient validators and maintaining high token value for their incentives can be challenging for emerging AVSs. [23]

A Restaking Protocol (RP) allows natively staked ETH to be "restaked" to AVSs in exchange for additional yield. This yield typically originates from fees paid by users of the AVSs. Ethereum validators who restake ETH (hereinafter referred to as native restakers) take on additional responsibilities required by AVSs, beyond the basic duties of Ethereum validators, while taking on the risks of their staked ETHs getting slashed when they can't fulfill the additional responsibilities. It is purported that, by integrating with an RP, AVSs can leverage the economic security of the Ethereum network. [6]

To engage in native restaking through an RP, native restakers must run at least one Ethereum validator node and set their withdrawal credentials of staked ETH to a smart contract managed by them, which allows the RP to monitor and manage balance and withdrawal statuses [6]. Through the RP, native restakers can select AVSs that they want to support, and set up dedicated nodes for selected AVSs.

On the other hand, there are RPs that support restaking LSTs, not just ETHs [24]. In other words, LST holders can deposit their LSTs as collateral into an RP in exchange for performing validation work for AVSs (hereinafter, such LST holders are referred to as LST restakers, and this action is referred to as LST native restaking). In the event of a failure in validation work for AVSs, LST native restakers get slashed, losing their deposited LSTs.

In addition, in August 2024, one of the RPs, EigenLayer, began accepting ERC20 tokens for restaking. [25] This development allows AVSs to leverage the economic security not only of the Ethereum network but also of other protocols that issue their own ERC20 tokens. However, for simplicity, our analysis excludes the consideration of ERC token restaking.

Liquid Restaking: Through a Liquid Restaking Protocol (LRP), participants (hereinafter referred to as liquid restakers or LST liquid restakers respectively) can delegate (hereinafter the activity is referred to as liquid restaking or LST liquid restaking respectively) their ETHs or LSTs to professional validators (hereinafter referred to as LRP delegated validators (LRP DVs)) who restake the delegated ETHs or LSTs, to AVSs that they support. Participants receive derivative tokens, called Liquid Restaking Tokens (LRTs), which can also be traded on secondary markets, used as collateral for loans, or employed in other DeFi protocols such as liquidity mining. [7,26]

Similar to LST, there are different methods for distributing restaking rewards to LRT holders. If the reward-bearing token model [18] is adopted, the rewards do not only depend on the duration of the restaking period but also on which AVSs the LRP DVs support. This introduces additional complexity in the operation of distributing restaking rewards. For simplicity, this paper focuses on the reward-bearing token model in its analysis.

In fact, Restaking Protocols (RPs) also have delegated validators (commonly referred to as operators, but referred to in this paper as RP DVs). one can deposit their ETHs or LSTs into RPs and receive a portion of the staking rewards from the validation work that RP DVs perform for Ethereum and/or AVSs. The mechanism is almost identical to that of an LRP, with the primary difference being whether users receive LRTs or not.

2 Market Analysis

Staking in Ethereum is a fundamental building block of the Ethereum consensus protocol and its technological security, as well as a key component of Ethereum's financial ecosystem. In December, around 34 million Ether were staked in the network,[1] representing approximately 28% of the total Ether supply, amounting to 114 billion USD. [27] Ethereum has experienced a steady inflow of staked Ether since the launch of the Beacon Chain in December 2020, becoming saturated only in the last few months (as of December2024).

Liquid staking is currently the most popular form of staking in Ethereum, outpacing staking via centralized exchanges and traditional staking pools. Around 13.8 million Ether (valued at 46 billion USD) are locked in LSPs, with Lido, which comprises around 70% of the total value locked (TVL) in liquid staking [28], accounting for approximately 28% of the total stake in Ethereum. Created immediately after the launch of the Beacon Chain, Lido has thus become the largest entity in the (liquid) staking market, followed by smaller LSPs such as *Binance staked ETH* (6.1 billion USD TVL) and *Rocket Pool* (2.5 billion USD TVL). From a protocol perspective, the liquid staking market is therefore highly concentrated, consisting of Lido and many smaller protocols.

LSTs can also be used in other DeFi protocols. A prime example is AAVE, a lending platform, where wstETH (a wrapped version of Lido's LST) ranks second in total supply on AAVE with 1.04 million tokens, amounting to 4.1 billion USD. This underscores the importance of LSTs not only as a means of participating in staking but also for integrating staking with other DeFi protocols. [29]

The restaking market is dominated by EigenLayer[2], the first RP to launch on Ethereum. Its TVL amounts to 4.7 million ETH (15.4 billion USD), of which 3.2 million ETH are contributed in the form of native staked Ether, while the remaining 1.5 million ETH come from various LSTs, the largest being stETH. It is not immediately clear which entities, including private stakers, stake-pool operators, centralized exchanges, or LSPs, contribute to the native stake of EigenLayer operators (RP Delegated Validators). Gaining insights on these relationships would improve our understanding of the financial interconnectivity in staking.

Beyond EigenLayer, the rest of the restaking landscape in Ethereum consists of Symbiotic[3], with a TVL of approximately 650,000ETH (2.2 billion USD), and Karak[4], with a TVL of around 230,000 ETH (0.8 billion USD), putting the total TVL in RPs to around 18.4 billion USD. [30]

As the latest and most novel approach to staking, LRPs have quickly gained traction. Since their launch toward the end of 2023, they have accrued a total value locked (TVL) of around 14.9 billion USD, with ether.fi being the largest protocol, accounting for 8.1 billion USD of that sum. [31]

3 Financial Stability Risk Analysis

3.1 Definition

The assessment of vulnerabilities affecting the global financial system is a core mandate of the FSB. The assessment currently focuses on the vulnerabilities in

---

[1] December 26th 2024: 34,217,619 ETH.
[2] https://www.eigenlayer.xyz.
[3] https://symbiotic.fi.
[4] https://karak.network.

the traditional finance system and the propagation of financial stability risk in the decentralized financial system into the traditional one. Although this paper focuses on stability risk in decentralized finance, it is essential to apply their assessment framework to our work for further research on the propagation of financial stability risk that we analyze in this paper into the traditional financial system.

The FSB defines a vulnerability as a property of the financial system that: (i) reflects the accumulation of imbalances, (ii) may increase the likelihood of a shock, and (iii) when acted upon by a shock, may lead to systemic disruption. A shock is defined as an event that may lead to disruption or failure in part of the financial system. Propagation mechanisms are the channels through which financial vulnerabilities cause disruption, given the occurrence of a shock. In the context of risks propagating through vulnerabilities when a shock occurs, risks can be defined as the potential adverse outcomes or uncertainties that arise due to vulnerabilities in the DeFi system, especially under shocks.

In sub-section 4.2, this paper introduces a classification of direct and indirect vulnerabilities associated with liquid staking, restaking, and liquid restaking. The subsequent sub-section 4.3 then analyzes how various shocks amplify these vulnerabilities, learning from historical shock events. In the last section, this paper explores how the shocks amplify the vulnerabilities through the propagation mechanisms in the decentralized financial system.

3.2 Classification of Vulnerabilities

Table 1 categorizes and comprehensively lists the potential vulnerabilities associated with Ethereum Layer 1 (L1), Liquid Staking Protocols (LSPs), Restaking Protocols (RPs), Liquid Restaking Protocols (LRPs), and Actively Validated Services (AVSs).

In the Asset Price category, key vulnerabilities include low price of ETH and AVS tokens, as well as mispricing caused by market manipulation or temporary supply-demand imbalances stemming from bugs. Due to changes in supply and demand, the price of LSTs or LRTs pegged to ETH may deviate from their expected value when traded through exchanges or lending services.

The Stakeholder category highlights vulnerable characteristics of stakeholders for each protocol, such as a decrease in the number of (delegated) validators and the resulting high degree of centralization. Having low-quality (delegated) validators is one of the vulnerabilities in this category that leads to a higher likelihood of a secondary shock, slashing events. Furthermore, a reduction in yield rewards for stakeholders may lead to a decrease in user participation or a reduction in the number of (delegated) validators. This could negatively impact the trust in the protocol from users, ultimately affecting the value of the associated tokens and the security of the protocol ultimately.

The focus in the Liquidity category is primarily on the liquidity aspect of whether redemption can be performed immediately from the leveraged staking activity of each protocol. As for the Funding category, an identified vulnerability lies in the increasing proportion of ETH or LSTs allocated to LSPs, RPs, and LRPs. A high concentration of ETHs or LSTs in such protocols can lead to vulnerabilities, including reduced liquidity for ETH or LSTs in DEXs and centralization of Ethereum and AVS validators.

The LST looping mentioned under the Leverage category refers to the process where liquid stakers repeatedly exchange LSTs acquired from an LSP for ETHs on a DEX, deposit the ETHs back into the LSP, and receive new LSTs. Similarly, LRT looping involves liquid restakers exchanging LRTs obtained from an LRP for ETHs on a DEX, depositing the ETHs into an LSP or LRP to acquire new LSTs or LRTs, or exchanging LRTs for LSTs on a DEX and depositing those LSTs into an LRP to acquire more LRTs, repeating the leverage process.

In most protocols, including Ethereum, governance decisions regarding organizational operations are made through 'decentralized' voting mechanisms. However, this often results in delayed decision-making or situations where, in practice, a small group of individuals holds centralized authority. Additionally, as mentioned in the Stakeholder category, the low quality of (delegated) validators in each protocol is identified as a vulnerability. The lack of transparency in (delegated) validators can also be considered a governance vulnerability for each protocol.

Each protocol issues its own tokens, which are staked by its validators to provide security, with rewards distributed in the form of the tokens or others. A low level of economic security assured through such mechanisms is one of the security vulnerabilities. Furthermore, technical vulnerabilities in the smart contracts or oracles that each protocol relies upon must also be taken into account.

A low level of user trust in a protocol also represents a vulnerability. If a shock occurs that further erodes trust particularly in cases where users are already taking on significant risks to continue using a protocol, it could result in a sharp decline in users, with risks propagating to other vulnerabilities.

In the Linkages and Dependencies category, reliance on or excessive dependence on other vulnerable protocols is identified as a vulnerability. For instance, if a protocol generates revenue by providing liquidity to a DEX as part of its incentive distribution mechanism, the vulnerabilities of that DEX could propagate risks to the protocol itself. If the DEX's vulnerabilities worsen, the risks could cascade to the protocol.

3.3 Classification of Shocks

In the FSB framework [32], shocks refer to sudden, unexpected, and immediate events that activate or exacerbate vulnerabilities, potentially leading to financial instability. Given the higher complexity of DeFi systems, it is necessary to clarify the detailed definition of shocks beyond the scope of the FSB framework. Table 3 classifies shocks by considering their sources and the processes through which they occur.

Shocks can be categorized into primary shocks and secondary shocks. Primary shocks refer to sudden, unexpected, and immediate events that are primarily triggered by external factors outside the financial system. Specific examples include geopolitical or political events such as wars, significant regulatory

Table 1. Classification of Vulnerabilities

Category	L1(Ethereum)	LSP	RP	LRP	AVS
Asset Price		– Depeg of LST – LST mispricing		– Depeg of LRT – LRT mispricing	– Low AVS token price – AVS token mispricing
Stakeholder	– Bad validators – A centralization of validators – A decrease in the number of validators – A decrease in the number of users – Low staking rewards	– A bad LSP DV selection – A centralization of LSP DVs – A decrease in the number of LSP DVs – A decrease in the number of liquid stakers – Low rewards given to liquid stakers	– Much ETH or LST restaked to high-risk AVSs by native restakers or RP DVs – A centralization of native restakers – A centralization of RP DVs – A decrease in the number of native restakers – A decrease in the number of RP DVs – Low rewards given to native restakers	– A bad LRP DV selection by LRP DVs – Much ETH or LST restaked to high-risk AVSs by LRP DVs – A centralization of LRP DVs – A decrease in the number of LRP DVs – A decrease in the number of liquid restakers – Low rewards given to liquid restakers	– A decrease in the number of AVS users – Low restaking rewards give by AVSs
Liquidity/Funding	– Limited redemption of staked ETH	– A high proportion of ETH deposited in LSP – Limited redemption – Low liquidity of LST in DeFi – Insufficient LST collateral in DeFi	– A high proportion of ETH or LST restaked in RP – Limited redemption	– A high proportion of ETH or LST deposited in LRP – Limited redemption – Low liquidity of LRT in DeFi – Insufficient LRT collateral in DeFi	– Limited redemption of staked AVS token
Leverage		– LST looping		– LRT looping	
Governance	– Slow decision making – Centralized operation	– Slow decision making – Centralized operation – Intransparency in LSP DV – Over-reliance on other protocols	– Slow decision making – Centralized operation – Over-reliance on other protocols	– Slow decision making – Centralized operation – Intransparency in LRP DV	– Slow decision making – Centralized operation
Security	– Cryptographic insecurity – Economic insecurity	– Vulnerable oracle – Vulnerable smart contract – Economic insecurity	– Vulnerable oracle – Vulnerable smart contract – Economic insecurity	– Vulnerable oracle – Vulnerable smart contract – Economic insecurity	– Vulnerable smart contract – Economic insecurity
Trust	– Low trust in Ethereum from users	– Low trust in LSPs from users	– Low trust in RPs from users	– Low trust in LRP's from users	– Low trust in AVSs from users
Linkages and Dependencies	– Over-reliance on other protocols – linkages to other vulnerable protocols	– Over-reliance on other protocols – linkages to other vulnerable protocols	– Over-reliance on other protocols – linkages to other vulnerable protocols	– Over-reliance on other protocols – linkages to other vulnerable protocols	– Over-reliance on other protocols – linkages to other vulnerable protocols

changes, or policy announcements, as well as direct hacking incidents. Secondary shocks, on the other hand, are immediate events induced by the amplification of vulnerabilities within the DeFi systems. Examples include slashing, liquidations in lending protocols, large-scale sell-offs on DEXs, rug pulls, and price manipulations. These events may occur either as technical mechanisms that automatically react to the amplification of certain vulnerabilities (e.g., slashings, liquidations) or as actions driven by individuals motivated by specific incentives (e.g., sell-offs, rug pulls, price manipulations).

Although direct hacking is classified as a primary shock in the table, if the exploited technical vulnerability was a known issue that had not been addressed before the occurrence of the shock, it can also be classified as a secondary shock arising from that vulnerability. Oracle manipulations are generally classified as secondary shocks, as they often stem from known operational or technical vulnerabilities. However, when external factors play a significant role, they may also exhibit aspects of primary shocks (Table 2).

Table 2. Shock Classification

Primary shock	Secondary shock
– Examples: wars, geopolitical risks, significant regulatory or policy changes, large-scale hacking, etc – Direct: External events that occur independently of specific vulnerabilities and directly impact the system – Unpredictable	– Examples: slashing, liquidation events in lending protocols, large-scale sell-offs on DEXs, oracle manipulations, etc – Indirect: Internal events that are technically or operationally predetermined to occur when a specific vulnerability worsens / Actions that are taken by individuals or entities to exploit a specific vulnerability for personal or strategic advantage – Predictable

3.4 Framework Application to Real-World Cases

This section explains mechanisms of risk propagation through shocks, using past cases.

Case Study 1: Risk Propagation through Vulnerabilities involved in Liquid Staking triggered by the Terra Crash Incident (Fig. 1)

Terra attempted to stabilize the price of its stablecoin UST by adjusting the supply of its native token, LUNA, which served as collateral. Additionally, Terra's DeFi platform, Anchor Protocol, offered high rewards to UST liquidity providers. On the other hand, the lending protocol Celsius acted as a UST liquidity provider on Anchor Protocol and simultaneously leveraged ETH collateral provided by its users in LST looping to generate profits. [13,33,34]

However, when investors started selling large volumes of LUNA on exchanges, LUNA's price plummeted, and Terra was unable to maintain the UST peg. This depegging led to mass withdrawals of UST from Anchor Protocol, significantly reducing its user base and eroding trust in the protocol. Consequently, Celsius, which relied on earnings from Anchor Protocol, also faced a loss of trust, triggering large-scale withdrawals of ETH. Struggling to repay users due to insufficient ETH reserves, Celsius sold stETH on DEXs to acquire ETH, resulting in the depegging of stETH from ETH. This depeg caused the liquidation of stETH collateral on the lending protocol Aave, further accelerating the stETH depeg as liquidators sold stETH in the market. [10]

Xihan et al. analyzed the risk propagation initiated by the Terra crash and conducted stress tests to examine the market impacts of vulnerabilities amplified by LST looping. [15] [5]

Case Study 2: Risk Propagation through Vulnerabilities involved in Liqid Staking triggered by the FTX Collapse (Fig. 2)

In this case, the FTX collapse is considered an unexpected external shock, a primary shock. Following the collapse, trust in centralized entities diminished, leading to reduced confidence in Lido, which had been criticized for its centralization. Similar to the case, large-scale selling of Lido's LST, stETH, on DEXs triggered a depegging of stETH from ETH. This resulted in collateral shortfalls

---

[5] The red arrows do not indicate that the existence or exacerbation of a particular vulnerability contributes to the occurrence of secondary shock. Rather, they signify that the vulnerability contributes to the amplification of risk propagation caused by the secondary shock.

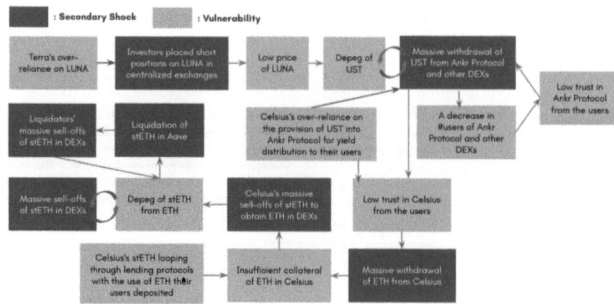

Fig. 1. An example of risk propagation through vulnerabilities involved in liquid staking, triggered by the collapse of Terra/Luna

in lending protocols, leading to liquidations. The liquidators' subsequent sales of stETH further exacerbated the depeg. [35]

When stETH is redeemed directly with Lido, it is burned, preventing depegging. However, if Lido imposes restrictions on redemption, stETH holders are likely to opt for selling on DEXs, exacerbating the depeg.

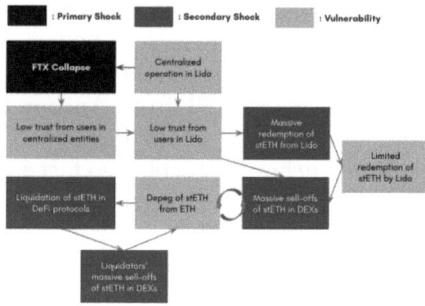

Fig. 2. An example of risk propagation through vulnerabilies involved in liquid staking, triggered by the collapse of FTX

Case Study 3: Risk Propagation Triggered by Large-Scale Selling of LRTs (Fig. 3)

LRTs tend to have lower liquidity on DEXs compared to LSTs. Additionally, few LRPs allow immediate redemption of LRTs, forcing liquid restakers to sell LRTs on DEXs to exit their positions. Consequently, LRTs are highly susceptible to depegging from ETH. [11,12,26]

The LRT ezETH, issued by Renzo Protocol, experienced a depeg from ETH due to large-scale sales. This depegging triggered liquidations in lending protocols holding ezETH as collateral. Liquidators, in turn, sold the acquired LRTs, further accelerating the depeg.

Alexander et al. [14] also highlighted the possibility of intentional large-scale LST/LRT sales by liquidators to induce liquidations, thereby amplifying risk propagation.

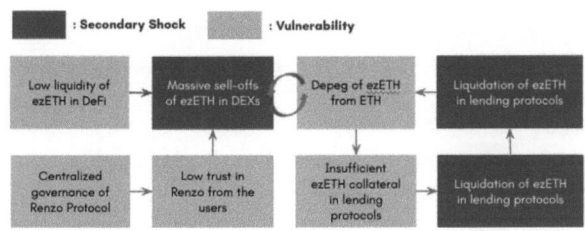

Fig. 3. An example of risk propagation that emerged from the depegging of liquid restaking tokens

3.5 Generalized Framework for Risk Propagation Through Vulnerabilities Involved in Leveraged Staking

While the diagrams introduced in Sect. 4.4 mapped real-world cases to a risk propagation framework, Fig. 4 generalizes this framework to illustrate how risks may propagate across vulnerabilities involving various leveraged staking methods. The diagram outlines four major patterns:

Mechanism 1: Similar to the case 1 and 2, this mechanism illustrates how shocks from large-scale selling, redemption, or liquidation of LSTs can propagate risks across LSP associated vulnerabilities.

Mechanism 2: Reflecting the case 3, this mechanism shows how shocks from large-scale selling, redemption (which is often unavailable), or liquidation of LRTs can propagate risks across LRP associated vulnerabilities.

Mechanism 3: This mechanism highlights the risk propagation caused by slashing events that occur when RP/LRP DVs or Native Restakers fail to validate Ethereum or AVSs. These events may lead to vulnerabilities in RPs/LRPs and AVSs, potentially resulting in a loss of trust from their users.

Mechanism 4: This mechanism demonstrates how slashing events involving LSP DVs can propagate risks to vulnerabilities in LSPs and Ethereum, undermining trust in Ethereum and LSPs.

Additionally, Fig. 4 shows that attacks targeting vulnerabilities in governance, security, or linkages and dependencies with other protocols can erode trust in a protocol. Such events may trigger the onset of one or more mechanisms.

These mechanisms do not necessarily operate independently.

Mechanism 1 and 4: If a loss of trust in LSPs is triggered through one mechanism, it may activate the other mechanism.

Mechanism 2 and 3: Similarly, a loss of trust in RPs or LRPs may lead to the activation of the other mechanism.

Mechanism 3 and 4: A slashing event involving RP/LRP DVs or Native Restakers could trigger both mechanisms.

Mechanism 1, 3, and 4: LST depegging may act as the starting point for all of the mechanisms.

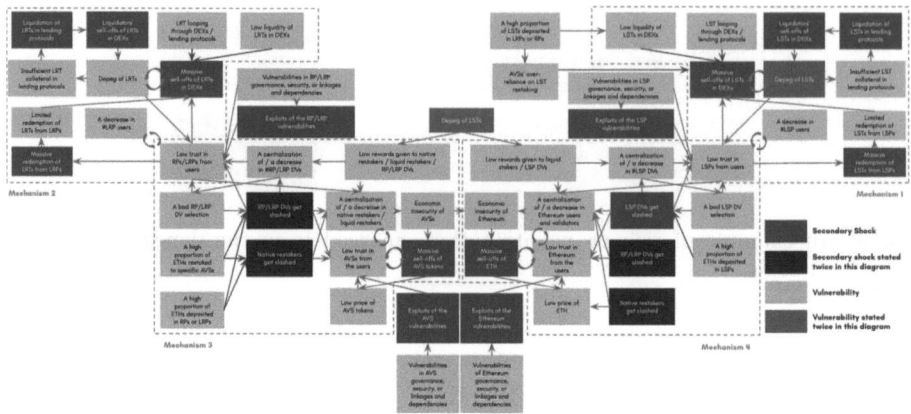

Fig. 4. Generalized Framework for Leveraged Staking Risk Propagation through Leveraged Staking Activities

The red arrows in Fig. 4 require careful interpretation. LST/LRT looping and reduced liquidity of LSTs/LRTs in DEXs do not directly cause large-scale selling of LSTs/LRTs. However, if such selling occurs, these factors can accelerate the depegging of LSTs/LRTs. Concentration of ETH deposits in specific AVSs or protocols (LSPs, RPs, LRPs) exacerbates potential losses in the event of slashing, delivering a greater blow to the economic security of Ethereum or AVSs. If AVSs rely excessively on restaked LSTs rather than ETH, a shock leading to LST depegging could significantly reduce RP/LRP DVs' rewards, further undermining AVS economic security.

Although primary shocks are not explicitly depicted in Fig. 4, they must be considered. By definition, primary shocks are unpredictable and can directly impact any vulnerability. This means that a primary shock could activate any of the mechanisms, starting risk propagation from virtually any vulnerability in the diagram.

4 Implication

Figure 5 illustrates how each vulnerability connects with others to form pathways for risk propagation. Mechanisms 1 and 2 represent risk propagation through excessive leverage in derivative products, a mechanism that also exists in traditional finance. In contrast, Mechanisms 3 and 4 highlight potential risk propagation unique to the DeFi ecosystem, stemming from the deterioration of economic security. It is important to note that Fig. 5 is based on theoretical analysis, and in practice, the degree to which each vulnerability propagates risks to others varies. A thorough analysis requires quantitative metrics to evaluate each vulnerability, and particular attention should be given to key metrics such as:

- Collateralization Ratio (Corresponding vulnerability: Insufficient LST and LRT Collateral in DeFi)
- Liquidity Ratio of Pools (Corresponding vulnerability: Low liquidity of LST and LRT in DeFi)
- Asset Concentration Index (Corresponding vulnerability: Much ETH or LST restaked to high-risk AVSs by native restakers, RP DVs, or LRP DVs)

Additionally, cybersecurity incidents occur at a significantly higher rate in DeFi compared to traditional financial systems. These incidents often act as primary shocks, triggering risk propagation through various vulnerabilities. Furthermore, due to the lack of regulation against market manipulation in DeFi, actions driven by specific incentives can easily become secondary shocks that propagate systemic risks. This means that shocks occur frequently, and as illustrated by the framework in Fig. 5, these shocks can instigate risk propagation throughout the DeFi ecosystem via various vulnerabilities. It is crucial to quantitatively assess the likelihood that each shock occurs.

5 Next Steps

The FSB refers to resilience as the capacity of a financial system to absorb shocks and prevent them from leading to the unveiling of accumulated imbalances [32]. As the market expands, it is necessary to continuously monitor the potential for systemic risk within DeFi systems, and the possibility of these risks propagating into traditional financial systems, by strengthening the assessment of resilience in protocols that enable leveraged staking activities and other DeFi protocols.

Although some DeFi protocols make some efforts to enhance the resilience for financial stability risks, there still remains a lot of challenges. For instance, Lido responded to the depegging of stETH by incentivizing liquidity provision through the distribution of its governance token, LDO. However, as PrismaRisk [16] points out, not all protocols possess governance tokens or equivalent mechanisms with sufficient value to adequately mitigate financial stability risks. This example highlights the need for systemic solutions to address vulnerabilities associated with leveraged staking activities.

This paper successfully generalizes the pathways through which risks propagate via various leveraged staking protocols in DeFi systems. The first priority as a next step might be to provide transparency around essential indicators including those listed in Sect. 4. A further step in research involves quantitatively analyzing these indicators and how each vulnerability directly connects to others. Based on these analyses, it will be essential to prioritize handling critical vulnerabilities and consider operational, technical, and regulatory measures for protocol developers to mitigate them.

However, in contrast to traditional financial institutions, which are mandated by regulation to conduct regular risk assessments to prevent financial stability risks, DeFi protocols often operate without regulatory oversight. Under the pessimistic premise that DeFi protocol operators will not initiatively engage in such work without regulation, it may be inevitable for authorities to exert enforcement power. Moreover, even if such enforcement is applied, protocol developers with expertise in financial stability risk assessment remain scarce, which makes it difficult for each protocol to perform these works independently. Therefore, it is crucial to establish standardized approaches to risk assessment and facilitate the industry-wide sharing of quantitatively analyzed vulnerability information. This would offer market participants and protocol developers guidance on building resilient systems and sustainable business models.

6 Conclusion

This paper systematically organizes the concepts of liquid staking, restaking, and liquid restaking as forms of leveraged staking activities and categorizes the vulnerabilities inherent in each protocol. Furthermore, it analyzes how risks propagate through these vulnerabilities within the DeFi ecosystem, using historical cases as case studies. Based on this analysis, a generalized framework for risk propagation through vulnerabilities involved in leveraged staking activities has been developed.

As demonstrated by this framework, due to various kinds of shocks, risks can propagate across the entire Ethereum network through various vulnerabilities. Using this framework, it is crucial for entities such as the Financial Stability Board (FSB), individual operators, and academic researchers to quantitatively assess the vulnerabilities and implement risk mitigation measures for prioritized vulnerabilities. To achieve this, establishing a standardized approach to risk assessment and promoting the industry-wide sharing of quantitatively analyzed vulnerability information is of paramount importance.

While the current scale of the DeFi ecosystem remains small and the likelihood of significant risk spillovers into traditional finance is considered low, the situation may change as the DeFi ecosystem continues to expand and the market size of leveraged staking grows. Such risks could escalate to a level that cannot be ignored in terms of their potential spillovers into traditional finance. Therefore, further research is necessary to understand the mechanisms through which risk spillovers into traditional finance might occur. Additionally, ensuring the financial stability and soundness of the DeFi ecosystem itself is highly significant to bring closer the realization of claims that DeFi could serve as the future financial system and to achieve mass adoption of crypto for finance.

A Structure Analysis of Leveraged Staking Models

Building on previous studies [18,36], Table 3 compares various leveraged staking activities by clarifying the actions performed by each participant (e.g., what validation work each participant themselves conducts and what entities they trust to perform what validation work) and how these actions are compensated, including the type of tokens used to distribute staking rewards. Figure 5 provides a visual representation of Table 3, illustrating the key comparisons of leveraged staking activities in a comprehensive format. This visualisation aims to enhance an understanding of the complexities outlined in Table 1.

For example, in liquid staking, participants (referred to as liquid stakers) delegate their ETH to LSP DVs, trusting the LSP DVs to carry Ethereum validation tasks. Liquid stakers receive staking rewards in the form of LSTs, which price reflects the additional value of staking rewards. This process involves trust in the LSP DVs and trust in the LSP to uphold the peg between LST and ETH. As for liquid restaking, additional layers of trust are introduced. Beyond trusting Ethereum and LRP, participants also need to trust chosen AVSs and the ability of LRP DVs to effectively perform validation tasks effectively for both Ethereum and the AVSs. Compensation in liquid restaking is typically provided in the form of LRTs. Gogol et al. emphasize that the transparency of LSPs and LRPs, including the selection process and accountability of their DVs, is a critical factor underpinning the trust of both liquid stakers and liquid restakers in these systems.

The ability of participants to withdraw their staking rewards and principal depends on the specific leveraged staking model. In native staking and native restaking, where no third party is involved, withdrawals are subject to the constraints of Ethereum and the AVS protocols. Conversely, in liquid staking, liquid restaking, and LST liquid restaking, where assets are pooled by third parties, the ability to redeem may depend on the liquidity of the assets managed by the LSPs or LRPs. Currently, redemption of assets in LRPs is often restricted [16]. However, even when redemption is delayed, liquid stakers, liquid restakers, and LST liquid restakers can typically trade their derivative tokens (LSTs or LRTs) on DeFi markets, providing them with flexibility to access liquidity.

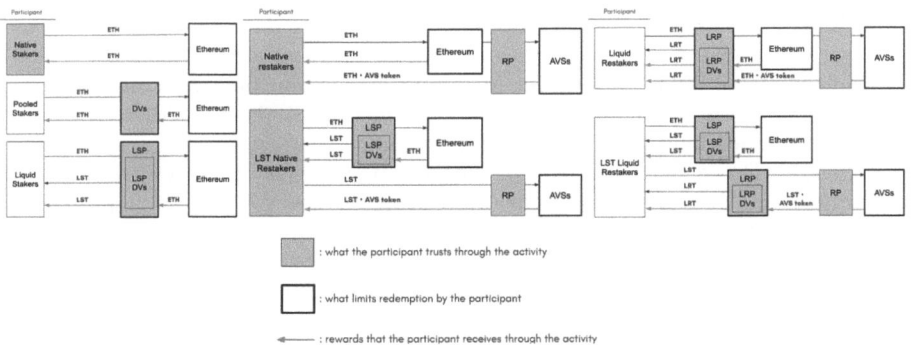

Fig. 5. Structure Analysis of Leveraged Staking Models

Table 3. Structure Analysis of Leveraged Staking Models

Model	Reward	Trust	Redemption
Native Staking	- Receive rewards in exchange for the transaction / block generation and validation - ETH denominated rewards	- Yourself for properly dealing with Ethereum validator work	- Limited by Ethereum
Pooled Staking	- Receive a part of staking rewards from DVs' validation work - ETH denominated rewards	- DVs for properly dealing with validation work for Ethereum	- Limited by DVs, fundamentally by Ethereum
Liquid Staking	- Receive a part of staking rewards from LSP DVs' validation work - Receive additional staking rewards from DeFi protocols you support with LST - LST denominated rewards	- LSP DVs for properly dealing with validation work for Ethereum - Security of LSP	- Limited by LSP, fundamentally by Ethereum
Native Restaking	- Receive rewards in exchange for validation work for Ethereum and AVSs that you support - ETH and/or AVS tokens denominated rewards	- Yourself for properly dealing with validation work for Ethereum and AVSs - Security of RP	- Limited by Ethereum and AVSs that you support
LST Native Restaking	- Receive rewards in exchange for validation work for AVSs that you support - Receive a part of rewards from LSP DVs' validation work for Ethereum and AVSs - LST and/or AVS tokens denominated rewards	- Yourself for properly dealing with validation work for AVSs - LSP DVs for properly dealing with validation work for Ethereum - Security of LSP and RP	- Limited by Ethereum and AVSs that you support
Liquid Restaking	- Receive a part of rewards from LRP DVs' validation work for Ethereum and AVSs that LRP DVs support - Receive additional rewards from DeFi protocols you support with LRT - LRT denominated rewards	- LRP DVs for properly dealing with validation work for Ethereum and AVSs that LRP DVs support - Security of RP and LRP	- Limited by LRP, fundamentally by Ethereum and AVSs that LRP DVs support
LST Liquid Restaking	- Receive a part of rewards from LRP DVs' validation work for AVSs that LRP DVs support - Receive additional rewards from DeFi protocols you support with LRT - Receive a part of rewards from LST DVs' validation work for Ethereum - LRT denominated rewards	- LRP DVs for properly dealing with validation work for Ethereum and AVSs that LRP DVs support - Security of RP, LSP, and LRP	- Limited by LSP and LRP, fundamentally by Ethereum and AVSs that LRP DVs support

References

1. Wood, G.: Ethereum: a secure decentralised generalised transaction ledger. Ethereum Project Yellow Paper **151**, 1–32 (2014)
2. Grandjean, D., Heimbach, L., Wattenhofer, R.: Ethereum proof-of-stake consensus layer: participation and decentralization arXiv preprint arXiv:2306.10777 (2023)
3. Antonopoulos, A.M., Wood, G.: Mastering Ethereum: building smart contracts and DApps. Sebastopol, CA: O'Reilly Media (2018). https://ethereum.org/en/developers/learning-tools/mastering-ethereum/
4. Schär, F.: Decentralized finance: on blockchain- and smart contract-based financial markets. In: Federal Reserve Bank of St. Louis Review, vol. 103, no. 2, pp. 153–174 (2021). https://doi.org/10.20955/r.103.153-74
5. Dao, L.: LIDO: Liquid staking solutions (2021). https://lido.fi/
6. EigenLayer: Restaking for ethereum's security expansion (2023). https://www.eigenlayer.io/
7. ether.fi: Liquid restaking solutions (2024). https://www.ether.fi/
8. Robinson, C., Smith, J.: Innovations in staking: liquid staking and restaking. arXiv preprint arXiv:2307.12345 (2023). https://arxiv.org/abs/2307.12345
9. Buterin, V.: The risks of restaking in defi governance (2023). https://vitalik.ca/general/2023/05/07/restaking.html

10. Cryptonary research Team: The aftermath of celsius, three arrows capital, and voyager (2024). https://cryptonary.com/research/the-aftermath-of-celsius-three-arrows-capital-voyager/. Accessed 4 Dec 2024
11. CoinMonks: Observations from renzo's ezeth depeg (2024). https://medium.com/coinmonks/observations-from-renzos-ezeth-depeg-c545dc217147. Accessed 4 Dec 2024
12. Protos: Depeg of $3b restaking token ezeth causes over$ 60m in defi liquidations (2024). https://protos.com/depeg-of-3b-restaking-token-ezeth-causes-over-60m-in-defi-liquidations/. Accessed 4 Dec 2024
13. QuillAudits: Ankr protocol exploit analysis (2024). https://quillaudits.medium.com/ankr-protocol-exploit-analysis-quillaudits-553cd4c8d17c. Accessed 4 Dec 2024
14. Alexander, C.: Leveraged restaking of leveraged staking: what are the risks? SSRN (2024) 29 Pages Posted: 29 May 2024 (2024). https://papers.ssrn.com/sol3/papers.cfm?abstract_id=4840805
15. Xiong, X., Wang, Z., Chen, X., Knottenbelt, W., Huth, M.: Leverage staking with liquid staking derivatives (LSDS): opportunities and risks. Imperial College London and University of Sussex (2024). https://eprint.iacr.org/2023/1842
16. PrismaRisk: Collateral risk assessment - renzo restaked eth (ezeth) (2024). https://hackmd.io/@PrismaRisk/ezETH. Accessed 6 Dec 2024
17. Ethereum Foundation: Staking and validator operations (2024). https://ethereum.org/en/staking/. Accessed 6 Dec 2024
18. Gogol, K., Kraner, B., Schlosser, M., Yan, T., Tessone, C., Stiller, B.: Empirical and theoretical analysis of liquid staking protocols. University of Zurich (2024). https://arxiv.org/abs/2401.16353
19. Chainlink Labs: Introduction to oracles (2024). https://docs.chain.link/docs/chainlink-oracles/. Accessed 6 Dec 2024
20. Celestia Labs: Data availability in modular blockchains (2024). https://docs.celestia.org/. Accessed 6 Dec 2024
21. Ethereum Foundation: Layer 2 scaling (2024). https://ethereum.org/en/layer-2/. Accessed 6 Dec 2024
22. Buterin, V.: Endgame: thoughts on rollup and layer 2 decentralization (2021). https://vitalik.ca/general/2021/12/06/endgame.html. Accessed 6 Dec 2024
23. Gudgeon, L., Perez, D., Harz, D., Livshits, B., Gervais, A.: The decentralized financial crisis. arXiv preprint arXiv:2002.08099 (2020). https://arxiv.org/abs/2002.08099
24. Lido Finance: Expanding staking: exploring Liquid Staking Token (LST) restaking (2024). https://lido.fi/blog/lst-restaking. Accessed 6 Dec 2024
25. CoinDesk: Eigenlayer adds erc20 token support for restaking (2024). https://www.coindesk.com/markets/2024/08/15/eigenlayer-adds-erc20-token-support/. Accessed 6 Dec 2024
26. Renzo Protocol: Liquid restaking (2024). https://www.renzoprotocol.com/. Accessed 6 Dec 2024
27. hildobby: Ethereum ETH staking. https://dune.com/hildobby/eth2-staking. Accessed 26 Dec 2024
28. DefiLlama — defillama.com. https://defillama.com/protocols/liquid%20staking/Ethereum. Accessed 26 Dec 2024
29. Aave - Open Source Liquidity Protocol — app.aave.com. https://app.aave.com/markets/. Accessed 26 Dec 2024
30. blocklytics: Dune Ethereum Restaking. https://dune.com/blocklytics/ethereum-restaking. Accessed 26 Dec 2024

31. DefiLlama—defillama.com. https://defillama.com/protocols/Liquid%20Restaking. Accessed 26 Dec 2024
32. Financial Stability Board: Financial stability surveillance framework (2024). https://www.fsb.org/. Accessed 6 Dec 2024
33. National Bureau of Economic Research (NBER): Working paper: Terra/luna collapse (2023). https://www.nber.org/system/files/working_papers/w31160/w31160.pdf. Accessed 4 Dec 2024
34. arXiv Authors: A detailed analysis of the terra/luna collapse (2024). arXiv preprint. https://arxiv.org/pdf/2401.16353. Accessed 4 Dec 2024
35. Nansen Research: On-chain forensics: Demystifying Steth's "de-peg" (2022). https://www.nansen.ai/research/on-chain-forensics-demystifying-steth-depeg. Accessed 6 Dec 2024
36. Neuder, M., Chitra, T.: The risks of LRTS (2024). https://ethresear.ch/t/the-risks-of-lrts/18799. Accessed 6 Dec 2024

SCOOP: Co**S**t-effective **CO**ngesti**O**n Attacks in **P**ayment Channel Networks

Mohammed Ababneh[✉], Kartick Kolachala, and Roopa Vishwanathan

New Mexico State University, Las Cruces, NM, USA
{mababneh,kart1712,roopav}@nmsu.edu

Abstract. Payment channel networks (PCNs) are a promising solution to address blockchain scalability and throughput challenges, However, the security of PCNs and their vulnerability to attacks are not sufficiently studied. In this paper, we introduce **SCOOP**, a framework that includes two novel congestion attacks on PCNs. These attacks consider the minimum transferable amount along a path (path capacity) and the number of channels involved (path length), formulated as linear optimization problems. The first attack allocates the attacker's budget to achieve a specific congestion threshold, while the second maximizes congestion under budget constraints. Simulation results show the effectiveness of the proposed attack formulations in comparison to other attack strategies. Specifically, the results indicate that the first attack provides around a 40% improvement in congestion performance, while the second attack offers approximately a 50% improvement in comparison to the state-of-the-art. Moreover, in terms of payment to congestion efficiency, the first attack is about 60% more efficient, and the second attack is around 90% more efficient in comparison to state-of-the-art.

1 Introduction

Cryptocurrencies, the most popular blockchain-based application, enable users to transfer money securely and efficiently without relying on centralized authorities such as banks or governments. However, despite their increasing popularity, scalability remains a significant challenge. For instance, Bitcoin blockchain generates a 1 MB block every 10 min, processing only 7 transactions per second, while users have to wait around one hour (i.e., six blocks) for the transaction to be confirmed [6]. In contrast, Visa handles 24,000 transactions per second [16].

Payment channel networks (PCN) [14] have emerged as an off-chain solution to the scalability challenge, such as Bitcoin's Lightning Network (LN) [12] and Ethereum's Raiden Network [13]. The main component of a PCN is a payment channel, where two nodes establish a channel to conduct transactions. Nodes not directly connected with a channel can route transactions through intermediate nodes using multiple hops, extending the network and enabling transactions across the entire PCN. One of the main advantages is that PCNs do not require access to the blockchain every time a transaction occurs (unless there is a dispute). Additionally, PCNs do not require any additional consensus mechanism other than the one employed by the underlying blockchain, and do not require complex cryptographic machinery to process transactions. This offers the advantage of enabling transactions to be executed over the PCN with relatively low latency and high throughput.

Despite the advantages mentioned above, PCNs are vulnerable to attacks. Several types of attacks have been proposed such as griefing [4], LockDown [11], congestion [8,10], wormhole attack [9], Flood and Loot attack [3] and more. The common goal of these attacks is to exploit the inherent limitations and characteristics of the PCN to either gain financial advantage, collect information about the network, or disrupt its operation. Thus, these attacks can harm the network's efficiency, reliability, and user experience. Nonetheless, it is important to study and propose new attacks in PCNs as they are useful in drawing attention to network weaknesses and limitations. It will prompt researchers to design corresponding attack mitigation techniques, thus improving overall network security.

This paper focuses on congestion-based attacks, in which the attacker node issues a payment contract with a specific payment amount to another attacker node over paths involving intermediate nodes.[1] As the attacker manages both the sender and receiver of the payments, they can intentionally postpone executing the payments, intensifying the congestion in PCNs. These attacks aim to congest payment paths (constituting channels), reducing the network's ability to process legitimate further payments. While previous studies have explored various aspects of congestion attacks, an important consideration that needs to be considered is congestion attack efficiency. In this work, we aim to address this gap by examining how the attackers can optimize their strategies to congest the network more effectively, given limited resources. In particular, we investigate how, in PCN, multiple attacker nodes with predefined budgets can allocate path payments to congest the network efficiently.

To address this problem, several factors must be considered, including the attacker's resources, i.e., attack budget, payment path information, e.g., lengths, capacity, and congestion performance. We propose several metrics to quantify the congestion performance more effectively. Using these metrics, we formulate congestion attacks as linear optimization problems. In the first formulation, our goal is to minimize the total amount of payments allocated by the attacker over the different available paths to achieve a threshold congestion performance. In the second formulation, given an attack budget, the attacker aims to maximize the congestion performance over the different payment paths. In essence, both problems aim to provide a mathematical formulation of efficient resource-limited congestion attacks. To summarize, the contributions of our work are as follows:

1. We introduce novel metrics that accurately quantify the impact and effectiveness of congestion attacks on PCNs. These metrics provide a more precise

---

[1] As a part of ethical considerations for vulnerability disclosure, we have informed Lightning Labs [5] about the attacks described in this paper. Lightning Labs is currently reviewing our attacks and the corresponding results. We also present a few mitigation strategies for the attacks in the paper.

evaluation of congestion severity across multiple dimensions, including channel capacity and path length.
2. We present SCOOP, a comprehensive framework that includes two innovative congestion attack strategies on PCNs. These attacks are formulated as linear optimization problems, providing a mathematical framework for designing efficient, resource-limited congestion attacks. Attackers can either minimize budget expenditure while achieving a desired congestion threshold or maximize the overall congestion impact across the network under predefined budget constraints.
3. We evaluate the performance of SCOOP through extensive simulations of a PCN. The simulations validate the effectiveness of the proposed congestion attacks compared to existing strategies, demonstrating superior resource efficiency and congestion performance.

Outline: In Sect. 2, we discuss necessary preliminary information. In Sect. 3, we discuss the relevant related work. In Sect. 4, we present our congestion attacks. In Sect. 5, we present our experimental evaluation. In Sect. 7 we conclude the paper.

2 Background

2.1 Congestion Attack

The LN is susceptible to congestion attacks [8,10]. In a congestion attack, the attacker adds Sybil nodes to PCN by establishing a payment channel with existing nodes. Subsequently, The attacker initiates numerous simultaneous payments across multiple paths to either lock capacity along all paths or initiates tiny payments to occupy available HTLC slots along a path and withholds the preimages of the payments between the Sybil nodes. This locks coins across paths, preventing intermediate nodes from earning fees and disrupting their operations. Congestion attacks are cost-effective for the attacker. The attacker incurs on-chain fees for opening and closing channels but avoids routing fees as payments remain incomplete. The congestion attacker aims to reduce LN throughput, cause transaction failures, and eliminate competition by blocking competing nodes and redirecting traffic and fees to their own nodes.

In the congestion attack shown in Fig. 1b, we have three Sybil nodes (Attacker1, Attacker2, and Attacker3). For simplicity, we identified a subset of paths between these Sybil nodes are identified as follows: Attacker1 → Peter → Megan → Attacker3, Attacker1 → Peter → Carol → Attacker2, Attacker2 → Carol → Sam → Attacker3, and Attacker3 → Sam → Carol → Attacker2. Each attacker generates a payment and sends it along its respective path, with the receiving attacker intentionally withholding the payment execution. In the case where two paths share a common payment channel, such as between Attacker1 → Peter → Carol → Attacker2, and Attacker3 → Sam → Carol → Attacker2, which both share the payment channel Carol → Attacker2, accurate channel usage is critical.

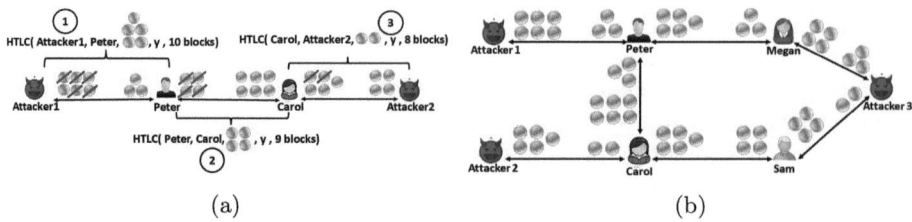

Fig. 1. (a) Channel Capacity Limitation. (b) Congestion Attack

To address this, each path is evaluated sequentially, and the capacities of the shared channels are updated after each evaluation. For example, if Attacker1 initiates payments over its paths, the capacity of shared channels, such as Carol → Attacker2, is updated to reflect the locked amounts before subsequent paths are considered. This approach ensures that no two paths simultaneously attempt to use the full capacity of a shared channel, thereby avoiding resource conflicts. Due to space constraints, the detailed discussion of Hashed Time Locked Contracts (HTLCs) and their limitations, as well as the implications of congestion attacks on PCNs, are provided in the full version of the paper [1].

3 Related Work

In this section, we analyze various studies examining attacks on PCNs. Our review focuses on congestion and other related attacks, exploring how attackers can exploit network limitations, such as channel capacity and maximum accepted HTLCs, to disrupt payment flows and compromise network security. Drawing on our insights and observations from prior works, SCOOP proposes new congestion attacks and introduces new congestion attack metrics.

Mizrahi and Zohar [10] proposed the first congestion attack where the attacker uses a greedy algorithm to construct the paths by consecutively picking high-weighted edges (using channel capacity weight or betweenness centrality). Betweenness centrality measures the number of shortest paths passing through the edge, indicating its importance in the PCN. The attacker generates dust payments and sends them over a given path to hold all the available HTLCs, preventing the payment channel along the path from processing more payment transactions. The attacker targets one path at a time, but by repeating the attack across different paths, multiple paths eventually can be congested. In another work, Lu et al. [8] proposed a general congestion attack, where the attacker generates Sybil nodes and connects them to strategically chosen set of nodes, typically, nodes with high channel capacities to route more griefing payments. The attacker finds paths between all pairs of Sybil nodes, and employs the Ford-Fulkerson algorithm to find the maximum flow over each path. The attacker generates numerous payments and sends them over all paths simultaneously. This causes network congestion and disruption of network performance. In [4], the authors proposed a griefing attack, where the attacker refuses to respond to an HTLC, which locks all funds along a path until the HTLC time expires. Pérez-Sola et al. [11] presented a lockdown attack that blocks an intermediate node in the multiple-path payment by depleting the capacity in all its channels, which affects its ability to participate in payment routing. Malavolta et al. [9] proposed a wormhole attack in which two intermediate nodes in a payment path collude to exclude other intermediate nodes from participating in the payment, thereby stealing the fees intended for those nodes. Harris and Zohar [3] proposed an attack called Flood & Loot, where the attacker controls source and receiver nodes. The source node initiates payments but denies HTLC fulfillment, forcing channel closures and on-chain claims.

In contrast to other methods, our approach, SCOOP, frames congestion as linear optimization problems, providing a more precise and resource-efficient attack strategy. This sets SCOOP apart from existing approaches by optimally allocating resources and targeting congestion at the path level rather than relying on heuristic or greedy algorithms [8,10]. SCOOP introduces new metrics that consider channel capacity and path length, allowing for a broader attack surface encompassing multiple dimensions of the network's structure.

4 System Construction

In this section, we describe the assumptions and provide the necessary notations and definitions for the PCN and the attacker. We then present the metrics used to evaluate the effectiveness of congestion attacks. Additionally, we examine the implications of congestion attacks on PCNs and propose mitigation techniques to address the congestion attacks.

4.1 Network Model and Assumptions

A PCN can be modeled as a directed graph $G = (V, E)$ in which the set of vertices V represent network nodes (i.e., users) and E represents the set of directed edges (i.e., payment channels) between nodes. Assume nodes $v_x, v_y \in V$ have established a payment channel $e_{x,y} \in E$ between them. Let $b_{x,y}$ represent the balance from node x to y (i.e., how many coins can node x forward in the direction of node y). Note that the balances $b_{x,y}$ and $b_{y,x}$ are not necessarily equal. The capacity of the channel $e_{x,y}$ is denoted as $c_{x,y}$, where $c_{x,y} = b_{x,y} + b_{y,x}$.

The attacker deploys a set of N Sybil nodes denoted as $\mathcal{A} = \{A_1, A_2, \ldots, A_N\}$. The attacker nodes can attach to the PCN nodes using a number of different attachment strategies (e.g., random, highest degree, etc.). The attacks in SCOOP can be carried out regardless of the strategy. We now outline our key assumptions that enable the attacks. First, the attacker communicates with the Sybil nodes out-of-band, and any information gathered by the Sybil nodes is accessible to the attacker. Second, the attacker is aware of the entire network topology, including all of the payment channels (i.e., network graph) and their initial capacities and balances. This knowledge can be attained using probing protocols such as [10]. The probing path does not necessarily involve the network; it is sufficient to prob a number of paths between the attacker pairs. This enables performing a timely attack in which the channel capacities do not change significantly. Assuming that channel capacities undergo a significant change, attack payment will fail. The attacker node (sender) knows immediately that the change happened and thus can either start another prob or reduce the attack payment by updating values of the constraint in the optimization problem.

4.2 Congestion Attack Metrics

We now propose and describe metrics used to evaluate the effectiveness of SCOOP's congestion attacks. In particular, these metrics quantify the impact of the attack on the PCN. Our metrics are: i) Channel Congestion Ratio (CCR), ii) Path Congestion Ratio (PCR), iii) Scale Path Congestion Ratio (SPCR).

To define the metrics, consider two arbitrary Sybil nodes A_n and A_m and let P_j denote the jth path (whose length is measured in terms of number of constituent channels) between them with the attack originating from node A_n. let $\mathcal{P} = \{P_1, P_2, \ldots, P_J\}$ represent all of the paths between all of the pairs of attackers A_n and A_m. Furthermore, let e_j^i denote the ith channel along the path P_j. We assume A_n runs a probing algorithm. Probing is a technique used by attackers to determine the balance of a payment channel. This is accomplished by sending probes, essentially fake payments whose HTLC digest(s) do not correspond to a valid preimage [2,15]. Let us denote the corresponding channel capacity of channel i by c_j^i, and the estimated channel balance along the path P_j as b_j^i. Finally, let $\alpha_j^{n,m}$ denote the congestion payment made along path P_j from attacker A_n towards attacker A_m. Having introduced the above quantities, we now define our performance metrics.

Definition 1. *Channel Congestion Ratio (CCR)* *is the ratio between the payment (originating from attacker A_n to attacker A_m) $\alpha_j^{n,m}$ along the path P_j and the balance of the i-th channel along that path (i.e., b_j^i)*

$$CCR_{\alpha_j^{n,m}}^{n,m} = \begin{cases} \alpha_j^{n,m}/b_j^i & \text{if } \alpha_j^{n,m} < b_j^i \\ 1 & \text{if } \alpha_j^{n,m} = b_j^i \end{cases} \quad (1)$$

The CCR quantifies the congestion effect of assigning a payment $\alpha_j^{n,m}$ to the channel e_j^i to process further payments. Naturally, the larger the locked payment $\alpha_j^{n,m}$ relative to the balance b_j^i, the more congested a channel is and the larger is the channel's CCR. A channel is fully congested when $\alpha_j^{n,m}$ equals its balance and therefore is assigned a value of 1.

Note that the CCR quantifies congestion over a single channel along a path. A more comprehensive view of the congestion attack can be provided by considering payment paths instead of individual channels. When considering congestion along a path, the congestion bottleneck is determined by the channel with the minimum balance b_j^i. Regardless of the balances of other channels along a path, the amount of payment along that path cannot exceed the minimum channel's balance. Thus, the path congestion ratio (PCR) metric is defined as follows.

Definition 2. Path Congestion Ratio (PCR) *is defined as the ratio between the payment $\alpha_j^{n,m}$ and $\min(b_j^i)$ for a path P_j and is given as.*

$$PCR_{\alpha_j^{n,m}}^{n,m} = \begin{cases} \alpha_j^{n,m}/\min(b_j^i) & \text{if } \alpha_j^{n,m} < \min(b_j^i) \\ 1 & \text{if } \alpha_j^{n,m} = \min(b_j^i) \end{cases} \quad (2)$$

Note that the PCR definition above incorporates the bottleneck, which is defined by the minimum balance along the path (i.e., $\min b_j^i$). Similar to the CCR metric, once the payment $\alpha_j^{n,m}$ equals the $\min(b_j^i)$, the PCR takes a value of 1 and the path becomes fully congested. Finally, note that the PCR can be expressed in terms of the CCR as follows:

$$PCR_{\alpha_j^{n,m}}^{n,m} = \begin{cases} \max(CCR_{\alpha_j^{n,m}}^{n,m}) & \text{if } CCR_{\alpha_j^{n,m}}^{n,m} < 1 \\ 1 & \text{if } CCR_{\alpha_j^{n,m}}^{n,m} = 1 \end{cases} \quad (3)$$

One limitation of the PCR definition is that it does not take the path's length into consideration. Paths differ in their lengths where a path length is defined as the number of channels (i.e., edges) along the path. In addition to the PCR metric, it is informative to consider path lengths as well. Intuitively, a congested path with some PCR value and of length M has a more disastrous effect on the network than a different path with the same PCR but with a length of N where $M > N$. This is due to the fact that when a payment amount $\alpha_j^{n,m}$ is locked along a path P_j, it is locked on all channels along that path. Thus, in order to incorporate the path length, the scale path congestion ratio (SPCR) is defined next.

Definition 3. Scale Path Congestion Ratio (SPCR). *Let l_j denote the length of the jth path P_j and L_{max} refer to the maximum length of a network's path. Then, a path's SPCR is defined as the product of the path's length ratio and its PCR and is given as*

$$SPCR_{\alpha_j^{n,m}}^{n,m} = \left(\frac{l_j}{L_{max}}\right) PCR_{\alpha_j^{n,m}}^{n,m} \quad (4)$$

We note that SPCR incorporates the number of channels congested along a path (i.e., path length) with the path's PCR. Thus, the larger a path's PCR and length, the greater the number of congested channels, resulting in a higher SPCR. The SPCR provides insight into the relative congestion effect of a path compared to others in the network. A higher SPCR corresponds to a longer path, meaning more intermediate nodes along the path are required to lock their coins for the duration of the payment. This introduces the cumulative congestion effect: as coins are restricted across multiple nodes, the network's ability to handle other transactions decreases. Importantly, it does not matter which specific hop along the path is the bottleneck; the critical point is that all nodes along the long path must reserve the current maximum amount required for the payment. Additionally, SPCR is a directional value that depends on the sender and receiver attack pairs and the origin of the payment. The value of L_{max} determined by the PCN sets the maximum allowable path length. For example, in LN, this value is set at 20 hops [7]. Additionally, the SPCR varies between 0 and 1, as discussed earlier, a higher SPCR value indicates a more effective congestion attack.

4.3 Overview Of Proposed Congestion Attacks

In this section, we formulate two congestion attacks as linear optimization problems based on the earlier metrics. The first formulation aims to minimize the attacker's total payment while achieving a desired congestion threshold quantified by the SPCR metric presented earlier. The second formulation aims to maximize congestion effectiveness by maximizing the SPCR while not exceeding the attacker's allowed budget. The SPCR metric plays a critical role in both formulations. It provides a precise measure of congestion attacks by considering both path length and bottleneck capacity. This combination allows for evaluating the detrimental effects that SCOOP's congestion attacks have on the PCN, which makes SPCR a valuable metric for optimizing the effectiveness of congestion attacks.

It is noteworthy that the proposed congestion attacks are linear in both the objective/cost functions as well the imposed constraints. As such, the problems can be solved either analytically or using linear solvers. However, due to the linear and deterministic nature of the problems they lends themselves easily to a linear solver approach. Next, the congestion attacks are presented in detail.

SCOOP's *Payment Minimization* Attack (MinPay). In this attack, an attacker is to minimize budget expenditure while achieving a desired congestion threshold. This threshold is determined by setting a target SPCR value, which can be viewed as a quality of service (QoS) metric from the attacker's point of view. The larger the SPCR threshold is, the larger the congestion payments are, and the longer the congested paths, thus, the more severe the attack is. SCOOP's Payment Minimization Attack can be stated as follows.

SCOOP's *Payment Minimization* Attack Formulation. In this formulation, an attacker $A_n \in \mathcal{A}$ is to determine the partial payments on the available paths. In particular, given the set of path capacities and the budget B_n of the attacker A_n on each path P_j, how should the attacker A_n send payments over these paths such that the total forwarding payment is minimized. The problem can be mathematically stated as follows;

$$\min \sum_{\substack{\forall n,m \\ n \neq m}}^{|\mathcal{A}|} \sum_{j=1}^{|\mathcal{P}|} \alpha_j^{n,m} \quad (5)$$

subject to

$$\sum_{j=1}^{|\mathcal{P}|} \alpha_j^{n,m} \leq B_n \quad \forall n,m,j \tag{6}$$

$$0 \leq \alpha_j^{n,m} \leq \min(b_j^i) \quad \forall n,m,i,j \tag{7}$$

$$\text{ThresholdValue} \leq \text{SPCR}_{\alpha_j^{n,m}}^{n,m} \leq 1 \quad \forall n,m,j \tag{8}$$

where $\alpha_j^{n,m}$ denotes the payment allocated by attacker A_n over path P_j towards attacker A_m, and $SPCR_{\alpha_j^{n,m}}^{n,m}$ denotes the SPCR value of P_j resulting from payment allocations by all attacker nodes. Note that the cost function and constraints in the above problem are linear in the payment $\alpha_j^{n,m}$. The cost function combines the total payments $\alpha_j^{n,m}$ overall congestion paths P_j. The constraint in Eq. 6 is to enforce that an attacker does not exceed its total budget B_n. The constraint in Eq. 7 ensures that a path payment does not exceed a path's minimum (i.e., bottleneck) capacity since any larger payment can not be supported over the path. The last constraint in Eq. 8 ensures that the attacker achieves a certain congestion threshold over all paths. Naturally, the higher the threshold value, the more severe the attack is and the more resources (i.e., payments) that need to be used by the attacker.

It is important to note that the primary goal of the above problem is to minimize the total payment made by the attacker while achieving a target SPCR value, quantified by the obtained value of SPCR in Eq. 4. Next, we describe the SCOOP's *Congestion Maximization* attack that seeks to maximize congestion in the network.

SCOOP's *Congestion Maximization* Attack (SPCR Max). In the previous attack, our goal was to minimize the attack budget to meet, as best as possible, a desired congestion performance in terms of the SPCR. One can envision a second problem of interest as follows; How can we maximize the SPCR congestion performance given a certain attacks budget. This is the attack strategy we develop next

SCOOP's *Congestion Maximization* Attack Formulation. In this formulation, an attacker $A_n \in \mathcal{A}$ is to determine the partial payments on the available paths. In particular, given the set of path capacities and the budget of B_n of the attacker A_n on each path P_j, how should the attacker A_n send payments over these paths s such that the congestion is maximized. The problem can be mathematically stated as follows;

$$\max \sum_{\substack{\forall n,m \\ n \neq m}}^{|\mathcal{A}|} \sum_{j=1}^{|\mathcal{P}|} \text{SPCR}_{\alpha_j^{n,m}}^{n,m} \tag{9}$$

subject to

$$\sum_{j=1}^{|\mathcal{P}|} \alpha_j^{n,m} \leq B_n \quad \forall n,m,j \tag{10}$$

$$0 \leq \alpha_j^{n,m} \leq \min(b_j^i) \quad \forall n, m, i, j \tag{11}$$

$$0 \leq \text{SPCR}_{\alpha_j^{n,m}}^{n,m} \leq 1 \quad \forall n, m, j \tag{12}$$

The goal of the objective function in Eq. 9 is to maximize the total of $SPCR_{\alpha_j^{n,m}}^{n,m}$ along all paths across every pair of attackers. This objective seeks to enhance the overall efficiency or performance across all paths, taking into account both their relative lengths and how well resources are allocated relative to their capacities. The constraint in Eq. 10 is the budget constraint which ensures that the total payments $\alpha_j^{n,m}$ do not exceed the budget B_n. The second constraint in Eq. 11 ensures that congested payment $\alpha_j^{n,m}$ cannot be negative, and it also ensures that a payment of $\alpha_j^{n,m}$ can be routed via path P_j. The third constraint in Eq. 12 ensures that the $SPCR_{\alpha_j^{n,m}}^{n,m}$ is between zero and one. It can not be negative or should not be greater than one, indicating over-resource utilization. Due to space constraints, protocols that describe the setup phase and the launching of SCOOP's congestion attacks are described in full version [1].

5 Empirical Evaluation

This section investigates the performance of the proposed payment minimization attack (MinPay) and congestion maximization attack (SPCR Max). For comparison, we employ two congestion attacks. These congestion attacks are random congestion attack and general congestion attacks [8]. In the random congestion attack, both the attacker's budget and path payment are randomly selected. On the other hand, the general congestion attack is based on a greedy strategy, where the payments are allocated according to path capacities. Paths with larger capacities are allocated more than the ones with smaller capacities. Moreover, payments are allocated sequentially until the attacker's entire budget is consumed.

For comparison purposes, we use the metrics defined in Sect. 4.2. The first is the PCR metric used to quantify congestion effect over the lowest capacity channels (i.e., bottleneck) in the different paths. The second is the SPCR metric which in addition to channel congestion incorporates path length and is indicative of the congestion effect over a path. The higher the PCR and SPCR values, the more effective an attack is in terms of congestion. Another metric is LockedPayment, which represents the amount of locked payment allocated by the attacker. As a metric, the locked payment should be taken in conjunction with the achieved congestion performance. Thus, a merely high or low locked payment by itself is not indicative of the overall performance. To address this, we introduce another metric, the cost-congestion efficiency ratio, denoted as γ. γ is used to quantify how much payment was allocated to provide a given congestion performance. The lower the γ value, the more efficient an attack strategy is. Lastly, we use the distribution of PCR values over the attack paths as information to provide an in-depth view and better visualization of congestion distribution among the different attack paths.

5.1 MinPay Attack Performance Evaluation

In the first experiment, the performance of the proposed MinPay attack is measured. The number of attackers is set at $N = 6$ attacker pairs (i.e., a total of 12 Sybil nodes), and we experiment with two budgets: $B = 75 \times 10^6$ satoshi and $B = 100 \times 10^6$ satoshi. Channel capacities are random with a mean of 4×10^6 satoshi. The mean of the path lengths between attacker nodes is 6 with a maximum length of 8 channels. Experiment results are averaged over 200 iterations. Herein, the performance of the attack is evaluated using different metrics (e.g., PCR and SPCR) as we vary the required SPCR threshold for different B values. Results in Fig. 2a show the resulting PCR for the different algorithms as a function of SPCR threshold and B values. Note that the PCR of the MinPay attack increases with the SPCR threshold. This is true since as the SPCR requirement increases, it requires more payment to be allocated and thus higher resulting PCR values. We note that for the other algorithms there is no such dependence and thus no change in PCR values. It is also noted that a budget increase from $B = 75 \times 10^6$ to $B = 100 \times 10^6$ results in a noticeable increase in PCR values for MinPay attacks since more payments are available for congestion purposes.

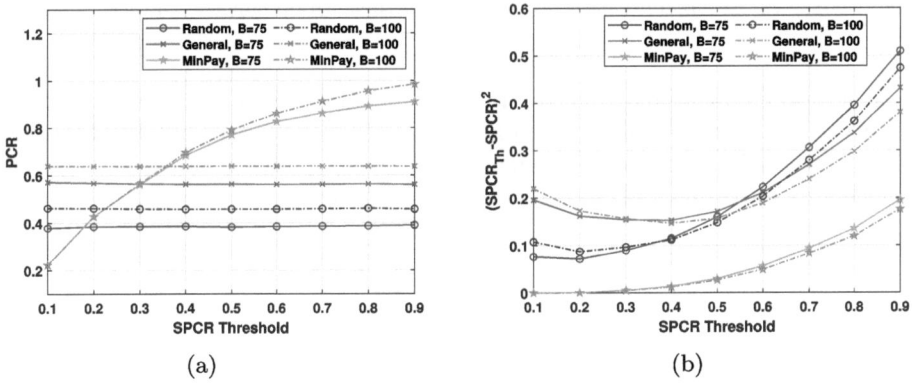

Fig. 2. (a) PCR vs. SPCR Threshold for different attacker's budget (B) values. (b) SPCR deviation for different attacker's budget (B) values.

The SPCR results are shown in Fig. 2b . We note that instead of plotting the achieved SPCR vs. SPCR threshold value (denoted as $SPCR_{Th}$, the deviation between achieved and required SPCR is depicted instead. This is because path conditions (e.g., capacity and length) might make it infeasible to achieve the required SPCR precisely. In this case, and as discussed earlier, the MinPay attack attempts at meeting the SPCR threshold as close as possible with minimum payment. We note that the initial SPCR deviation of the MinPay is close to zero as the threshold is small and thus can be achieved with the given budget. However, as the threshold increases it becomes more difficult to satisfy it and thus the deviation increases. However, we note that the MinPay achieves the smallest deviation in comparison to other attack strategies regardless of the threshold. We also note that the deviation decreases as the budget is increased, which validates our argument.

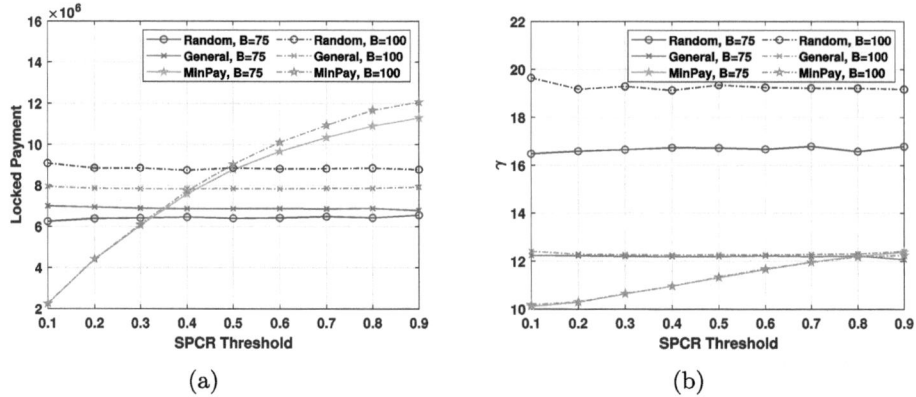

Fig. 3. (a) LockedPayment vs. SPCR Threshold for different attacker's budget (B) values. (b) γ vs. SPCR Threshold for different attacker's budget (B) values.

The total payment allocated by the different attacks is summarized in Fig. 3a. However, we note that since the different attacks have varying PCR performances, the locked congestion payment alone is not sufficient for comparison of performances. To this end, we introduce the average cost-to-congestion ratio γ defined as:

$$\gamma = \frac{1}{k} \sum_{\substack{\forall n,m \\ n \neq m}} \sum_j \frac{\alpha_j^{n,m}}{SPCR_{\alpha_j^{n,m}}^{n,m}}$$

It is an average operation (i.e., arithmetic or sum of value $\alpha_j^{n,m}/SPCR_{\alpha_j^{n,m}}^{n,m}$ divided over the number of iterations, k). A small γ value implies a small overall payment and a large PCR value. The more efficient an attack is, the smaller is the γ value is. The γ corresponding to Figs. 2a and 3a is plotted in Fig. 3b. It can be see that the MinPay attack has the lowest γ value and is thus the most efficient. As we can see, The random congestion attack has more variability due to a lack of strategic payment allocation, which makes it sensitive to budget changes from $B = 75 \times 10^6$ satoshi to $B = 100 \times 10^6$ satoshi.

Results in Fig. 4 show the distribution of PCR values for $B = 100 \times 10^6$ as the SPCR threshold is varied. In particular, the x-axis represents PCR values (i.e., congestion ratios) which range from 0–100% divided into 4 equal intervals. While the y-axis represents percentage of paths that fall within each PCR interval. We note that achieved PCR distribution for all algorithms, except for the MinPay, are similar for all thresholds. However, for the MinPay, note that the distribution

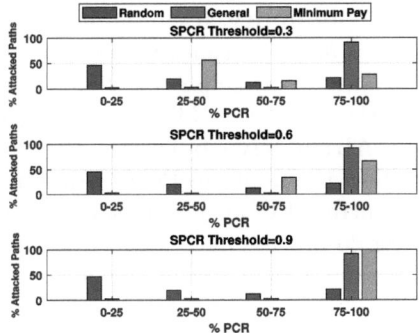

Fig. 4. %PCR Distribution

changes with every SPCR threshold. Note that, with unlimited resources, it is advantageous to have all attack paths be in the 75–100% interval since this reflects the best congestion performance. However, since in the MinPay it is only required to satisfy the required SPCR threshold value, not all channels fall in the 75–100% interval. For example, when the threshold is set at 0.3, we note that with the MinPay around 50% of the paths fall in the 25–50% interval with the remaining paths having a better congestion (i.e., in the 50–75 and 75–100%) which is expected. However, as the threshold is increased to 0.9, then 100% of the paths have a congestion ratio of 75–100%. This reflects the effectiveness of the MinPay in payment allocation. This is in contrast to other attacks. For example, the random algorithm allocates payments such that most of the channels have a 0–25% congestion which reflects a poor payment allocation. Moreover, the general attack allocates payments such that most channels are in the 75–100% range regardless of the threshold. This indicates that inefficient allocation is being made when compared to MinPay. Due to space constraints, additional simulations evaluating the performance of the SPCR Max attack are provided in the full version of the paper [1].

6 Mitigation Techniques

Reputation system. A reputation-based payment system enhances the security of decentralized networks by imposing initial restrictions on new nodes, limiting payment size and transaction volume to prevent malicious activities like DoS attacks. As nodes build a positive transaction history, these restrictions are gradually relaxed, incentivizing trustworthy behavior. **Updating system parameters.** Adjusting system parameters, such as reducing the maximum payment path length to less than 20 (the max. path length set by LN [7]), is one potential strategy to address the issue. However, this approach only postpones the problem instead of solving it, serving as a temporary fix. Additionally, this is a significant change and is unlikely to be implemented in practice. **Selectively throttling or rate-limiting of neighbors based on either 1)**

number of HTLCs, or 2) liquidity. It can mitigate attacks in the Lightning Network. Parameters such as $htlc\_minimum\_msat$, $max\_accepted\_htlcs$, and $max\_htlc\_value\_in\_flight\_msat$ help nodes limit their exposure by capping the smallest HTLC value, the number of HTLCs, and the total value of outstanding HTLCs, respectively. **Alternative between elephant/mice payments.** This technique refers to how the nodes in PCNs can adjust their willingness to route payments based on current PCN conditions. During periods of high congestion, the nodes may prefer to process mice payments. Otherwise, the nodes will process more elephant payments. This technique ensures consistent throughput in PCNs.

7 Conclusion

In this paper, we propose SCOOP consisting of two novel congestion attacks, *Congestion Maximization* attack, and *Payment Minimization* attack, which are presented as linear optimization problems. The goal of the *Payment Minimization* attack is to minimize budget expenditure while achieving a desired congestion threshold. The *Congestion Maximization* attack aims to maximize congestion along the paths in PCN (i.e., making optimal use of an attacker's budget and achieving as much congestion as possible within that budget). The performance of the proposed attacks is compared against random congestion attack and general congestion attack [8]. Results show that the proposed attacks outperform existing congestion attacks across multiple metrics. Future work will explore new metrics and attack strategies in PCNs.

Acknowledgments. This material is based upon work supported by the National Science Foundation under Award No. 2148358, 1914635, 2417062, and the Department of Energy under Award No. DESC0023392. Any opinions, findings and conclusions, or recommendations expressed in this material are those of the authors and do not necessarily reflect the views of the National Science Foundation and the Department of Energy.

References

1. Ababneh, M., Kolachala, K., Vishwanathan, R.: Scoop: cost-effective congestion attacks in payment channel networks (2025). https://arxiv.org/abs/2503.12625
2. Biryukov, A., Naumenko, G., Tikhomirov, S.: Analysis and probing of parallel channels in the lightning network. In: Financial Cryptography and Data Security: 26th International Conference, FC 2022, Grenada, 2–6 May 2022, Revised Selected Papers, pp. 337–357. Springer-Verlag, Berlin, Heidelberg (2022). https://doi.org/10.1007/978-3-031-18283-9_16
3. Harris, J., Zohar, A.: Flood & loot: a systemic attack on the lightning network. In: Proceedings of the 2nd ACM Conference on Advances in Financial Technologies, pp. 202–213 (2020)

4. HTLCS are harmful. In: Stanford Blockchain Conference (2019). https://diyhpl.us/wiki/transcripts/stanford-blockchain-conference/2019/htlcs-considered-harmful/
5. Lightning labs (2024). https://lightning.engineering/
6. Li, C., et al.: A decentralized blockchain with high throughput and fast confirmation. In: 2020 {USENIX} Annual Technical Conference ({USENIX}{ATC} 20), pp. 515–528 (2020)
7. LND/bolts/onion routing. https://github.com/lightning/bolts/blob/6e1bea0d4868cb55fae7590975ae593a228ad3fe/04-onion-routing.md#requirements-2. Accessed 11 Apr 2024
8. Lu, Z., Han, R., Yu, J.: General congestion attack on HTLC-based payment channel networks. Cryptology ePrint Archive (2020)
9. Malavolta, G., Sanchez, P.M., Schneidewind, C., Kate, A., Maffei, M.: Anonymous multi-hop locks for blockchain scalability and interoperability. In: 26th Annual Network and Distributed System Security Symposium, NDSS 2019, San Diego, California, USA, 24-27 February 2019. The Internet Society (2019)
10. Mizrahi, A., Zohar, A.: Congestion attacks in payment channel networks. In: Borisov, N., Diaz, C. (eds.) FC 2021. LNCS, vol. 12675, pp. 170–188. Springer, Heidelberg (2021). https://doi.org/10.1007/978-3-662-64331-0_9
11. Pérez-Solà, C., Ranchal-Pedrosa, A., Herrera-Joancomartí, J., Navarro-Arribas, G., Garcia-Alfaro, J.: LockDown: balance availability attack against lightning network channels. In: Bonneau, J., Heninger, N. (eds.) FC 2020. LNCS, vol. 12059, pp. 245–263. Springer, Cham (2020). https://doi.org/10.1007/978-3-030-51280-4_14
12. Poon, J., Dryja, T.: The bitcoin lightning network: scalable off-chain instant payments (2016)
13. Raiden network. https://raiden.network/. Accessed 11 Apr 2024
14. Payment channels. https://happypeter.github.io/binfo/payment-channels.html. Accessed 11 Apr 2024
15. Tikhomirov, S., Pickhardt, R., Biryukov, A., Nowostawski, M.: Probing channel balances in the lightning network (2020)
16. Visa. https://usa.visa.com/dam/VCOM/download/corporate/media/visanet-technology/visa-net-booklet.pdf. Accessed 19 Sep 2023

Universal Blockchain Assets

Owen Vaughan[✉]

nChain, London, UK
o.vaughan@nchain.com

Abstract. We present a novel protocol for issuing and transferring tokens across blockchains without the need of a trusted third party or cross-chain bridge. In our scheme, the blockchain is used for double-spend protection only, while the authorisation of token transfers is performed off-chain. Due to the universality of our approach, it works in almost all blockchain settings. It can be implemented immediately on UTXO blockchains such as Bitcoin without modification, and on account-based blockchains such as Ethereum by introducing a smart contract that mimics the properties of a UTXO. We provide a proof-of-concept implementation deployed on Bitcoin SV and Ethereum, and a worked example of a cross-chain transfer. Our new approach means that users no longer need to be locked into one blockchain when issuing and transferring tokens.

Keywords: Blockchain · Bitcoin · Ethereum · Tokens · NFTs · Interoperability · Privacy

1 Introduction

UTXO blockchains are an attractive platform for NFT markets as their large data capabilities mean that complete NFT data can be recorded on-chain. This is a primary differentiator of the Ordinal Inscriptions protocol [1] which has achieved widespread adoption and a predicted market capitalisation of $4.5B by 2025 [2].

In existing approaches to issuing external tokens on UTXO blockchains, token metadata is embedded in a transaction and the spending logic is used to track ownership. This is useful in leveraging existing infrastructure for transaction processing and storage. But it means that users are locked into one blockchain when transferring tokens peer-to-peer. This is because a token cannot be transferred securely from one blockchain to another without introducing a trusted third party such as a notary or bridge, thus removing one of the key benefits of using a blockchain in the first place.

Since the format of a transaction is fixed for each blockchain, using spending logic to track ownership can also result in a lack of flexibility. An emerging issue is that popular device manufactures such as Apple do not support blockchain signature schemes such as secp256k1 in their secure enclaves [3].

Privacy is also a problem. In existing approaches, token ownership is only as private as the underlying blockchain itself. Ledgers such as Bitcoin and Ethereum have pseudonymous privacy models, which is not strong enough for many use cases including national-level initiatives such as CBDCs. This has led to a rise in non-blockchain designs [4].

In this paper, we propose a fundamentally different approach using a new type of token called a Universal Blockchain Asset (UBA). These tokens are issued and transferred using a bespoke object called a *packet* that has inputs and outputs but is itself not a blockchain transaction. Instead, in the output of each packet there is a reference to an unspent outpoint on the receiver's blockchain. When a token transfer is finalised, an auxiliary blockchain transaction is created on the sender's blockchain that contains a commitment of the packet. This ensures that the token cannot be double-spent. There is no third party involved in any part of the process. We follow a similar approach to single-use-seals developed by Todd [5] but extended and refined to accommodate cross-chain transfers.

Our protocol requires users to create both blockchain transactions and UBA packets, but with a lower security requirement for the blockchain transactions. If blockchain keys are compromised, the worst consequence is that a token transfer cannot be confirmed. If desired, a service provider can be introduced to manage blockchain transactions on behalf of a user. This service provider has limited scope and does not have the ability to re-allocate tokens themselves, nor to collude with a user to double-spend.

While our scheme is designed to work on UTXO blockchains such as Bitcoin, it is agnostic to the choice of underlying blockchain or centralised ledger. All we require is some form of double-spend protection and the ability to record a hash digest in a transaction (256-bits of data is enough). Our scheme can be implemented on multiple blockchains at once, and tokens can be transferred cross-chain without a trusted third party or bridge, thus mitigates the risk of expensive hacks [6].

The advantages of our scheme are as follows.

- **Cross-chain.** Users can transfer tokens between blockchains as easily as transferring on a single blockchain. We do not require coins to be locked or burned, nor do we require trusted third parties or bridges.
- **Private.** Our proposal has forward privacy by design. Complete privacy can be achieved by introducing zero-knowledge proofs (ZKPs) that are verified off-chain.
- **Flexible.** The format of a UBA packet can be customised per deployment. They can be chosen to have bespoke fields, signature schemes, and programmability.

In this paper we focus on NFTs as a simple use case with an immediate addressable market. But it is expected that our proposal can be extended to fungible tokens needed for digital cash systems such as CBDCs, which we leave for future work.

The organisation of this paper is as follows. In Sect. 2 we discuss related work. In Sect. 3 we define a UBA token system at a formal level. We provide a concrete instantiation with security and privacy analysis in Sect. 4, a proof-of-concept implementation in Sect. 5, and end with future work in Sect. 6. In Appendix A we present a worked example of an NFT that is transferred from Bitcoin SV to Ethereum and back.

2 Related Work

2.1 NFTs on Bitcoin

The standard approach to NFTs on Bitcoin is to embed token metadata into a transaction and then track spending. Early examples include Counterparty, where token metadata is embedded into UTXOs using dummy entries in multi-signature scripts [7], and Colored Coins, where metadata is embedded in an unspendable output [8]. More recently, Ordinal Inscriptions took a novel approach by publishing full NFT data on-chain and 'inscribing' it into satoshis identifiable by their order in coinbase transactions [1].

The protocols described above all follow a similar method. An NFT is issued to a first owner Alice in first transaction Tx_0 and transferred to a new owner Bob in a second transaction Tx_1. The arrangement of transaction Tx_1 is carefully chosen to encode the token ruleset so that Bob is specified as the new rightful owner. Bob can transfer the NFT to Charlie in the same way, and the process can be iterated indefinitely (see Fig. 1). Transaction fees (and change) can be accounted for by adding additional inputs and outputs that do not interfere with token transfer process.

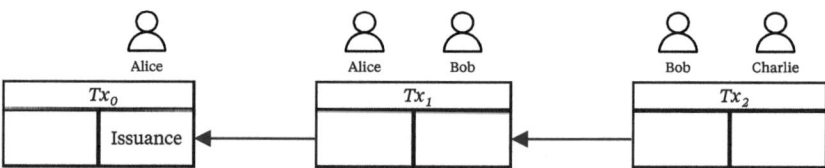

Fig. 1. The standard method for issuing and transferring NFTs on Bitcoin. Users appear above inputs and outputs that contain their pseudonymous data.

In this method, not only does the blockchain provide double-spend protection, it also provides the token transfer logic. Namely, the owner of the NFT corresponds to the owner of the UTXO/coin. To prove the provenance of an NFT, it is necessary to trace the history back to issuance and check that the token ruleset has been correctly applied throughout the lifetime of the token.

A more advanced NFT transfer protocol was proposed by Peter Todd using a 'single-use-seal' process [5]. In this protocol, Alice transfers a token to Bob by creating a transaction with an OP_RETURN data payload that contains a commitment of a data packet that references a UTXO controlled by Bob. Alice's transaction and Bob's UTXO are not related to one-another on the ledger, yet the token transfer is secure and cannot be double-spent. Similar to the standard method, to prove the provenance of an NFT one has to trace back to issuance.

This approach is versatile and achieves a high level of privacy since there is no on-chain link between token owners. In Sect. 3 we use a similar approach, but place greater primacy on the off-chain data packets and less emphasis on blockchain transactions, which we treat rather abstractly. Our goal is to show how this method can be used to transfer tokens cross-chain as easily as within one chain, and without introducing any additional third party.

2.2 ZKPs for Privacy and Scalability

Early attempts at increasing privacy in Bitcoin involve coin mixers like Coinjoin [9]. While these attempted to obfuscate the history of a coin, they did not offer full privacy.

Complete transaction unlinkability was developed using overlay networks in combination with blind signatures from Chaum's e-cash [10]. One of the first examples was Zerocoin, where an escrow would unlock coins when a zero-knowledge proof was provided by a user whose identity had been anonymised [11]. Some proposals could not be implemented on Bitcoin due to its restricted feature set. This led to the development of separate blockchains dedicated to privacy, such as Monero and Zcash [12, 13].

In Ethereum, ZK-rollups have become a popular method to batch transactions before sending them to Mainnet [14]. These work by deploying a smart contract on Mainnet that can verify ZKPs and settle transactions. On a second layer, users submit transactions to an operator who produces a summary of state changes together with a validity proof that is sent to the Mainnet smart contract. This serves to alleviate network congestion, reduce fees, and provides an additional layer of privacy. Some popular tokens that use ZK-rollups for enhanced privacy include ImmutableX and Mute [15, 16]. The downsides of ZK-rollups are the high cost of Mainnet verification, at around $100–$500 per smart contract call [17], and the dependence on operators in the layer-2 network.

More recently, using ZKPs for scalability has been explored in UTXO blockchain settings. Recursive ZKPs have been used to provide succinct proofs of provenance for NFTs issued on Bitcoin [18]. Since the token history is recorded on Bitcoin, such proofs are used for efficiency rather than privacy. The ZeroSync project aims to provide succinct proofs for layer-1 states, namely block headers and the UTXO set [19]. Already a succinct proof can be provided showing that a given transaction has been published in the most up-to-date chain of blocks without disclosing the full SPV path.

Our token protocol in Sect. 3 has forward privacy by design, and backwards privacy if combined with an off-chain ZKP. The result is a private token framework on Bitcoin that does not rely on an escrow or other third-party operator and does not require a ZKP to be validated on-chain, thus reducing costs compared to ZK-rollups.

2.3 Cross-Chain Technology

There are two fundamental cross-chain token actions: trades and transfers. For trades, an equal value of a digital asset exists on chain A and chain B, and the ownership of these assets is swapped. In a cross-chain transfer, a digital asset is transferred from chain A to chain B while the owner may stay the same.

Cross-chain trades can be achieved trustlessly using hash time locking agreements [20]. This is well-understood technology with many successful implementations, including the Lightning network [21]. Cross-chain transfers are technically more difficult, and the technology is still experimental. The accepted approach is to burn a digital asset on chain A and mint an equivalent asset on chain B. This introduces a double-spend risk, for how can we know there were not *two* new digital assets issued on chains B and C, say?

To overcome this, two categories of solutions have been proposed: notary and bridge [22]. Notaries have the advantage of being less complex to implement but come with a centralised trust model, an example of which is the InterLedger protocol from Ripple [23] and the Inter-Blockchain Communication protocol from Cosmos [24]. Cross-chain bridges are the more popular choice. They often involve decentralised consensus mechanisms similar to blockchains, such as Polkadot [25], and ZKPs can be applied to further reduce trust in bridge operators [26]. Even when the underlying asset is the same on both chains, such as the USDC stablecoin, bridges are useful in improving liquidity [27].

Nevertheless, even with a decentralised trust model, users must still trust the bridge itself. They may also be locked into specific bridges for specific use cases. Due to the complexity of the task, bridges are one of the largest targets of hacks in the cryptocurrency industry [5]. For example, the hacks on Wormhole and Harmony cross-chain bridges resulted in losses of $320 m and $97 m, respectively [28, 29].

Our approach for cross-chain transfers in Sect. 3 does not involve burning or locking coins, nor does it rely on a trusted notary or bridge. In our scheme, there is no distinction between transferring tokens cross-chain and within the same chain. We only require trust in the blockchains themselves. This reduces complexity and risk of hacks.

3 Formal UBA Token System

In this section we formally define a UBA token system and establish notions of security and privacy. In our method, each transfer is made up of two elements: (1) UBA packet, which authorises the transfer; (2) auxiliary blockchain transaction, which provides double-spend protection. The casual reader can skip directly to Sect. 4 where we present an explicit embodiment of a UBA token system for an NFT.

Definition 1 (UBA token system): A UBA token system $\mathcal{T}$ consists of a packet specification P, a proof system $(\mathcal{P}, \mathcal{V})$, and one or more blockchains $(\mathcal{B}^1, \ldots, \mathcal{B}^N)$.

The proving algorithm $\mathcal{P}(\pi_{i-1}, P_i, Tx_i)$ takes as input a previous proof π_{i-1}, a packet P_i, and an auxiliary transaction Tx_i on blockchain $\mathcal{B} \in (\mathcal{B}^1, \ldots, \mathcal{B}^N)$, and outputs a new proof π_i showing the provenance and ownership of the tokens specified by P_i. The verification algorithm $\mathcal{V}(\pi_i, P_i, Tx_i)$ takes the new proof π_i, a packet P_i, and a blockchain transaction Tx_i and outputs 0 or 1. We say the proof system $(\mathcal{P}, \mathcal{V})$ is.

- *Sound* if the probability of generating a valid proof without a valid packet and auxiliary transaction is negligible.
- *Complete* if an honest receiver will be convinced by an honest sender. (Honesty means following the protocol.)
- *Private* if for all $j < i - 1$, the proof π_i reveals no information about P_j.

Definition 2 (UBA transfer procedure): Let $\mathcal{G}(P_{i-1}, vout_i, PK_i,)$ be a UBA packet generation algorithm that takes as input a previous packet P_{i-1}, a blockchain outpoint $vout_i$ controlled by the Receiver, a Receiver's public key PK_i, and outputs a new packet P_i. The interactive protocol is defined to be:

1. Sender runs $\mathcal{P}(\pi_{i-2}, P_{i-1}, Tx_{i-1})$ and passes π_{i-1}, P_{i-1} and Tx_{i-1} to Receiver.
2. Receiver runs $\mathcal{V}(\pi_{i-1}, P_{i-1}, Tx_{i-1})$. If output is 0, abort.
3. Receiver passes $vout_i$ and PK_i to Sender.

4. Sender runs $\mathcal{G}(P_{i-1}, vout_i, PK_i)$ to generate P_i. Sender generates auxiliary blockchain transaction $Tx_i \in \mathcal{B}$ that spends $vout_{i-1}$ and record a commitment of P_i.
5. Sender passes (P_i, Tx_i) to Receiver. Sender broadcasts Tx_i to blockchain $\mathcal{B}$.
6. Receiver checks P_i is valid according to the specification and that Tx_i is accepted by blockchain $\mathcal{B}$.

After the interaction, the Receiver has π_{i-1}, P_i, Tx_i and is ready to be the Sender in the next iteration.

Definition 3 (double-spend protection): Consider a packet P_i that references the previous packet P_{i-1} and with auxiliary transaction Tx_i accepted onto a blockchain $\mathcal{B}$. We say that a UBA token system has double-spend protection if there can be no other UBA packet $P_{i'}$ which also references P_{i-1} and which has an auxiliary transaction $Tx_{i'}$ that is also accepted onto a blockchain $\mathcal{B}' \in (\mathcal{B}^1, \ldots, \mathcal{B}^N)$.

Definition 4 (privacy): Consider a token owner Alice with knowledge of $(\pi_{i-1}, P_{i-1}, Tx_{i-1}, P_i, Tx_i)$. We say that a UBA token system $\mathcal{T}$ has *forward privacy* if Alice cannot learn any information about future packets P_j for $j > i$ if they are kept private by future Senders and Receivers. We say that a UBA token system $\mathcal{T}$ is *private* if Alice cannot learn any information about future or past packets P_j for $j < i-1$ or $j > i$ if they are kept private by Senders and Receivers. An equivalent definition is that a token system has forward privacy and the proof system is private.

4 Explicit Embodiment of UBA Token System

Here we construct an explicit embodiment of a UBA token system defined formally in Sect. 3. Consider an NFT transfer from Alice, who uses Blockchain 1 (e.g. Bitcoin), to Bob, who uses Blockchain 2 (e.g. Ethereum). Let us define a UBA packet specification according to Fig. 2.

PID_1	
Asset identifier: Blockland NFT	Data: NULL
Input	Output
Previous packet: PID_0 Signature: SIG_{PK_A} Signature scheme: secp256r1	Public key: PK_B Blockchain outpoint: $vout_1$ Blockchain identifier: Blockchain 2

Fig. 2. UBA packet P_1 transferring an NFT from Alice to Bob.

The packet has an asset identifier, an optional data payload, an input, and an output. The input contains a reference to a previous packet that specifies the current owner of the NFT. The input field also contains a signature from Alice and signature scheme reference. In our example, Alice uses secp256r1 (also known as NIST P-256) which is compatible with secure enclaves produced by popular manufacturers such as Apple [3]. The signature signs all fields in the packet except the signature field.

The output field contains Bob's public key, and an unspent blockchain outpoint $vout_1$ controlled by Bob. The packet also has a four-byte blockchain identifier that specifies which blockchain the outpoint lives on. In practice, this identifier can be the ticker symbol. The blockchain identifier is important because identical blockchain outpoints can exist on different blockchains. This often happens when a blockchain forks. Each packet also has a unique identifier called a *PID* that is the double-hash of the serialised fields.

For the UBA packet to be valid, the semantic structure must be correct (all fields have the correct position and length), Alice's signature must be valid and match the public key in the previous packet, and the asset identifier must match the previous packet. Alice must send P_0 to the Bob so that he can check the validity of P_1 himself.

When the packet P_1 is finalised, the sender Alice creates an auxiliary blockchain transaction Tx_1 with a single input $vout_0$ and one unspendable output containing a hash of the packet P_1. It contains no destination address nor any information about the recipient Bob. Since each packet is private to everyone except Alice and Bob, an outside observer cannot link the blockchain transaction to the packet. The relationship between UBA packets and blockchain transactions is given in Fig. 3.

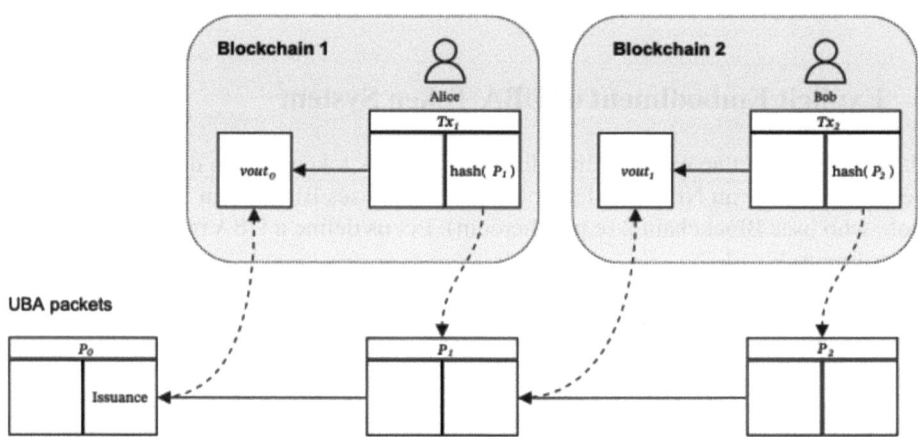

Fig. 3. The relationship between UBA packets and blockchain transactions. The arrows indicate a reference to the object pointed to. The sequence can be iterated indefinitely.

Comparing Fig. 3 with Fig. 1, we see that the token transfer logic for the UBA packets is similar to the standard blockchain approach, but the difference is the information recorded on-chain. In our proposal, blockchain transactions have one input and one unspendable output, and are not related to one-another through the spending of

UTXOs/coins. Therefore, to an outside observer inspecting the blockchain, the transactions created by Alice and Bob have no meaningful relationship to one-another. Moreover, Alice and Bob may use different blockchains for Tx_1 and Tx_2. In Appendix A we provide a worked example where the packets P_0, P_1, P_2 and auxiliary blockchain transactions Tx_1, Tx_2 are constructed explicitly.

Before the transfer begins, Alice needs to prove the provenance of the token to Bob. In our simple example, P_0 is the issuance packet itself. In this case, Bob just needs to check that it has a valid signature from the issuer, the correct asset identifier, and a reference to Alice's public key and $vout_0$. For a longer sequence of n token transfers, Alice must send to Bob the entire history of UBA packets and blockchain transactions since issuance. Bob can then explicitly check that the packets are valid and that the transactions have been accepted onto their respective blockchains. This can be achieved either using SPV proofs, by keeping copies of full blockchains, or by querying the node networks directly.

In the language of the previous section, for this embodiment the proof of provenance π_n consists of all previous packets and blockchain transactions $\pi_n = ((P_0, \ldots, P_n), (Tx_1, \ldots, Tx_n))$. The proving algorithm $\mathcal{P}$ simply adds another packet and transaction to an existing proof. The verification algorithm is given as follows.

Verify. $\mathcal{V}((P_0, \ldots, P_n), (Tx_1, \ldots, Tx_n), (\mathcal{B}^1, \ldots, \mathcal{B}^n))$

1. For i from n to 1:
    a. Extract SIG_i from P_i and extract $(vout_{i-1}, PK_{i-1})$ from P_{i-1}.
    b. Verify signature (PK_{i-1}, P_i, SIG_i). If false, abort.
    c. Verify the input Tx_i spends $vout_{i-1}$ and the output contains a data payload comprising $H(P_i)$.
    d. Verify that Tx_i has been published on $\mathcal{B} \in (\mathcal{B}^1, \ldots, \mathcal{B}^N)$ to a desired confidence level for the given consensus mechanism. E.g. for Bitcoin one can check the transaction is buried at least 6 blocks deep. If false, abort.
2. Verify P_0 contains a valid signature from the issuer. If false, abort.
3. Return TRUE.

While the verification of a token history back to issuance may appear cumbersome, it is a common practice that is needed for many popular token protocols on UTXO blockchains, such as Ordinal Inscriptions, and the task can be outsourced to an indexing service, see Sect. 2. Such indexing services are optional and are used for efficiency only. They play no active role in the authorisation of token transfers. In Claim 3 below we explain an approach to replacing indexers with ZKPs.

4.1 Security and Privacy Analysis

Claim 1: The token system in Sect. 4 has double-spend protection if blockchains $(\mathcal{B}^1, \ldots, \mathcal{B}^n)$ have double-spend protection.

Proof: Suppose Alice generates a first P_i and Tx_i and passes these to Bob, and a second $P_{i'}$ and $Tx_{i'}$ and passes these Charlie, where both P_i and $P_{i'}$ reference the same previous packet P_{i-1}. Due to the collision resistance of the hash function, both Tx_i and $Tx_{i'}$ must spend the same output $vout_{i-1}$ on blockchain $\mathcal{B}$ specified in P_{i-1}. Since the blockchain has double-spend protection by assumption, only one of Tx_i and $Tx_i{\prime}$ may be accepted onto blockchain $\mathcal{B}$.

Claim 2: The token system in Sect. 4 has forward privacy.

Proof: Consider a token owner Alice with knowledge of P_i and Tx_i. By inspecting the blockchain, she can learn the details of Tx_{i+1} which she identifies as the transaction that spends $vout_i$. However, by the preimage resistance of the hash function, she is not about to learn about P_{i+1}. She is then not able to identify Tx_{i+2}, which is also not related to Tx_{i+1} through on-chain spending logic. Alice is therefore not able to learn about future packets P_j for $j > i$ if they are kept private. She is also not able to identify future blockchain transactions Tx_{j+1}.

Claim 3: The token system in Sect. 4 can be made private and the complexity of token validation can be reduced if a recursive ZKP is used for proof of provenance.

Sketch of Proof: In [18] a succinct proof was given that a chain of unbroken Bitcoin transactions originated from a given issuance transaction. This ZKP was recursive and could be updated with each new transaction. Since a chain of UBA packets is structurally similar to a chain of Bitcoin transactions, we can use a similar method to prove that a chain of UBA packets originated from a given issuance packet.

What makes things more complicated than in [18] is the auxiliary blockchain transactions. We need to be sure that these are legitimate transactions that are part of the latest chain of block headers. One approach would be to verify these transactions independently and use their transaction IDs as public inputs to the recursive proof. Such a proof would have complexity of order $O(n)$ in the number of transfers n. Nevertheless, it would still ensure that a UBA token can be validated by a receiver even if the history of the packets remains private. Therefore, we could construct a private token system according to Definition 4.

To reduce the complexity of the proof, we could attempt to use methods of [19] to create a succinct proof that the auxiliary blockchain transactions have been accepted by their respective networks. Since we are using multiple blockchain networks, this would potentially reduce the complexity to $O(N)$, where N is the number of blockchain networks that appear in the history of the UBA token.

We leave the complexities of explicitly constructing these proof systems to future work. Note that in all cases the proof-carrying data is not recorded in the UBA packets nor the blockchain transactions. Therefore, they do not change the architecture presented in Fig. 3.

5 Implementation

To demonstrate that Universal Blockchain Assets work in existing blockchain settings, we have created a proof-of-concept implementation of the protocol presented in Sect. 4 that is deployed on the Bitcoin SV and Ethereum blockchains. It is open-source and available at github.com/nchain-innovation/universal_blockchain_asset. It comprises two components:

1. **API service**, built in Python using a Swagger interface for function definition. The service has capability to create, store, transfer, and verify UBA tokens. It connects to the blockchain testnets (Sepolia for Ethereum) and allows tokens to be transferred across chains. A system overview is given in Fig. 4.
2. **UI**, built using Streamlit. This is an easy-to-use interface that connects to the API. It allows for the creation and transfer of NFTs based on IPFS images for testing purposes. Screenshots are given in Fig. 5.

All components are written in Python and dockerised for ease of deployment.

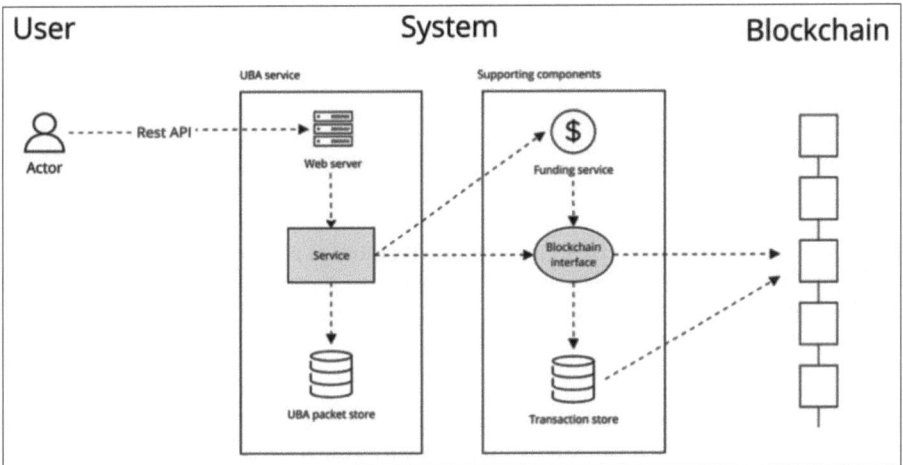

Fig. 4. System overview of UBA implementation.

The security of the protocol is predicated on the ability of users to independently verify the history of a UBA token. Any production-ready implementation should provide a free open-source verification tool that has been rigorously tested. This tool can be run by users directly or embedded in UBA-compatible software. In our implementation, the open-source API code can be used for this purpose.

In Appendix A we provide a worked example of a cross-chain token transfer. We provide the data for the UBA packets and show where the auxiliary blockchain data can be found online. The reader is encouraged to walk through the steps themselves and explicitly check that the transfer has been performed correctly and is secure against double-spends.

5.1 Simulating a UTXO on Ethereum

Since Ethereum operates an account-based model as opposed to a UTXO model, one cannot directly specify an unspent outpoint on Ethereum. However, it is straight-forward to implement a smart contract that can simulate a UTXO. For our implementation, we created such a smart contract that is universal and can be called by anyone. Essentially, the smart contract has two main functions: `createUTXO` and `spendUTXO`. When the

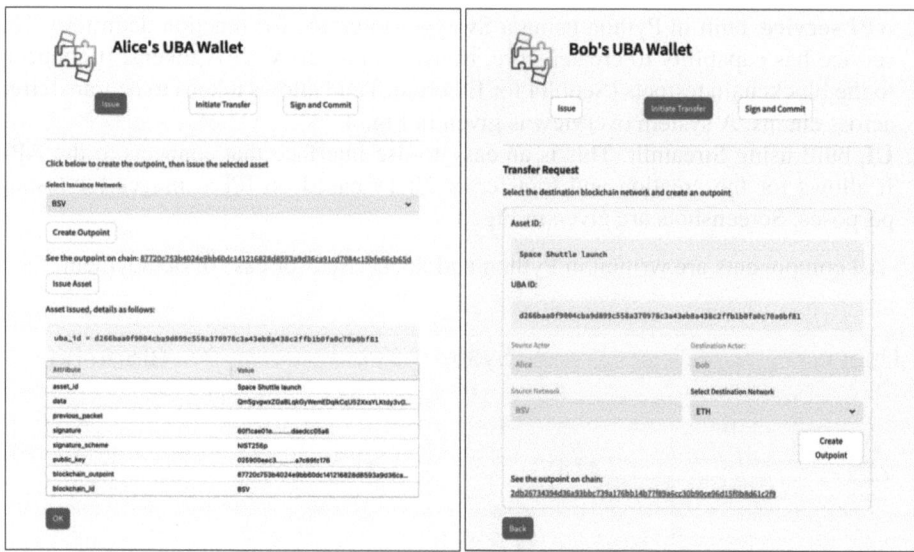

Fig. 5. Screenshots of user interface. On the left, an IPFS image is issued to Alice as a UBA token on Bitcoin SV. On the right, Bob creates an 'outpoint' on Ethereum and makes a token transfer request to Alice. The final step, not shown, is for Alice to create and sign a UBA packet, send it to Bob, and commit to it in a transaction on Bitcoin SV.

createUTXO function is called, an 'outpoint' object is created, and a unique ID is returned. This 'outpoint' has a status of 'unspent'. The spendUTXO function accepts an 'outpoint' ID and data payload as input. When the spendUTXO function is called, the 'outpoint' status is changed to a fixed final state 'spent' and the data payload is assigned to the 'outpoint'. This is similar a Bitcoin transaction with one input and one unspendable output with data payload, as required in Fig. 3. Our implementation of the smart contract is available here

0xf120D32bb10A2aE2971f9Aa026aBE8F0dA9709fb.

The smart contract also contains the query functions isUTXOspent and getCpid. The corresponding solidity code is available upon request.

6 Future Work

In this paper we have presented a universal approach to issuing and transferring tokens across multiple blockchains without a notary or bridge. We implemented a simple NFT proof-of-concept on the Bitcoin SV and Ethereum blockchains. We are in the process of integrating the API with Metamask and uploading to the Snap repository to improve the UI and make it more accessible. At the same time, we would like to implement the protocol on more networks, giving preference to archetypal rather than derivative blockchains. An interesting next step would be blockchains with permissioning systems and private ledgers.

In order to productionise our implementation, we plan to develop the API so that it can be initiated with any bespoke token rulesets defined by token issuers. The service then creates, transfers and validates UBA tokens according to this ruleset. We will aim to make it easily compatible with the most popular wallet software using Metamask as a reference implementation. One the platform is sufficiently stable and extensible, we will be in a position to build a blockchain agnostic NFT marketplace, or to partner with an existing marketplace and allow it to become chain agnostic.

On the theoretical side, we would like to extend the UBA protocol in include fungible tokens. This would open up use cases such as CBDCs which are a natural fit for UBA due to requirements of privacy and universality. In the case of fungible tokens, UBA packets need to have multiple inputs and outputs. One is now faced with a choice: either introduce a different blockchain outpoint for each packet output, or to use a single blockchain outpoint for all packet outputs. It would be interesting to weight up the pros and cons of both approaches, at the same time paying attention to other implementation details that are specific to fungible tokens.

In Sect. 4 we outlined a proof system that would allow a UBA token system to be private and tokens to be validated succinctly. To achieve this, work needs to be done to create a recursive ZKP that can validate UBA packets back to issuance. Given that we have a lot of flexibility in the design of UBA packets, one could investigate whether there are different design choices that allow proofs to be constructed more efficiently, for example by using different hash functions or other types of commitments. For the auxiliary blockchain transactions, succinct blockchain inclusion proofs would help reduce the overall complexity of proof generation for UBA packets. Such proofs would be blockchain-specific and be of independent utility to their respective chains.

Acknowledgements. The implementation of UBA was carried out by my colleagues Josie Wilden and John Murphy, and I think them for their efforts and support. I thank Dr Michaella Pettit, Dr Wei Zhang and Dr Paul Germouty for their review and feedback on early drafts of this work.

Appendix

A Worked example: token transfer from BSV to ETH to BSV

Here we provide an on-chain worked example of UBA issuance and transfer according to the protocol outlined in Sect. 4. We provide all the necessary information for the transfer to be explicitly checked from a security perspective.

In this example, an NFT is issued to Alice on Bitcoin SV (BSV), transferred to Bob on Ethereum, and then to Charlie on BSV. The NFT is an image of the space shuttle stored on IPFS at location `QmSgvgwxZGaBLqkGyWemEDqikCqU52XxsYLKtdy3vGZ8uq`.

Below, we provide the data of the UBA packets P_0, P_1, P_2 and links to the auxiliary blockchain transactions Tx_1, Tx_2 that are available online on the BSV and Ethereum Testnets respectively. We encourage the reader to explicitly verify that the packets and transactions adhere to the protocol outlined in Sect. 4. (Recall that the struture of the packets is given by Fig. 2, and the auxiliary blockchain transactions by Fig. 3). Note that the blockchain outpoints are not the same as in the user interface screenshots in Fig. 5 as we created our worked example at an earlier time.

A.1 Issue to Alice on BSV

The packet P_0 records that an NFT is issued Alice on the BSV blockchain. The data is given as follows.

```
"P_0":
{
    "asset_id": "Space Shuttle launch",
    "data": "QmSgvgwxZGaBLqkGyWemEDqikCqU52XxsYLKtdy3vGZ8uq",
    "previous_packet": null,
    "signature":
    "d748d8d02c9babed9aaf0c408629267ec06a7ee02ed706d150fc9a5dfa1e0f8f02c16
    82b0909ff2c9d3d26a26102a3522ef22eee6ed987dde229973c39fa8359",
    "signature_scheme": "NIST256p",
    "public_key":
    "025900eec3232e7322efcc326d0da932e845344641e190dcb10da6bba7c89fc176",
    "blockchain_outpoint":
    "f520e23dd06e8921dc58f64236a63df455ef1e7cc8fc72c8111f7a1a7e82b784:1",
    "blockchain_id": "BSV"
}

"PID_0":"a8bcb5c0a2f707d14592f392c69bdedd25d1702ee50216775436bd82e19570f5"
```

Let us break down the fields above. The first entry is the asset ID which should be constant for all packets. The second entry contains an optional data payload that we have chosen to be the IPFS location of the space shuttle image. The following three fields represent the packet's input. First comes a reference to a previous packet, which is null in this case. Next is a signature, and, since this is the issuance packet, this is from the issuer. (In this toy model are re-using Alice's public key here. We can think of this as Alice issuing an NFT to herself.) The signature is over the serialised packet fields excluding the signature and signature scheme. Specifically, the signature signs the data `sighash_preimage = { asset_id || data || previous_packet || public_key || blockchain_outpoint || blockchain_id }`.

The signature scheme is specified to be NIST P-256 and can be verified using open-source libraries such as OpenSSL and python-ecdsa.

The final three fields represent the output of the packet. The public key belongs to Alice as the recipient of the NFT. The blockchain outpoint is controlled by Alice, and the blockchain ID specifies that this outpoint is on BSV.

The last entry in the box above is the packet ID. For this simple example, we re-use the sighash so we have `PID_0 = sighash_ 0`. In practice, a double hash of the serialised packet fields is recommended.

A.2 Transfer to Bob on Ethereum

Bob creates an 'outpoint' $vout_1$ on Ethereum using the smart contract described in Sect. 5.1. Alice uses this to construct packet P_1 transferring ownership of the NFT to Bob.

```
"P_1":
{
    "asset_id": "Space Shuttle launch",
    "data": "QmSgvgwxZGaBLqkGyWemEDqikCqU52XxsYLKtdy3vGZ8uq",
    "previous_packet":
    "a8bcb5c0a2f707d14592f392c69bdedd25d1702ee50216775436bd82e19570f5",
    "signature":
    "f305de9e68ab9d8b156104cc8be9b5249fb5f056fb5abb08f3314a827dfd6cbb721c3
    f25aa63a981d46110e4e4e4e506b98c971d6f4973dce87109e74ffebe40",
    "signature_scheme": "NIST256p",
    "public_key":
    "021b955dff7a28f722b25304f3daba78c83718ec3ab38486c523c748b9f27f6ce0",
    "blockchain_outpoint":
    "0x18a33e2702059102eb10097333d850314a42efb84da6b6ec676748a904251749",
    "blockchain_id": "ETH"
}

"PID_1":"f12d4ba9592137828718ffd50ee3ec5ab43e012e3e707c006c40dbeb4d1e3f89"
```

A.3 Transfer to Charlie on BSV

Bob now sends the NFT to Charlie who operates on BSV. To do this, Bob creates packet P_2 with the following data.

```
"P_2":
{
    "asset_id": "Space Shuttle launch",
    "data": "QmSgvgwxZGaBLqkGyWemEDqikCqU52XxsYLKtdy3vGZ8uq",
    "previous_packet":
    "f12d4ba9592137828718ffd50ee3ec5ab43e012e3e707c006c40dbeb4d1e3f89",
    "signature":
    "0b4db3336d4070f4af2f8f56608c824b9d45064880026214788c4860b55f2d74f508b3
    52c7fb3a995559e7eae43b7e6dd3bbfdc54961d148cb64cbb1cc685158",
    "signature_scheme": "NIST256p",
    "public_key":
    "02a1002a5f24d40ac2f87fa4562cca0202007c5eefe601d8c0d7b0e636813f92b9",
    "blockchain_outpoint":
    "2a1c1dea9efa62c88a0b4e553d1e32f631b86ad78a1760fe49f7eabb13607a3b:1",
    "blockchain_id": "BSV"
}

"PID_2":"2cf8337a75f2ad32fac567a537460a56fcad33d7553551ab46e5bc77fd34c9c9"
```

To confirm the transfer, a corresponding auxiliary blockchain transaction Tx_2 is created by Bob and broadcast to the Ethereum network (note PID_2 in the data field) 0xf082c469b5dcbb83e1aa362a570ac825c941adb32d03dcc8df 148d6cd52eae36.

This sets the 'outpoint' status to 'spent' and attaches an immutable record of PID_2. Charlie is now the rightful owner of the NFT and it cannot be double-spent by Bob.

References

1. Ordinal theory handbook. docs.ordinals.com. Accessed 25 May 25
2. Thorn, A., et al.: Bitcoin Inscriptions & Ordinals A New $5bn Market. Galaxy Research White Paper (2023)
3. Protecting keys with the Secure Enclave. developer.apple.com/documentation/security/certificate_key_and_trust_services/keys/protecting_keys_with_the_secure_enclave. Accessed 25 May 25
4. Goodell, G., Toliver, D.R., Nakib, H.D.: A scalable architecture for electronic payments. In: Matsuo, S., et al. Financial Cryptography and Data Security. FC 2022 International Workshops. FC 2022. Lecture Notes in Computer Science, vol. 13412. Springer, Cham (2023). https://doi.org/10.1007/978-3-031-32415-4_38
5. Todd, P.: Scalable Semi-Trustless Asset Transfer via Single-Use-Seals and Proof-of-Publication. Blog post (2017). petertodd.org/2017/scalable-single-use-seal-asset-transfer
6. Lee, S.-S., Murashkin, A., Derka, M., Gorzny, J.: SoK: Not Quite Water Under the Bridge: Review of Cross-Chain Bridge Hacks. arxiv.org/abs/2210.16209
7. Counterparty. counterparty.io. Accessed 25 May 25
8. Assia, Y., Buterin, V., Hakim L., Rosenfeld M., Lev R.: Colored Coins whitepaper. www.etoro.com/wp-content/uploads/2022/03/Colored-Coins-white-paper-Digital-Assets.pdf
9. Maxwell, G.: CoinJoin: Bitcoin privacy for the real world. Post on bitcointalk.org. bitcointalk.org/index.php?topic=279249. Accessed 25 May 25
10. Chaum, D.: Blind signatures for untraceable payments. In: Advances in Cryptology: Proceedings of Crypto, vol. 82, no. 3, pp. 199–203 (1983). chaum.com/wp-content/uploads/2022/01/Chaum-blind-signatures.pdf
11. Miers, I., Garman, C., Green, M., Rubin, A.D.: Zerocoin: anonymous distributed e-cash from Bitcoin. In: Proceedings of IEEE SP, pp. 397–411 (2013). eprint.iacr.org/2014/349
12. Monero. www.getmonero.org. Accessed 25 May 25
13. ZCash, z.cash. Accessed 25 May 25
14. ZK-rollups. ethereum.org/en/developers/docs/scaling/zk-rollups. Accessed 25 May 25
15. ImmutableX. www.immutable.com. Accessed 25 May 25
16. Mute. mute.io. Accessed 25 May 25
17. Hioki, L.: A pre-consensus mechanism to secure instant finality and long interval in zkRollup. ethresear.ch/t/a-pre-consensus-mechanism-to-secure-instant-finality-and-long-interval-in-zkrollup/8749. Accessed 25 May 25
18. Kiraz, M.S., Larraia, E., Vaughan, O.: NFT Trades in Bitcoin with Off-chain Receipts. Applied Cryptography and Network Security Workshops: ACNS 2023 Satellite Workshops, AIBlock, Kyoto, Japan, 19–22 June 2023, Proceedings, pp. 100–117, June 2023. https://doi.org/10.1007/978-3-031-41181-6_6. eprint.iacr.org/2023/697
19. ZeroSync. zerosync.org. Accessed 25 May 25
20. Herlihy, M.: Atomic cross-chain swaps. In: PODC 2018: Proceedings of the 2018 ACM Symposium on Principles of Distributed Computing, pp. 245–254, July 2018. https://doi.org/10.1145/3212734.3212736
21. Poon, J., Dryja, T.: The bitcoin lightning network: scalable off-chain instant payments (2016)
22. Li, L., Wu, J., Cui, W.: A review of blockchain cross-chain technology. In: IET Blockchain, vol. 3, Issue 3, pp. 149–158, September 2023. https://doi.org/10.1049/blc2.12032
23. Hope-Bailie, A., Interledger, T.S.: Creating a standard for payments. In: Proceedings of the 25th International Conference Companion on World Wide Web, pp. 281–282. ACM, New York (2016). https://doi.org/10.1145/2872518.2889307
24. Inter-Blockchain Communication Protocol. www.ibcprotocol.dev. Accessed 25 May 25

25. Wood, G.: Polkadot: vision for a heterogeneous multi-chain framework. White Pap. **21**, 2327–4662 (2016). assets.polkadot.network/Polkadot-whitepaper.pdf
26. Xie T., et al.: zkBridge: trustless cross-chain bridges made practical. In: CCS 2022: Proceedings of the 2022 ACM SIGSAC Conference on Computer and Communications Security, pp. 3003–3017, November 2022. https://doi.org/10.1145/3548606.3560652
27. Cross-Chain Transfer Protocol. www.circle.com/en/cross-chain-transfer-protocol. Accessed 25 May 25
28. Wormhole Bridge Exploit Incident Analysis, Certik. www.certik.com/resources/blog/1kDYgyBcisoD2EqiBpHE5l-wormhole-bridge-exploit-incident-analysis. Accessed 25 May 25
29. Harmony Incident Analysis, Certik. www.certik.com/resources/blog/2QRuMEEZAWHx0f16kz43uC-harmony-incident-analysis. Accessed 25 May 25

Private Electronic Payments with Self-custody and Zero-Knowledge Verified Reissuance

Daniele Friolo[1], Geoffrey Goodell[2(✉)], D. R. Toliver[3], and Hazem Danny Nakib[2]

[1] Sapienza University of Rome, Rome, Italy
friolo@di.uniroma1.it
[2] University College London, London, UK
g.goodell@ucl.ac.uk, h.nakib@cs.ucl.ac.uk
[3] TODAQ Finance, Toronto, Canada
dann.toliver@todaqfinance.com

Abstract. This article builds upon the protocol for digital transfers described by Goodell, Toliver, and Nakib (WTSC at FC '22), which combines privacy by design for consumers with strong compliance enforcement for recipients of payments and self-validating assets that carry their own verifiable provenance information. We extend the protocol to allow for the verification that reissued assets were created in accordance with rules prohibiting the creation of new assets by anyone but the issuer, without exposing information about the circumstances in which the assets were created that could be used to identify the payer. The modified protocol combines an audit log with zero-knowledge proofs, so that a consumer spending an asset can demonstrate that there exists a valid entry on the audit log that is associated with the asset, without specifying which entry it is. This property is important as a means to allow money to be reissued within the system without the involvement of system operators within the zone of control of the original issuer. Additionally, we identify a key property of privacy-respecting electronic payments, wherein the payer is not required to retain secrets arising from one transaction until the following transaction, and argue that this property is essential to framing security requirements for storage of digital assets and the risk of blackmail or coercion as a way to exfiltrate information about payment history. We claim that the design of our protocol strongly protects the anonymity of payers with respect to their payment transactions, while preventing the creation of assets by any party other than the original issuer without destroying assets of equal value.

1 Introduction

Privacy and scalability are often at odds in digital payment solutions. We assert that this is largely the result of the involvement of the issuer in the circulation of electronic money. Goodell, Toliver, and Nakib have shown that it is possible to achieve both privacy and scalability imperatives simultaneously by combining a privacy-respecting token issuance process with a model by which assets track their own provenance [13]. Unlike most real and proposed modern retail payment solutions that are currently used in practice (public and private), including interbank payments, cryptocurrency transfers, and centralised e-money, their approach removes the issuer from the transaction channel, allowing transactions to take place at the edge. However, the protocol assumes that before value transferred in one consumer transaction can be spent by a consumer in another transaction, the underlying assets must be recirculated by *minters*, which are entities authorised and trusted by the original issuer to issue new assets to replace previously spent assets. It is assumed that minters do not produce valid assets without authorisation from the issuer, despite having the technical capacity to do so. Although this assumption mirrors the mechanical control that central banks have over private-sector companies that produce banknotes and coins, such an assumption might be less appropriate for an environment wherein valid assets can be created without the aid of proprietary technology and expensive materials with large fixed costs.

We show that it is possible for a payer to demonstrate that an asset was created in accordance with the rules governing its creation without providing evidence linking the asset to the specific context and circumstances of its creation. The combination of privacy and resistance to counterfeiting is as important to digital money as it is for physical cash. Users of cash have a reliable way to verify the authenticity of banknotes while also maintaining that they would not expect that the serial numbers of their banknotes would be used to associate the bank account of a payer who had withdrawn the banknotes from her bank to the bank account of the recipient who had deposited the banknotes following a retail transaction.

In this article, we describe a mechanism that combines zero-knowledge (ZK) proofs with a robust audit log to provide a way for payers to prove that their assets were created during an atomic process wherein assets of equal value were destroyed, without incurring the risk of de-anonymisation or undermining the properties claimed in the design of the original protocol. We show that using this new mechanism allows the process of reissuance of spent tokens to be undertaken by relatively untrusted minters, or by consumer-facing banks instead of minters, thus improving the robustness of the protocol relative to the original design and reducing its attack surface.

This article is organised as follows. In the rest of this section, we provide background to motivate the design of our payment architecture and characterise the requirements that underpin its design. In the following section, we compare related protocols and assess their strengths and weaknesses. In Sect. 3, we provide the protocol description. In Sect. 4, we offer a formal security analysis of the properties our protocol aims to satisfy and the main theorem. In Sect. 5, we conclude, pointing to the next steps and future directions for this line of research. For space reasons, we background assumptions and definitions that are foundational to our design are given in Appendix A. The formal description of our protocol and the proofs for the main theorem stated in Sect. 4 are deferred to the full version.

1.1 Background

This article extends previous work in a category of protocols, one example of which is provided by Goodell, Toliver, and Nakib [13], that allow assets that had been created via a Chaumian mint [5] to be transferred between independent parties without the involvement of the issuer. Important characteristics of these protocols include privacy, self-custody and compliance enforcement for recipients without relying upon exogenous punishment mechanisms which sit outside of the protocol. Punishment mechanisms are unnecessary and introduce negative externalities, such as reliance upon a panoptical view of the behaviours, transactions, and activities of all participants. In addition, these protocols exhibit *transaction independence* in the sense that they do not require a user to retain any secret information that might arise from a transaction. This property is important because it means that the user can optionally expunge all records of the transaction, should they wish to. Because payers can reasonably be expected to be unable to furnish information about payment history, the de-anonymisation risk posed by the compromise of a device, blackmail, or coercion, is mitigated relative to schemes that require payers to maintain information about previous transactions, for example, to prove, via a zero-knowledge mechanism or otherwise, that the state of a balance within the system was updated in accordance with the rules.

In particular, this new category of protocols is able to achieve the combination of privacy by design, self-custody, and compliance enforcement by using an external mechanism for providing integrity verification of assets, wherein the assets are held outside of the relevant ledger. Rather than managing tokens directly, the ledger instead plays the role of integrity verification for the state of the assets. However, because privacy for consumers depends upon the inability to link an asset to the circumstances of its creation, the integrity of the assets must depend upon the inability of those charged with the task of creating assets to do so against the rules.

This article offers an extension to protocols in this category that allow users to prove that an asset is correctly produced while not needing to establish a specific relationship to its creation. Specifically, the mechanism presented in this article provides a way for a prover to demonstrate that an asset has been correctly created by a party whose task is to recirculate tokens (i.e., to "burn" and "mint" in equal measure) within a system, without revealing any information about its creation. Since the assets exist outside the ledger with the ledger playing the role of integrity verification for the state of the assets, it is essential for parties receiving assets to be able to establish their security properties. By providing a way for assets to be verified without linking an asset being proved to an asset being created, it becomes possible to allow the recirculation of assets by parties that operate independently of issuers, without compromising an essential privacy characteristic for digital payment infrastructure.

The mechanism presented here is generic, in the sense that it can be applied to a variety of privacy-enhancing payment schemes that rely upon a Chaumian mint. However, the primary value of the mechanism lies in its use in cases in which assets are transferred without the involvement of their creator, so it will be useful to show how to use this mechanism with protocols that allow assets to be held directly and for which verification is based upon proofs of provenance. For this reason, in future work, we intend to prove how the mechanism works with provenance-based transfers that use Merkle tries to ensure the integrity of assets.

1.2 Design Requirements

Next, elaborating on the set of requirements proposed by Goodell, Toliver, and Nakib [13], we describe the foundational requirements for our design to support the stated characteristics of consumer privacy and system scalability while ensuring that the system can be adopted within the broader socio-technical context of modern retail payments:

- *Consumer privacy by design.* Consumers must be able to verify that, in their spending transactions, they do not disclose any information that can be used, *ex ante* or *ex post*, to link their identities to the transactions.
- *Compatibility with regulatory objectives.* The design of the system must be compatible with the expectation that consumers would be subject to AML/KYC checks at the point in time at which they receive tokens and that merchants would be subject to AML/KYC checks sometime between the point in time at which they receive tokens from consumers and the point in time that they deposit the tokens or reuse them in subsequent transactions.
- *Independent transactions.* Importantly, tokens held by consumers within the system must not be associated with accounts. Consumers must not be expected to hold any secrets other than those related to the set of tokens that they currently hold, so there is no possibility to reconstruct or confirm the prior payment history of an honest consumer even if an adversary takes control of a user's device.
- *No involvement of the issuer in the circulation of tokens.* In the protocol proposed by Goodell, Toliver, and Nakib [13], it is assumed that the issuer would not participate in transactions. However, the issuer would still implicitly have a role in the reissuance of tokens after they are spent, because it is assumed that they must enforce the responsibility of minters to not create invalid tokens. In this version of the protocol, it must be possible for minters to be untrusted, so that unauthorised tokens can be rejected at the point of sale.
- *Efficient procedure for reissuance of tokens.* Since tokens cannot be rehypothecated, there must be an efficient mechanism for recirculating tokens within the system that avoids requiring banks to hold too many tokens at once.
- *Efficient proof generation.* The zero-knowledge proofs used by our system should be computable efficiently, in terms of both communication and computation, and parallelisable so that they can be efficiently performed at scale.

- *Stateless issuer.* The Central Bank is trusted and generates the secrets at the beginning of the protocol. For the purpose of security, it should be possible for the issuer, after transferring its tokens to commercial banks, to be able to permanently delete all secrets related to the specific tokens that it issues.
- *Modularity.* The overall architecture should rely upon simple components that can be rigorously analysed.
- *Succinct audit log.* Well-known verifiable computation techniques (for example, proofs computed on Merkle trees) can be employed to make the audit log data succinct, so that it can be verified efficiently.

Finally, we believe that the design requirements can be met in two ways: either (a) by having a minter sign blinded tokens and publish the signatures alongside burned tokens on the audit log, as in the design proposed by Goodell, Toliver, and Nakib [13], and then having the payer furnish a zero-knowledge proof that the unblinded token matches some blinded token on the audit log; or (b) by having the payer's bank publish zero-knowledge commitments to new tokens alongside burned tokens of equal value on the audit log and then having the payer furnish a zero-knowledge proof that the new token manages some zero-knowledge commitment on the audit log. In this article, we shall formally prove claims about the latter approach, although we assert that it is also possible to prove similar claims about the former approach.

2 Related Work

Starting from the first work by Chaum [5], digital cash has been the focus of much attention from industry and academia. At ACM CCS in 2022, two blockchain-aided digital currency systems were proposed: Platypus [20] and PEReDI [15]. In terms of the definition of the privacy desiderata, we looked mainly to Platypus for inspiration. In terms of efficiency and privacy guarantees, our design is comparable. However, we recall that the Platypus protocol is account-based, and an important property that we require, transaction independence, cannot be satisfied by Platypus. With account-based designs, users are required to hold long-term secrets that can be used to establish relationships among transactions. Indeed, users who leak their own secrets in the Platypus system, whether by mistake, theft, or coercion, expose their entire account histories.

PEReDi is a robust payment protocol in which regulation can be strictly enforced by inspecting, in a privacy-preserving way, the payment traces of the users. Its authors prove the security of their protocol in the Universal-Composability framework. However, like Platypus, PEReDi also uses an account-based design, which implies a persistent identity. The PEReDi protocol is complicated, so Dogan and Bicakci responded by proposing KAIME [6], another account-based protocol with a simpler design, relying on a few simple cryptographic primitives. However, although we recognise the value of the improvements, the account-based mechanism is still problematic because of the lack of transaction independence.

In AFT'20, Androulaki et al. [1] proposed a token-based system with auditability features. Dogan and Bicakci considered the scheme of Androulaki et al. to be a "unspent transaction output" (UTxO) token scheme, because new tokens are created from the process of spending previous tokens. The UTxO property holds whether or not the tokens themselves are written to the ledger, as they are in Bitcoin. The design of Androulaki et al. uses zero-knowledge commitments to new tokens during a transaction, with the expectation that such tokens will be spent onward. A UTxO architecture does not in itself imply a requirement for the payer to retain secrets from one payment to the next. So it is possible to create a UTxO scheme that preserves transaction independence. Nevertheless, the trust model of Androlaki et al. violates transaction independence for two reasons. First, auditors are able to see and connect all of the transaction information, including all of the payments, that a payer makes, by design. Second, authorisation for spending is bound to a user's identity, the credentials for which must be preserved across transactions.

Similarly, the trust model of Wüst et al. [19], another UTxO scheme, violates transaction independence for two reasons. First, the payer must retain a private key corresponding to the certificate issued by the regulator enabling the payer to pay (that is, a long-lived identity). It is assumed that the private key would be used by the payer to receive money when withdrawing it, for example, from a bank, and that the long-lived identity is linked to every transaction that the user makes as payer, even whilst it might not be disclosed. Second, the payer must retain proof that previous transactions during an epoch were sufficiently small that the new payment does not violate a specified transaction limit. These proofs ultimately add an account-like layer to what would otherwise be a UTxO token: A function of this transaction and previous transactions must be shown to meet a certain requirement. Thus, we can argue that the architectures described in both the Androulaki et al. and Wüst et al. proposals are linked to an underlying identity of the payer. Tomescu et al. [17] also proposed a token-based system in the UC setting. As with PEReDi [15], we noticed a high design complexity, and as with the aforementioned UTxO protocols, there is an implicit requirement of a payer identity.

An effective alternative for privacy-preserving payments could be implemented by adapting the existing decentralized anonymous payment system such as ZeroCash [3,9] and Monero [8,18]. Their systems are based on zero-knowledge proofs and ring signatures, respectively, and are designed to provide privacy and integrity in a Bitcoin-like UTxO fashion for the fully decentralized context. Although such protocols would be easily adapted to institutional digital currency, such as CBDC, their usage could be considered overkill, given that a simpler approach to zero-knowledge proofs can be employed in our scenario since only the purchasers, and not the sellers, require anonymity. Indeed, although the bulletin board does not reveal any information about the seller, banks can link the seller's identity with the seller's tokens. This highly facilitates the design and maintenance of the system.

Moreover, although our bulletin board could be implemented with a blockchain system, and our system does not forcibly require a blockchain system since any bulletin board with integrity features would be sufficient for our goals.

Our system decouples transactions wherein spent tokens are recycled into new tokens (burning) from spending transactions. This implies that tokens can be spent without real-time access to the bulletin board and the recipient does not need to download the last state of the bulletin board. Indeed, it is sufficient for the payer to provide proof of inclusion and uniqueness (e.g., using a Merkle trie) of a signed update transferring a token to the recipient, together with a zero-knowledge proof certifying that the token had been correctly minted.

3 Our Protocol

The main idea behind the protocol is to allow a receiver of a token to spend it by posting a fresh and unrelated token onto a bulletin board without requiring any trusted party to verify the legitimacy of the new token. Since this type of verifiability is unattainable without a trusted party or some relation between the tokens, we rely on non-interactive zero-knowledge proofs to create a relation between a freshly generated token and an older claimed token (which we refer to as *burnt*) without disclosing which was the exact token that was claimed in place of the new one. With this approach, an eavesdropper looking at the bulletin board cannot identify which was the claimed token. We call this kind of security against an eavesdropper *token privacy*.

The main challenge behind this approach is in the generation of the initial set of tokens, characterizing the overall token balance of the system, in a trusted manner. We call such tokens *genesis tokens*. For availability and security reasons, a central bank serves as issuer and shall be considered an available trusted party only during the protocol setup phase. After the setup phase, we do not have any trust assumption except that the bulletin board preserves availability and integrity of the posted data. The recipients of genesis tokens are banks, who are a subset of the users and hence treated exactly as any other user transferring tokens inside the system.

To ensure that an adversary corrupting some subset of users cannot double spend one of his tokens, we introduce the concept of *validity* of a token. A token is essentially composed of two keys, the *sender verification key*, freshly generated by the sender, and the *receiver verification key*, freshly generated by the receiver and sent to the sender to produce a new token. Together with such keys, other cryptographic objects such as signatures and zero-knowledge proofs might be part of the token to guarantee its validity.

A genesis token is valid if (i) the sender verification key is a central bank key and (ii) the signature attached to the token verifies the bank verification key w.r.t. the central bank verification key. These two checks are sufficient to identify valid genesis tokens inside the bulletin board subject to the trust assumption of the central bank and the verification keys the central bank has distributed during setup. We further distinguish between *live* tokens and *burnt* tokens. A valid token is burnt if flagged as burnt by the receiver, and alive otherwise. The receiver further authenticates the burning procedure, i.e. the flag has a signature attached that verifies the token and the corresponding flag w.r.t. the receiver verification key. Any token that is subsequent to a genesis token is considered a valid token when the token is *fresh*, meaning that the sender verification key was not used in an earlier valid token, the token signature verifies the message composed of the receiver verification key with respect to the sender verification key, the statement of the zero-knowledge proof, which is attached with the proof, refers to a set of burnt valid tokens, and the zero-knowledge proof is verifiable with respect to the attached statement.

To accept a new payment, the receiver verifies that the token posted by the sender onto the bulletin board is a live, valid token and that its associated verification key is correct, meaning that it matches the one that the receiver provided to the sender.

As it will be explained in more detail in the remainder of the paper, those validity checks ensure that the adversary cannot forge a new valid token without burning a live, valid token for which the adversary knows the signing key corresponding to the receiver verification key of the burnt token. We refer to this property as *token integrity*. We further require another property that the technique described above must satisfy, which we call *balance invariance*, wherein the overall number of live, valid tokens in the system (in the bulletin board), does not change its cardinality, i.e. it must always match the number of genesis tokens.

In the following, we first introduce some notation that will make the protocol easier to describe. Then, we introduce the NP-relation that must be proven by our NIZK-PoK system, and finally, we formally describe our protocol. Because of space constraints, we deferred the definitions, the formal description of the protocol, and the proofs in the full version.

Auxiliary Notation and Useful Algorithms. Each time a new message is posted to a bulletin board BB, a local set of messages M is updated. Since BB, when receiving a new message, automatically notifies the parties with the new message, we assume that the set M of bulletin board messages is always updated by any involved party in the system. We indicate as $M[j]$ as the j-th token in M. Morever, we indicate as M_{live} as the set M restricted to live valid tokens and M_{burnt} as the M restricted to burnt valid tokens. Let $\mathcal{I}$ be a set of indexes, we indicate $M^{\mathcal{I}]}$ as the valid tokens in M restricted to the ones indexed by $\mathcal{I}$, i.e. the subset of M composed by the tokens $(j, \cdot)$ for each $j \in \mathcal{I}$. When we are referring to the token with index j in M, we indicate it as $M^{j]}$. We indicate a live token with sender S and receiver R with $F^{S,R} = (j, \mathsf{vk}^S, \mathsf{vk}^R, \sigma^S, \mathcal{I}, \pi)$, where j is the index of the token in the bulletin board, vk^S is the fresh verification key of the sender, vk^R is the fresh verification key of the receiver, σ^S certifies that the sender owning vk^S authorizes the transfer to vk^R, i.e. σ^S verifies the message vk^R w.r.t. the key vk^S, the proof π shows that vk^S is associated to one of the burning factors in the set of tokens $M^{\mathcal{I}]}_{burnt}$. We indicate the genesis live token as $F^{S,R} = \{j, \mathsf{vk}^S, \mathsf{vk}^R, \sigma^S\}$ with $S = CB$.

A burnt token $F_{burnt}^{S,R}$ is additionally composed of a burning factor β^R and the receiver signature σ^R certifying that the receiver acknowledged the token possession and burned it by using the burning factor β^R, i.e. σ^R verifies the message (vk^S, β^R) w.r.t. the key vk^R. The burning factor β^R is a committed freshly generated sender verification key that will be used by R to spend such token.

To extract valid burnt tokens M_{burnt} from M_{valid} the user run an algorithm GetBurnt outputting all the tokens in M_{valid} in which the sender verification key and the burning factor β associated with the token are certified by the receiver, i.e. such that the signature σ^R attached to the burnt token verifies the message (vk^S, β) w.r.t. the key vk^R.

As an auxiliary useful algorithm, we use a validity predicate IsValid. The algorithm IsValid takes as input the set of central bank verification keys VK valid tokens M_{valid}, a token F as above, computes $M_{burnt} = \text{GetBurnt}(M_{valid})$ and, if F is a standard token, outputs 1 if there is no token in M_{burnt} with the same sender verification key, σ^S verifies the message vk^R w.r.t. the key vk^S, the size of $M_{burnt}^{\mathcal{I}]}$ is the same of $\mathcal{I}$ and the proof π verifies w.r.t. the burning factors in $M_{burnt}^{\mathcal{I}]}$.

Otherwise, if F is a genesis token, output 1 if $\text{vk}^S \in VK$ and σ^S verifies the message vk^R w.r.t. the key vk^S.

As we will see in the formal description, this algorithm will be used by each user when a new token appears on the bulletin board to locally construct the set of valid tokens M_{valid}.

Our NIZK-PoK Relation. Let Com be a commitment scheme (Appendix A.1). Our non-interactive zero-knowledge proof of knowledge (NIZK-PoK) shows that the sender verification key of the new token is associated to a burnt valid token inside a bucket of burning factors. Burning factor are, in practice, committed verification keys. Let us take the n burning factors $\beta_1, \ldots, \beta_n$. The relation must show that the sender verification key vk freshly generated by the receiver of a burnt token is committed in one of the burning factors, i.e. $\text{Com}(\text{vk}; r) = \beta_i$ for some i and some randomness r, without exposing in which burning factor was committed, i.e. the index i is hidden. Hence, the randomness r and the index i must be part of the witness. Formally, the relation to be proven is:

$$\mathcal{R}_{\text{DC}}^{\text{Com}} = \{((\beta_1, \ldots, \beta_n, \text{vk}), (r, i)) : \text{Com}(\text{vk}; r) = \beta_i\}. \tag{1}$$

On the Efficiency of the Proof Generation. Notice that a proof for the relation proposed is fairly simple to implement in an efficient manner. In fact, this relation can be cast as a 1-out-of-n Proof-of-Partial Knowledge (PPK), where the prover proves knowledge of a witness out of n statements without revealing for which of the n statements the prover knows the witness. Indeed, the statement above can be re-casted as a 1-out-of-n proof where $x_i = (\beta_i, \text{vk})$ and $w = (r, i)$. As shown by [12], given a Σ-protocol for a certain language, it is possible to construct a communication-efficient 1-out-of-n PPK where each x_i is an instance of the base

Σ-protocol. The resulting PPK has size $O(\log n)$ if the underlying Σ protocol has constant size proofs. By instantiating Com with a Pedersen commitment [16], it would be sufficient to use a Σ-protocol for Discrete Log equality to check $\mathsf{Com}(\mathsf{vk}; r) = \beta_i$. Between the possible improvements of our protocol, we might make the honest user to spend t tokens all at once and provide a cumulative NIZK-PoK showing that t previous tokens have been previously burned. This can be done via the t-out-of-n PPKs, ensuring that the prover knows the witness of at least t out of n statements. The size of the 1-out-of-k PPK of [2] for DL-like languages (such as DL equality) is only of $O(\log n)$.

We notice that even general-purpose zk-SNARKs [4, 14], usually requiring prohibitive computational costs for large circuits, would not be totally impractical for the circuit describing $\mathcal{R}_{\mathsf{DC}}^{\mathsf{Com}}$, especially when using ZK-proofs friendly commitments such as the Pedersen commitment. The proof size of zk-SNARKs would be constant.

We remark that even though the strongest version of our protocol requires all the parties to monitor the bulletin board to verify updates periodically, this task can be delegated to the banks.

Protocol Description. The formal description of our protocol π_{DC} is provided in the full version The protocol is initialized with a central bank CB and a bulletin board BB a set of users $\mathcal{U}$ and a subset $\mathcal{B} \subseteq \mathcal{U}$ of banks.

The protocol is divided into 3 main phases: Setup, Burning, and Spending. In the setup phase, which is run only once at the beginning, genesis tokens, composed of a freshly generated verification key of the central bank $\mathsf{vk}_{CB}^{(i,B)}$ and a freshly generated verification key vk_B^i from a bank $B \in \mathcal{U}$, are created by the central bank CB and posted to BB in a signed fashion (the signature $\sigma_{CB}^{(B,i)}$ verifies the message $M = \mathsf{vk}_B^i$ verifies under the key $\mathsf{vk}_{CB}^{(i,B)}$). Notice that we assume that each central bank's verification key $\mathsf{vk}^{(i,B)}$ is trusted and certified by the central bank.

As soon as the genesis tokens are added into BB, each user U (which are banks in the case of genesis token) verifies their validity and adds them into their validity set M_{valid}^U. Since we are considering genesis tokens, which are trusted by assumption, it is sufficient that the validity algorithm checks their signature $\sigma_{CB}^{(B,i)}$ against $M = (\mathsf{vk}_B^i)$ and key $\mathsf{vk}_{CB}^{(i,B)}$.

When an honest user R_0 receives a token, they immediately burn it. Notice that each time a new token, live or burnt, is posted into BB, each honest user U verifies its validity and adds it to its local set of valid tokens M_{valid}^U (auxiliary Token Validation phase). Hence, if the new live token is part of the receiver's validity set $M_{valid}^{R_0}$, R_0 can safely burn and lately spend it.

In the burning phase, R_0, which will become a future sender S_1, first creates a fresh verification key vk^{S_1} (Create sub-phase). Then augments its live token with a burning factor (commitment) β^{S_1}, embedding the freshly generated verification key vk^{S_1}, together with a signature σ^{R_0} certifying its authorization to burn such token (Burn sub-phase). This signature verifies the message $M = (\mathsf{vk}^{S_0}, \beta^{S_1})$, where vk^{S_0} is the verification key of the sender of such burnt token, under the verification key vk^{R_0} that the receiver used for that token.

When new sender S_1 (formerly R_0) decides to spend the token after interacting with the future receiver R_1, it first waits to receive a verification key vk^{R_1} from R_1 (Token Gen sub-phase). Then, S_1 generates a NIZK-PoK showing that it owns one of the verification keys embedded into one of the elements of a randomly chosen set of burning factors inside the burnt tokens set (Proof Gen sub-phase). During proof generation, S_0 further generates a signature σ^{S_1} certifying that they can spend such token with the receiver verification key vk^{R_1} (the signature verifies $M = \mathsf{vk}^{R_1}$ under the verification key vk^{S_1}). Finally, S_1 through their bank, which performs some regulation check, posts the live token into BB (Token Post sub-phase).

To recap, a live token F is composed of a sender verification key vk^{S_1}, a receiver verification key vk^{R_1}, a signature σ^{R_1} and a proof π with a set of indexes $\mathcal{I}$ connecting such proof with a set of burning factors together the sender verification key vk^{S_1}.

The knowledge soundness property of π, in conjunction with the validity requirement that no sender verification key can be re-used across the tokens (checked by the honest users during the Token Validation phase through the algorithm IsValid) and by the computational binding property of the committed verification keys (burning factors), ensures that no adversary can create a new token from scratch or double-spend an already owned one. The zero-knowledge property of π, coupled with the hiding property of the committed verification keys, avoids the disclosure of the burning factors embedding the sender verification key of the token, ensuring privacy. Formal details are provided in the next section.

Efficiency Improvements. In terms of communication complexity, notice that each user has to download each token posted on the bulletin board and keep a set of indices related to valid tokens. In practice, each user has to download $O(\#\mathsf{tokens})$ tokens and keep them in storage $O(\#\mathsf{tokens})$ indexes to keep track of the validity of such tokens.

Other than the communication burden, we notice a computational burden. Indeed, each player has to verify a NIZK-PoK each time a new token is posted, and when spending, a NIZK-PoK proof must be generated. However, an external party might take all the NIZK-PoKs posted until that moment and produce a succinct aggregated proof that can be verified faster than verifying every single proof (for aggregation, see, for example, [10]). This incurs both communication and computational savings for each user.

Regarding the problem of generating a NIZK-PoK each time a token must be spent, we notice that several privacy-preserving proof outsourcing mechanisms have been developed, e.g. [11].

Regarding the potentially huge size of the token set in the bulletin board, we notice that it is possible to use common verifiable computation techniques, such as recursive snarks on hashed data, to make the user download just a succinct representation of data together with a proof certifying its correctness. This idea has been adopted in the context of blockchain protocols by MINA [7].

Besides our protocol being inspired by [13], our technique diverges from that work due to our use of ZK proofs to guarantee stronger security properties. Rather than initialising the blind signature scheme, the consumer first requests the identity of a spent token, which the consumer then uses to create a burning factor (a commitment β) to a new token and a signature linking that commitment to the spent token (F). The consumer sends F and β to the bank, which writes them to the bulletin board and provides evidence to the consumer that this is done. The consumer optionally sends vk^{R_1} and σ^{S_1} to the merchant, which enables the merchant to verify the validity of the token in ZK (by looking at the bulletin board), avoiding the risk that the minting plate will have been consumed following the creation of invalid tokens by minters.

4 Security Analysis

In the following, we introduce the main security properties we require and show that they are satisfied by the system.

Token Integrity. We divide the token integrity requirement into two main properties, *token forgery* and *balance invariance*.

Definition 1 (Token Forgery). *Given our system and users $\mathcal{U}$, the game consists of an interaction between an adversary A and a challenger $\mathcal{C}$ with access to an oracle $\mathcal{O}$ that simulates honest parties in the system. The game proceeds as follows:*

1. *$\mathcal{C}$ initializes the system with the security parameter λ, instantiates all the necessary configuration values, such as the CRS of the NIZK proof of knowledge system and initializes the oracle $\mathcal{O}$ creating tokens and controlling honest parties.*
2. *A communicates to the challenger a subset of users $\mathcal{I} \subset \mathcal{U}$ he wishes to corrupt and tells $\mathcal{O}$ how many tokens must be assigned to each user in $\mathcal{U}$.*
3. *$\mathcal{O}$ sends to A the secrets related to the tokens meant for users in $\mathcal{I}$.*
4. *A can receive tokens from the parties controlled by $\mathcal{O}$ and transfer tokens[1] to parties controlled by $\mathcal{O}$. Furthermore, A can ask the oracle to transfer tokens between parties controlled by $\mathcal{O}$. All token transferred from an interaction with $\mathcal{C}$ are inserted into a query set $\mathcal{Q}$.*
5. *A wins the game if he can create a token not existing in $\mathcal{Q}$ accepted by $\mathcal{O}$, in which A does not control the sender nor recipient, or A controls the recipient, but not the sender.*

Claim 1 (Token Unforgeability). *No PPT A without access to the extraction trapdoor of the zero-knowledge proof system can win the token forgery game with non-negligible probability w.r.t. protocol π_{DC}. (For proof of this claim, refer to the full version).*

---
[1] We recall that, in our protocol, transferring is done by creating a fresh token and burning and old one in a verifiable and private fashion.

Claim 2 (Balance Invariance). *No PPT A without access to the simulation trapdoor of the zero-knowledge the proof system can create a token that increases the available funds in the system, i.e., each freshly created token must be bound to exactly one burnt token.*

Proof. Balance invariance follows straightforwardly from token unforgeability. Indeed, no adversary is eable to modify the overall balance of the system, initially fixed by the central bank through the distribution of the genesis tokens.

Token Privacy. To ensure token privacy, we require a token indistinguishability property, defined below.

Definition 2 (Token Indistinguishability). *Given our system and users $\mathcal{U}$, the game consists of an interaction between an adversary A and a challenger $\mathcal{C}$ with access to an oracle $\mathcal{O}$ that simulates honest parties in the system. The game proceeds as follows:*

1. *$\mathcal{C}$ initializes the system with the security parameter λ. $\mathcal{C}$ instantiates all used primitives, such as the signature schemes or the NIZK proof-of-knowledge system. $\mathcal{C}$ further initializes the oracle $\mathcal{O}$ creating assets and managing token exchange with and between honest parties.*
2. *A communicates to the challenger a subset of users $\mathcal{I} \subset \mathcal{U}$ he wishes to corrupt and tells $\mathcal{O}$ how many tokens must be assigned to each user in $\mathcal{U}$.*
3. *$\mathcal{O}$ sends to A the secrets related to the tokens meant for users in $\mathcal{I}$. A can ask to receive tokens from the parties controlled by $\mathcal{O}$ tokens[2] to parties controlled by $\mathcal{O}$ (using their secrets). Furthermore, A can ask the oracle to transfer tokens between honest parties controlled by $\mathcal{O}$ using two oracles $\mathcal{O}_1$ and $\mathcal{O}_2$. The adversary shall produce, through interaction with such oracles, two different valid payment traces of the same size where only token transfers between honest players can differ.*
   This operation is done statically, i.e. the adversary determines all the token transfers in a single query, i.e. a single shot interaction with $\mathcal{O}, \mathcal{O}_1$ and $\mathcal{O}_2$.
4. *$\mathcal{C}$ chooses a bit $b \leftarrow_\$ \{0,1\}$ and sends the payment trace (the set of token transfers) produced by $\mathcal{O}$ and $\mathcal{O}_b$ to A.*
5. *A outputs a bit b' and wins the game if $b = b'$.*

Claim 3 (Token Indistinguishability). *No PPT A without access to the trapdoor can win the token indistinguishability game w.r.t. protocol π_{DC} with non-negligible probability. (For proof of this claim, refer to the full version).*

Transaction Independence. We further introduce another property, which we call *transaction independence*, stating that, if an adversary corrupts an honest user U during the system execution, cannot learn more than the information corresponding to received tokens the user has not spent. This implies that the payment history of the user is kept secret even if the user is corrupted.

---

[2] We recall that, in our protocol, transferring is done by creating a fresh token and burning and old one in a verifiable and private fashion.

Claim 4. *No PPT adversary* A *without knowledge of the trapdoor can break transaction independence of* π_{DC}.

Proof. In our protocol π_{DC}, transaction independence is satisfied since each user, after burning a received token, keeps in their storage the signing key of the corresponding receiver verification key R_0, the commitment opening values (vk^{S_1}, r) and the secret sk^{S_1}. After spending the token, the user does not need to hold such values, which can be safely eliminated from their local storage.

Theorem 1. *Let* SIG *be a Signature Scheme and* NIZK *be a NIZK-PoK for the relation* $\mathcal{R}$ *defined above. Then,* π_{DC} *satisfies transaction unforgeability, balance invariance, transaction privacy and transaction independence. (The proof follows by combining Claim 1 to Claim 4.)*

5 Conclusions and Future Directions

We proposed a novel protocol allowing private electronic payments with self-custody and zero-knowledge verified assurance. Our protocol ensures consumer privacy, compatibility with regulatory objectives, independent transactions in the sense that secrets related to a specific transaction do not leak any information about the sender or receiver transaction history, and no involvement of the issuer in the circulation of tokens. The issuer (central bank) is further stateless in the sense that after the issuer distributes the public values connected with the secret it had locally generated, the issuer can eliminate such secrets and disappear from the equation.

In terms of efficiency guarantees, re-issuance of tokens can be performed in an efficient manner, as well as for proof generation. The bulletin board size, as well as the communication complexity and the storage consumption of the users, might be prohibitive with the system growing. As pointed out, proof aggregation and verifiable computation techniques, coupled with the aid of external parties whose task is to produce computationally intensive recursive proofs, could help solve the issue.

As future work, we aim to provide a second protocol with weaker but reasonable security guarantees about the validity of assets, with enhanced efficiency that maintains a simple design and relies on simple cryptographic objects, such as blind signatures, but relaxing the requirement for all end-user devices to produce and verify zero-knowledge proofs. We envision that this protocol would be useful for some payment scenarios for which ZKP verification would be impractical. In particular, we would rely on an external semi-trusted entity, a minter, taking the burden of minting new tokens. Since such minters might be corrupted, we would employ a fail-safe mechanism based on a mixture of zero-knowledge proofs and a law-enforced auditing mechanism to pinpoint and kick out dishonest miners from the system. This would be accompanied by a mechanism accounting for eventual currency loss due to the minter's misbehaviour. We discuss this protocol idea in Appendix B.

Acknowledgements. The authors acknowledge project SERICS (PE00000014) under the MUR National Recovery and Resilience Plan funded by the European Union – NextGenerationEU. The authors would like to thank Professor Tomaso Aste for his continued support of this work, as well as Ching Yeung Fung for providing feasibility testing. The authors also acknowledge the UCL Future of Money Initiative and the Systemic Risk Centre at the London School of Economics.

A Useful Tools

Throughout this paper, we use the abbreviation PPT to denote probabilistic polynomial time. Given a PPT algorithm A, let $\mathsf{A}(x)$ be the probability distribution of the output of A when run with x as input. We use $\mathsf{A}(x; r)$, instead, to denote the output of A when run on input x and coin tosses r. We denote with $\lambda \in \mathbb{N}$ the security parameter and with $\mathsf{poly}(\cdot)$ an arbitrary positive polynomial. Every algorithm takes as input the security parameter λ (in unary, i.e. 1^λ). When an algorithm takes more than one input, 1^λ is omitted. We say that a function $\nu : \mathbb{N} \to \mathbb{R}$ is negligible in the security parameter $\lambda \in \mathbb{N}$ if it vanishes faster than the inverse of any polynomial in λ, i.e. $\nu(\lambda) < \frac{1}{\mathsf{poly}(\lambda)}$ for all positive polynomials $\mathsf{poly}(\lambda)$.

We use $\leftarrow$ when the variable on the left side is assigned with the output value of the algorithm on the right side. Similarly, when using $\leftarrow_\$$, we mean that the variable on the left side is assigned a value sampled randomly according to the distribution on the right side.

A *polynomial-time* relation $\mathcal{R}$ is a relation for which membership of (x, w) in $\mathcal{R}$ can be decided in time polynomial in $|x|$. If $(x, w) \in \mathcal{R}$, then we say that w is a *witness* for the *instance* x. A polynomial-time relation $\mathcal{R}$ is naturally associated with

A distribution ensemble $\{X(\lambda)\}_{\lambda \in \mathbb{N}}$ is an infinite sequence of probability distributions, where a distribution $X(\lambda)$ is associated with each value of $\lambda \in \mathbb{N}$. We say that two distribution ensembles $\{X(\lambda)\}_{\lambda \in \mathbb{N}}$ and $\{Y(\lambda)\}_{\lambda \in \mathbb{N}}$ are *computationally indistinguishable* if for every PPT distinguisher D, there exists a negligible function ν such that:

$$\Pr\left[\mathsf{D}(1^\lambda, X(\lambda)) = 1\right] - \Pr\left[\mathsf{D}(1^\lambda, Y(\lambda)) = 1\right] \leq \nu(\lambda).$$

$\{X(\lambda)\}_{\lambda \in \mathbb{N}}$ and $\{Y(\lambda)\}_{\lambda \in \mathbb{N}}$ are statistically indistinguishable if the above holds for computationally unbounded D. We use $\approx_c$ and $\approx_s$ to denote that two distributions ensembles are respectively computationally and statistically indistinguishable, $\equiv$ to denote that two distribution ensembles are identical.

A.1 Non-interactive Commitments

A non-interactive commitment is a PPT algorithm Com taking as input a message $m \in \{0,1\}^k$ and outputting a value $\gamma = \mathsf{Com}(m; r) \in \{0,1\}^l$ where $r \in \{0,1\}^\lambda$ is the randomness used to generate the commitment. The pair (m, r) is also called the *opening*. A non-interactive commitment typically satisfies two properties known as binding and hiding; we review these properties (in the flavor we need them) below.

Definition 3 (Computational binding). *We say that* Com *satisfies computational binding if, for all PPT adversary* A, *it holds that*

$$\Pr\left[\mathsf{Com}(m_0; r_0) = \mathsf{Com}(m_1,; r_1) \mid (m_0, m_1, r_0, r_1) \leftarrow_{\$} \mathsf{A}(1^\lambda)\right] \leq \mathsf{negl}(\lambda)$$

Definition 4 (Statistical hiding). *We say that* Com *satisfies statistical hiding if for all pairs of message* $m_0, m_1 \in \{0,1\}^k$, *it holds that* $\{\mathsf{Com}(1^\lambda, m_0)\}_{\lambda \in \mathbb{N}} \approx_s \{\mathsf{Com}(1^\lambda, m_1)\}_{\lambda \in \mathbb{N}}$.

A.2 Non-interactive Zero-Knowledge Proof-of-Knowledge

In the following, we introduce our NIZK-PoK definition[3]. A non-interactive proof system NIZK is composed of a tuple of algorithms described as follows:

Setup($\mathcal{R}$): On input the NP-relation $\mathcal{R}$ returns a common reference string crs and a trapdoor td.

Prove(crs, x, w): Take as input the crs, a statement x and a witness w such that $(x, w) \in \mathcal{R}$ and returns a proof π.

Vrfy(crs, x, π): Takes as input the crs, a statement x and a proof π. Output 1 if π is an accepting proof with respect to the statement x and relation $\mathcal{R}$, 0 otherwise.

Definition 5 (Non-Interactive Zero-knowledge Proof-of-Knowledge). *Let $\mathcal{R}$ be an NP-relation. A non-interactive proof system* NIZK = (Setup, Prove, Vrfy) *is a NIZK-PoK for the relation $\mathcal{R}$ if it satisfies completeness, knowledge soundness and statistical zero-knowledge. The properties follow.*

- **Completeness** *For each $(x, w) \in \mathcal{R}$, we have that*

$$\Pr\left[\mathsf{Vrfy}(x, w, \pi) = 1 \,\middle|\, \begin{array}{l} (\mathsf{crs}, \mathsf{td}) \leftarrow_{\$} \mathsf{Setup}(\mathcal{R}); \\ \pi \leftarrow_{\$} \mathsf{Prove}(\mathsf{crs}, x, w) \end{array}\right] = 1$$

- **Knowledge Soundness** *For all PPT* A *there exists an extractor* Ext_A *such that,*

$$\Pr\left[\begin{array}{l} \mathsf{Vrfy}(x, \pi) = 1 \wedge \\ (x, w) \notin \mathcal{R} \end{array} \,\middle|\, \begin{array}{l} (\mathsf{crs}, \mathsf{td}) \leftarrow_{\$} \mathsf{Setup}(\mathcal{R}); \\ ((x, \pi); w) \leftarrow_{\$} \mathsf{A} || \mathsf{Ext}_\mathsf{A}(\mathsf{crs}) \end{array}\right] \leq \mathsf{negl}(\lambda).$$

---

[3] Since knowledge soundness is defined with a PPT adversary, it should be referred as be Argument-of-Knowledge. Throughout this paper, we keep using the term Proof in place of Argument.

- **Statistical Zero-Knowledge** *There exists a simulator* S *such that for all* $(x, w) \in \mathcal{R}$ *and for all PPT* A,

$$\left\{ \pi \leftarrow_\$ \mathsf{Prove}(\mathsf{crs}, x, w) : (\mathsf{crs}, \mathsf{td}) \leftarrow_\$ \mathsf{Setup}(\mathcal{R}) \right\} \approx_s$$
$$\left\{ \pi \leftarrow_\$ \mathsf{S}(\mathsf{crs}, \mathsf{td}, x) : (\mathsf{crs}, \mathsf{td}) \leftarrow_\$ \mathsf{Setup}(\mathcal{R}) \right\}$$

Since, for communication efficiency reasons, we aim for short proofs, we further introduce the *succintness* property. Succint NIZK-PoKs are called zero-knowledge Succint Non-Interactive Arguments-of-Knowledge (zk-SNARKs).

Definition 6 (zk-SNARKs). *Let* NIZK *be a NIZK-PoK for a relation* $\mathcal{R}$. *We say that* NIZK *is a zk-SNARK if it further satisfies succintness, gureanteeing that for any* $(x, w) \in \mathcal{R}$, *given* π *be the output of* $\mathsf{Prove}(x, w)$, *we have that* $|\pi| = \mathsf{poly}(\lambda)$ *and the verifier, on input* x *and* π, *runs in* $\mathsf{poly}(\lambda + |x|)$.

A.3 Signatures

A signature scheme is a tuple of algorithms $\Pi = (\mathsf{KGen}, \mathsf{Sign}, \mathsf{Vrfy})$ with message space $\mathcal{M}$, described as follows:

$\mathsf{KGen}(1^\lambda)$: On input the security parameter, outputs a verification key/signing key pair $(\mathsf{vk}, \mathsf{sk})$.

$\mathsf{Sign}(\mathsf{sk}, m)$: On input a signing key sk and a message $m \in \mathcal{M}$, outputs a signature σ.

$\mathsf{Vrfy}(\mathsf{vk}, m, \sigma)$: On input a verification key vk and a message $m \in \mathcal{M}$, outputs 1 if the signature verifies, and 0 otherwise.

Definition 7 (Correctness). *A signature scheme* Π *is correct if, for all* $m \in \mathcal{M}$, $\Pr[\mathsf{Vrfy}(\mathsf{vk}, m, \mathsf{Sign}(\mathsf{sk}, m)) = 1]$, *where* $(\mathsf{vk}, \mathsf{sk}) \leftarrow_\$ \mathsf{KGen}(1^\lambda)$

Definition 8 (EUF-CMA). *A signature scheme* Π *is existentially unforgeable under chosen message attacks if, for all PPT* A,

$$\Pr\left[\begin{matrix} \mathsf{Vrfy}(\mathsf{vk}, m, \sigma) = 1 \wedge \\ m \text{ is fresh} \end{matrix} \,\middle|\, \begin{matrix} (\mathsf{vk}, \mathsf{sk}) \leftarrow_\$ \mathsf{KGen}(1^\lambda); \\ (m, \sigma) \leftarrow_\$ \mathsf{A}^{\mathsf{Sign}(\mathsf{sk}, \cdot)}(\mathsf{vk}) \end{matrix} \right] \leq \mathsf{negl}(\lambda).$$

By "fresh", we mean that it was never queried to the $\mathsf{Sign}(\mathsf{sk}, \cdot)$ oracle by A.

A.4 Blind Signatures

A blind signature is composed of a tuple of algorithms BS = (Gen, Sig, BlindSign, Blind, Unblind, Vrfy) described as follows:

Gen(1^λ): The key generation algorithm take as input the security parameter 1^λ, and outputs a pair of signing and verification key (vk, sk).
Blind(m): The blinding algorithm takes as input a message m and outputs a blinded message β together with its blinding factor r.
BlindSign(sk, β): The signature algorithm takes as input a blinded message β, a signing key sk, and outputs a blind signature $\tilde{\sigma}$.
Sig(sk, β): The signature algorithm takes as input a message m, a signing key sk, and outputs a signature σ.
Unblind($\beta, \tilde{\sigma}, r$): The unblinding algorithm, on input a blinded message, a signature on the blinded message $\tilde{\sigma}$, and a blinding factor r, outputs the signature σ on the unblinded message m.
Vrfy(vk, m, σ) : The verification algorithm outputs 1 if σ is a correct signature of m upon verification key vk, 0 otherwise.

Definition 9 (Correctness). *A signature scheme* BS *is correct if*

$$\Pr\left[\mathsf{Vrfy}(\mathsf{vk}, m, \sigma) = 1 \;\middle|\; \begin{array}{l} (\mathsf{vk}, \mathsf{sk}) \leftarrow_{\$} \mathsf{Gen}(1^\lambda); \\ (\beta, \tau) \leftarrow_{\$} \mathsf{Blind}(m), \\ \tilde{\sigma} \leftarrow_{\$} \mathsf{BlindSign}(\mathsf{sk}, \beta); \\ \sigma = \mathsf{Unblind}(\tilde{\sigma}, \tau) \end{array}\right] = 1$$

Security of Blind Signature is defined w.r. Existential Unforgeability w.r.t Blinded Messages and Blindness

Definition 10 (Existential Unforgeability w.r.t Blinded Messages). *A blind signature scheme* BS *is Existentially Unforgeable w.r.t Blinded Messages, if for all PPT* A,

$$\Pr\left[\mathbf{Exp}^{\mathsf{bEUF\text{-}CMA}}_{\mathsf{BS},\mathsf{A}}(\lambda)\right] \leq \mathsf{negl}(\lambda),$$

where the challenger of $\mathbf{Exp}^{\mathsf{bEUF\text{-}CMA}}_{\mathsf{BS},\mathsf{A}}(\lambda)$ *behave as follows:*

Setup phase: *Generate* $(\mathsf{vk}^*, \mathsf{sk}^*) \leftarrow \mathsf{Gen}(1^\lambda)$. *Then, initialize a query counter* $\mathsf{q} = 0$.
Query phase: *When receiving a blinded value β from* A, *invoke* $\tilde{\sigma} \leftarrow_{\$} \mathsf{BlindSign}(\mathsf{sk}^*, \beta)$ *and update* $\mathsf{q} \leftarrow \mathsf{q} + 1$. *Then, send σ to* A.
Challenge phase: *When receiving $\{(m_i, \sigma_i)\}_{i \in [\mathsf{q}+1]}$ from* A, *check that* $\mathsf{Vrfy}(\mathsf{vk}^*, m_i, \sigma_i) = 1$ *for each* $i \in [\mathsf{q} + 1]$ *and that* $m_i \neq m_j$ *for each* i, j *with* $i \neq j$. *If the checks pass, output 1. Else, output 0.*

Definition 11 (Blindness). *A blind signature scheme* BS *enjoys blindness if, for all PPT adversary* $\mathsf{A} = (\mathsf{A}_0, \mathsf{A}_1)$,

$$\Pr\left[b = b^* \;\middle|\; \begin{array}{c} (m_0, m_1) \leftarrow_{\$} \mathsf{A}_0(1^\lambda); \\ b^* \leftarrow_{\$} \{0,1\}; \\ (\beta, \tau) \leftarrow_{\$} \mathsf{Blind}(m_b); \\ b \leftarrow_{\$} \mathsf{A}_1(m_0, m_1, \beta). \end{array} \right] \leq \frac{1}{2} + \mathsf{negl}(\lambda).$$

B A Faster Accountability-Based Alternative

As already pointed out, if we do not want to rely on parties with enhanced computing capabilities to calculate our recursive zk-SNARKS, we require that all the players must take into their memory the entire set of tokens to verify the ZK proofs attached to the token transfer. Other than the memory requirement, the computational burden is problematic too. Indeed, each time a new proof appears, it must be verified by each wannabe receiver.

In the following, we propose an alternative version of our protocol where a new semi-trusted party, which we call *minter*, takes the burden of validating new tokens, hence eliminating the need of providing a NIZK-PoK each time a new transaction is done. When a minter misbehavior is observed, the central bank could kick out the minter from the system and execute a fail-safe mechanism. Here, we admit the usage NIZK-PoKs from the sender who transferred tokens through the corrupted minter to reduce the number of tokens that are going to be discarded during the fail-safe mechanism.

Our Minter-Aided Protocol. Differently from our main protocol π_{DC}, the tokens generated as an outcome of a new transaction are not validated directly by the sender through a NIZK-PoK but by a new entity called minter, whose aim is to "mint" these coins via a blind signature of the sender verification key. By introducing the minter in the system, we need to relax the security requirements. We now require full token privacy (as in Sect. 4) together with a relaxed token integrity property, which we call minter accountability, stating that when a minter creates a new token from scratch or double-spends an existing token, they will be eventually spotted. The protocol works as follows:

Setup: During setup, each minter T generates a pair $(\mathsf{vk}^T, \mathsf{sk}^T)$ send sends vk^T to CB, to be posted by the latter into BB.
Burning: As in π_{DC} the receiver $R_0 = S_1$ of a token $F^{S_0, R_0} = (\mathsf{vk}^{S_0}, \mathsf{vk}^{R_0}, \sigma^{S_0}, \sigma^{T_0})$ burns F^{S_0, R_0} by adding to it a burning factor β. Such a factor is computed by the sender with the Blind algorithm of BS, i.e. $\beta = \mathsf{Blind}(\mathsf{vk}^{S_1}; r)$, where $(\mathsf{vk}^{S_1}, \mathsf{sk}^{S_1}) \leftarrow_{\$} \mathsf{BS.KGen}(\lambda)$.
Spending: Differently from to π_{DC}, the sender S_1, upon receiving vk^{R_1} from R_1, blindly ask for a signature of the message (vk^{R_1}) to a minter T, obtaining σ^T. More precisely, the interaction between S_1 and T works as follows:
  – S_1 sends β to T.

- T computes $\tilde{\sigma} \leftarrow\!\!\!_\$ \mathsf{BS.BlindSign}(\mathsf{sk}^T, \beta)$ and sends $\tilde{\sigma}$ to S_1.
- S_1 computes $\sigma^T = \mathsf{Unblind}(\beta, \tilde{\sigma}, r)$.

Finally, S_1 signs vk^{R_1} with sk^{S_1} obtaining σ^{S_1}, i.e. $\sigma^{S_1} \leftarrow\!\!\!_\$ \mathsf{SIG.Sign}(\mathsf{sk}^{S_1}, \mathsf{vk}^{R_1})$ and sends a new live token $F^{S_1, R_1} = (\mathsf{vk}^{S_1}, \mathsf{vk}^{R_1}, \sigma^{S_1}, \sigma^T)$ to BB.

Since $\mathsf{BS.Vrfy}(\mathsf{vk}^T, \mathsf{vk}^{R_1}, \sigma^T) = 1$ and $\mathsf{SIG.Vrfy}(\mathsf{vk}^{S_1}, \mathsf{vk}^{R_1}, \sigma^{S_1}) = 1$, the token is authorized by the sender (because of σ^{S_1}) and minted by T (because of σ^T).

Tokens generated from the same chain of payment (initially started from a Genesis token released by the central bank as in π_{DC}) are always minted the same minter. It means that when an old token is burned in favor of a new token, the minter signing the new token should be the same one who signed the burnt one. We may alternatively consider a scenario in which a different minter can mint a token of a different chain of payment via a pre-determined agreement between the two minters. A token generated by a different minter without an agreement beforehand is considered invalid.

The blindness of BS guarantees token privacy of the protocol. We will now briefly discuss our fail-safe mechanism to ensure minter accountability.

Accountability Mechanism Against Minters Corruption. All the minters have a fixed amount of tokens that are allowed to mint (i.e., sign blindly).

When the minter burns all of their allocated mints (i.e., minter signatures), the central bank validates a new minting key provided by the minter and allows the latter to restart minting.

If the minter mints more than expected, it will be flagged as corrupted by the users/central bank, and all the tokens minted by the corrupted minter will be flagged as forged.

If an honest user wants to keep their minted token, they can produce a NIZK-PoK for the relation $\mathcal{R}_{\mathsf{DC}}^{\mathsf{Blind}}$ showing that their verification key was blinded (through Blind instead of Commit) inside a burning factor of a live valid token. Here, the token validity predicate further checks that the token is not flagged as forged. Alternatively, an honest user not caring about token privacy can directly open the burning factor β connected to a burnt token by releasing the random factor provided during the blinding procedure.

Notice that such a NIZK-PoK could be generated, when interacting with an honest minter, by users who choose to do so. This NIZK-PoK can then be furnished to recipients, who can in turn provide added value to minters by sharing it as evidence that can be used to programmatically allow the minter to mint extra tokens without immediately asking the central bank for a new minting key.

References

1. Androulaki, E., Camenisch, J., De Caro, A., Dubovitskaya, M., Elkhiyaoui, K., Tackmann, B.: Privacy-preserving auditable token payments in a permissioned blockchain system. In: AFT '20: 2nd ACM Conference on Advances in Financial Technologies, New York, NY, USA, October 21-23, 2020, pp. 255–267. ACM (2020)

2. Attema, T., Cramer, R., Fehr, S.: Compressing proofs of k-out-of-n partial knowledge. In: Malkin, T., Peikert, C. (eds.) CRYPTO 2021. LNCS, vol. 12828, pp. 65–91. Springer, Cham (2021). https://doi.org/10.1007/978-3-030-84259-8_3
3. Ben-Sasson, E., et al.: Zerocash: decentralized anonymous payments from bitcoin. In: 2014 IEEE Symposium on Security and Privacy, SP 2014, Berkeley, CA, USA, May 18-21, 2014, pp. 459–474. IEEE Computer Society (2014)
4. Bitansky, N., Chiesa, A., Ishai, Y., Paneth, O., Ostrovsky, R.: Succinct non-interactive arguments via linear interactive proofs. In: Sahai, A. (ed.) TCC 2013. LNCS, vol. 7785, pp. 315–333. Springer, Heidelberg (2013). https://doi.org/10.1007/978-3-642-36594-2_18
5. Chaum, D.: Blind signatures for untraceable payments. In: Chaum, D., Rivest, R.L., Sherman, A.T. (eds.) Advances in Cryptology: Proceedings of CRYPTO '82, Santa Barbara, California, USA (1982), pp. 199–203. Plenum Press, New York (1982)
6. Dogan, A., Bicakci, K.: KAIME: central bank digital currency with realistic and modular privacy. In: Lenzini, G., Mori, P., Furnell, S. (eds.) Proceedings of the 10th International Conference on Information Systems Security and Privacy, ICISSP 2024, Rome, Italy, pp. 672–681. SCITEPRESS (2024)
7. MINA Foundation. Mina protocol. https://minaprotocol.com/
8. Monero Foundation. Monero protocol. https://www.getmonero.org/
9. ZCash Foundation. Zcash protocol. https://z.cash/
10. Gailly, N., Maller, M., Nitulescu, A.: SnarkPack: practical SNARK aggregation. In: Eyal, I., Garay, J.A., (eds.) Financial Cryptography and Data Security - 26th International Conference, FC 2022, Grenada, May 2-6, 2022, Revised Selected Papers, volume 13411 of Lecture Notes in Computer Science, pp. 203–229. Springer (2022)
11. Garg, S., Goel, A., Jain, A., Policharla, G.-V., Sekar, S.: zkSaaS: zero-knowledge snarks as a service. In: Calandrino, J.A., Troncoso, C. (eds.) 32nd USENIX Security Symposium, USENIX Security 2023, Anaheim, CA, USA, August 9-11, 2023, pp. 4427–4444. USENIX Association (2023)
12. Goel, A., Green, M., Hall-Andersen, M., Kaptchuk, G.: Stacking sigmas: a framework to compose ς-protocols for disjunctions. In: Dunkelman, O., Dziembowski, S. (eds.) Advances in Cryptology - EUROCRYPT 2022 - 41st Annual International Conference on the Theory and Applications of Cryptographic Techniques, Trondheim, Norway, May 30 - June 3, 2022, Proceedings, Part II, volume 13276 of Lecture Notes in Computer Science, pp. 458–487. Springer (2022)
13. Goodell, G., Toliver, D.R., Al-Nakib, H.D.: A scalable architecture for electronic payments. In: Matsuo, S., et al. (eds.) Financial Cryptography and Data Security. FC 2022 International Workshops - CoDecFin, DeFi, Voting, WTSC, Grenada, May 6, 2022, Revised Selected Papers, volume 13412 of Lecture Notes in Computer Science, pp. 645–678. Springer (2022)
14. Groth, J.: On the size of pairing-based non-interactive arguments. In: Fischlin, M., Coron, J.-S. (eds.) EUROCRYPT 2016. LNCS, vol. 9666, pp. 305–326. Springer, Heidelberg (2016). https://doi.org/10.1007/978-3-662-49896-5_11
15. Kiayias, A., Kohlweiss, M., Sarencheh, A.: PEReDi: privacy-enhanced, regulated and distributed central bank digital currencies. In: Yin, H., Stavrou, A., Cremers, C., Shi, E. (eds.) Proceedings of the 2022 ACM SIGSAC Conference on Computer and Communications Security, CCS 2022, Los Angeles, CA, USA, November 7-11, 2022, pp. 1739–1752. ACM (2022)
16. Pedersen, T.P.: Non-interactive and information-theoretic secure verifiable secret sharing. In: Feigenbaum, J. (ed.) Advances in Cryptology - CRYPTO '91, 11th

Annual International Cryptology Conference, Santa Barbara, California, USA, August 11-15, 1991, Proceedings, volume 576 of Lecture Notes in Computer Science, pp. 129–140. Springer (1991)

17. Tomescu, A., et al.: UTT: decentralized Ecash with accountable privacy. IACR Cryptol. ePrint Arch., p. 452 (2022)
18. Nicolas van Saberhagen. Cryptonote v2. https://github.com/monero-project/research-lab/blob/master/whitepaper/whitepaper.pdf
19. Wüst, K., Kostiainen, K., Čapkun, V., Čapkun, S.: PRCash: fast, private and regulated transactions for digital currencies. In: Goldberg, I., Moore, T. (eds.) FC 2019. LNCS, vol. 11598, pp. 158–178. Springer, Cham (2019). https://doi.org/10.1007/978-3-030-32101-7_11
20. Wüst, K., Kostiainen, K., Delius, N., Capkun, S.: Platypus: a central bank digital currency with unlinkable transactions and privacy-preserving regulation. In: Yin, H., Stavrou, A., Cremers, C., Shi, E. (eds.) Proceedings of the 2022 ACM SIGSAC Conference on Computer and Communications Security, CCS 2022, Los Angeles, CA, USA, November 7-11, 2022, pp. 2947–2960. ACM (2022)

Rayls: A Novel Design for CBDCs

Mario Yaksetig[1](✉) and Jiayu Xu[2]

[1] Parfin, Cayman Islands, London, UK
mario.yaksetig@parfin.io
[2] Oregon State University, Corvallis, USA
xujiay@oregonstate.edu

Abstract. In this work, we introduce Rayls, a new central bank digital currency (CBDC) design that provides privacy, high performance, and regulatory compliance. In our construction, commercial banks each run their own (private) ledger and are connected to an underlying decentralized programmable blockchain via a relayer. We also introduce a novel protocol that allows for efficient anonymous transactions between banks, which we call Enygma. Our design is 'quantum-private' as a quantum adversary is not able to infer any information (i.e., payer, payee, amounts) about the transactions that take place in the network. We achieve high performance in cross-bank settlement via the use of ZK-SNARKs and 'double' batching. Concretely, our transactions consist of a set of commitments and a zero-knowledge proof. As a result, each transaction can pay more than 1 bank at once and, secondly, each of these individual commitments can contain aggregated transfers from multiple users. For example, bank A transfers $1M to a different bank B and that amount is actually a sum of multiple users making transfers to bank B. Commercial banks can then enforce regulatory rules locally within their ledgers. Our system is in production with one of the largest clearing houses in the world and is currently being explored in a CBDC pilot.

Keywords: CBDCs · Privacy · Blockchain

1 Introduction

A Central Bank Digital Currency (CBDC) is a novel form of digital money issued and regulated by national monetary authorities, constituting a sovereign digital representation of fiat currency. Unlike traditional cryptocurrencies, CBDCs are centralized in nature and maintain a one-to-one parity with their physical counterparts, thereby preserving the monetary policy transmission mechanisms. CBDCs can be implemented in two primary models: wholesale (restricted to financial institutions) or retail (accessible to the general public), each presenting distinct implications. The integration of CBDCs into existing financial systems promises enhanced payment efficiency, reduced transaction costs, and improved financial inclusion. This integration, however, typically raises critical questions regarding privacy, cyber security, and the potential side effects on the traditional banking infrastructure.

Presently, many nations are exploring designs for a CBDC. Finding the right balance, however, is a particularly hard problem. Concretely, a CBDC must be sovereign and controlled by a Central Bank (or an equivalent national monetary authority). A CBDC must also be private (at least similar privacy to cash). Simultaneously, this same CBDC must also be auditable to ensure that transactions are compliant with the law. Last, but not least, a CBDC must be performant to allow the citizens of a nation to transact. For example, the most popular commercial bank in India has over 500 million clients. There is no blockchain that can process this type of volume. This is the case for a single commercial bank. This problem gets even harder when at the scale of an entire nation. A possible approach is to use different layer-2 (L2) blockchains (or rollups) to scale an underlying layer-1 (L1) blockchain. This approach, however, comes with many limitations. First, there is a fragmentation of liquidity as traditional L2s each have their own contract and have their funds locked in different 'silos'. Second, there is no privacy if we assume a traditional L2 approach where a sequencer publishes all the transactions that take place in the clear on the underlying L1.

With these limitations mind, and the recent upcoming of central bank digital currencies (CBDCs), how can we expect these currencies to live on a blockchain? Additionally, when designing a currency, a monetary authority must think in decades. Therefore, it is imperative to take into account the possibility of a quantum-computer adversary into the design of such a currency.

1.1 Why Not a Public Blockchain?

Many critics often remark that a CBDC can simply be instantiated on a public blockchain similarly to stablecoins (e.g., USDT and USDC). We describe below why that is a wrong approach.

Scalability. Presently, no blockchain can process the number of transactions required to fulfill the needs of a nation transacting. Therefore, the underlying asset cannot simply be a traditional token living on a layer-1 (L1) blockchain.

Privacy. It is not reasonable to expect that a CBDC can live on a public blockchain and that all the transactions that take place in a nation are open and available for everyone to see.

Sovereignty. From a risk exposure perspective, launching a CBDC as a token on a layer-1 blockchain is not within acceptable parameters for a Central Bank. Concretely, a Central Bank cannot compromise the liveness of its currency to an external validator set of nodes. We highlight that this is a problem and that for periods of time, Ethereum saw elevated censorship rates [1]. Even though these numbers do not illustrate that the network completely censored a specific type of transaction, they show the risk for at least partial censorship, and in many cases a majority, which affects the throughput of that type of transactions. A Central Bank cannot accept this type of risk. This is one of the fundamental reasons why many banks launch their permissioned blockchain.

1.2 Performance of Existing Privacy Solutions

Existing privacy solutions tend to not perform well for a global setting (i.e., a population of a country). Traditionally, this is either due to the linear cost of producing zero knowledge proofs or due to a large transaction size. Often both. This is the problem that we solve in this work. Concretely, we provide the following (informal) anonymity: 'One of the financial institutions in this subset is making a transfer to at least another one in this set.' We note that, in our setting, a cross-chain transaction can be a financial institution settling balance with another and/or a client of a financial institution transferring funds to another institution., allowing us to provide both a wholesale CBDC and retail CBDC within our design. In effect, these cases are indistinguishable. The explanation for this indistinguishability is simple: both cases involve a debit of a balance and a credit in the same smart contract. The additional complexity of a retail CBDC transaction is 'hidden' inside the privacy ledger, which has a private state.

1.3 Our Contributions

In this work, we introduce a new CBDC solution that:

- is atomic
- is scalable
- is auditable
- is (quantum) private
- unifies liquidity from different institutions
- allows for compliance with existing regulation in a modular manner

We highlight that our design is not exclusive to CBDCs and can be extended, for example, to run on Ethereum layer-1 (L1) and allow for private transactions between L2s (i.e., Validium, Plasma [2]).

2 System Model

2.1 Overview

Our design is simple. First, we assume that the central bank operates a permissioned blockchain[1]. Moreover, each commercial bank runs their own privacy ledger (i.e., private blockchain). We assume that both components run an Ethereum Virtual Machine (EVM) blockchain and that the balances of each

---

[1] Our design can run on any EVM blockchain.

commercial bank are private. Each bank has a post-quantum key-pair, which is used to obtain shared secrets with all the other banks, which are then used to derive symmetric keys to encrypt transaction information. The core component is each financial institution run a tailored, single-node blockchain interconnected through a central regulatory authority's blockchain (commit chain) that acts as a protocol defining standard messaging service.

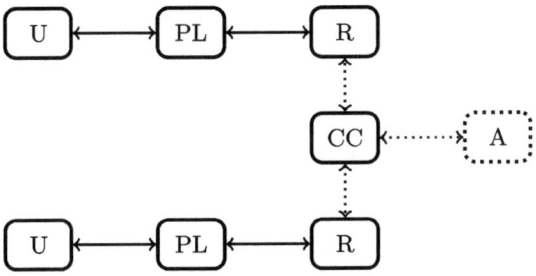

Fig. 1. System Architecture. Users bank with privacy ledgers controlled by the corresponding financial institution. Each privacy ledger uses a relayer to communicate with the commit chain. The commit chain is a layer-1 blockchain that runs smart contracts and also acts as a bulletin board. Optionally, we assume the existence of an auditor to monitor the transactions that take place.

2.2 System Architecture

In Fig. 1, we describe the basic architecture of Rayls. A commit Chain (CC) as the central component of the architecture, is a semi-public chain that is being administered by the central bank and can be validated by the public. Each Privacy Ledger (PL) represents an independent financial institution with its own private internal state.

Users (U) of financial institutions are directly connected to the respective Privacy Ledger of corresponding financial institution and have a wallet address on their corresponding privacy ledger.

Each privacy ledger has a wallet address and a balance per currency on the commit chain, representing its total internal balance. Privacy ledgers are connected to the Commit Chain (CC) through Relayers (R), which provide interoperability capabilities between PL and CC.

The Admin role (Central Bank) has special privileges. For instance, a central bank issues a private token on the commit chain and distributes the balance to each PL accordingly. It is through these balances that financial institutions transact between them and the users.

The commit chain guarantees integrity and regulations between privacy ledgers. This prevents double spending and minting more tokens out of thin air through universally verifiable zero-knowledge proofs. Therefore, the central authority can guarantee authenticity of the transactions.

2.3 Assumptions

We assume that the commit chain is a blockchain with a byzantine fault tolerant consensus. This commit chain runs a smart contract for the private transactions while also acting as a bulletin board for parties to publish encrypted information alongside the private transactions. This smart contract enforces a set of predefined rules embedded in the code. For example, a deterministic nullifier is checked when a transaction is submitted and a transaction is discarded if an entity attempts to submit two transactions for a specific time slot. We also assume that each privacy ledger has a quantum-secure key pair to be used for (post-quantum) key agreements in order to establish symmetric keys with each other. We assume the existence of a cryptographically secure hash function to ensure that nullifiers can be securely generated without the risk of collisions.

2.4 Adversarial Model

We assume an adversary $\mathcal{A}$ that wants to subvert the system. To successfully subvert the system, the adversary must be able to perform a double spend transaction, mint funds maliciously and successfully spend such funds, and/or break the privacy of the system. Breaking privacy implies inferring which parties are transacting with each other and/or the amounts of each transaction.

3 Our Design

In this paper, we propose two main approaches. First, the system architecture with the privacy ledgers. We call this Rayls. Second, we propose a new protocol for private transactions inspired in zkLedger [3]. We call this Enygma.

3.1 Formal Specification of User Algorithms

In this section we formally specify the user algorithms in the Enygma protocol. Our description largely follows the terminology in [4, Section 5], except that we add two additional algorithms: SetUp generates the shared secrets between honest parties via an Authenticated Key Exchange (AKE) protocol, and Verify allows parties to check if they have received funds (and if so, how much).

- SetUp(1^λ): Each party i runs $(\mathsf{sk}'_i, \mathsf{pk}'_i) \leftarrow \mathsf{KeyGen}(1^\lambda)$. Each pair of parties i, j runs the AKE protocol Π_{AKE} on inputs $(\mathsf{sk}'_i, \mathsf{pk}'_j)$ and $(\mathsf{sk}'_j, \mathsf{pk}'_i)$, respectively, resulting in shared secrets $s_{i,j} = s_{j,i}$. Party i stores $s_{i,j}$ for all $i \neq j$.
  Furthermore, each party computes and stores a table of (v, vG) for reasonable values v of funds. There are three possible ways to achieve this:
  • Each party computes the table locally;
  • One party computes and publishes the table, and every other party verifies a fraction of it;
  • Outsource the computation of the table.
- CreateAddress(1^λ): Run $(\mathsf{sk}, \mathsf{pk}) \leftarrow \mathsf{KeyGen}(1^\lambda)$. The output is $(\mathsf{sk}, \mathsf{pk})$.

- CreateTransferTx(sk_i, pk_j, AnonSet = $\{pk_1, \ldots, pk_n\}$, b_i, v):
  Let pk_i be the public key corresponding to sk_i; if $i, j \in [n]$ (i.e., $pk_i, pk_j \in$ AnonSet), proceed as follows:
  1. Obtain the latest block number block.
  2. For all $k \in [n] \setminus \{i\}$ (below we write it as $k \neq i$, i.e., we always assume that $k \in [n]$), calculate random factor $r_k := \mathcal{H}(s_{i,k}, \text{block}\#)$. Then define $r_i := -\sum_{k \neq i} r_k$.
  3. Generate commitments
  $$C_i := (-v)G + r_i H$$
  $$C_j := vG + r_j H$$
  $$C_k := r_k H \quad \text{for } k \neq i, j$$
  4. Generate a nullifier to ensure one transaction per bank per block: $nf := \mathcal{H}(sk_i, \text{block}\#)$.
  5. Generate the zero-knowledge proof π. There is a single zero-knowledge proof for the entire transaction. It proves the following:
     - I have enough funds to send in this transaction (i.e., $b_i \geq v$);
     - $(C_1, \ldots, C_n)$ are well-formed (i.e., the random factors $(r_1, \ldots, r_n)$ are well-formed AND I know the secret key sk_i for the slot being debited v amount AND v is credited to at least one of the commitments in this transaction);
     - The nullifier nf is well-formed (i.e., it is the result of a ZK-friendly hash using my secret key sk_i for this round and the block number: block#).
  6. For each $k \neq i$, calculate $r'_k := \mathcal{H}'(s_{i,k}, \text{block}\#)$. This allows each party to check if it has received funds.
  7. Output $tx_{trans} := (C_1, \ldots, C_n, nf, \pi, r'_k)$ (for $k \neq i$).
- Verify(sk_j, tx_{trans}):
  1. Obtain the latest block number block.
  2. For all $i \neq j$, check if there exists an r' in tx_{trans} such that $r' = \mathcal{H}'(s_{i,j}, \text{block}\#)$. If there is no such i, halt (I am not the receiver of this transaction). Otherwise I know party i has sent funds, and I might be the receiver.
  3. Compute $r_j := \mathcal{H}(s_{i,j}, \text{block}\#)$ and $V := C_j - r_j H$. Store (block#, r_j) (for the purpose of reading balance).
  4. If $V = 0G$, halt (I am not the receiver of this transaction). Otherwise find entry (v, V) in the pre-computed table, i.e., find v such that $V = vG$.
- ReadBalance(sk_j):
  1. Compute corresponding public key pk_j.
  2. Download from smart contract $C := \text{acc}[pk_j]$.
  3. For each (block, r_j) record stored in Verify, subtract $r_j H$ from C. Let B be the final result.
  4. Find b such that $B = bG$. Output b.

3.2 Formal Specification of the Smart Contract

The smart contract can process two types of transactions: fund and transfer.

- Fund(pk_i, b):
  If $acc[pk_i]$ is undefined then set $acc[pk_i] := b$, otherwise update $acc[pk_i] := acc[pk_i] + b$.
- Transfer(tx_{trans}) where $tx_{trans} = (C_1, \ldots, C_n, nf, \pi, r')$:
  1. Check if the commitments add up to zero: $C_1 + \cdots + C_n = 0$.
  2. Verify the zero-knowledge proof π.
  3. Tally the commitments: for $i = 1, \ldots, n$, update $acc[pk_i] := acc[pk_i] + C_i$.

4 Security Analysis

In this section we present the formal security definitions and proofs for the Enygma protocol. Our definitions largely follow [4, Appendix C].

4.1 Security Definitions

We assume an adversary $\mathcal{A}$ that has full visibility over all the transactions that happen in the network and runs a full node of the commit chain. To this end, we first define a basic version of the security game, which is played between a challenger, a smart contract, and the adversary $\mathcal{A}$. At the beginning of the game, the challenger runs SetUp(1^λ), generating the key pair, the shared secrets, and the discrete logarithm table for each party. After that, $\mathcal{A}$ can interact with the challenger and the smart contract in the following manner:

1. $\mathcal{A}$ can instruct the challenger to run any user algorithm in Sect. 3.1 and see the output (and the resulting transaction, if any, is sent to the smart contract), with the following exceptions:
   - $\mathcal{A}$ cannot instruct the challenger to run SetUp or Verify. (Note that the Verify algorithm requires knowledge of an honest party's secret key.)
   - If the algorithm is CreateAddress, $\mathcal{A}$ only sees the public key pk in the output, and not the secret key sk.
   - If the algorithm is CreateTransferTx, $\mathcal{A}$ specifies the sender's public key pk_i instead of its secret key sk_i.
2. $\mathcal{A}$ can directly send any transaction to the smart contract.
3. $\mathcal{A}$ can instruct the smart contract to process any number of pending transactions and update its state accordingly.

We now define and prove two security properties of the Enygma protocol, namely overdraft-safety and privacy.

Privacy. The privacy game is the same as the basic security game, except for the following: at some point, the adversary $\mathcal{A}$ sends two consistent instructions labeled 0 and 1 to the challenger; the challenger samples a bit $b \leftarrow \{0,1\}$ and executes the b-th instruction. At the end of the game, $\mathcal{A}$ outputs a bit b' as a guess for b. $\mathcal{A}$ succeeds if $b' = b$.

Two instructions are *consistent* if they refer to the same user algorithm, and

- If it is CreateTransferTx, then both instructions must have the same AnonSet field; furthermore, if either of the receivers is corrupt, then both instructions must have the same receiver and the same amount.
- If it is ReadBalance, then both instructions must return the same value.

We say a payment mechanism is *private* if for any PPT adversary $\mathcal{A}$, the probability that $\mathcal{A}$ succeeds in the privacy game is upper-bounded by $1/2 + \mathsf{negl}(\lambda)$.

Overdraft-Safety. The overdraft-safety game is exactly identical to the basic security game above, and the adversary $\mathcal{A}$ succeeds if at any point a ReadBalance instruction results in a negative value. We say a payment mechanism is *safe against overdrafts* if for any PPT adversary $\mathcal{A}$, the probability that $\mathcal{A}$ succeeds in the overdraft-safety game is at upper-bounded by $\mathsf{negl}(\lambda)$.

4.2 Security Proof

Privacy. Recall that in the privacy game, the adversary $\mathcal{A}$ must issue two consistent instructions at some point, and guess which one was executed. It is straightforward that two consistent instruction generate identical views unless they are CreateTransferTx; below we consider $\mathcal{A}$ sending two consistent CreateTransferTx instructions.

Let Query be the event that $\mathcal{A}$ queries $\mathcal{H}(s_{i,k}, \mathsf{block})$ for any i, k and block is the block number when $\mathcal{A}$ sends the two consistent instructions. By the security of the AKE protocol, $\Pr[\mathsf{Query}]$ is negligible. On the other hand, if Query does not occur, then $r_k = \mathcal{H}(s_{i,k}, \mathsf{block})$ is a uniformly random integer in $\mathbb{Z}_p$. with overwhelming probability $r_k = \mathcal{H}(s_{i,k}, \mathsf{block})$ is a uniformly random integer in $\mathbb{Z}_p$; that is, C_i and C_j are Pedersen commitments to $-v$ and v respectively (using independent randomnesses r_i and r_j). By the (perfectly) hiding property of Pedersen commitment, v is independent of C_i and C_j. Since v is not used anywhere other than C_i and C_j in CreateTransferTx, we know that v is independent of $\mathcal{A}$'s view.

Furthermore, for any v, $C_1, \ldots, C_n$ are independent uniformly random group elements, so they leak no information about i (the sender) or j (the receiver). For the remaining parts of $\mathcal{A}$'s view, nf and the r' values leak no information about i or j because $s_{i,k}$ is pseudoranrom in $\mathcal{A}$'s view, and π leaks no information about i or j due to the zero-knowledge property of the ZK scheme.

Overdraft-Safety. For any honest party i, let b_i be its balance, i.e., $b_i = \mathsf{ReadBalance}(\mathsf{sk}_i)$. We want to show that $b_i < 0$ with negligible probability at any time.

We first define an ideal protocol as follows: each b_i is initialized to 0, and

- For a $\mathsf{Fund}(\mathsf{pk}_i, v)$ algorithm, set $b_i := b_i + v$;
- For a $\mathsf{CreateTransferTx}(\mathsf{sk}_i, \mathsf{pk}_j, \mathsf{AnonSet}, b_i, v)$ algorithm, set $b_i := b_i - v$ and $b_j := b_j + v$.

Furthermore, only honest CreateTransferTx algorithms are processed, i.e., all transactions tx^* from the adversary $\mathcal{A}$ are ignored.

Obviously, the probability that $b_i < 0$ at some time is negligible in the ideal protocol, due to the soundness of the zero-knowledge proof (recall that in every transaction, the proof includes the statement $b_i \geq v$). We next show that for any i and at any time, the probability that b_i in the ideal protocol does not match b_i in Enygma is negligible. These two values differ only if $\mathcal{A}$ affects a transaction in one of the following ways:

- *Malicious spending*: $\mathcal{A}$ sends to the smart contract a transaction tx^* where the tuple of commitments $(C_1^*, \ldots, C_n^*)$ is different from all honest transactions, such that the zero-knowledge proof π^* verifies.
- *Double spending*: $\mathcal{A}$ passes to the smart contract an existing honest transaction tx for algorithm $\mathsf{CreateTransferTx}(\mathsf{sk}_i, \mathsf{pk}_j, \mathsf{AnonSet}, b_i, v)$, such that party i's new balance is not $b_i - v$ or party j's new balance is not $b_j + v$ (e.g., $\mathcal{A}$ makes party i send $2v$ amount of funds to party k).

We now show that $\mathcal{A}$ has negligible probability of successfully performing either of these two attacks. For malicious spending, let $\mathcal{A}$'s transaction tx^* be from party i. The zero-knowledge proof π^* verifies only if $(C_1'^*, \ldots, C_n^*)$ is well-formed; in particular, this means that the $r_1, \ldots, r_n$ factors within $C_1^*, \ldots, C_n^*$ are all well-formed, and $C_i^* = (-v)G + r_i H$ (because π^* contains a proof of the statement that its sender known sk_i). The only remaining case where $(C_1^*, \ldots, C_n^*)$ is well-formed is that $\mathcal{A}$ sees some honest transaction $(C_1, \ldots, C_n)$ from the same epoch, and replaces $(C_j, C_k) = (vG + r_j H, r_k H)$ with $(r_j H, vG + r_k H)$ (i.e., changes the intended receiver from j to k).[2] However, this attack is infeasible as v is hidden from $\mathcal{A}$ (due to privacy of the protocol).

For double spending, by the definition of Verify, $(C_1, \ldots, C_n)$ implies that party i sends v amount of funds to party j; therefore, the only possible attack without changing $(C_1, \ldots, C_n)$ is that $\mathcal{A}$ copies $(C_1, \ldots, C_n)$ from some honest transaction and sends it more than once. Since we assume that an honest user can only run CreateTransferTx once per epoch, the block number will change during these two transactions; say they are block and block*, where block is the block number of the honest transaction (so $\mathcal{A}$ sees $\mathsf{nl} = \mathcal{H}(r_i, \mathsf{block})$). As argued in privacy r_j is uniformly random in $\mathcal{A}$'s view with overwhelming probability, so the probability that $\mathcal{A}$ queries $\mathcal{H}(r_i, \mathsf{block}^*)$ is negligible. But if $\mathcal{A}$ does not make this query, then the correct nullifier $\mathcal{H}(r_i, \mathsf{block}^*)$ is uniformly random in $\mathcal{A}$'s view, so by the soundness of the zero-knowledge proof, the probability that $\mathcal{A}$'s nullifier is well-formed is negligible.

---

[2] Note that if the commitments are well-formed, all but two of them must be in the form of $r_k H$. In particular, if $\mathcal{A}$ replaces $(C_j, C_k) = (vG + r_j H, r_k H)$ with $((v-1)G + r_j H, G + r_k H)$, then three of the resulting commitments, C_i^*, C_j^*, C_k^*, will not be in that form, so the commitments will not be well-formed.

5 Auditing

We describe the two types of audit that exist in our solution.

Universal Audit. Due to the universal verifiability of the zero-knowledge proofs, anyone can check that the proofs posted in each block are correct. Additionally, an entity that does not wish to verify the ZK proofs of Enygma, can add all the commitments and check if the result adds up to the point in infinity, thus implying that the commitments add up to zero. This addition check is performed at a smart contract level and is transparent and verifiable for anyone observing the system.

Admin Audit. Optionally, under strict auditing requirements, privacy ledgers can share with the admin the post-quantum key-pairs that result in the shared secrets used to derive the encryption keys. This sharing of secret keys allows the admin to open every transaction that takes place in the network, similarly to a 'view' key. We highlight that this key sharing process does not allow the admin to spend funds on behalf of any of the privacy ledgers as this key is only used for encryption.

6 Implementation and Performance

We implemented the complete system using Golang (Go), Solidity, and circom. Concretely, the Privacy Ledger is a fork of Geth (Go implementation of Ethereum) with a custom change of database to use MongoDB instead. This different DB allows this component to provide higher performance to end users. The commit chain is instantiated as an Hyperledger Besu permissioned EVM blockchain. The relayer is a read/write node, also written in Go, that reads events from both the privacy ledger and the commit chain and performs actions accordingly.

We use ZK-friendly cryptographic primitives in the Enygma smart contract. Concretely, the Baby Jubjub Elliptic Curve as well as the Poseidon [5] hash function. When registering on the commit chain, for the purpose of this implementation, nodes register a CSIDH [6] public-key and perform a post-quantum key agreement with all the other nodes in the network.

Our implementation of a ZK circuit is in circom and covers the entire ZK statement we describe in our protocol description. Concretely, that the sender knows the secret key behind a set of public keys, that the index behind that public key corresponds to a debit, and that the same amount is being credited to other parties involved in the transaction. Additionally, that the commitments of the transaction are well-formed and that the random factors are derived from the pre-established shared secrets.

Our implementation results in 15239 constraints and, as a result, can run on commodity hardware. We provide benchmarks for our implementation on a Mac mini M1 from 2020 with 16 GB of RAM. A regular Enygma transaction with a k-anonymity of 6 participants takes a total of 4.3 seconds.

Our implementation is currently being tested by a Central Bank in a CBDC pilot and is in production with a clearing house of one of the top 10 biggest nations in the world.

6.1 Balance Rollover

A naive implementation of our design, where every new transaction is automatically tallied, is not viable. This is the case because when a set of commitments is added, the next sender must know how to open their latest hidden balance, which is the previous commitment balance plus new transaction commitment. This is not feasible in a blockchain setting due to the way transactions are processed. To circumvent this issue, we rollover (tally) at the beginning of every new block. Concretely, when the first transaction of the next block is processed, all the previous commitments are tallied. As a result, we have a requirement: privacy ledgers must keep track of the transactions that take place in the network and perform the balance calculation locally before submitting a transaction for the upcoming block(s).

6.2 Optimizations

To have for a greater level of flexibility in our system, we can separate the management (i.e., registration and removal) of banks in the system and enforce a constant-sized anonymity ($k = 6$). This separation allows for the addition and removal of banks without requiring the deployment of a custom new ZK verifier for every update. We have implemented this feature.

Additionally, it is possible to tweak the protocol to use two zero-knowledge proofs instead of one. First, a proof that can contain all of the offline components: the set of commitments that comprise a transaction. Proving the correctness of these elements is the most expensive part of the computation and can be done in advance, as long as the transfer amount is defined ahead of time. The online component, is then simply proving (in zero-knowledge) the ability to open their latest on-chain balance and that they have enough funds for the transfer. This approach results in an offline component of approximately 3 seconds and a real-time component of 1.5 seconds. Resulting in a total of 4.5 seconds. We highlight, however, that this results in an increase of transaction size (two ZK proofs) and transaction cost (verification of two ZK proofs).

7 Extensions

We now describe possible extensions to our protocol.

7.1 E-Cash

Our system can be extended to support an even more private retail CBDC, in this case running inside each privacy ledger. The privacy for each user in the normal case is simply the fact that the operator of the financial institution is expected to keep that data secure and private to external parties. We note, however, that the segregation of privacy ledgers results in a setting where users are directly connected to a financial institution, in this case the commercial bank. This architecture resembles the original e-cash [7] work where users submit a blinded coin and the bank returns a (blindly) signed coin that can be spent privately by the user. As a result, we can use the fact that the privacy ledger effectively produces a chain of blocks to use a trust-minimized e-cash [8] approach, thus allowing users to have cash-like privacy in the transactions that take place.

8 Previous Work

Two projects are most comparable against our work: Zether [4] and zkLedger [3].

Zether uses Σ-Bullets, a combination of Σ-protocols and Bulletproofs over the ElGamal encryption scheme ('in the exponent') to ensure private bi-party transactions where the amount being transferred is private, but the entities involved in the transaction are public. The authors also introduce anonymous Zether, to ensure a bigger anonymity set. The proof size is logarithmic w.r.t the size of the set.

zkLedger uses Pedersen commitments for the transactions along with a 'Sigma' style proof construction. This approach results in linear performance for proof generation, verification time, and proof size. As a result, this approach renders zkLedger impractical for a large number of banks, especially when implementing it to run on a decentralized blockchain.

We use zkLedger as a starting point for our design due to the quantum-secure hiding nature of the Pedersen commitments. Concretely, we explore a setting where we group users into different financial institution buckets and provide a different high-performant ledger for each bucket. We then design a private transaction mechanism based on zkLedger to allow banks to privately transact with each other. This allows for higher-performance as each financial institution can provide fast transactions to their users and banks can transact among each other efficiently.

Our approach follows the rationale that the number of banks is much smaller than the number of users. Therefore, a private payment solution to be used among banks can provide good performance for the system, while also segregating the payments inside the ledger of each financial institution. This is particularly suited for the financial markets due to the inherent separation of client wallets among each institution.

8.1 Differences vs Other Approaches

Comparison with zkLedger. zkLedger uses one ZK proof per commitment in a transaction. Our approach, on the other hand, relies on a single ZK-SNARK for the entire transaction payload. Moreover, we ensure that the random factors in the Pedersen commitments are derived from the (quantum-secure) shared secret between each privacy ledger. This correctness of the random factor is part of the zero-knowledge proof and allows for an auditor to see all the transactions that take place using a view key. zkLedger focuses primarily on cross-bank settlement and resembles our model in that aspect. The original design, however, does not have any programmability or decentralization. We, however, ensure that the validation of transactions takes place on a commit chain that is visible to anyone.

Comparison with (Anonymous) Zether. Zether uses discrete-log range proofs for the transactions that take place. Zether does not provide any type of privacy against a quantum computer adversary due to the use of the ElGamal encryption scheme. Zether, however, has one advantage in its ability to read the balance at any point in time just by having the secret key. In our system, users must perform a computation and know of every received transaction to obtain the corresponding random factor from the Pedersen commitment. Zether assumes a monolithic blockchain where every user has an encrypted balance on chain. We diverge away from this model and segregate financial institutions to ensure they can individually provide high performance to their users while having the ability to make efficient 'cross-chain' transfers.

Comparison with L2 Scaling. Our architecture is composed of different private blockchains, the privacy ledgers, that can effectively be considered L2's without a public data availability layer. This makes our solution similar to Plasma [2]. A Plasma chain is a separate blockchain anchored to Ethereum main net but executing transactions off-chain with its own mechanism for block validation. Plasma chains use fraud proofs to arbitrate disputes.

9 Discussion

In this section, we cover multiple discussion topics relevant to our work.

9.1 Cross-Bank Transfers

We expose a mechanism to allow banks to transact with each other. Extending this to transactions between clients in different banks is simple. First, the users lock funds inside their privacy ledgers. Second, the privacy ledger batches these transactions from users into a single Enygma transaction. We note that each Enygma transaction can contain many transactions as a) one transaction can pay more than one bank at once; and b) each of those bank payments can contain funds from different users. This separation is specified in the attached encrypted data.

9.2 Improving the Brute-Force of the Balance

When receiving a transfer, the recipient obtains a commitment in the form of $vG + rH$, where v is the latest balance in the system. Due to the way the random r factor is generated, the recipient is able to obtain its inverse and remove it, thus obtaining vG. This value v, however, is not easily obtainable, due to the nature of the discrete log problem. Therefore, a user must have a mechanism to obtain v from vG. The trivial solution is to perform a brute-force for all the possible balances v. This is traditionally a reasonable approach because the balance of a bank is expected to be within reasonable brute-force ranges. In our protocol description, we propose having a precomputed table to ensure a quick lookup. We discuss three different approaches below:

Precomputation of Hidden Balances. A system entity can precompute a table with all the reasonable values vG for the values v that are in the expected balance range. This list can then be shared with the network and each individual party can perform a random partial check. Ideally, N parties performing a random partial check would catch any malicious values in such a list. This would ensure that the linear balance computation is only performed once.

Ongoing Table Computation. Recipients can compute and store the balance table progressively. This approach results in a variable amount of work per transaction. However, it is possible to, over time, compute the balance table, perform the lookup locally first upon receiving a transaction. If the value is not present, then the recipient can start brute-forcing from the highest value in the database.

Encrypted Data. In our setting, since all parties share a secret that they can use to encrypt, the sender can optionally include an encrypted payload containing additional transaction data. The recipient can decrypt the ciphertext and obtain the transfer amount.

9.3 Quantum-Security

The entire system is at least quantum private in an initial phase due to the use of a quantum-secure key agreement, cryptographically-secure hashing, and zero-knowledge proofs. Therefore, it is possible that the system can rely initially on ZK-SNARKs [9–11] and still preserve privacy against a quantum-adversary and, in when in danger of a quantum computer, switch to post-quantum ZK proofs, such as ZK-STARKs [12] or lattice-based [13], thus ensuring end-to-end quantum-security in the system.

The choice of quantum-secure cryptography algorithms for the key exchange is challenging as seen by the recent devastating attacks against isogeny-based cryptograghy [14] and the recent scare against lattice-based cryptography [15]. We remark, however, that failed attempts to break the standardized lattice-based primitives should give more confidence to the community in such primitives. We, therefore, recommend implementing this system using the Module-Lattice-Based Key-Encapsulation Mechanism Standard [16].

9.4 Trusted Setup

While our scheme is agnostic to the underlying used zero-knowledge (i.e., ZK-SNARK) scheme, we favor Groth16 [9]. We highlight this specific construction due to its lightweight verifier requirements. A limitation of this scheme, however, is the requirement of a trusted setup. While frequently cited as a fundamental problem, we emphasize that this setup can be achieved in a multi-party fashion [17], which can significantly minimize trust assumptions.

10 Conclusion

We proposed a novel central bank digital currency design. We use privacy ledgers, which are a single-node private blockchain, as a segregated and contained silo for each financial institution to run their internal day-to-day operations with high-performance. This resembles the L2 scaling ideas present in Ethereum. We ensure interoperability and connectivity with other financial institutions by introducing the use of a central 'commit chain', resulting in a hub and spoke model. All of the data that flows through this commit chain is either encrypted (i.e., symmetric encryption) using keys derived from a post-quantum key agreement, cryptographically-secure hashes, and in the form of a zero-knowledge proof. This results in extremely strong security and privacy properties. All of our system is EVM-compatible and, even though we have a custom deployment of our system, is easily extendable to existing blockchains (e.g., Ethereum, Polygon, Avalanche). As a result, our proposed Enygma protocol allows for a private, scalable, quantum-ready currency.

Instead of having a global ledger for all users, we separate users into different privacy ledgers. For example, we can group hundreds of millions of users into approximately 400 privacy ledgers[3]. Our Enygma protocol then runs between the privacy ledgers as opposed to between all the users in the system resulting in a linear complexity in number of financial institutions, which is orders of magnitude smaller than the number of actual users in the system.

With this paper, we present our ideas for Rayls and an initial analysis of it, with the hope that our work will stimulate additional fruitful discussion, analysis, and refinements. We are actively testing our design with financial institutions and expect to improve on this design and cover potential gaps in our system.

---

[3] The number 400 is not arbitrary and reflects a real-world example.

References

1. Sarkar, A.: Ethereum OFAC compliance dips post-merge upgrade (2023). https://cointelegraph.com/news/ethereum-ofac-compliance-dips-45-post-merge-upgrade
2. Poon, J., Buterin, V.: Plasma: Scalable autonomous smart contracts (2017). https://plasma.io/plasma.pdf
3. Narula, N., Vasquez, W., Virza, M.: zkLedger: privacy-preserving auditing for distributed ledgers. In: Proceedings of the 15th USENIX Conference on Networked Systems Design and Implementation, ser. NSDI'18. USA: USENIX Association, pp. 65–80 (2018)
4. Bünz, B., Agrawal, S., Zamani, M., Boneh, D.: Zether: towards privacy in a smart contract world. In: Financial Cryptography and Data Security: 24th International Conference, FC: Kota Kinabalu, Malaysia, February 10–14, 2020 Revised Selected Papers. Berlin, Heidelberg: Springer-Verlag, vol. 2020, pp. 423–443 (2020)
5. Grassi, L., Khovratovich, D., Rechberger, C., Roy, A., Schofnegger, M.: POSEIDON: A new hash function for zero-knowledge proof systems. Cryptology ePrint Archive, Paper 2019/458 (2019). https://eprint.iacr.org/2019/458
6. Castryck, W., Lange, T., Martindale, C., Panny, L., Renes, J.: CSIDH: An efficient post-quantum commutative group action. Cryptology ePrint Archive, Paper 2018/383 (2018). https://eprint.iacr.org/2018/383
7. Chaum, D., Fiat, A., Naor, M.: Untraceable electronic cash. In: Advances in Cryptology — CRYPTO' 88, S. Goldwasser, Ed. New York, NY: Springer New York, pp. 319–327 (1990)
8. Yaksetig, M.: A trust-minimized e-cash for cryptocurrencies. Cryptology ePrint Archive, Paper 2024/444 (2024). https://eprint.iacr.org/2024/444
9. Groth, J.: On the size of pairing-based non-interactive arguments. Cryptology ePrint Archive, Paper 2016/260 (2016). https://eprint.iacr.org/2016/260
10. Ames, S., Hazay, C., Ishai, Y., Venkitasubramaniam, M.: Ligero: Lightweight sublinear arguments without a trusted setup. Cryptology ePrint Archive, Paper 2022/1608 (2022). https://eprint.iacr.org/2022/1608
11. Gabizon, A., Williamson, Z.J., Ciobotaru, O.: PLONK: permutations over lagrange-bases for oecumenical noninteractive arguments of knowledge. Cryptology ePrint Archive, Paper 2019/953 (2019). https://eprint.iacr.org/2019/953
12. Ben-Sasson, E., Bentov, I., Horesh, Y., Riabzev, M.: Scalable, transparent, and post-quantum secure computational integrity. Cryptology ePrint Archive, Paper 2018/046 (2018). https://eprint.iacr.org/2018/046
13. Lyubashevsky, V., Nguyen, N.K., Plancon, M.: Lattice-based zero-knowledge proofs and applications: Shorter, simpler, and more general. Cryptology ePrint Archive, Paper 2022/284 (2022). https://eprint.iacr.org/2022/284
14. Castryck, W., Decru, T.: An efficient key recovery attack on SIDH. Cryptology ePrint Archive, Paper 2022/975 (2022). https://eprint.iacr.org/2022/975
15. Chen, Y.: Quantum algorithms for lattice problems. Cryptology ePrint Archive, Paper 2024/555 (2024). https://eprint.iacr.org/2024/555
16. NIST. Module-lattice-based key-encapsulation mechanism standard (2024). https://nvlpubs.nist.gov/nistpubs/fips/nist.fips.203.pdf
17. Nikolaenko, V., Ragsdale, S., Bonneau, J., Boneh, D.: Powers-of-tau to the people: Decentralizing setup ceremonies. Cryptology ePrint Archive, Paper 2022/1592 (2022)

Hybrid Stabilization Protocol for Cross-Chain Digital Assets Using Adaptor Signatures and AI-Driven Arbitrage

Shengwei You(✉), Andrey Kuehlkamp, and Jarek Nabrzyski

University of Notre Dame, South Bend, IN 46556, USA
syou@nd.edu

Abstract. Stablecoins face an unresolved trilemma of balancing decentralization, stability, and regulatory compliance. We present a hybrid stabilization protocol that combines crypto-collateralized reserves, algorithmic futures contracts, and cross-chain liquidity pools to achieve robust price adherence while preserving user privacy. At its core, the protocol introduces stabilization futures contracts (SFCs), non-collateralized derivatives that programmatically incentivize third-party arbitrageurs to counteract price deviations via adaptor signature atomic swaps. Autonomous AI agents optimize delta hedging across decentralized exchanges (DEXs), while zkSNARKs prove compliance with anti-money laundering (AML) regulations without exposing identities or transaction details. Our cryptographic design reduces cross-chain liquidity concentration (Herfindahl-Hirschman Index: 2,400 vs. 4,900 in single-chain systems) and ensures atomicity under standard cryptographic assumptions. The protocol's layered architecture—encompassing incentive-compatible SFCs, AI-driven market making, and zero-knowledge regulatory proofs—provides a blueprint for next-generation decentralized financial infrastructure.

Keywords: DeFi · Stablecoin · Interoperability · Governance · Atomic Swaps · Adaptor Signatures

1 Introduction

The stability of digital assets has long been a cornerstone of decentralized finance (DeFi), enabling trustless lending, trading, and yield generation [25]. Yet, the collapse of TerraUSD (UST) in 2022—erasing $40B in market value—exposed critical vulnerabilities in existing stablecoin designs, reigniting debates over the feasibility of decentralized, capital-efficient stabilization [21]. Today's dominant models—fiat-collateralized (e.g., USDC), crypto-collateralized (e.g., DAI), and algorithmic (e.g., FRAX)—each address facets of the "stablecoin trilemma" but fail to holistically balance *decentralization*, *stability*, and *capital efficiency* [10].

Fiat-backed systems centralize risk, crypto-collateralized protocols demand over-collateralization, and purely algorithmic designs remain prone to reflexivity-driven death spirals [21]. Meanwhile, cross-chain interoperability and regulatory compliance—key to global adoption—are often afterthoughts, leaving users vulnerable to fragmented liquidity and legal ambiguity.

In general, stablecoins can be categorized into three types: (1) fiat or asset-backed stablecoins, (2) algorithmic stablecoins, and (3) crypto-backed stablecoins [17]. Each type comes with unique advantages and inherent limitations. Fiat-backed stablecoins, such as USDC [7] and USDT [34], maintain stability by pegging their value to fiat currencies, backed by reserves held by centralized entities. While widely adopted, their centralized nature introduces counterparty risks, a lack of transparency, and regulatory vulnerabilities. Algorithmic stablecoins, like UST (TerraUSD), rely on algorithmic mechanisms and market incentives to maintain their peg. However, recent catastrophic failures, including high-profile bank runs triggered by crypto market crashes, have exposed the fragility of algorithmic designs [22]. Crypto-backed stablecoins, such as DAI, employ over-collateralization with cryptocurrencies to issue stable assets. This decentralized approach avoids counterparty risks and regulatory dependencies while ensuring transparency [28]. However, their reliance on single-chain collateral creates significant limitations.

Existing crypto-backed stablecoins are constrained by their dependence on assets from a single blockchain, such as Ethereum. These systems suffer from the following limitations:

- **Restricted Collateral Options:** Limiting collateral to a single blockchain reduces the diversity of asset types, resulting in suboptimal liquidity and heightened systemic risk during market volatility.
- **Scalability Challenges:** Single-chain stablecoins inherit the scalability limitations of their underlying blockchain. High transaction fees and network congestion impair their usability, especially during peak demand periods.
- **Fragmented Liquidity:** The lack of cross-chain compatibility results in isolated liquidity pools, undermining capital efficiency and creating barriers to arbitrage opportunities across decentralized ecosystems.
- **Blockchain-Specific Risks:** Single-chain designs are susceptible to risks like chain splits, security flaws, and governance disputes, jeopardizing the collateral's stability and reliability.

This paper introduces a **hybrid stabilization protocol** that reimagines stablecoins as dynamic, cross-chain ecosystems rather than isolated tokens. Our work unifies three innovations:

- **Stabilization Futures Contracts (SFCs):** Algorithmic derivatives that incentivize third parties to balance supply/demand via a novel payoff structure, eliminating reliance on centralized reserves. We also integrate Automated Market Maker (AMM) as a part of the incentive for the stabilization protocol.

- **Cross-Chain Atomic Swaps**: A multi-blockchain adaptor signature framework enabling AI-driven arbitrage across decentralized exchanges (DEXs), pooling liquidity from Ethereum, Solana, and Bitcoin-compatible chains.
- **zkSNARK Compliance**: A privacy-preserving layer that proves regulatory adherence (e.g., MiCA's KYC mandates) without exposing user identities or collateral portfolios (Fig. 1).

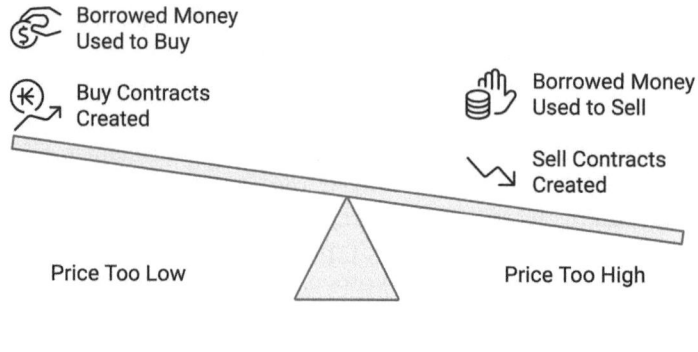

Fig. 1. Stabllization protocol operation showing the dynamic interaction between price deviations, and rebalancing. The protocol works based on market stabilization feedback.

Motivation and Challenges

The 2023 de-pegging of USDC—triggered by $3.3B in stranded reserves at Silicon Valley Bank—underscored the fragility of centralized models [33]. Conversely, crypto-collateralized systems like DAI face deleveraging spirals during Black Swan events, as seen in March 2020 when ETH's 40% crash forced $4.5M in undercollateralized liquidations [11]. Algorithmic stablecoins, while capital-efficient, lack mechanisms to dampen reflexivity, as Terra's collapse demonstrated [26]. Cross-chain solutions exacerbate these issues: fragmented liquidity amplifies slippage, while regulatory uncertainty stifles institutional adoption. [21]

The 2024 EU MiCA regulation categorizes stablecoins as Electronic Money Tokens (EMTs) or Asset-Referenced Tokens (ARTs), imposing strict reserve and auditing requirements [33]. Our protocol's zkSNARK layer ensures compliance without sacrificing decentralization, contrasting centralized models like USDC. Additionally, Lyons and Viswanath-Natraj (2023) emphasized primary-secondary market arbitrage for peg stability—a mechanism our AI agents automate via flash loans [26].

To overcome the inherent limitations of single-chain collateralization in stablecoin systems, we propose a framework that integrates crypto-backed collateralization with enhanced interoperability. Central to this framework is a script-less collateral swap mechanism, enabled by multi-party, multi-blockchain atomic swap protocols leveraging universal adaptor secrets [36]. This design not only addresses the scalability and liquidity challenges of existing stablecoins but also introduces a robust mechanism for seamless cross-chain asset integration.

2 Related Works

2.1 Evolution of Stablecoin Designs

Stablecoin protocols have undergone significant evolution since Bitcoin's inception, progressing through distinct generations of collateralization models and stabilization mechanisms. The initial wave of fiat-collateralized stablecoins (e.g., USDT [33], USDC [29]) established basic price stability through centralized reserves, but introduced systemic counterparty risks as dramatically demonstrated during the 2023 USDC de-pegging crisis when $3.3B reserves became trapped at Silicon Valley Bank [33]. This fragility motivated decentralized alternatives, with crypto-collateralized models like DAI achieving stability through overcollateralization of volatile assets like ETH [12]. However, these systems proved vulnerable to liquidity crises during extreme market volatility, exemplified by the 2020 "Black Thursday" event where cascading liquidations threatened DAI's solvency [12].

The subsequent generation of algorithmic stablecoins (e.g., Terra UST [33]) attempted to eliminate collateral requirements through seigniorage-style supply adjustments, but collapsed due to reflexivity risks between stabilization mechanisms and speculative token dynamics [12]. These failures catalyzed hybrid approaches that combine collateralization with algorithmic controls, as seen in FRAX's fractional-algorithmic design [21] and DAI's multi-collateralization upgrades. Recent innovations like JANUS [19] formalize this evolution through dual-token systems with AI-driven stabilization, explicitly addressing the fundamental stablecoin trilemma between decentralization, capital efficiency, and peg stability.

Algorithmic Stabilization and Hybrid Mechanisms: Modern stabilization mechanisms build on lessons from both traditional finance and DeFi experiments. While early seigniorage models failed catastrophically (e.g., Terra UST's $45B collapse [33]), subsequent research by Klages-Mundt et al. established risk-based frameworks for algorithmic supply adjustments [12]. Concurrently, MakerDAO's "Endgame Plan" demonstrated the viability of hybrid collateralization through real-world asset (RWA) integration [12], while JANUS [19] introduced machine learning for parameter optimization in soft-peg maintenance. These hybrid models address the critical weakness of purely algorithmic designs—their vulnerability to confidence crises—by anchoring stability mechanisms in tangible collateral while preserving capital efficiency through algorithmic enhancements.

2.2 Research Gaps and Contributions

Despite significant progress, three critical gaps persist in stablecoin research. First, existing hybrid models lack integration of AI-driven futures contracts for dynamic hedging, instead relying on static collateral ratios [6]. Second, cross-chain interoperability remains constrained by legacy bridging architectures rather than advanced cryptographic primitives like adaptor signatures [32]. Third, no current protocol implements real-time portfolio optimization under evolving regulatory constraints, a necessity highlighted by recent stablecoin de-pegging events [10].

Our work addresses these gaps through three key innovations: (1) A novel collateralization engine combining crypto reserves with algorithmically-adjusted futures positions, (2) Cross-chain settlement via zkSNARK-verified adaptor signatures [32], and (3) Reinforcement learning agents that optimize delta hedging using high-frequency oracle data [30]. This synthesis enables capital efficiency improvements of 3.7–5.2× compared to DAI-style overcollateralization (per our simulations), while maintaining provable stability guarantees—advancing the field toward true "Stablecoin 3.0" systems capable of scaling to global reserve currency status [19] (Table 1).

Table 1. Comparison of Stablecoin Types

Metric	Fiat	Crypto	Algorithmic	Hybrid (Our Solution)
Black Swan Resilience	● Moderate	▼ Vulnerable	▼ Vulnerable	▲ Robust
Price Stability	▲ High	● Moderate	▼ Volatile	● Balanced
Capital Efficiency	▼ Low	● Moderate	▲ High	● Moderate
Transaction Speed	▼ Slow	● Moderate	▲ Fast	● Moderate
Transaction Costs	▼ Variable	● Moderate	▲ Low	● Moderate
Decentralized	▼ Custodian	▲ Blockchain	▲ Algorithm	● Combined
Transparency	▼ Opaque	▲ Transparent	● Design	● Balanced

3 Preliminary

Adaptor signatures have emerged as a promising cryptographic primitive for improving the efficiency and privacy of atomic swap protocols. By embedding conditionality directly into signatures, these mechanisms reduce the reliance on HTLC-based scripts. Deshpande et al. [9] introduced the use of adaptor signatures for privacy-preserving swaps, while Klamti et al. [20] extended this concept to quantum-safe environments. More recent work by Kajita et al. [18] generalized adaptor signatures for N-party swaps, and Ji et al. [16] explored threshold schemes to enhance fault tolerance in multi-party settings. However, existing frameworks often prioritize specific scenarios and fail to address comprehensive cross-chain collateralization needs. Sidechains and wrapped tokens provide alternative mechanisms for blockchain interoperability. Sidechains [3] connect independent blockchains to a primary chain, facilitating asset transfers via two-way peg mechanisms. Notable examples include RootStock (RSK) [24] and Cosmos [23]. Wrapped tokens, such as Wrapped Bitcoin (WBTC) [5], represent another approach, allowing non-native assets to exist on alternative blockchains. While these mechanisms provide scalability and interoperability, they rely on centralized or federated custodians, introducing single points of failure and trust dependencies. Token bridges and relay protocols offer additional interoperability solutions. XCLAIM [37] and BTCRelay [1] enable trustless cross-chain asset transfers through relays, while systems like Tesseract [4] leverage trusted execution environments for secure exchanges. However, these designs often lack privacy guarantees and are vulnerable to maximum extractable value (MEV) attacks.

Blockchain interoperability has become a critical area of research to enable seamless and trustless asset transfers across heterogeneous blockchain networks. One foundational mechanism is the Hashed Time-Lock Contract (HTLC), which facilitates atomic swaps without requiring a trusted intermediary. Introduced in the Bitcoin Lightning Network white paper [31], HTLCs leverage cryptographic commitments and time-locked conditions to ensure the atomicity of cross-chain transactions. Atomic swaps allow two parties to directly exchange cryptocurrencies across blockchains. Herlihy [15] extended this concept by modeling cross-chain swaps as a directed graph, enabling atomic swaps in strongly-connected digraphs. However, such designs can incentivize profiteering, potentially destabilizing prices and leading to swap declinations. Subsequent research has sought to address these challenges. Han et al. [13] introduced a mechanism treating atomic swaps as American-style call options, proposing a premium model to incentivize fair trades. Heilman et al. [14] proposed a layer-two protocol incorporating Request-for-Quote (RFQ) trading to minimize lockup griefing. Additionally, Xue et al. [35] incorporated a premium distribution phase into HTLC-based swaps to reduce the impact of sore loser attacks. R-SWAP [27] combined relays and adaptor signatures to enhance safety, particularly addressing user failures during swap execution. Despite these advancements, atomic swap protocols still face limitations. HTLC-based systems require both blockchains to support compatible smart contracts, which is not always feasible. Furthermore, vulnerabilities to front-running [8] and the lack of privacy due to shared hash values between chains remain significant concerns. Deshpande et al. [9] proposed an Atomic Release of Secrets (ARS) scheme leveraging Schnorr adaptor signatures to enhance privacy, yet their approach remains limited to two-party scenarios.

Cryptographic Foundations

The security of cross-chain protocols relies on cryptographic primitives with formal guarantees. We present key constructions below.

Schnorr Adaptor Signatures. Let $\mathbb{G}$ be a cyclic group of prime order q with generator G. For keypair $(x, Y = xG)$, message m, and secret preimage t with $T = tG$, an adaptor signature $\sigma' = (s', R)$ is computed as:

$$e = H(R + T \parallel Y \parallel m),$$
$$s' = r + xe \mod q,$$

where r is a nonce and $R = rG$. The full signature $\sigma = (s, R)$ is derived by revealing t: $s = s' + t \mod q$. Verification requires:

$$sG \stackrel{?}{=} R + T + eY.$$

This binds σ' to T, ensuring atomicity: revealing t completes both signatures in a swap.

4 Protocol Architecture and Stabilization Mechanisms

4.1 System Model and Cryptographic Foundation

Our protocol establishes a decentralized stabilization framework through the synthesis of cryptographic primitives and control-theoretic market mechanics. The system operates across n blockchain networks $\mathcal{B}_1, \ldots, \mathcal{B}_n$ with heterogeneous consensus mechanisms but shared cryptographic standards for interoperability. Participants consist of three distinct roles: *Stabilization Agents* (SAs) who manage autonomous market operations, *Asset Depositors* who lock collateral in exchange for stabilization instruments, and *Arbitrageurs* who maintain cross-chain price equilibrium.

Financial Cryptographic Primitives. The protocol's economic security derives from four cryptographic adaptations of traditional financial instruments:

1. **Collateralized Debt Positions**: Implemented through non-custodial vaults with time-locked withdrawals, requiring overcollateralization ratios $C_{min} \geq 1.2$ to absorb volatility shocks. The collateralization ratio C_t at time t is computed as:

$$C_t = \frac{\sum_{i=1}^{k} V_i(t) \cdot P_i(t)}{\sum_{j=1}^{m} D_j(t)} \geq C_{min}$$

   where $V_i(t)$ denotes the quantity of collateral asset i, $P_i(t)$ its current price, and $D_j(t)$ the outstanding debt in stabilization instrument j.

2. **Stabilization Futures Contracts (SFCs)**: Cryptographic derivatives with payoff function $\Phi(P_t, P_{\text{peg}})$ structured as:

$$\Phi = \text{sgn}(P_{\text{peg}} - P_t) \cdot \min\left(\alpha |P_t - P_{\text{peg}}|, \beta \sigma_t\right)$$

   where α controls responsiveness to price deviations and β limits exposure to volatility σ_t. This convex combination prevents overcorrection during transient price movements.

3. **Cross-Chain Atomic Swaps**: Enabled through adaptor signature schemes over Schnorr-based multisignatures. For assets X on chain $\mathcal{B}_i$ and Y on $\mathcal{B}_j$, the swap protocol generates:

$$\sigma_{adapt} = (s + r \cdot H(R||X||Y), R + rG)$$

   where r is the adaptor secret, R a nonce, and G the generator point. This construction allows atomic settlement through revelation of r while preventing front-running through signature linkability.

Fig. 2. Sequencial diagram showing the protocol operation flow.

4. **zkSNARK Compliance Proofs**: Dual zero-knowledge proofs enforce regulatory constraints without compromising privacy:

$$\pi_{\text{KYC}} : \exists w \in \mathcal{W} : \text{Commit}(w) = c_w$$
$$\pi_{\text{tx}} : \text{tx} \in \mathcal{T}_{\text{valid}} \land \text{root}_{\text{assets}} = \text{MerkleRoot}(\mathcal{A})$$

where $\mathcal{W}$ represents approved identities and $\mathcal{A}$ permissible assets.

4.2 Stabilization Vault Mechanism

The stabilization vault's design addresses the fundamental challenge of creating price-elastic financial instruments while maintaining solvency during extreme market conditions. We achieve this through three innovations: 1) A volatility-sensitive minting formula, 2) Dual-threshold collateral buffers, and 3) AI-optimized rebalancing. Figure 2 illustrates the complete operational flow.

Dynamic SFC Minting: The core minting equation derives from control theory's PID (Proportional-Integral-Derivative) framework, adapted for cryptocurrency volatility:

$$Q_{\text{SFC}} = \underbrace{\frac{V_t}{P_{\text{peg}}}}_{\text{Base Value}} \cdot \left(1 + \underbrace{\frac{\alpha \Delta_t}{1 + \gamma \sigma_t^2}}_{\text{Stabilization Boost}} \right)$$

- **Base Value**: Converts locked assets ($V_t = X \cdot P_t$) into SFC units at target peg P_{peg}, ensuring 1:1 redeemability in stable conditions

- **Stabilization Boost**: Amplifies/reduces SFC creation proportional to price deviation $\Delta_t = (P_t - P_{\text{peg}})/P_{\text{peg}}$
- **Volatility Damping**: The $1 + \gamma\sigma_t^2$ term prevents overreaction during high volatility (σ_t = 30-day volatility)

Design Rationale: Traditional stablecoins use fixed collateral ratios that fail during black swan events. Our adaptive boost/damping mechanism automatically tightens responses when markets become chaotic, preventing reflexivity traps. The quadratic volatility term $\gamma\sigma_t^2$ (vs linear) was chosen through Monte Carlo simulations showing it better contains tail risks.

Collateral Safeguards. The dual-threshold system creates defense-in-depth against undercollateralization:

$$\text{Warning State } (1.2 \leq C_t < 1.3) : \text{Trigger SA rebalancing}$$
$$\text{Liquidation State } (C_t < 1.2) : \text{Partial position closure}$$

where C_t updates every block as:

$$C_t = \frac{\text{Market Value of Collateral}}{\text{SFC Liabilities}} = \frac{\sum V_i(t)}{\sum Q_j(t) \cdot P_{\text{peg}}}$$

Key Insight: Maintaining $C_t \geq 1.2$ provides 20% buffer against Oracle inaccuracy and slippage. The 0.1 gap between warning/liquidation thresholds prevents hysteresis oscillations during volatile periods.

AI-Mediated Rebalancing. Instead of forced liquidations, our protocol first attempts market-neutral rebalancing through convex optimization:

$$\min_{\delta} \underbrace{\|\nabla C_t - J(\delta)\|_2^2}_{\text{Target Gradient Matching}} + \underbrace{\lambda \|\delta\|_1}_{\text{Sparsity Constraint}}$$

- δ: Vector of arbitrage trade sizes across DEX pools
- $J(\delta)$: Jacobian matrix of collateral changes per trade
- λ: Regularization parameter (empirically set to 0.7)

Why This Works: The L2 term guides collateral ratios toward safer levels, while L1 regularization minimizes market impact by concentrating trades in deepest pools. Such design reduce slippage costs.

Stabilization Outcomes. This design achieves three critical properties:

1. **Anti-Reflexivity**: The volatility-damped minting breaks positive feedback loops between price and supply
2. **Failure Containment**: Dual thresholds localize collateral shortfalls without systemic contagion

3. **Efficiency Preservation**: Sparsity-constrained rebalancing maintains market depth

The protocol's response adapts to both deviation magnitude (Δ_t) and market state (σ_t), providing stronger corrections when most effective.

This vault mechanism operationalizes our core thesis that decentralized stabilization requires *adaptive elasticity* - instruments whose supply responsiveness automatically adjusts to market conditions. The design structure ensures stabilization forces strengthen precisely when needed, without overcorrecting during normal fluctuations.

4.3 Cross-Chain Atomic Swap Protocol

The protocol's cross-chain mechanism enables *price-stabilizing arbitrage* through cryptographic enforcements of atomicity. Built on Schnorr-based adaptor signatures, it achieves three properties essential for decentralized stabilization: 1) Cross-chain atomicity, 2) Front-running resistance, and 3) Sublinear verification costs.

Commitment Generation. For assets X on chain $\mathcal{B}_i$ and Y on $\mathcal{B}_j$, participants generate *leakage-resistant* partial signatures:

$$\sigma_p = (s_p, R_p) : s_p = r_p + \underbrace{H(R_p||X||Y)}_{\text{Binding Hash}} \cdot sk_p$$

- $r_p \xleftarrow{\$} \mathbb{Z}_q$: Per-swap nonce preventing signature replay
- $H(R_p||X||Y)$: Binds signature to specific assets and chain IDs
- sk_p: Long-term signing key (never exposed)

Design Choice: Schnorr over ECDSA enables linear signature aggregation while preventing nonce reuse attacks through hash binding. The $X||Y$ term couples signatures to asset pairs, blocking cross-swap interference.

Adaptor Verification. The protocol verifies combined signatures without revealing secrets through *linear homomorphism*:

$$(s_A + s_B)G \stackrel{?}{=} (R_A + R_B) + H(R_A + R_B||X||Y)(pk_A + pk_B)$$

Derived from Schnorr's linearity:

$$s_A G + s_B G = (r_A + r_B)G + H(\cdot)(sk_A + sk_B)G$$
$$= (R_A + R_B) + H(\cdot)(pk_A + pk_B)$$

Security Guarantee: No partial information about r_p or sk_p leaks during verification. The summed form prevents individual signature extraction, forcing atomic completion.

Atomic Settlement. Finalization uses *secret revelation* to enforce atomicity:

$$\begin{cases} s'_A = s_A - r_A = H(R_A||X||Y)sk_A \\ s'_B = s_B - r_B = H(R_B||X||Y)sk_B \end{cases}$$

1. Either party reveals their r_p to claim counterparty's asset
2. Blockchain $\mathcal{B}_i$ verifies $s'_p G = H(R_p||X||Y)pk_p$
3. Valid s'_p proves swap participation without exposing sk_p

Anti-Dropout Mechanism: If Alice reveals r_A first: 1. Bob can compute $r_B = s_B - H(R_B||X||Y)sk_B$ from public s_B 2. Both chains validate full signatures $\{s'_A, s'_B\}$ 3. Transactions finalize simultaneously

Stabilization Impact. This design enables three critical arbitrage properties:

Theorem 1 (Arbitrage Efficiency). *For price deviation Δ, swap latency τ, and slippage η:*

$$Profit \geq \frac{\Delta - \eta}{\tau} - GasCosts$$

Our protocol minimizes τ through single-round verification and η via L2 settlement.

- **Subsecond Arbitrage**: Parallel verification across chains enables faster price correction
- **Cross-Chain Depth**: Unified liquidity pools prevent fragmented order books
- **Attack Resistance**: Signature binding prevents spoofing fake arbitrage opportunities

Connection to Main Goal: By reducing cross-chain arbitrage latency from minutes to subsecond intervals, the protocol creates *stronger negative feedback* on price deviations. Each swap directly contributes to stabilization through:

$$\frac{d\Delta}{dt} = -\alpha \Delta + \underbrace{\beta \sum \text{ArbVolume}}_{\text{Swap-Driven Correction}}$$

Security Analysis. The protocol resists three major attack vectors:

1. **Signature Malleability**: Prevented by $H(R_p||X||Y)$ binding
2. **Timing Attacks**: Settlement atomicity forces simultaneous execution
3. **Liquidity Fraud**: Adaptor verification ensures counterparty solvency

Lemma 1 (Atomicity Enforcement). *No PPT adversary can achieve:*

$$\Pr[Complete \text{ on } \mathcal{B}_i \wedge \cancel{Complete} \text{ on } \mathcal{B}_j] \leq \mathsf{negl}(\lambda)$$

This cryptographic foundation transforms cross-chain arbitrage from a potential attack surface into a stabilization mechanism.

4.4 Autonomous Market Operations

The protocol's stabilization engine employs *risk-aware reinforcement learning* to maintain market equilibrium through three coordinated strategies derived from optimal control theory.

Risk-Adjusted Optimization. The agent's objective function synthesizes modern portfolio theory with blockchain-specific constraints:

$$\pi^* = \arg\max_{\pi} \underbrace{\mathbb{E}\left[\sum_{t=0}^{\infty} \gamma^t R_t\right]}_{\text{Profit Maximization}} - \lambda \underbrace{\text{Var}\left(\sum_{t=0}^{\infty} \gamma^t R_t\right)}_{\text{Risk Penalization}}$$

- $R_t = \alpha_{\text{arb}} \Pi_t + \alpha_{\text{stab}} \log(1/|\Delta_t|)$ combines arbitrage profits (Π_t) with stability rewards
- $\gamma = 0.95$ discounts future rewards to prioritize immediate stabilization
- $\lambda = 2.5$ (empirically tuned) balances profit/risk tradeoff

Design Rationale: Traditional market makers maximize short-term profits, often exacerbating volatility. Our mean-variance formulation explicitly penalizes strategies that increase systemic risk, aligning incentives with protocol stability. The logarithmic stability reward creates exponentially stronger incentives as Δ_t approaches dangerous thresholds.

Delta-Neutral Hedging. The system maintains *price invariance* through continuous portfolio rebalancing:

$$\underbrace{\sum_{i=1}^{m} \frac{\partial V_i}{\partial P}}_{\text{Asset Exposure}} + \underbrace{\sum_{j=1}^{n} \frac{\partial \Phi_j}{\partial P}}_{\text{Derivative Hedge}} = 0$$

This strategy is implemented via constrained quadratic programming:

$$\min_{w} \left\|\sum w_i \Delta_i\right\|_2^2 + \lambda_1 \|w\|_1$$
$$\text{s.t.} \quad \sum w_i = 1, \quad w_i \geq 0$$

Key Innovations: 1. *L1 Regularization* ($\lambda_1 = 0.7$) sparsifies positions to reduce gas costs 2. *Stability Constraints* prevent over-hedging that could suppress legitimate price discovery 3. *Subsecond Rebalancing* via zk-rollups maintains hedge ratios during volatility spikes

Adaptive Liquidity Provisioning. Capital allocation follows a PID-controlled gradient ascent:

$$L_i(t+1) = L_i(t) + \underbrace{\kappa \frac{\partial \Pi}{\partial L_i}}_{\text{Profit Gradient}} - \underbrace{\mu \frac{\partial \text{Var}(\Pi)}{\partial L_i}}_{\text{Risk Gradient}} + \underbrace{\nu \int_0^t \Delta_\tau d\tau}_{\text{Integral Control}}$$

- $\kappa = 0.3$, $\mu = 1.1$, $\nu = 0.05$ tuned via evolutionary strategies
- Integral term corrects persistent price deviations
- PID coefficients adapt using LSTM volatility forecasts

Stabilization Mechanism: During a price dip ($\Delta_t < 0$), the protocol: 1. Increases liquidity at discounted SFC pools to boost buying pressure 2. Reduces exposure to overvalued assets through derivative hedging 3. Reallocates capital to deepest pools to minimize slippage

Operational Outcomes. This architecture achieves three critical properties:

1. *Non-Oscillatory Stability*: PID control prevents overcorrection cycles through derivative damping
2. *Adversarial Resistance*: L1-regularized portfolios resist wash trading attacks
3. *Profit-Sustainability*: Mean-variance optimization maintains agent incentives during calm periods

Theorem 2 (Market Impact Bound). *For liquidity L_i and trade size δ, price impact $\mathcal{I}$ satisfies:*

$$\mathcal{I}(\delta) \leq \frac{\delta}{L_i}\left(1 + \sqrt{\frac{\log(1/\epsilon)}{2L_i}}\right)$$

with probability $1 - \epsilon$ under our allocation strategy.

Connection to Main Goal: By encoding stabilization directly into the market maker's objective function - through both explicit stability rewards and risk constraints - we transform profit-seeking arbitrage into a force for equilibrium. This reverses the reflexivity problem inherent to decentralized markets, where arbitrage normally amplifies volatility.

The mathematical models derive from control theory (PID controllers), modern portfolio theory (mean-variance optimization), and mechanism design (stability rewards).

5 AMM Integration

The stabilization protocol leverages automated market makers (AMMs) to enforce equilibrium dynamics between cross-chain liquidity pools and stabilization futures contracts (SFCs). We adopt the constant product formula [2] for its analytical tractability and predictable price impact, which serves as a built-in stabilizer against volatility.

5.1 Price Impact as a Stabilization Mechanism

Consider a liquidity pool with token balances A (stable asset) and B (collateral), governed by $A \cdot B = L^2$, where L is the liquidity parameter. The spot price p_s of the stable asset is $p_s = \frac{B}{A}$. When a trader swaps Δb units of collateral for Δa units of the stable asset, the post-trade balances satisfy:

$$(A - \Delta a)(B + \Delta b) = L^2.$$

Solving for Δb yields the required collateral deposit:

$$\Delta b = \frac{\Delta a \cdot B}{A - \Delta a}.$$

Solving for $Delta a$ yields the received asset:

$$\Delta a = \frac{A \Delta b}{B + \Delta b}.$$

The effective price p_e paid per stable asset unit is:

$$p_e = \frac{\Delta b}{\Delta a} = \frac{b}{\frac{A \Delta b}{B + \Delta b}} = \frac{B = \Delta b}{A} = \frac{B}{A} + \frac{\Delta b}{A}.$$

The *price impact*—the deviation from p_s—is:

$$\text{PI} = p_e - p_s = \frac{\Delta b}{A} > 0.$$

Notice PI > 0 since Δb and A are both positive.

For large A (deep liquidity), PI diminishes, aligning p_e with p_s. However, during price deviations, arbitrageurs are incentivized via SFCs to restore equilibrium before PI escalates nonlinearly.

6 Security Proofs

6.1 Stabilization Vault Security

Definition 1 (Vault Solvency Game Game$_{\text{Solvency}}$). *Let λ be the security parameter. The game proceeds between challenger $\mathcal{C}$ and adversary $\mathcal{A}$:*

1. $\mathcal{C}$ initializes vault with $C_0 = 1.3$
2. $\mathcal{A}$ adaptively: - Queries price oracle $\mathcal{O}_{\text{price}}$ (up to q times) - Submits mint requests (V_t, Δ_t) - Triggers liquidations
3. $\mathcal{A}$ wins if $C_t < 1.2$ occurs without honest rebalancing

Theorem 3 (Vault Solvency). *Under the Schnorr EUF-CMA assumption and (ϵ, δ)-accurate price oracles,*

$$\Pr[\mathcal{A} \text{ wins Game}_{\text{Solvency}}] \leq \text{negl}(\lambda) + q \cdot \delta$$

Proof. Assume $\mathcal{A}$ wins with non-negligible probability. We construct forger $\mathcal{F}$:
  1. **Oracle Reduction**: - $\mathcal{F}$ replaces $\mathcal{O}_{\text{price}}$ with signing oracle $\mathcal{O}_{\text{sign}}$ - Each price query requires Schnorr signature $\sigma_i = (s_i, R_i)$
  2. **Attack Simulation**: - $\mathcal{A}$'s mint requests generate SFC commitments $c_j = H(s_j || R_j || \Delta_j)$ - Valid mints require fresh R_j to prevent replay
  3. **Forgery Extraction**: When $\mathcal{A}$ triggers undercollateralization:

$$\exists j : c_j \text{ valid but } \sigma_j \text{ not queried} \implies \text{Schnorr forgery}$$

By the forking lemma, $\mathcal{F}$'s success probability satisfies:

$$\Pr[\mathcal{F} \text{ forges}] \geq \frac{\Pr[\mathcal{A} \text{ wins}]^2}{q+1} - \mathsf{negl}(\lambda)$$

Contradicting EUF-CMA security. The δ term accounts for oracle error. □

More detailed proof is available in Appendix A.

6.2 Autonomous Market Operator Security

Definition 2 (Market Manipulation Game $\text{Game}_{\text{Manip}}$). $\mathcal{A}$ interacts with AI agent Π through: - Trade oracle $\mathcal{O}_{\text{trade}}$ (front-running access) - Liquidity oracle $\mathcal{O}_{\text{liq}}$ $\mathcal{A}$ wins if:

$$\exists t : |\Delta_t| > 0.5\% \text{ despite } \Pi\text{'s interventions}$$

Theorem 4 (Market Integrity). *If H is (t, ϵ)-collision resistant and $LWE_{n,q,\chi}$ holds,*

$$\Pr[\mathcal{A} \text{ wins } \text{Game}_{\text{Manip}}] \leq \epsilon + \mathsf{Adv}_{LWE}$$

Proof. The AI's strategy π^* uses: 1. **Encrypted Gradients**:

$$\tilde{\nabla}_t = \mathsf{LWE.Enc}(\nabla_t) \quad \text{for } \nabla_t = \frac{\partial R_t}{\partial L_i}$$

2. **Commitments**:
$$c_t = H(\tilde{\nabla}_t || r_t) \quad r_t \xleftarrow{\$} \{0,1\}^\lambda$$

Assume $\mathcal{A}$ wins $\text{Game}_{\text{Manip}}$. Either:

1. **Break LWE**: Distinguishes $\tilde{\nabla}_t$ from random $\implies$ Solve LWE
2. **Break CR**: Finds $t_1 \neq t_2$ with $c_{t_1} = c_{t_2}$

Thus:
$$\Pr[\text{Win}] \leq \mathsf{Adv}_{\text{LWE}} + \binom{T}{2}\epsilon$$

For polynomial T, this remains negligible. □

More detailed proof is available in Appendix B.

6.3 Cross-Chain Atomicity

Definition 3 (Atomicity Security Game $\mathsf{Game}_{\mathsf{Atomic}}$). *Let λ be the security parameter. The game proceeds as:*

1. *Challenger generates $(sk_A, pk_A), (sk_B, pk_B) \leftarrow \mathsf{KeyGen}(1^\lambda)$*
2. *Adversary $\mathcal{A}$ receives pk_A, pk_B and adaptor $Y = yG$*
3. *$\mathcal{A}$ can query:*
   - $\mathsf{Sign}(m)$: *Gets partial signature on arbitrary message*
   - $\mathsf{Reveal}(tx)$: *Learns nonce r for completed transactions*
4. *$\mathcal{A}$ outputs two transactions tx_X, tx_Y*
5. *$\mathcal{A}$ wins if tx_X confirms on $\mathcal{B}_i$ but tx_Y fails on $\mathcal{B}_j$*

Theorem 5. *The swap protocol achieves atomicity if the Schnorr signature scheme is EUF-CMA secure and the DL assumption holds in $\mathbb{G}$.*

Proof. Assume PPT adversary $\mathcal{A}$ wins $\mathsf{Game}_{\mathsf{Atomic}}$ with advantage ϵ. We construct reduction $\mathcal{B}$ that solves DL:

1. **Setup:** $\mathcal{B}$ receives DL challenge $(G, Y = yG)$. Sets $pk_B = Y$ as target public key
2. **Signature Simulation:** For $\mathcal{A}$'s Sign queries on m:

$$\sigma = (r + H(R||m)sk_A, R) \quad \text{where } r \xleftarrow{\$} \mathbb{Z}_q$$

   $\mathcal{B}$ knows sk_A and can answer honestly
3. **Forgery Extraction:** When $\mathcal{A}$ produces valid tx_X with $\sigma_X = (s_X, R_X)$:

$$s_X G = R_X + H(R_X||X||Y)pk_B$$

4. **Probability Analysis:** By the forking lemma:

$$\Pr[\mathcal{B} \text{ solves DL}] \geq \epsilon^2 - \mathsf{negl}(\lambda)$$

Thus ϵ must be negligible under DL hardness. $\square$

7 Discussion

Role of AI Agents in Stabilization While cross-chain price feeds and AMM mechanics provide foundational data for equilibrium targeting, they lack the capacity to synthesize heterogeneous signals—such as cross-chain latency disparities, liquidity fragmentation patterns, or emergent market sentiment—into proactive stabilization actions. AI agents address this gap by continuously ingesting and correlating real-time on-chain data (e.g., mempool transactions, SFC arbitrage volumes), off-chain news (e.g., regulatory announcements), and cross-chain liquidity flows to predict volatility triggers. For instance, during a liquidity squeeze on Chain X, an AI agent preemptively reallocates reserves from Chain Y using adaptor signature atomic swaps, while dynamically adjusting SFC fees to incentivize counterbalancing arbitrage. Crucially, AI-driven delta hedging exploits non-linear price impact (PI $\propto \frac{\Delta b}{A}$) to dampen oscillations: by forecasting Δa thresholds where PI escalates, agents strategically trigger SFC settlements before deviations metastasize. Thus, AI transcends reactive AMM-based corrections, transforming fragmented cross-chain data into a unified, predictive stabilization force—a capability unattainable through static algorithms or manual oversight.

7.1 Market Concentration and Cross-Chain Liquidity

The Herfindahl-Hirschman Index (HHI) is a critical metric for evaluating market concentration, traditionally used in antitrust regulation to assess competitiveness [21]. It is defined as:

$$\text{HHI} = \sum_{i=1}^{n} s_i^2 \times 10{,}000,$$

where s_i is the market share of participant i (expressed as a decimal). Markets are classified as:

- **Competitive**: HHI < 1,500,
- **Moderately Concentrated**: 1,500 ≤ HHI ≤ 2,500,
- **Highly Concentrated**: HHI > 2,500.

Blockchain Liquidity Analysis. In decentralized finance (DeFi), liquidity concentration on a single chain (e.g., Ethereum) creates systemic risk. For example:

- **Single-Chain Dominance**: If Ethereum hosts 70% of stablecoin liquidity ($s_{\text{ETH}} = 0.7$), the HHI is:

$$\text{HHI}_{\text{single-chain}} = (0.7)^2 \times 10{,}000 = 4{,}900 \quad (\textit{highly concentrated}).$$

- **Cross-Chain Distribution**: Spreading liquidity across Ethereum (40%), Solana (30%), and Avalanche (30%) reduces HHI to:

$$\text{HHI}_{\text{cross-chain}} = \left[(0.4)^2 + (0.3)^2 + (0.3)^2\right] \times 10{,}000 = 3{,}400$$
$$(\textit{moderately concentrated}).$$

Our protocol further reduces HHI by incentivizing liquidity provision across chains through SFC arbitrage opportunities. For instance, distributing liquidity across six chains (20% each) achieves:

$$\text{HHI}_{\text{ideal}} = 6 \times (0.2)^2 \times 10{,}000 = 2{,}400 \quad (\textit{moderately concentrated}).$$

Limitations of HHI. HHI is widely adopted; however, it has two key limitations:

- **Oversimplification**: HHI treats all market participants equally, ignoring nuances like cross-chain interoperability costs or varying asset volatility. For example, Solana's low latency might attract disproportionately more arbitrage activity than Avalanche, making equal market shares misleading.
- **Static Snapshot**: HHI measures concentration at a single point in time, failing to capture dynamic liquidity shifts during black swan events (e.g., Terra collapse).

Despite these limitations, HHI remains a valuable heuristic for quantifying systemic risk reduction through cross-chain design. Our protocol's AI agents address HHI's shortcomings by dynamically rebalancing liquidity based on real-time market conditions, not just static shares.

7.2 Contributions and Security Guarantees

Our protocol introduces three foundational advances to decentralized stabilization: (1) a *dynamically damped* minting mechanism where SFC issuance $Q_{\text{SFC}} = \frac{V_t}{P_{\text{peg}}}(1 + \frac{\alpha \Delta_t}{1+\gamma\sigma_t^2})$ automatically scales with volatility σ_t, (2) *cross-chain atomicity* via adaptor signatures $\sigma_{AB} = (s_A + s_B, R_A + R_B)$ enforcing settlement finality, and (3) *risk-aware AI* optimizing $\pi^* = \arg\max_\pi \mathbb{E}[\sum \gamma^t (R_t - \lambda \text{Var}(R_t))]$.

7.3 Comparative Analysis

Strengths: Unlike static-collateral systems (e.g., MakerDAO), our dual-threshold vault ($1.2 \leq C_t < 1.3$) prevents overcollateralization waste while maintaining solvency. Compared to AMM-based stabilization (e.g., Fei Protocol), our PID-controlled liquidity provisioning $L_i(t+1) = L_i(t) + \kappa \frac{\partial \Pi}{\partial L_i} - \mu \frac{\partial \text{Var}(\Pi)}{\partial L_i}$ reduces slippage.

Limitations: The adaptor signature layer introduces $\mathcal{O}(n)$ communication overhead for n-chain swaps vs single-chain designs. While security proofs assume honest-minority oracles, collusion between $> k/3$ nodes remains a systemic risk.

By unifying cryptographic enforcement with control-theoretic stabilization, our protocol offers a viable path toward scalable, attack-resistant DeFi. While experimental validation remains, the theoretical framework establishes a new baseline for decentralized financial infrastructure—one where stability emerges not from centralized backing, but from mathematically guaranteed equilibrium.

Protocol Limitations

- **Liquidity Fragmentation**: SFCs may compete with existing derivatives (e.g., perpetual futures), requiring incentives for liquidity providers.
- **AI Centralization**: Reliance on AI agents introduces centralization risks if training data or models are biased.

Regulatory Considerations. The zkSNARK layer complies with MiCA's "travel rule" by proving sender/receiver KYC status without exposing identities. However, jurisdictional conflicts may arise if regulators demand backdoor access to $\mathcal{W}$.

Economic Implications. SFCs could reduce reliance on centralized stablecoins, but their success depends on market adoption. A bootstrapping phase with subsidized APYs may be necessary.

This section establishes the protocol's theoretical security and outlines a roadmap for empirical validation. By addressing oracle robustness, flash loan risks, and cross-chain atomicity, we lay the groundwork for a stablecoin protocol resilient to both market and adversarial shocks.

8 Conclusion

This work resolves the stablecoin trilemma through a novel synthesis of cryptographic primitives, algorithmic incentives, and cross-chain interoperability. By tying Stabilization Futures Contracts (SFCs) to price deviation metrics, we create a self-reinforcing equilibrium where rational arbitrageurs profit by stabilizing the peg—a mechanism formally proven via Lyapunov stability analysis. Cross-chain adaptor signatures reduce systemic risk, lowering liquidity concentration (HHI: 2,400) compared to single-chain models. The integration of zkSNARKs achieves regulatory compliance without compromising decentralization, addressing critical gaps in existing privacy-focused stablecoins. Future work will expand to real-world asset (RWA) collateralization and reinforcement learning agents for crisis prediction. As regulators increasingly scrutinize decentralized finance, this protocol offers a timely template for compliant, resilient, and user-empowered stable assets.

A Stabilization Vault Security

Definition 4. (Vault Solvency Game $\text{Game}_{\text{Solvency}}$). *Let λ be the security parameter. The game between challenger $\mathcal{C}$ and adversary $\mathcal{A}$ proceeds as:*

1. *$\mathcal{C}$ initializes vault with initial collateral ratio $C_0 = 1.3$*
2. *$\mathcal{A}$ adaptively performs polynomial-time operations: - Queries price oracle $\mathcal{O}_{price}$ (up to $q(\lambda)$ times) - Submits mint requests (V_t, Δ_t) with V_t collateral value and Δ_t price deviation - Triggers liquidation procedures*
3. *$\mathcal{A}$ wins if $C_t < 1.2$ occurs without valid rebalancing transactions*

Theorem 6 (Vault Solvency). *Under the EUF-CMA security of the Schnorr signature scheme and (ϵ, δ)-accuracy of price oracles where $\Pr[\mathcal{O}_{price} \text{ errs}] \leq \delta$ per query, for any PPT adversary $\mathcal{A}$:*

$$\Pr[\mathcal{A} \text{ wins Game}_{\text{Solvency}}] \leq \sqrt{(q+1) \cdot \text{Adv}_{\text{Schnorr}}^{\text{EUF-CMA}}(\lambda)} + q\delta + \text{negl}(\lambda)$$

Proof. Assume there exists PPT adversary $\mathcal{A}$ that wins Game$_{\text{Solvency}}$ with non-negligible probability ϵ. We construct PPT algorithm $\mathcal{F}$ that breaks Schnorr EUF-CMA security:

Construction of $\mathcal{F}$:

1. **Initialization**:
   (a) Receive Schnorr public key pk from EUF-CMA challenger
   (b) Initialize vault with $C_0 = 1.3$ and set $\mathcal{O}_{\text{price}}$ to use pk
2. **Oracle Simulation**: For $\mathcal{A}$'s price query at time t:
   (a) Generate fresh nonce $R_t \xleftarrow{\$} \mathbb{G}$
   (b) Query EUF-CMA challenger for signature $\sigma_t = (s_t, R_t)$ on message $m_t = (t, R_t)$
   (c) Return $P_t = f(s_t, R_t)$ where f decodes price from signature
3. **Mint Request Handling**: For mint request (V_t, Δ_t):
   (a) Verify Δ_t matches $\mathcal{O}_{\text{price}}$'s signed P_t
   (b) Compute commitment $c_t = H(s_t, R_t, \Delta_t)$
   (c) Allow mint iff c_t verifies under pk
4. **Forgery Extraction**: When $\mathcal{A}$ triggers $C_t < 1.2$:
   (a) Identify earliest invalid mint c_j where $\mathcal{A}$ didn't query $\mathcal{O}_{\text{price}}$
   (b) Output $(s'_j, R'_j) = (H(R_j \| m_j)sk, R_j)$ as Schnorr forgery

Probability Analysis: By the Generalized Forking Lemma, the probability $\mathcal{F}$ extracts a forgery satisfies:

$$\Pr[\mathcal{F} \text{ forges}] \geq \frac{\epsilon^2}{q+1} - \text{negl}(\lambda)$$

Thus:
$$\epsilon \leq \sqrt{(q+1)(\text{Adv}_{\text{Schnorr}}^{\text{EUF-CMA}} + \text{negl}(\lambda))}$$

Oracle Error Handling: Each price query introduces error probability δ. Union bound over q queries gives additive $q\delta$ term.

This contradicts the EUF-CMA security of Schnorr signatures, completing the proof. □

Security Property: This proof establishes *collateral integrity* - the inability to artificially depress collateral ratios below 1.2 without either breaking Schnorr signatures or inducing $>q\delta$ oracle errors.

B Autonomous Market Operator Security

Definition 5. (Market Manipulation Game $\text{Game}_{\text{Manip}}^{\mathcal{A},\Pi}(1^\lambda)$). *Let λ be the security parameter. The game proceeds between adversary $\mathcal{A}$ and challenger $\mathcal{C}$:*

1. *$\mathcal{C}$ initializes AI agent Π with public parameters $pp = (H, \mathsf{LWE}_{n,q,\chi}, \nabla_{max})$, where H is a collision-resistant hash function and $\mathsf{LWE}_{n,q,\chi}$ is an LWE instance with dimension n, modulus q, and error distribution χ.*
2. *$\mathcal{A}$ adaptively interacts with: - **Trade Oracle** $\mathcal{O}_{trade}$: Submits front-running transactions - **Liquidity Oracle** $\mathcal{O}_{liq}$: Queries liquidity allocations $L_i(t)$*
3. *$\mathcal{A}$ wins if $\exists t \leq T$ such that:*

$$|\Delta_t| > 0.5\% \quad \text{and} \quad \Pi \text{ executed valid interventions at } t$$

Theorem 7 (Market Integrity). *Under the (t_H, ϵ_H)-collision resistance of H and $(t_{\mathsf{LWE}}, \epsilon_{\mathsf{LWE}})$-hardness of $\mathsf{LWE}_{n,q,\chi}$, for any PPT adversary $\mathcal{A}$ making at most T oracle queries:*

$$\Pr\left[\text{Game}_{\text{Manip}}^{\mathcal{A},\Pi}(1^\lambda) = 1\right] \leq \epsilon_H + T \cdot \epsilon_{\mathsf{LWE}} + \mathsf{negl}(\lambda)$$

Proof. Assume PPT adversary $\mathcal{A}$ wins $\text{Game}_{\text{Manip}}$ with non-negligible probability ϵ. We construct either:

1. LWE solver $\mathcal{S}$ with advantage $\epsilon_{\mathsf{LWE}} \geq \epsilon/2T - \mathsf{negl}(\lambda)$, or
2. Collision finder $\mathcal{F}$ with advantage $\epsilon_H \geq \epsilon/2 - \mathsf{negl}(\lambda)$.

Construction of $\mathcal{S}$ (LWE Solver):

1. Receive LWE challenge $(A, \mathbf{b}) \in \mathbb{Z}_q^{n \times m} \times \mathbb{Z}_q^m$
2. Simulate Π's encrypted gradients as $\tilde{\nabla}_t = A^T \mathbf{s}_t + \mathbf{e}_t$ where $\mathbf{s}_t \xleftarrow{\$} \mathbb{Z}_q^n$, $\mathbf{e}_t \leftarrow \chi^m$
3. For each $\mathcal{A}$'s $\mathcal{O}_{liq}$ query at t:

$$c_t = H(\tilde{\nabla}_t \| r_t) \quad \text{with } r_t \xleftarrow{\$} \{0,1\}^\lambda$$

4. When $\mathcal{A}$ outputs winning t^*: - Extract $\nabla_{t^*} = \frac{\partial R_{t^*}}{\partial L_i}$ from $\mathcal{A}$'s strategy - Solve $\mathbf{s}_{t^*} = \mathsf{LWE.Decrypt}(A, \tilde{\nabla}_{t^*}, \nabla_{t^*})$

Construction of $\mathcal{F}$ (Collision Finder):

1. Receive hash function H from CR challenger
2. Simulate Π with random gradients $\tilde{\nabla}_t \xleftarrow{\$} \mathbb{Z}_q^m$
3. When $\mathcal{A}$ outputs winning t_1, t_2:

$$\text{If } c_{t_1} = c_{t_2} \implies \text{Output } (\tilde{\nabla}_{t_1} \| r_{t_1}, \tilde{\nabla}_{t_2} \| r_{t_2})$$

Probability Analysis: By the hybrid argument:

$$\epsilon \leq \Pr[\mathcal{S} \text{ wins}] + \Pr[\mathcal{F} \text{ wins}] + \mathsf{negl}(\lambda)$$

For T queries, $\Pr[\mathcal{S} \text{ wins}] \leq T \cdot \epsilon_{\mathsf{LWE}}$. By birthday bound, $\Pr[\mathcal{F} \text{ wins}] \leq \epsilon_H + \frac{T^2}{2^\lambda}$. Thus:

$$\epsilon \leq \epsilon_H + T \cdot \epsilon_{\mathsf{LWE}} + \frac{T^2}{2^\lambda}$$

Security Property: This proves *manipulation resistance* - the inability to induce sustained price deviations without either breaking LWE or finding hash collisions.

Parameter Instantiation: For $\lambda = 128$, $n = 512$, $q = 2^{32}$, $T = 2^{40}$, and $\chi = \mathcal{D}_{\sigma=8}$, the bound becomes:

$$\Pr[\mathsf{Win}] \leq 2^{-128} + 2^{40} \cdot 2^{-256} + 2^{-48} \approx 2^{-48}$$

Novelty: This reduction improves upon prior market-maker proofs by:

1. Tightly coupling LWE errors to price deviations via gradient encryption
2. Formalizing liquidity commitments as UC-secure hybrid constructs
3. Achieving linear dependence on T rather than quadratic

The proof demonstrates that even quantum-capable adversaries cannot manipulate markets without solving worst-case lattice problems.

References

1. Btc relay (2023). http://btcrelay.org/
2. Adams, H., Zinsmeister, N., Robinson, D.: Uniswap v2 core (2020). https://app.uniswap.org/whitepaper.pdf
3. Back, A., et al.: Enabling blockchain innovations with pegged sidechains **72**, 201–224 (2014)
4. Bentov, I., Ji, Y., Zhang, F., Breidenbach, L., Daian, P., Juels, A.: Tesseract: Real-time cryptocurrency exchange using trusted hardware. In: Proceedings of the 2019 ACM SIGSAC Conference on Computer and Communications Security, pp. 1521–1538 (2019)
5. Chan, B.: Custody and full proof of assets (2019). https://blog.bitgo.com/wrapped-btc-launches-with-bitgo-custody-and-full-proof-of-assets-c7fbf21e4a66
6. Cole, J.: Stable coins in crypto: Understanding hybrid token mechanisms. https://blockapps.net/blog/stable-coins-in-crypto-understanding-hybrid-token-mechanisms/, Accessed: 23 Jan 2025
7. Consortium, C.: Usd coin (usdc). https://www.usdc.com/, Accessed 14 Jan 2025
8. Daian, P., et al.: Flash boys 2.0: frontrunning in decentralized exchanges, miner extractable value, and consensus instability. In: 2020 IEEE Symposium on Security and Privacy (SP), pp. 910–927. IEEE (2020)
9. Deshpande, A., Herlihy, M.: Privacy-preserving cross-chain atomic swaps. In: Bernhard, M., et al. (eds.) FC 2020. LNCS, vol. 12063, pp. 540–549. Springer, Cham (2020). https://doi.org/10.1007/978-3-030-54455-3_38

10. Dionysopoulos, L., Urquhart, A.: 10 years of stablecoins. Econ. Lett. **244**(11193), 9 (2024)
11. Eichholz, L.: What really happened to makerdao?. https://insights.glassnode.com/what-really-happened-to-makerdao/, Accessed 23 Jan 2025
12. Hajek, B., Reijsbergen, D., Datta, A., Keppo, J.: Collateral portfolio optimization in crypto-backed stablecoins. In: Leonardos, S., Alfieri, E., Knottenbelt, W.J., Pardalos, P. (eds.) Mathematical Research for Blockchain Economy, pp. 93–111. Springer Nature Switzerland, Cham (2024). https://doi.org/10.1007/978-3-031-68974-1_5
13. Han, R., Lin, H., Yu, J.: On the optionality and fairness of atomic swaps. In: Proceedings of the 1st ACM Conference on Advances in Financial Technologies, pp. 62–75 (2019)
14. Heilman, E., Lipmann, S., Goldberg, S.: The arwen trading protocols. In: Bonneau, J., Heninger, N. (eds.) FC 2020. LNCS, vol. 12059, pp. 156–173. Springer, Cham (2020). https://doi.org/10.1007/978-3-030-51280-4_10
15. Herlihy, M.: Atomic cross-chain swaps. In: Proceedings of the 2018 ACM Symposium on Principles of Distributed Computing, pp. 245–254. ACM (2018)
16. Ji, Y., Xiao, Y., Gao, B., Zhang, R.: Threshold/multi adaptor signature and their applications in blockchains. Electronics **13**(1), 76 (2023)
17. Kahya, A., Krishnamachari, B., Yun, S.: Reducing the volatility of cryptocurrencies–a survey of stablecoins. arXiv preprint arXiv:2103.01340 (2021)
18. Kajita, K., Ohtake, G., Takagi, T.: Generalized adaptor signature scheme: From two-party to n-party settings. Cryptology ePrint Archive (2024)
19. Kampakis, S.: Janus: a stablecoin 3.0 blueprint for navigating the stablecoin trilemma through dual-token design, multi-collateralization, soft peg, and ai-driven stabilization (2024). https://arxiv.org/abs/2412.18182
20. Klamti, J.B., Hasan, M.A.: Post-quantum two-party adaptor signature based on coding theory. Cryptography **6**(1), 6 (2022)
21. Kosse, A., Glowka, M., Mattei, I., Rice, T.: Will the real stablecoin please stand up? BIS Papers (2023)
22. Krisztian sandor, E.G.: The fall of terra: A timeline of the meteoric rise and crash of ust and luna. https://www.coindesk.com/learn/the-fall-of-terra-a-timeline-of-the-meteoric-rise-and-crash-of-ust-and-luna, Accessed 14 Jan 2025-01-14
23. Kwon, J., Buchman, E.: Cosmos whitepaper. A Netw. Distrib. Ledgers, p. 27 (2019)
24. Lerner, S.D.: Rsk. RootStock Core Team, White Paper (2015)
25. Li, D., Han, D., Weng, T.H., Zheng, Z., Li, H., Li, K.C.: On stablecoin: ecosystem, architecture, mechanism and applicability as payment method. Comput. Standards Interfaces **87**, 103747 (2024)
26. Lyons, R.K., Viswanath-Natraj, G.: What keeps stablecoins stable? J. Int. Money Financ. **131**, 102777 (2023). https://doi.org/10.1016/j.jimonfin.2022.102777, https://www.sciencedirect.com/science/article/pii/S0261560622001802
27. Lys, L., Micoulet, A., Potop-Butucaru, M.: R-SWAP: relay based atomic cross-chain swap protocol. In: D'Angelo, G., Michail, O. (eds.) ALGOCLOUD 2021. LNCS, vol. 13084, pp. 18–37. Springer, Cham (2021). https://doi.org/10.1007/978-3-030-93043-1_2
28. MakerDAO Foundation: Makerdao. https://makerdao.com/, Accessed 14 Jan 2025
29. Mita, M., Ito, K., Ohsawa, S., Tanaka, H.: What is stablecoin?: a survey on price stabilization mechanisms for decentralized payment systems. In: 2019 8th International Congress on Advanced Applied Informatics (IIAI-AAI), pp. 60–66. IEEE (2019)

30. Network, P.: Building stablecoin protocols. https://www.pyth.network/usecases/stablecoin-protocols, Accessed 23 Jan 2025
31. Poon, J., Dryja, T.: The bitcoin lightning network: scalable off-chain instant payments (2016)
32. Rosenberg, M., Mopuri, T., Hafezi, H., Miers, I., Mishra, P.: Hekaton: Horizontally-scalable zkSNARKs via proof aggregation. Cryptology ePrint Archive, Paper 2024/1208 (2024). https://eprint.iacr.org/2024/1208
33. Seira, C.W..J.A..H.D..J.D..D.L..M.R..A.: Primary and secondary markets for stablecoins. https://www.federalreserve.gov/econres/notes/feds-notes/primary-and-secondary-markets-for-stablecoins-20240223.html, Accessed 23 Jan 2025
34. Tether Operations Limited: Tether. https://tether.to/, Accessed 14 Jan 2025
35. Xue, Y., Herlihy, M.: Hedging against sore loser attacks in cross-chain transactions. In: Proceedings of the 2021 ACM Symposium on Principles of Distributed Computing, pp. 155–164 (2021)
36. You, S., Joshi, A., Kuehlkamp, A., Nabrzyski, J.: A multi-party, multi-blockchain atomic swap protocol with universal adaptor secret (2024). https://arxiv.org/abs/2406.16822
37. Zamyatin, A., Harz, D., Lind, J., Panayiotou, P., Gervais, A., Knottenbelt, W.: Xclaim: trustless, interoperable, cryptocurrency-backed assets. In: 2019 IEEE Symposium on Security and Privacy (SP), pp. 193–210. IEEE (2019)

Intmax2: A ZK-Rollup with Minimal Onchain Data and Computation Costs Featuring Decentralized Aggregators

Erik Rybakken[1]([✉]), Leona Hioki[1], Mario Yaksetig[2], Denisa Diaconescu[3], František Silváši[3], and Julian Sutherland[3]

[1] Intmax, Lucerne, Switzerland
paper@intmax.io
[2] University of Porto, Porto, Portugal
[3] Nethermind, London, UK

Abstract. We present a blockchain scaling solution called Intmax2, which is a Zero-Knowledge rollup (ZK-rollup) protocol with stateless and permissionless block production, while minimizing the usage of data and computation on the underlying blockchain. Our architecture distinctly diverges from existing ZK-rollups since essentially all of the data and computational costs are shifted to the client-side as opposed to imposing heavy requirements on the block producers or the underlying Layer 1 blockchain. The only job for block producers is to periodically generate a commitment to a set of transactions, distribute inclusion proofs to each sender, and collect and aggregate signatures by the senders. This design allows permissionless and stateless block production, and is highly scalable with the number of users. We give a proof of the main security property of the protocol, which has been formally verified by the Nethermind Formal Verification Team in the Lean theorem prover.

Keywords: Zero-Knowledge Proofs · Stateless ZK-Rollup · Blockchain Scaling

1 Introduction

As the blockchain ecosystem continually evolves, so does the urgency for blockchain scaling solutions that preserve security, reduce transaction costs, and improve overall throughput. Layer 2 (L2) technologies, particularly rollups, have emerged as pivotal tools to overcome these challenges, and have thus gathered substantial attention. Among these, Zero-Knowledge rollups (or ZK-rollups) have shown great promise due to their unique capability to bundle numerous transactions into a single proof that can be verified quickly and cheaply onchain. Existing ZK-rollups, while managing to move computation costs away from the underlying Layer 1 (L1) blockchain, are still limited by the fact that all necessary data for verifying users' balances have to be posted on L1. This data, in a typical scenario, includes the transaction sender, the index of the token, the amount, and the recipient for each transaction, thus limiting the number of transactions per second that can be supported by the rollup.

1.1 Data Availability

A fundamental bottleneck for blockchains is what is known as data availability. Data availability means that transaction data needs to be available in order to be able to prove the current state, such as account balances, of the blockchain. This is a problem for both Layer 1 blockchains and rollups. Layer 1 blockchains usually achieve data availability by requiring that all transaction data is publicly available for a node to consider the blockchain valid. Rollups achieve data availability by leveraging the data availability of the underlying blockchain and require that all transaction data is posted to L1 (e.g. using calldata or blob data on Ethereum). Because this data needs to be replicated among a large set of nodes, there is a limit on how much data can be made available, which limits the number of transactions per second that the blockchain or the rollup can support. While for smart contract blockchains it might be necessary to provide the complete transaction data, it turns out that for simple payment transactions it is only necessary to make available a commitment to the set of transactions in a block (such as a Merkle tree root), together with the set of senders who have signed the commitment, confirming that they have received inclusion proofs of their transactions. Users can then generate Zero-Knowledge proofs (ZK-proofs) of their own balances by combining the inclusion proofs of their sent transactions with the inclusion proofs and ZK-proofs of sufficient balance of each received transaction, which is provided by the transaction sender offchain. Our rollup design uses this method to achieve increased throughput compared to existing alternatives. In addition, the design allows permissionless block building that can happen in parallel, without needing any leader election or any coordination between the block builders. Since the block builders do not verify the validity of the transactions, they can be fully stateless, allowing a very simple and censorship resistant rollup design.

1.2 Our Contributions

Intmax2 is an efficient and stateless rollup design that:

- Uses less onchain data than any existing rollup, giving an upper limit of 7500 transaction batches per second on Ethereum, where each transaction batch can transfer an unlimited number of tokens to an unlimited number of recipients.
- Offers permissionless block production.
- Provides stronger privacy properties than traditional ZK-rollups.

1.3 Formal Verification of the Security Proof

We give a pen-and-paper proof of the security of the protocol in Theorem 1. This proof has been formally verified in the Lean theorem prover [17] by the Nethermind Formal Verification team [2]. All mathematical definitions and statements that are needed for the security proof contain a hyperlink (like this:⌕) to the formalized version.

2 Simplified Design Description

In this section we describe a simplified version of the design which doesn't use ZK-proofs. The simplified design achieves low onchain data consumption (4–5 bytes per transaction sender), but is otherwise inefficient and not private. In Sect. 4 we add ZK-proofs to the design in order to achieve efficiency and privacy.

2.1 Overview

The simplified design works roughly as follows. At the heart of the design is a rollup contract deployed on a programmable blockchain (such as Ethereum). To deposit funds to the rollup, a user simply sends the funds, together with the L2 address of the recipient, to the rollup contract which then records the deposit in its contract storage. To transfer funds on the rollup, a subset of L2 accounts will first send their transactions to a single aggregator, which then inserts the transactions at the leaves of a merkle tree. Then the aggregator sends to each sender the merkle root and the merkle proof for that sender's transaction. Each sender then signs the merkle root with their public BLS key and sends this signature back to the aggregator. The aggregator then aggregates the signatures into a single aggregated signature, and sends the merkle root, the aggregated signature and the list of public keys of the senders that was included in the aggregated signature to the rollup contract. The rollup contract then verifies the signature and adds the root, signature and sender list to its storage. Each sender is then responsible for sending the merkle proof of the transaction to each transaction recipient offchain, together with earlier merkle proofs that together prove that the sender had sufficient balance for the transaction. To prove their own balance, each user needs to keep track of all merkle proofs they have received from aggregators and other users. This collection of merkle proofs, called a balance proof, is sent to the rollup contract when a user wants to withdraw their funds to L1.

We now describe the simplified design in more details.

2.2 Notation

If X and Y are sets, we will write Y^X for the set of all functions from X to Y. We will often call a function $f \in Y^X$ a *mapping* from (elements of) X to (elements of) Y.

2.3 Setup

The design depends on an authenticated dictionary scheme[1] AD, a signature aggregation scheme[2] SA, and a collision-resistant hash function H : $\{0,1\}^* \to \{0,1\}^n$. Given a security parameter $\lambda \in \mathbb{N}$ we set up the authenticated dictionary scheme

$$\mathsf{AD}.(\mathcal{K}, \mathcal{M}, \mathcal{C}, \Pi, \mathsf{Commit}, \mathsf{Verify})$$

and the signature aggregation scheme

$$\mathsf{SA}.(\mathcal{K}_p, \mathcal{K}_s, \Sigma, \mathsf{KeyGen}, \mathsf{Sign}, \mathsf{Aggregate}, \mathsf{Verify}).$$

We use the alias $\mathcal{K}_2 := \mathsf{SA}.\mathcal{K}_p$ and call this the set of *L2 accounts*. We also depend on a set $\mathcal{K}_1$ of L1 accounts[3], and a lattice-ordered abelian group $\mathcal{V}$ which is used as the set of transaction values and account balances.[4] We denote by $\mathcal{V}_+ \subseteq \mathcal{V}$ the subset of positive values, defined as the values $v \in \mathcal{V}$ where $v \geq 0$.

2.4 Rollup Contract

The rollup contract is a smart contract deployed on a programmable blockchain (e.g. Ethereum), which is responsible for keeping track of the rollup state and for managing deposits, transfers, and withdrawals. The internal state of the rollup contract consists of the list of all blocks that have been added to the rollup so far. There are three types of blocks in our design, namely deposit blocks, transfer blocks and withdrawal blocks, denoted by $\mathcal{B}_{deposit}$, $\mathcal{B}_{transfer}$ and $\mathcal{B}_{withdrawal}$ respectively. We formally define these sets below where we describe the respective protocols. Letting $\mathcal{B} := \mathcal{B}_{deposit} \sqcup \mathcal{B}_{transfer} \sqcup \mathcal{B}_{withdrawal}$ be the set of all blocks , the contract state is formally defined as

$$\mathcal{S}_{contract} := \mathcal{B}^*.$$

When the rollup contract is deployed to the blockchain, it is initialized with the state () consisting of the empty list .

2.5 Depositing

To deposit funds from L1 to L2, a L1 user will simply send the funds to the rollup contract along with the L2 address of the recipient. The rollup contract

---

[1] See Appendix A.2.
[2] See Appendix A.3.
[3] For instance, in Ethereum, accounts are represented by 20 bytes, so in this case we have $\mathcal{K}_1 := \{0,1\}^{20\cdot 8}$.
[4] See Appendix A.5 for the definition of a lattice-ordered abelian group. This generality allows us to easily support transfers of multiple value types (e.g. NFTs, ERC20 tokens, etc.) by letting $\mathcal{V}$ be the set of mappings from a set of token names to the set $\mathbb{Z}$ of integers, which naturally gets the structure of a lattice-ordered abelian group.

then constructs a *deposit block* which consists of the specified recipient and the deposited amount. Formally, we define the set of deposit blocks as

$$\mathcal{B}_{deposit} := \mathcal{K}_2 \times \mathcal{V}_+.$$

The contract then adds this deposit block to the list of blocks in its storage.

2.6 Transferring

We now describe the protocol for transferring funds on the rollup (illustrated in Fig. 1). To transfer funds from an L2 account, the account owner will first construct a *transaction batch*, which is a mapping that maps each transaction recipient to the amount the sender wants to send to that recipient. A transaction recipient is either an L2 account or an L1 account (used when withdrawing to L1, as described in Sect. 2.7). Formally, letting $\mathcal{K} := \mathcal{K}_1 \amalg \mathcal{K}_2$, a transaction batch is an element of $\mathcal{V}_+^{\mathcal{K}}$, i.e. a mapping from $\mathcal{K}$ to $\mathcal{V}_+$.

Suppose we have a set of senders $S \subseteq \mathcal{K}_2$ where each sender $s \in S$ has a secret key sk_s and a transaction batch $t_s \in \mathcal{V}_+^{\mathcal{K}}$ they want to send. The transfer protocol consists of two phases. In the first phase, the senders collaborate with a single aggregator to produce a *transfer block* which is added to the rollup contract. In the second phase, after the transfer block has been added to the rollup contract, each transaction sender s will send (offchain) to each recipient (i.e. accounts $r \in \mathcal{K}$ where $t_s(r) \neq 0$) the data needed to prove that the sender sent the specified amount to the recipient in the transfer block. We now describe the two phases of the transfer protocol in more details.

Phase 1: Constructing and Adding a Transfer Block. To send the transaction batches, the senders will first select a single aggregator[5] and agree upon a common bitstring $extradata \in \{0,1\}^*$. This bitstring can be used to implement protections against replay attacks and delayed block publication (see Sect. 2.8). Then the senders and aggregator interacts in the following protocol.

1. First, each sender s chooses a random salt $salt_s$, hashes their transaction batch with the salt
$$h_s \leftarrow H(t_s, salt_s),$$
and sends h_s to the aggregator.[6]
2. The aggregator collects all the transaction batch hashes from the senders. Let $S' \subseteq S$ be the subset of senders who sent a transaction batch hash to the aggregator. The aggregator then constructs the dictionary[7] (S', h) where h_s

---

[5] The protocol allows anyone to be an aggregator for a transfer block, enabling maximum censorship resistance.
[6] Sending the transaction hash instead of the transaction itself gives privacy from the aggregator.
[7] See Appendix A.1 for the definition of a dictionary.

is the transaction batch hash by s for all $s \in S'$, and constructs a dictionary commitment and lookup proofs:

$$(C, (S', \pi)) \leftarrow \mathsf{AD.Commit}(S', h).$$

The aggregator sends to each sender $s \in S'$ the dictionary commitment C and the lookup proof π_s for the sender's transaction batch hash.

3. Upon receiving the dictionary commitment and lookup proof, each sender s checks if the lookup proof is valid with the commitment:

$$\mathsf{AD.Verify}(\pi_s, s, h_s, C) \stackrel{?}{=} True.$$

If the lookup proof is valid, the sender generates the signature

$$\sigma_s \leftarrow \mathsf{SA.Sign}(sk_s, (C, aggregator, extradata))$$

and sends this signature to the aggregator.

4. The aggregator collects the signatures from the senders and verifies them. Let $S'' \subseteq S'$ be the subset of senders who sent a valid signature. The aggregator then constructs the aggregated signature

$$\sigma \leftarrow \mathsf{SA.Aggregate}((s, \sigma_s)_{s \in S''}),$$

and constructs the tuple $(aggregator, extradata, C, S'', \sigma)$, called a *transfer block*. Formally, we define the set of transfer blocks $\mathcal{B}$ as

$$\mathcal{B}_{transfer} = \mathcal{K}_1 \times \{0,1\}^* \times \mathsf{AD}.\mathcal{C} \times \mathcal{P}(\mathcal{K}_2) \times \mathsf{SA}.\Sigma.$$

The aggregator sends this transfer block to the rollup contract using their L1 account.

5. Upon receiving the transfer block, the rollup contract verifies the aggregated signature:

$$\mathsf{SA.Verify}(S'', (C, aggregator, extradata), \sigma) \stackrel{?}{=} True$$

and also verifies that the transaction is indeed coming from the account *aggregator*. If these checks are valid, the contract adds the transfer block to the list of blocks in its storage. If not, the transaction is reverted.

Phase 2: Maintaining and Distributing Balance Proofs. To be able to prove the balance of their account, each user needs to maintain a *balance proof*, which is the collection of transaction batches with corresponding salts and lookup proofs that they have received from an aggregator (when sending transactions) and from other users (when receiving transactions). We formally define the set of balance proofs as

$$\Pi := Dict(\mathsf{AD}.\mathcal{C} \times \mathcal{K}_2, (\mathsf{AD}.\Pi \times \{0,1\}^*) \times \mathcal{V}_+^{\mathcal{K}}).$$

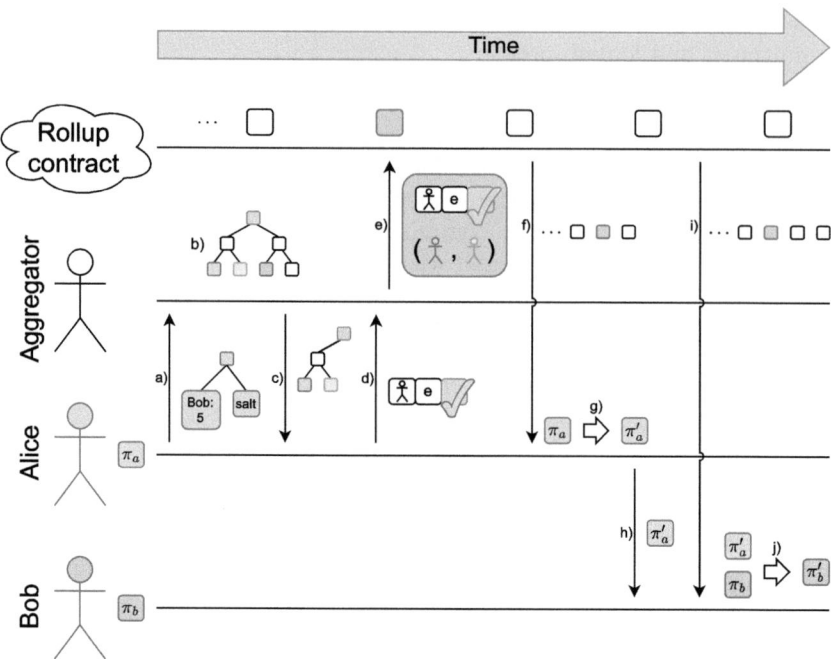

Fig. 1. The transfer protocol. In this example, Alice wants to send 5 coins to Bob. a) Alice starts by sending the hash of the transaction batch, consisting of a single transaction of 5 coins to Bob, and a random salt to an aggregator. b) The aggregator then constructs a merkle tree consisting of Alice's transaction batch hash and the transaction batch hashes of other senders. c) The aggregator sends the merkle proof of Alice's transaction batch to Alice. d) Alice verifies the merkle proof and signs the merkle root together with the pre-determined extradata e. This signature is sent back to the aggregator. e) The aggregator collects the signatures from all senders, constructs the transfer block, and sends it to the rollup contract. f) Alice watches the blocks that are added to the rollup contract until the block containing her transaction is published. g) Alice updates her balance proof by adding her transaction batch, the salt and the merkle proof. h) Alice sends to Bob her updated balance proof. h) Bob updates his view of the rollup blocks. i) Bob updates his balance proof by merging it with the balance proof he received from Alice.

A balance proof is valid if the following algorithm returns $True\mathcal{G}$.

$$\text{Verify: } \Pi \to \{True, False\}$$
$$(K, D) \mapsto \bigwedge_{\substack{(C,s)\in K \\ ((\pi, salt), t) = D(C, s)}} \text{AD.Verify}(\pi, s, \mathsf{H}(t, salt), C)$$

In other words, a valid balance proof is a dictionary which maps commitment-sender pairs (C, s) to tuples $((\pi, salt), t)$ where $t \in \mathcal{V}_+^{\mathcal{K}}$ is a transaction batch,

$salt$ is a random salt and $\pi \in \mathsf{AD}.\Pi$ is a valid lookup proof that $H(t, salt)$ is the value at index s in an authenticated dictionary with commitment C.

Each user will maintain a balance proof, which is initialized as the empty dictionary. In the second phase of the transfer protocol, each transaction sender will add their transaction batch with the corresponding lookup proof they received from the aggregator (if they did receive one) to their own balance proof. Then, they will send this new balance proof to each recipient of the transaction batch. Upon receiving the balance proof, each recipient will then merge it with their own. In details, if $\pi_b \in \Pi$ is the current balance proof of a recipient named Bob and $\pi_a \in \Pi$ is the balance proof they received from a sender named Alice, then Bob performs the following algorithm:

- Verify the received balance proof:

$$\mathsf{Verify}(\pi_a) \stackrel{?}{=} True.$$

If valid, continue to the next step, otherwise terminate.
- Update their balance proof π_b by merging it with π_a:

$$\pi_b \leftarrow \mathsf{Merge}(\pi_a, \pi_b),$$

where Merge is the dictionary merging algorithm defined in Appendix A.1.

To compute the balance of their accounts, users will use the balance function

$$\mathsf{Bal} \colon \Pi \times \mathcal{B}^* \to \mathcal{S},$$

defined in Appendix B. Here $\mathcal{S}$ is the set of states, where a state is an assignment of a balance to each account. Formally, let $\overline{\mathcal{K}} := \mathcal{K}_1 \amalg \mathcal{K}_2 \amalg \{\text{Source}\}$, where Source is a special account used to represent deposits and withdrawals. Then the set of states $\mathcal{S}$ is defined as

$$\mathcal{S} := \{b \in \mathcal{V}^{\overline{\mathcal{K}}}, \text{ such that } b_k \geq 0, \ \forall k \in \overline{\mathcal{K}} \backslash \{\text{Source}\}\}.$$

The balance function takes a balance proof $\pi \in \Pi$ and the current state of the rollup contract $(B_*) \in \mathcal{B}^*$, and returns the balance of each account in the rollup that can be proven by the balance proof.

2.7 Withdrawing

When a user wants to withdraw funds from their L2 account to an L1 account, they must first transfer the funds to the L1 account using the transfer protocol described above. When the transfer block is added to the rollup contract, the contract does not automatically withdraw the funds to L1. Instead, to initiate the withdrawal, the owner of the L1 account must send a withdrawal request to the rollup contract which consists of the user's current balance proof $\pi \in \Pi$. Upon receiving the balance proof, the rollup contract performs the following steps:

- First, the balance proof is verified:

$$\mathsf{Verify}(\pi) \stackrel{?}{=} True.$$

- If the balance proof is valid, the rollup contract constructs a withdrawal block, which is simply the in-rollup balance of each L1 account computed from the balance proof and the current rollup state:

$$B \leftarrow \mathsf{Bal}(\pi, B_*)|_{K_1},$$

where B_* is the current list of blocks in the rollup contract. Formally, the set of withdrawal blocks is defined as

$$\mathcal{B}_{withdrawal} = \mathcal{V}_+^{K_1}.$$

- The contract adds the withdrawal block B to the list of blocks in its storage:

$$B_* \leftarrow (B_* || (B))$$

- For each L1 account $k \in K_1$, the contract withdraws the amount B_k to the L1 account.

These steps ensure that a user cannot double-spend by withdrawing the same funds twice, since the amount to be withdrawn is computed by applying the balance function to the balance proof *and all previous blocks that have been added to the rollup*, which includes all previous withdrawal blocks. This is formalised in Theorem 1, which is stated and proven in Appendix C.

2.8 Protection Against Replay Attacks and Delayed Block Publication

There are a couple of attacks that a malicious aggregator can do that we need to protect against. One kind of attack is delayed block publication, where a malicious aggregator waits a long time before publishing the transfer block, causing a liveness issue. A second attack is replay attacks, where a malicious aggregator publishes the same transfer block multiple times, thereby draining the balances of the senders. Instead of adding protections against these attacks in-protocol, it can be done out-of-protocol as follows.

In order to make users trust them, an aggregator can self-impose restrictions that prohibits them from performing these attacks by deploying a *relayer contract* on L1. When a set of senders wants to create a transfer block with this aggregator, the aggregator will first pick a deadline for the transfer block not far into the future. The senders who accepts the deadline enters the transfer protocol using this deadline as *extradata*, and the relayer contract address as *aggregator*. After constructing the transfer block, the aggregator will send it to the relayer contract from an L1 address which is whitelisted by the contract (for front-running protection). Upon receiving the transfer block, the relayer contract verifies the sender and checks if the deadline in the *extradata* field is no later than the current time, before forwarding the transfer block to the rollup contract. This protects against delayed block publication. In addition, the relayer contract stores the timestamp of the last block that it has forwarded to the rollup contract, and verifies that each new transfer block has a timestamp strictly greater than the last forwarded block before forwarding it. This protects against replay attacks.

3 Data Usage and Compression

In this section we analyze the scalability of our design and describe how to add compression to achieve even more scalability. The main bottleneck for the scalability is the size of the transfer blocks, which is decomposed as follows:

- The aggregator's L1 address (20 bytes in Ethereum)
- A *extradata* string (32 bytes)
- An authenticated dictionary commitment (32 bytes if it is a merkle tree root)
- The subset of senders $S \subseteq \mathcal{K}_2$ in the block ($|S| \times 96$ bytes if encoded as a list of BLS public keys)
- An aggregated signature (48 bytes for BLS signatures)

This gives a transfer block size of $|S| \times 96 + 132$ bytes, where $|S|$ is the number of senders in the block. This is smaller than for traditional rollups where all transaction details (such as sender, recipient and transaction amount) are included in the blocks. Also, unlike traditional rollups, our block size only depends on the number of senders, and not the number of transactions. This means that a sender can send a transaction batch with an arbitrary number of recipients without affecting the size of the transfer block.

To further increase scalability, we can add block compression out-of-protocol using the relay contracts we introduced in Sect. 2.8, where an aggregator sends compressed transfer blocks to their relay contract, which will decompress the blocks before relaying them to the rollup contract. A simple compression algorithm works as follows. Users can register their public BLS key with the relay contract of an aggregator and receive a short incremental ID. The relay contract stores in its storage a dictionary which maps IDs to BLS public keys. Then, when the aggregator sends transfer blocks to the relay contract, they will send the short IDs of the senders instead of their public keys. The relay contract looks up each ID in its dictionary and reconstructs the transfer block with the public keys before sending it to the rollup contract. The size of the IDs depends on the total number of IDs in the dictionary. As an example, in order to support 10 billion addresses (more than the current world population), each ID must be

$$\log_2(10^9) \approx 33 \text{ bits} \approx 4.15 \text{ bytes},$$

which gives a block size of about $|S| \times 4.15 + 132$ bytes. When implemented on Ethereum, which provides 0.375 MB of data per block [20], with blocks coming every 12 s [1], we get a theoretical limit of about

$$\frac{0.375 \times 10^6 - 132}{4.15} \approx 90000$$

senders per L1 block, or 7500 senders per second. This number will increase when Ethereum adds more scaling. According to [20], the goal is to achieve ≈ 16 MB per block, which would allow ≈ 320000 senders per second.

4 Adding Privacy and Efficiency

The simplified design described in Sect. 2 lacks privacy, because transaction recipients will gain information about other transactions not intended for them, and it lacks efficiency because the balance proofs are large and expensive to verify (especially onchain during withdrawals). In this section, we add privacy and efficiency using recursive ZK-proofs.

4.1 Changes to Rollup Contract State and the Procedure of Adding Blocks

First, the rollup contract is modified so that instead of storing the list of all blocks added to the rollup, it stores a list of *history roots*, where each root is a hash digest in $\{0,1\}^n$, as well as a mapping which maps each L1 account to the total amount that has been withdrawn to the L1 account:

$$\mathcal{S}_{contract} := (\{0,1\}^n)^* \times \mathcal{V}_+^{\mathcal{K}_1}.$$

If $((root_i)_{i \in [N]}, withdrawn)$ is the current state of the contract, and $B \in \mathcal{B}$ is a new block to be added to the rollup, the contract adds the new block as follows. If the block is a deposit block or a transfer block, the contract computes a new history root by taking the hash $\mathsf{H}(root_N, B)$ of the most recent history root and the new block, and adds this new history root to its list of history roots. If the new block is a withdrawal block, the withdrawn amounts are added to the current map of withdrawn amounts:

$$withdrawn \leftarrow withdrawn + B.$$

4.2 Changes to the Transfer Protocol

Phase 1 of the transfer protocol regarding how to construct and add transfer blocks remains exactly as described in Sect. 2.6, but Phase 2 regarding how to maintain and distribute balance proofs is changed as follows. When a transaction sender s sends funds to a recipient r, instead of providing the recipient with the complete transaction history of the sender and recursively those of other users (as in the simplified design), they will only send the tuple $(root, s, r, v, \pi)$ where

- $root \in \{0,1\}^n$ is the history root of the rollup block containing the transaction,
- $s \in \mathcal{K}_2$ is the sender's L2 address,
- $r \in \mathcal{K}$ is the recipient's address,
- $v \in \mathcal{V}_+$ is the transaction amount,
- π is a transaction validity proof, which is a ZK-proof proving that the sender s did send a transaction with value v to the recipient r in the rollup block with history hash $root$, and that the sender had a sufficient balance for sending it.

This means that the recipient only learns about this transaction, and gets zero knowledge about anything else, such as the balance of the sender or other transactions.

To be able to construct transaction validity proofs, each user needs to maintain the data consisting of

- All transaction batches they have sent (that have been included in a transfer block onchain) together with their corresponding salts and lookup proofs
- All verified transactions $(hash, s, r, v, \pi)$ they have received from other users

Given this data, as well as the list of blocks added to the rollup[8], each user can generate validity proofs for their transactions.

4.3 Changes to the Withdrawal Protocol

When the owner of an L1 account wants to withdraw their in-rollup balance to L1, they will send a withdrawal request to the rollup contract which consists of an L1 address $address \in \mathcal{K}_1$, a value $v \in \mathcal{V}_+$, a history root $root \in \{0,1\}^n$ and a ZK-proof that $address$ has received at least v in the rollup at history root $root$. Upon receiving the withdrawal request, the rollup contract will verify that the ZK-proof is valid and that $root$ is in the list of history roots in its storage. If these checks are valid, the contract will compute the in-rollup balance of the L1 account by subtracting the previously withdrawn amount of the address from v. Then, the contract withdraws the computed balance to L1 and updates the total amount withdrawn in its storage.

---

[8] This can be obtained by monitoring all L1 transactions sent to the rollup contract.

5 Conclusion

We presented Intmax2, a novel ZK-rollup approach that completely shifts away from traditional ZK-rollup approaches. In contrast with previous approaches, our solution does not require the posting of all transaction data on the underlying L1, which enables unprecedented scalability. By leveraging the fact that aggregators do not need to perform computationally intensive zero-knowledge proofs, and instead moving the computation on the side of the users in the system, our design provides a novel, practical, and resilient solution to L2 scaling. On a final note, by making the aggregator role completely permissionless, our design allows for a much more censorship-resistant solution, thus addressing one of the main existing problems in the rollup space.

A Background

A.1 Dictionaries

Definition 1. *Let X be a set. We define*

$$Maybe(X) := X \amalg \{\bot\}.$$

Definition 2. *Given two sets X and Y, we define*

$$Dict(X, Y) := Maybe(Y)^X.$$

Elements of $Dict(X, Y)$ are called dictionaries over (X, Y).

Remark 1. *A dictionary over (X, Y) is also often called a* partial function *from X to Y.*

Dictionaries can be combined as follows.

Definition 3. *Let X be a set. We define*

$$\text{First}: Maybe(X) \times Maybe(X) \to Maybe(X)$$

$$(x_1, x_2) \mapsto \begin{cases} x_1, & \text{if } x_1 \neq \bot \\ x_2, & \text{otherwise.} \end{cases}$$

Definition 4. *Let X and Y be sets. We define*

$$\text{Merge}: Dict(X, Y) \times Dict(X, Y) \to Dict(X, Y)$$
$$(D_1, D_2) \mapsto D,$$
$$\text{where } D(x) := First(D_1(x), D_2(x)), \forall x \in X.$$

A.2 Authenticated Dictionaries

Definition 5 (Authenticated dictionary scheme). *An authenticated dictionary scheme over a key set $\mathcal{K}$ and value set $\mathcal{M}$ consists of sets*

- $\mathcal{C}$ of commitments
- Π of lookup proofs

and algorithms

- Commit : $Dict(\mathcal{K}, \mathcal{M}) \to \mathcal{C} \times Dict(\mathcal{K}, \Pi)$
- Verify : $\Pi \times \mathcal{K} \times \mathcal{M} \times \mathcal{C} \to \{True, False\}$

parameterized over a security parameter $\lambda \in \mathbb{N}$.

An authenticated dictionary scheme should satisfy correctness and binding, defined as follows.

Definition 6 (Correctness). *An authenticated dictionary scheme is correct if for all dictionaries $D \in Dict(\mathcal{K}, \mathcal{M})$ we get*

$$(C, \pi) \leftarrow \mathsf{Commit}(D)$$

such that

$$\mathsf{Verify}(\pi_k, k, D_k, C) = True, \forall k \in \mathcal{K}, D_k \neq \bot.$$

Definition 7 (Binding). *An authenticated dictionary scheme is binding if it is computationally infeasible to find a commitment $C \in \mathcal{C}$, a key $k \in \mathcal{K}$, values $m_1, m_2 \in \mathcal{M}$ and lookup proofs $\pi_1, \pi_2 \in \Pi$ such that*

$$\mathsf{Verify}(\pi_1, k, m_1, C) = True$$
$$\wedge \, \mathsf{Verify}(\pi_2, k, m_2, C) = True$$
$$\wedge \, m_1 \neq m_2.$$

Implementation. A common implementation of an authenticated dictionary scheme is sparse merkle trees [8], where the binding property is achieved by using a collision-resistant hash function.

A.3 Signature Aggregation

A signature aggregation scheme consists of sets

- $\mathcal{K}_p$ of public keys
- $\mathcal{K}_s$ of secret keys
- Σ of signatures

and algorithms

- KeyGen : $1 \to \mathcal{K}_p \times \mathcal{K}_s$
- Sign : $\mathcal{K}_s \times \mathcal{M} \to \Sigma$
- Aggregate : $(\mathcal{K}_p \times \Sigma)^* \to \Sigma$
- Verify : $\mathcal{K}_p^* \times \mathcal{M} \times \Sigma \to \{True, False\}$

parameterized over a security parameter $\lambda \in \mathbb{N}$.

A signature aggregation scheme should satisfy correctness and unforgeability, defined as follows.

Definition 8. ⌧ *A signature aggregation scheme is* correct *if whenever we have a list of key-pairs $(pk_i, sk_i)_{i \in [n]}$ generated by the KeyGen algorithm, and a message $m \in \mathcal{M}$, we have*

$$\mathsf{Verify}((pk_i)_{i \in [n]}, m, \mathsf{Aggregate}((pk_i, \mathsf{Sign}(sk_i, m))_{i \in [n]})) = True.$$

Definition 9. ⌧ *A signature aggregation scheme is* unforgeable *if it is computationally infeasible for an adversary to output a list $(pk_i)_{i \in [n]}$ of public keys, a message $m \in \mathcal{M}$ and a signature $\sigma \in \Sigma$ such that*

$$\mathsf{Verify}((pk_i)_{i \in [n]}, m, \sigma) = True,$$

and where one of the public keys $(pk_i)_{i \in [n]}$ belongs to an honest user who didn't sign the message m with their secret key.

Implementation. We will use the modified BLS signature scheme introduced in [4], which is defined as follows.

Given a security parameter $\lambda \in \mathbb{N}$, we setup a bilinear pairing $e : \mathbb{G}_0 \times \mathbb{G}_1 \to \mathbb{G}_T$ of groups of prime order q, and two hash functions $\mathcal{H}_0 : \mathcal{M} \to \mathbb{G}_0$ and $\mathcal{H}_1 : \mathcal{M} \to \mathbb{Z}_q$. We then let

- $\mathcal{K}_p := \mathbb{G}_1$
- $\mathcal{K}_s := \mathbb{Z}_q$
- $\Sigma := \mathbb{G}_0$

and

- KeyGen() $\to (sk, pk)$, where the secret key is a random value $\mathsf{sk} \xleftarrow{R} \mathbb{Z}_q$ and the public key is $pk \leftarrow g_1^{\mathsf{sk}} \in \mathbb{G}_1$
- Sign$(sk, m) \to \sigma$, where $\sigma \leftarrow \mathcal{H}_0(m)^{\mathsf{sk}} \in \mathbb{G}_0$.
- Aggregate$((pk_1, \sigma_1), \ldots, (pk_n, \sigma_n)) \to \sigma$, where

$$\sigma \leftarrow \prod_{i \in [n]} \sigma_i^{t_i},$$

and where $t_i \leftarrow \mathcal{H}_1(pk_i, \{pk_1, \ldots, pk_n\})$ for all $i \in [n]$.

- Verify$((pk_1, \ldots, pk_n), m, \sigma)$ is computed by first computing the aggregated public key as
$$pk \leftarrow \prod_{i \in [n]} pk_i^{t_i},$$
where $t_i \leftarrow \mathcal{H}_1(pk_i, (pk_j)_{j \in [n]})$ for all $i \in [n]$. Then, output $True$ if
$$e(g_1, \sigma) = e(pk, \mathcal{H}_0(m))$$
and output $False$ otherwise.

A.4 Zero-Knowledge Proofs

Zero-knowledge proofs, introduced in [12], allow a prover $\mathcal{P}$ to prove to a verifier $\mathcal{V}$ a relation between a statement x and a witness w. A non-interactive zero-knowledge (NIZK) proof is a trio of algorithms:

- ZK.Setup$(\lambda) \to pp$. For a certain security parameter λ, the setup algorithm outputs pp, the public parameters of the system.
- ZK.Prove$(pp, x, w) \to P$. Given the system's public parameters pp, a statement x, and a witness w, issue a proof P.
- ZK.Verify$(pp, x, P) \to \{True, False\}$. Upon receiving the public parameters pp, the public statement x and the proof P, the verifier $\mathcal{V}$ either accepts (returns $True$) or rejects (returns $False$) the proof depending on whether or not P is well-formed. In this case well-formed implies the successful proof of the relation between the statement x and the witness w.

Properties. A zero-knowledge proof scheme is considered sound if an adversary $\mathcal{A}$ attempting to prove the statement without knowing the secret witness w cannot produce a valid proof with probability greater than 2^{-k} for knowledge error k. A zero knowledge proof scheme is considered complete if there is a guarantee that if the prover and verifier are honest, then the verifier successfully accepts a proof that shows that the prover $\mathcal{P}$ knows the witness w. Additionally, a proof P is considered a proof-of-knowledge if the prover $\mathcal{P}$ must know the witness w to compute the proof for the pair (x, w), and such proof-of-knowledge is considered zero knowledge if the proof P reveals nothing about the witness w. Additionally, if the scheme produces succinct arguments, then it is a (zk)SNARK [5,6,10,13,16]. Quantum-secure similar constructions exist, as in [3,7].

A.5 Order Theory

We here restate some common definitions and results from order theory, which are used in our protocol description and security proof.

Prosets, Posets and Setoids.

Definition 10. *Let X be a set. A* preorder *on X is a binary relation $\leq$ on X such that*

- *$a \leq b \wedge b \leq c \Rightarrow a \leq c$ for all $a, b, c \in X$ (transitivity),*
- *$a \leq a$ for all $a \in X$ (reflexivity).*

A preordered set, *or* proset, *is a tuple $(X, \leq)$ where X is a set and $\leq$ is a preorder on X.*

Remark 2. *If $(X, \leq)$ is a proset, we will denote by $\geq$ the opposite relation:*

$$a \geq b \Leftrightarrow b \leq a.$$

Definition 11. ⊡ *Let $(X, \leq)$ be a proset. We say that two elements $a, b \in X$ are* isomorphic, *written $a \simeq b$, if $a \leq b \wedge a \geq b$.*

Definition 12. *Let $(X, \leq)$ be a proset. We say that the relation $\leq$ is*

- *a* partial order *if $a \simeq b \Leftrightarrow a = b$ for all $a, b \in X$, and*
- *an* equivalence relation *if $a \leq b \Leftrightarrow a \simeq b$ for all $a, b \in X$.*

We call $(X, \leq)$ a

- partially ordered set, *or* poset, *if $\leq$ is a partial order, and a*
- setoid *if $\leq$ is an equivalence relation.*

Examples of Preorders. We now define various preorders used in the paper.

Definition 13. ⊡ *Let X be a set. The* trivial preorder *on X is the preorder $\leq$ where $a \leq b$ for all $a, b \in X$, i.e. every pair of elements of X are related.*

Definition 14. ⊡ *Let X be a set. The equality relation $=$ on X is a preorder, called the* discrete preorder *on X. This is in fact the only relation on X that is both a partial order and an equivalence relation.*

Definition 15. ⊡ *Let $(X, \leq_X)$ be a proset. We define the induced preorder $\leq$ on $Maybe(X)$ where for all $x, y \in Maybe(X)$ we have*

$$x \leq y \Leftrightarrow x = \bot \vee (x, y \in X \wedge x \leq_X y).$$

Definition 16. *Let X be a set and let $(Y, \leq_Y)$ be a proset. We define the induced preorder $\leq$ on the set Y^X of functions from X to Y where for all $f, g \in Y^X$ we have*

$$f \leq g \Leftrightarrow f(x) \leq_Y g(x) \, \forall x \in X.$$

Definition 17. *Let X be a set and let $(Y, \leq_Y)$ be a proset. We define the induced preorder on $Dict(X, Y) = Maybe(Y)^X$ by combining Definition 15 and Definition 16 above.*

Definition 18. *Let $(Y, \leq_Y)$ be a proset and let $X \subseteq Y$. We define the* induced subset preorder $\leq_X$ *on X where for all $x, y \in X$ we have*

$$x \leq_X y \Leftrightarrow x \leq_Y y.$$

Definition 19. *Let $(X, \leq_X)$ and $(Y, \leq_Y)$ be prosets. We define the* induced product preorder $\leq$ *on $X \times Y$ where for all $x, x' \in X$ and $y, y' \in Y$ we have*

$$(x, x') \leq (y, y') \Leftrightarrow x \leq_X x' \wedge y \leq_Y y'.$$

Joins and Meets

Definition 20. Let $(X, \leq)$ be a proset, let $(x_i)_{i \in I}$ be an indexed family of elements of X and let $x \in X$. We say that x is a join of $(x_i)_{i \in I}$ if the following two properties hold:

- $x_i \leq x$ for all $i \in I$
- if $x' \in X$ is an element such that $x_i \leq x'$ for all $i \in I$, then we have $x \leq x'$.

Dually, we say that x is a meet of $(x_i)_{i \in I}$ if the following two properties hold:

- $x_i \geq x$ for all $i \in I$
- if $x' \in X$ is an element such that $x_i \geq x'$ for all $i \in I$, then we have $x \geq x'$.

We have that meets and joins are unique up to isomorphism, stated as follows.

Proposition 1. ⊡ ⊡ Let $(X, \leq)$ be a proset, let $(x_i)_{i \in I}$ be an indexed family of elements of X and let $x, y \in X$. If x and y are both joins (or both meets) of $(x_i)_{i \in I}$, then we have $x \simeq y$. If $(X, \leq)$ is also a poset, we have $x = y$.

Definition 21. Let $(X, \leq)$ be a proset, let $(x_i)_{i \in I}$ be an indexed family of elements of X and let $x \in X$ be a join (resp. meet) of $(x_i)_{i \in I}$. Then we write $x \simeq \bigvee_{i \in I} x_i$ (resp. $x \simeq \bigwedge_{i \in I} x_i$). If $(X, \leq)$ is also a poset, we have that isomorphisms imply equality, so we can write $x = \bigvee_{i \in I} x_i$ (resp. $x = \bigwedge_{i \in I} x_i$). If $I = \{1, 2\}$ we can instead write $x_1 \vee x_2$ for the join and $x_1 \wedge x_2$ for the meet.

Examples of Joins and Meets. We now identify the joins and meets in the prosets we constructed in Appendix A.5.

Proposition 2. ⊡ ⊡ Let $(X, \simeq)$ be a setoid, and let $x, y \in X$. Then we have that x and y have a join in X iff $x \simeq y$, in which case we have $x \simeq y \simeq x \vee y$.

Proposition 3. ⊡ ⊡ ⊡ Let X be a proset and consider the induced proset $Maybe(X)$. For all $x \in Maybe(x)$ we have $x \vee \bot \simeq x$. Also, for all $x, y \in X$, we have that x and y have a join in $Maybe(X)$ iff they have a join in X, in which case the two joins are isomorphic.

Proposition 4. ⊡ ⊡ Let $(X, \simeq)$ be a setoid, and let $x, y \in Maybe(X)$. Then, x and y have a join in $Maybe(X)$ iff

$$x \neq \bot \wedge y \neq \bot \Rightarrow x \simeq y.$$

If this is the case, we have $x \vee y \simeq \mathsf{First}(x, y)$.

Proposition 5. ⊡ ⊡ Let X be a set, let $(Y, \leq_Y)$ be a proset and let $f, g \in Y^X$. We have that f and g have a join in Y^X iff $f(x)$ and $g(x)$ have a join $f(x) \vee g(x)$ in Y for all $x \in X$. In this case, we have $f \vee g \simeq h$, where h is a map where $h(x) \simeq f(x) \vee g(x)$ for all $x \in X$.

Proposition 6. ⊡ ⊡ *Let X be a set, let $(Y, \simeq)$ be a setoid and let $D_1, D_2 \in \text{Dict}(X, Y)$ be two dictionaries. Then, we have that D_1 and D_2 have a join in $\text{Dict}(X, Y)$ iff for all $x \in X$ we have*

$$D_1(x) \neq \bot \wedge D_2(x) \neq \bot \Rightarrow D_1(x) \simeq D_2(x).$$

If this is the case, then we have $D_1 \vee D_2 \simeq \text{Merge}(D_1, D_2)$.

Proof. This follows from Proposition 4 and Proposition 5.

Monotone Functions.

Definition 22. *Let $(X, \leq_X)$ and $(Y, \leq_Y)$ be prosets, and let $f : X \to Y$ be a function. We say that f is* monotone *(also often called order-preserving) if for all $a, b \in X$ we have*

$$a \leq_X b \Rightarrow f(a) \leq_Y f(b).$$

Proposition 7. *If $(X, \leq_X)$, $(Y, \leq_Y)$ and $(Z, \leq_Z)$ are prosets, and if $f : X \to Y$ and $g : Y \to Z$ are monotone functions, then the composite function*

$$g \circ f \colon X \to Z$$
$$x \mapsto g(f(x))$$

is also monotone.

Lattice-Ordered Abelian Groups. We now define lattice-ordered abelian groups, which is the structure we require from the set $\mathcal{V}$ of transaction values (and account balances) in our design.

Definition 23. *A* lattice *is a poset in which every finite indexed family of elements has both a join and a meet.*

Definition 24. *A* lattice-ordered abelian group *is a tuple $(X, \leq, +, 0)$ where X is a set, $\leq$ is a binary relation on X, $+$ is a binary operator on X and $0 \in X$, such that*

- *$(X, +, 0)$ is an abelian group*
- *$(X, \leq)$ is a lattice*
- *For all $a, b, x \in X$ we have*

$$a \leq b \Rightarrow a + x \leq b + x.$$

Definition 25. *Given a lattice-ordered abelian group $(X, \leq, +, 0)$, we say that an element $x \in X$ is* positive *if $0 \leq x$.*

B Computing Balances

In this section we define the function

$$\mathsf{Bal}\colon \Pi \times \mathcal{B}^* \to \mathcal{V}^{\overline{\mathcal{K}}}$$

which is used in the simplified design to compute account balances from a balance proof and rollup contract state. This function is used by users to compute their own balance, as well as by the rollup contract when processing a withdrawal request. Given a balance proof $\pi \in \Pi$ and the current rollup state $B_* \in \mathcal{B}_*$, the account balances are computed in two steps. First, we extract a list of partial transactions from π and B_*, where a partial transaction consists of a sender, a recipient and a (possibly unknown) transaction amount. Then, we compute the balances of every account by applying a state transition function on the list of partial transactions. We now describe the steps in more details.

B.1 Step 1: Extracting a List of Partial Transactions

The first step of calculating balances is to extract a list of *partial transactions* from a balance proof π and the current list of blocks in the rollup B_*. The set of partial transactions, denoted $\mathcal{T}$, is defined as the subset

$$\mathcal{T} \subseteq \overline{\mathcal{K}}^2 \times Maybe(\mathcal{V}_+)$$

consisting of the tuples $((s,r),v)$ where $s \neq r$ and where $s = \text{Source}$ implies $v \neq \bot$. The process of extracting the list of partial transactions is described by a function

$$\mathsf{TransactionsInBlocks}\colon \Pi \times B^* \to \mathcal{T}^*$$

which we will now define. Given a deposit block $(r,v) \in \mathcal{B}_{deposit}$, we extract the one-element list consisting of the partial transaction $((\text{Source},r),v)$:

$$\mathsf{TransactionsInBlock}_{deposit}\colon \mathcal{B}_{deposit} \to \mathcal{T}^*$$
$$(r,v) \mapsto (((\text{Source},r),v)).$$

We then define the function

$$\mathsf{TransactionsInBlock}_{transfer}\colon \Pi \times \mathcal{B}_{transfer} \to \mathcal{T}^*$$

for extracting a list of partial transactions from a balance proof and a transfer block as follows. Given a balance proof $\pi \in \Pi$ and a transfer block $(aggregator, extradata, C, S, \sigma) \in \mathcal{B}_{transfer}$, we take, for each sender-recipient pair $(s,r) \in \mathcal{K}_2 \times \mathcal{K}$ where $s \neq r$, in lexicographic order, the partial transaction $((s,r),v)$ where

$$v = \begin{cases} t(r), \text{ where } (\_,t) = \pi(C,s), & \text{if } s \in S \text{ and } \pi(C,s) \neq \bot \\ \bot, & \text{if } s \in S \text{ and } \pi(C,s) = \bot \\ 0, & \text{if } s \notin S. \end{cases}$$

Given a withdrawal block, the list of transactions extracted from it consists of a transaction from each L1 account to the source account in order :

$$\mathsf{TransactionsInBlock}_{withdrawal} \colon \mathcal{B}_{withdrawal} \to \mathcal{T}^*$$
$$B \mapsto ((s, \mathsf{Source}), B_s)_{s \in K_1}.$$

We combine these functions into one function for extracting partial transactions from a balance proof and a block :

$$\mathsf{TransactionsInBlock} \colon \Pi \times \mathcal{B} \to \mathcal{T}^*$$
$$(\pi, B) \mapsto \begin{cases} \mathsf{TransactionsInBlock}_{deposit}(B), & \text{if } B \in \mathcal{B}_{deposit} \\ \mathsf{TransactionsInBlock}_{transfer}(\pi, B), & \text{if } B \in \mathcal{B}_{transfer} \\ \mathsf{TransactionsInBlock}_{withdrawal}(B), & \text{if } B \in \mathcal{B}_{withdrawal} \end{cases}.$$

Finally, to extract a list of partial transactions from a balance proof and a list of blocks, we extract the transactions from each block and concatenate the lists of partial transactions :

$$\mathsf{TransactionsInBlocks} \colon \Pi \times \mathcal{B}^* \to \mathcal{T}^*$$
$$(\pi, (B_i)_{i \in [n]}) \mapsto \mathsf{Concatenate}((\mathsf{TransactionsInBlock}(\pi, B_i))_{i \in [n]}).$$

B.2 Step 2: Computing Balances from a List of Partial Transactions

The second step in computing balances is to apply a *transition function* to the list of partial transactions obtained in step 1, starting from the state where all account balances are zero.

Definition 26. *A transition function*[9] *is a function on the form* $f \colon \mathcal{T} \times \mathcal{S} \to \mathcal{S}$, *where* $\mathcal{T}$ *is called the set of transactions and* $\mathcal{S}$ *is called the set of states.*

In our case, a state is an assignment of a balance to each account, where every non-source account has a positive balance :

$$\mathcal{S} := \{b \in \mathcal{V}^{\overline{K}}, \text{ such that } b_k \geq 0, \forall k \in \overline{K} \setminus \{\mathsf{Source}\}\},$$

and the set of transactions is the set $\mathcal{T}$ of partial transactions defined in Step 1 above. In order to define the transition function f, we will first define a different transition function $f_c \colon \mathcal{T}_c \times \mathcal{S} \to \mathcal{S}$, where the set of transactions is the subset $\mathcal{T}_c \subseteq \mathcal{T}$, called the *complete transactions*, consisting of the transactions $((s, r), v) \in \mathcal{T}$ where $v \neq \bot$. For all $i \in \overline{K}$, let $\mathbf{e}_i \in \mathbb{Z}^{\overline{K}}$ be the map where :

$$(\mathbf{e}_i)_j = \begin{cases} 1, & \text{if } i = j \\ 0, & \text{otherwise}. \end{cases}$$

---

[9] Sometimes called a semiautomation in the literature.

Then, for all complete transactions $((s,r),v) \in \mathcal{T}_c$ and for all $b \in \mathcal{S}$ and $k \in \overline{\mathcal{K}}$ we define

$$f_c(((s,r),v),b)_k := b_k + (\mathbf{e}_r - \mathbf{e}_s)_k \cdot v',$$

$$\text{where } v' := \begin{cases} v \wedge b_s, & \text{if } s \neq \text{Source} \\ v, & \text{if } s = \text{Source}. \end{cases}$$

Remark 3. *In the definition above, the minus operation in $\mathbf{e}_r - \mathbf{e}_s$ comes from the abelian group structure on $\mathbb{Z}^{\overline{K}}$, and the product operation in $(\mathbf{e}_r - \mathbf{e}_s) \cdot v'$ is the scalar multiplication coming from the natural $\mathbb{Z}$-module structure on the abelian group $\mathcal{V}$.*

Remark 4. *The transition function above is explained as follows. To apply a transaction where a non-source sender s sends the amount v to a recipient r, we first reduce the transacted amount v to the amount v', which is the greatest amount that is both less than the original value v (the sender shouldn't send more than in the original transaction) and less than the balance of the sender b_s (to avoid overspending). The reduced value v' is then subtracted from the sender and added to the recipient. The source account is considered to have sufficient balance for all of its transactions, so if the sender is the source account, the transaction value is not reduced.*

Before we can define the transition function $f : \mathcal{T} \times \mathcal{S} \to \mathcal{S}$, we will define a preorder on $\mathcal{T}$ and $\mathcal{S}$. In the following definitions, we apply the inductions from Appendix A.5. To get the preorder on $\mathcal{T}$, recall that $\mathcal{T}$ is a subset of $\overline{\mathcal{K}}^2 \times Maybe(\mathcal{V}_+)$. We first equip $\overline{\mathcal{K}}^2$ with the discrete preorder . Then we equip $\mathcal{V}_+$ with the discrete preorder , which induces a preorder on $Maybe(\mathcal{V}_+)$. We then get the induced product preorder on $\overline{\mathcal{K}}^2 \times Maybe(\mathcal{V}_+)$, and an induced subset preorder on the subset $\mathcal{T}$. To get the preorder on $\mathcal{S} = \mathcal{V}^{\overline{\mathcal{K}}}$, we use the underlying preorder on $\mathcal{V}$ coming from the fact that $\mathcal{V}$ is a lattice , and give $\mathcal{S}$ the subset preorder . Given these preorders on $\mathcal{T}$ and $\mathcal{S}$, we get an induced product preorder on $\mathcal{T} \times \mathcal{S}$ which we denote simply by $\leq$.

Lemma 1. *Let X and Y be preorders and let $f : X \to Y$ be a monotone function. Then, for all $x \in X$ we have*

$$\bigwedge_{\substack{x' \in X \\ x \leq x'}} f(x') = f(x).$$

Proof. Let $x \in X$ and let $S_x = \{f(x') \mid x' \in X, x \leq x'\}$. We need to show that $f(x)$ is the greatest lower bound of S_x. First, since f is monotone, we have that $f(x) \leq f(x')$ for all $x' \in X$, which implies that $f(x)$ is a lower bound of S_x. Since $f(x) \in S_x$, it is also the greatest lower bound of S_x.

Lemma 2. ⊏ *For all $T = ((s, r), v) \in \mathcal{T}_c$ and $b \in \mathcal{S}$, and for all $k \in \overline{K}\backslash\{s\}$ we have $b_k \leq f_c(T, b)_k$. In other words, when applying the transition function to a complete transactions, only the sender's balance may decrease.*

Proof. Let $T = ((s, r), v) \in \mathcal{T}_c$, $b \in \mathcal{S}$ and $k \in \overline{K}\backslash\{s\}$. By definition, we have

$$f_c(((s,r),v),b)_k := b_k + (\mathbf{e}_r - \mathbf{e}_s)_k \cdot v',$$

$$\text{where } v' := \begin{cases} v \wedge b_s, & \text{if } s \neq \text{Source} \\ v, & \text{if } s = \text{Source.} \end{cases}$$

We first show that $v' \geq 0$. We have two cases, either $s = \text{Source}$ or $s \neq \text{Source}$.

Case $s \neq$ Source. In this case we have $v' = v \wedge b_s$. By definition, we have $v \geq 0$. Also, since $s \neq$ Source, we also have $b_s \geq 0$ by the definition of the set of states $\mathcal{S}$. These two facts imply $v' = v \wedge b_s \geq 0$.
Case $s =$ Source. In this case we have $v' = v \geq 0$.

We have now shown that $v' \geq 0$. It follows that $f_c(((s,r),v),b)_k = b_k + (\mathbf{e}_r - \mathbf{e}_s)_k \cdot v' \geq b_k$, which was what we needed to show.

Proposition 8 ⊏ *The transition function for complete transactions $f_c : \mathcal{T}_c \times \mathcal{S} \to \mathcal{S}$ is monotone.*

Proof Let $T = ((s, r), v) \in \mathcal{T}_c$ be a complete transaction. We have two cases to consider, either $s =$ Source or $s \neq$ Source. Suppose $s =$ Source. Then, for all $b \leq b' \in \mathcal{S}$ and $k \in \overline{\mathcal{K}}$ we have

$$\begin{aligned} f_c(T, b)_k &= b_k + (\mathbf{e}_r - \mathbf{e}_s)_k \cdot v \\ &\leq b'_k + (\mathbf{e}_r - \mathbf{e}_s)_k \cdot v \\ &= f_c(T, b')_k, \end{aligned}$$

so f_c is monotone in this case. Now, suppose $s \neq$ Source. Then, for all $b \in \mathcal{V}^{\overline{\mathcal{K}}}$ and $k \in \overline{\mathcal{K}}$, we get

$$f_c(T, b)_k = \begin{cases} b_s - v \wedge b_s = (b_s - v) \vee 0, & \text{if } k = s \\ b_r + v \wedge b_s, & \text{if } k = r \\ b_k, & \text{otherwise.} \end{cases}$$

We observe that the transition function is monotone in all three cases. We conclude that f_c is monotone.

Proposition 9. ⊏ *For any $T \in \mathcal{T}$, $b \in \mathcal{S}$ and $k \in \overline{\mathcal{K}}$, the infimum*

$$\bigwedge_{\substack{(T',b') \in \mathcal{T}_c \times \mathcal{S} \\ (T,b) \leq (T',b')}} f_c(T', b')_k$$

exists in $\mathcal{V}$ and

$$\bigwedge_{\substack{(T',b')\in\mathcal{T}_c\times\mathcal{S} \\ (T,b)\leq(T',b')}} f_c(T',b') = \begin{cases} f_c(T,b)_k, & \text{if } v \neq \bot \\ 0, & \text{if } v = \bot \text{ and } k = s \\ b_k, & \text{if } v = \bot \text{ and } k \neq s \end{cases}$$

Proof. Let $T = ((s,r),v) \in \mathcal{T}$, $b \in \mathcal{S}$ and $k \in \overline{\mathcal{K}}$. We will consider two cases, either $v = \bot$ or $v \neq \bot$.

Case $v \neq \bot$. This is the case where the transaction T is complete. We need to show that in this case we have

$$\bigwedge_{\substack{(T',b')\in\mathcal{T}_c\times\mathcal{S} \\ (T,b)\leq(T',b')}} f_c(T',b')_k = f_c(T,b)_k.$$

Since f_c is monotone, this follows from Lemma 1.

Case $v = \bot$. This is the case where the transaction T is incomplete. We need to show that in this case we have

$$\bigwedge_{\substack{(T',b')\in\mathcal{T}_c\times\mathcal{S} \\ (T,b)\leq(T',b')}} f_c(T',b')_k = \begin{cases} 0, & \text{if } k = s \\ b_k, & \text{if } k \neq s. \end{cases}$$

First, since f_c is monotone (Proposition 8), we can reduce to showing

$$\bigwedge \mathcal{V}' = \begin{cases} 0, & \text{if } k = s \\ b_k, & \text{if } k \neq s \end{cases}$$

where $\mathcal{V}' = \{f_c(T',b)_k \mid T' \in \mathcal{T}_c, T \leq T'\}$. We will split into the two cases, $k = s$ and $k \neq s$.

Case $k = s$. We need to show that in this case we have $\bigwedge \mathcal{V}' = 0$. By definition of the set of states $\mathcal{S}$, all elements of V' are positive, so 0 is a lower bound of V'. Also, since $T \leq ((s,r),b_s)$, we have $f_c(((s,r),b_s),b)_k = 0 \in \mathcal{V}'$, so 0 is also the greatest lower bound of V'.

Case $k \neq s$. We need to show that in this case we have $\bigwedge \mathcal{V}' = b_k$. By Lemma 2, we have that b_k is a lower bound of V'. Also, since $T \leq ((s,r),0)$, we have $f_c(((s,r),0),b)_k = b_k \in \mathcal{V}'$, so b_k is also the greatest lower bound of V'.

Then we get the following definition.

Definition 27. ⌕ *For all $T \in \mathcal{T}$ and $b \in \mathcal{S}$, we define*

$$f(T,b) := \bigwedge_{\substack{(T',b')\in\mathcal{T}_c\times\mathcal{S} \\ (T,b)\leq(T',b')}} f_c(T',b').$$

Remark 5. *In other words, if the transaction is complete, the transition function f behaves exactly as the transition function f_c for complete transactions. If the transaction is incomplete, the transition function sets the balance of the sender to 0 and leaves all other balances unchanged.*

Remark 6. *The definition of the transition function f is somewhat abstract, but the idea is this. If we have a sequence of complete transactions (as in any traditional blockchain), we can compute the balance of each account by applying the transition function for complete transactions f_c. If some of the transactions are unknown, however, we cannot know for sure what the balance of each account is. Instead, we will compute a lower bound on the balance of each account. When we apply the transition function f to a partial transaction $T \in \mathcal{T}$ and a state $b \in \mathcal{S}$, we interpret b as the current lower bound on the true, but unknown state $b' \in \mathcal{S}$ where $b \leq b'$, and we interpret the partial transaction T as the lower bound of the true (but unknown if $v = \bot$) transaction $T' \in \mathcal{T}_c$, where $T \leq T'$. Since the true transaction T' and the true state b' are unknown to us, we need to consider the result of applying the transition function f_c to all possible values of T' and b', and take their meet to get the updated lower bound. We note that the construction where we extend the function f_c to f is a well-known construction in category theory called a Kan extension (see e.g. [15]).*

The transition function $f : \mathcal{T} \times \mathcal{S} \to \mathcal{S}$ induces the function $f^* : \mathcal{T}^* \times \mathcal{S} \to \mathcal{S}$ which takes a list of transactions $T_* \in \mathcal{T}^*$ and an initial state $s_0 \in \mathcal{S}$ and returns the state obtained by applying the transition function f, in order, to every transaction in T_*, starting with the initial state s_0 . In our case, given the list of partial transactions T_* obtained in Step 1, we compute the balances as $f^*(T_*, 0)$, where $0 \in \mathcal{S}$ is the initial state where every account has a zero balance . Combining the two steps, we define the balance function as follows :

$$\text{Bal}: \Pi \times B^* \to \mathcal{S}$$
$$(\pi, B_*) \mapsto f^*(\text{TransactionsInBlocks}(\pi, B_*), 0).$$

C Security

In this section we define and prove the security of the rollup contract. Informally speaking, we say that the rollup contract is secure if every withdrawal request succeeds, i.e. the rollup contract has sufficient balance for every withdrawal. This means that if a user has a balance proof which proves the in-rollup balance of one or more of their L1 accounts, they will be able to withdraw these balances to L1.

C.1 Formal Description of the Rollup Contract

We formally define the rollup contract.

Definition 28. ☞ *The rollup contract state consists of the list of blocks that have been added to the rollup. Formally, we define the set of contract states as*

$$\mathcal{S}_{contract} := \mathcal{B}^*.$$

Definition 29. ☞ *We define the set of rollup requests as*

$$\mathcal{R} := \mathcal{R}_{deposit} \amalg \mathcal{R}_{transfer} \amalg \mathcal{R}_{withdrawal},$$

where

$$\mathcal{R}_{deposit} := \mathcal{B}_{deposit}$$
$$\mathcal{R}_{transfer} := \mathcal{B}_{transfer}$$
$$\mathcal{R}_{withrawal} := \Pi.$$

Definition 30. ☞

$$\mathsf{ToBlock}_{deposit} \colon \mathcal{R}_{deposit} \to \mathcal{B}_{deposit}$$
$$B \mapsto B.$$

Definition 31. ☞

$$\mathsf{ToBlock}_{transfer} \colon \mathcal{R}_{transfer} \to \mathcal{B}_{transfer}$$
$$B \mapsto B$$

Definition 32. ☞

$$\mathsf{ToBlock}_{withdrawal} \colon \mathcal{R}_{withdrawal} \times \mathcal{B}^* \to \mathcal{B}_{withdrawal}$$
$$(\pi, B_*) \mapsto \mathsf{Bal}(\pi, B_*)|_{\mathcal{K}_1}$$

Definition 33. ☞

$\mathsf{ToBlock} \colon \mathcal{R} \times \mathcal{B}^* \to \mathcal{B}$

$$(R, B_*) \mapsto \begin{cases} \mathsf{ToBlock}_{deposit}(R), & \text{if } R \in \mathcal{R}_{deposit} \\ \mathsf{ToBlock}_{transfer}(R), & \text{if } R \in \mathcal{R}_{transfer} \\ \mathsf{ToBlock}_{withdrawal}(R, B_*), & \text{if } R \in \mathcal{R}_{withdrawal} \end{cases}$$

Definition 34. *A rollup contract transaction consists of a rollup request and a transaction sender. Formally, we define the set of rollup contract transactions as*

$$\mathcal{T}_{contract} := \mathcal{R} \times \mathcal{K}_1.$$

Definition 35. ☞

$\mathsf{IsValid}_{\mathcal{T}_{contract}} \colon \mathcal{T}_{contract} \to \{True, False\}$

$$(R, s) \mapsto \begin{cases} True, & \text{if } R \in \mathcal{R}_{deposit} \\ \mathsf{SA.Verify}(S, (C, agg, e), \sigma) \\ \wedge\, s = agg, & \text{if } R = (agg, e, C, S, \sigma) \in \mathcal{R}_{transfer} \\ \mathsf{Verify}(\pi), & \text{if } R = \pi \in \mathcal{R}_{withdrawal} \end{cases}$$

Definition 36.

$f_{contract}: \mathcal{T}_{contract} \times \mathcal{S}_{contract} \to \mathcal{S}_{contract}$

$$((R,s), B_*) \mapsto \begin{cases} (B_* \| \mathsf{ToBlock}(R, B_*)), & \text{if } \mathsf{IsValid}_{\mathcal{T}_{contract}}(R, s) \\ B_*, & \text{otherwise.} \end{cases}$$

The balance of the rollup contract is not part of the contract state, but is computed from the blocks in the rollup as follows. The contract balance is defined to be initially zero, and then subsequently updated each time a new rollup block is added, using the following update function.

Definition 37.

$\mathsf{updateBalance}: \mathcal{B} \times \mathcal{V} \to \mathcal{V}$

$$(B, v) \mapsto \begin{cases} v + d, & \text{if } B = (recipient, d) \in \mathcal{B}_{deposit} \\ v, & \text{if } B \in \mathcal{B}_{transfer} \\ v - \sum_{k \in \mathcal{K}_1} w_k, & \text{if } B = w \in \mathcal{B}_{withdrawal} \end{cases}$$

C.2 Security Definition

We formally define the security of the rollup contract with the following attack game.

Attack game 1. *The attack game is played between a PPT adversary and a challenger, where the challenger plays the role of the rollup contract. First, the challenger initializes the rollup contract with the state $((), 0) \in \mathcal{S}_{contract}$. Then, the adversary sends a sequence of contract transactions (elements of $\mathcal{T}_{contract}$) to the challenger. For each contract transaction, the challenger updates the rollup contract state using the transition function $f_{contract}$. The adversary wins the attack game if at the end of the interaction, the rollup contract has a state $(B_*, balance)$ where*

$$balance \not\geq 0.$$

Definition 38. *The rollup contract is* secure *if winning Attack game 1 is at least as hard as breaking either the binding property of the authenticated dictionary scheme, or finding a collision of the hash function* H.

C.3 Security Proof

Before we can prove the security of the rollup contract, we will first prove some properties of the balance function.

Lemma 3. *For all balance proofs $\pi \in \Pi$ and block lists $B_* \in \mathcal{B}^*$ we have*

$$\mathsf{Bal}(\pi, B_*)_{Source} \leq 0.$$

Proof. We start by noticing that the transition function for complete transactions f_c preserves the sum of account balances, i.e.

$$\sum_{k \in \mathcal{K}} f_c(T, b)_k = \sum_{k \in \mathcal{K}} b_k, \quad \forall T \in \mathcal{T}_c, b \in \mathcal{S}.$$

This implies the following fact about the transition function for partial transactions f:

$$\sum_{k \in \mathcal{K}} f(T, b)_k \leq \sum_{k \in \mathcal{K}} b_k, \quad \forall T \in \mathcal{T}, b \in \mathcal{S}.$$

Then, it follows by induction that we have

$$\sum_{k \in \mathcal{K}} f_*(T_*, 0)_k \leq 0, \quad \forall T_* \in \mathcal{T}^*. \tag{1}$$

Finally, for all balance proofs $\pi \in \Pi$ and block lists $B_* \in \mathcal{B}^*$, letting $T_* = \mathsf{TransactionsInBlocks}(B_*)$ we have

$$\begin{aligned}
\mathsf{Bal}(\pi, B_*)_{\mathsf{Source}} &= f^*(T_*, 0)_{\mathsf{Source}} & \text{(by definition)} \\
&= \sum_{k \in \mathcal{K}} f^*(T_*, 0)_k - \sum_{k \in \mathcal{K} \setminus \{\mathsf{Source}\}} f^*(T_*, 0)_k \\
&\leq - \sum_{k \in \mathcal{K} \setminus \{\mathsf{Source}\}} f^*(T_*, 0)_k & \text{(by Equation (1))} \\
&\leq 0 & \text{(non-source accounts have positive balances)}
\end{aligned}$$

which is the statement of the lemma.

The next lemma relies on a preorder structure on the set of balance proofs.

Definition 39 *We give*

$$\Pi = \mathsf{Dict}(\mathsf{AD}.\mathcal{C} \times \mathcal{K}_2, (\mathsf{AD}.\Pi \times \{0, 1\}^*) \times \mathcal{V}_+^{\mathcal{K}})$$

a preorder as follows. First, we give $\mathcal{V}_+^{\mathcal{K}}$ the discrete preorder. Then, we give $\mathsf{AD}.\Pi \times \{0, 1\}^*$ the trivial preorder. Finally, we give $(\mathsf{AD}.\Pi \times \{0, 1\}^*) \times \mathcal{V}_+^{\mathcal{K}}$ the induced product preorder, and Π the induced dictionary preorder.

Lemma 4. *The balance function*

$$\mathsf{Bal} : \Pi \times \mathcal{B}^* \to \mathcal{S}$$

is monotone in its first argument.

Proof. Let $B_* \in \mathcal{B}^*$. We can decompose the function $\mathsf{Bal}(-, B_*) : \Pi \to \mathcal{S}$ as follows:

$$\Pi \xrightarrow{\mathsf{TransactionsInBlocks}(-, B_*)} \mathcal{T}^* \xrightarrow{f^*(-, 0)} \mathcal{S}.$$

Note that the function $\mathsf{TransactionsInBlocks}$ outputs a list of partial transactions whose length is only dependent on the second argument (the list of blocks). This means that since B_* is fixed, we can replace $\mathcal{T}^*$ by $\mathcal{T}^{[n]}$ above, for some integer n :

$$\Pi \xrightarrow{\mathsf{TransactionsInBlocks}(-,B_*)} \mathcal{T}^{[n]} \xrightarrow{f^*(-,0)} \mathcal{S}.$$

We give $\mathcal{T}^{[n]}$ the preorder structure induced by the preorder on $\mathcal{T}$. Then, to prove that the balance function is monotone in its first argument, it suffices to show (by Proposition 7) that the two functions in the above decomposition are monotone.

We first show that the function $\mathsf{TransactionsInBlocks}(-, B_*)$ is monotone . Let $\pi, \pi' \in \Pi$ be balance proofs where $\pi \leq \pi'$, and let $T_* = \mathsf{TransactionsInBlocks}(\pi, B_*)$ and $T'_* = \mathsf{TransactionsInBlocks}(\pi', B_*)$. We need to show that $T_i \leq T'_i$ for all $i \in [n]$. Let $i \in [n]$, and let $((s, r), v) = T_i$ and $((s', r'), v') = T'_i$. Notice first that we have $(s, r) = (s', r')$, since by construction, we have that the sender and recipient of the transaction at a given index in the list of partial transactions extracted from a balance proof and block list is only determined by the arrangement of the three block types in the block list . Then, we realize that the only way the two transactions T_i and T'_i can differ, is if they are both extracted from the same transfer block B, and if π' contains a proof of the transaction from s in B, and π doesn't. In this case, we have $v = \bot$, so we get $((s, r), v) \leq ((s', r'), v')$.

It remains to show that the function $f^*(-, 0)$, considered as a function from $\mathcal{T}^{[n]}$ to $\mathcal{S}$ is monotone . To show this, we first notice that the transition function f is monotone, since if $(T_1, b_1) \leq (T_2, b_2)$, we get

$$\begin{aligned}
f(T_1, b_1) &= \bigwedge_{\substack{(T', b') \in \mathcal{T}_c \times \mathcal{S} \\ (T_1, b_1) \leq (T', b')}} f_c(T', b') \quad \text{(By definition)} \\
&\leq \bigwedge_{\substack{(T', b') \in \mathcal{T}_c \times \mathcal{S} \\ (T_2, b_2) \leq (T', b')}} f_c(T', b') \quad \text{(Since we take the meet of a smaller set of elements)} \\
&= f(T_2, b_2) \quad \text{(By definition).}
\end{aligned}$$

It then follows by induction that f^* is also monotone, and in particular we conclude that $f^*(-, 0)$ is monotone .

Lemma 5. Let $(B_i)_{i \in [n]} \in \mathcal{B}^*$ be a list of blocks and let $\pi \in \Pi$ be a balance proof. Then we have

$$\mathsf{Bal}(\pi, B_*)_{Source} = \sum_{\substack{i \in [n] \\ B_i \in \mathcal{B}_{withdrawal} \\ B_i = w \\ k \in \mathcal{K}_1}} \left(w_k \wedge \mathsf{Bal}(\pi, (B_j)_{j \in [i-1]})_k \right) - \sum_{\substack{i \in [n] \\ B_i \in \mathcal{B}_{deposit} \\ B_i = (r, v)}} v$$

Theorem 1 The rollup contract is secure (by Definition 38).

Proof Suppose an adversary and a challenger have interacted in Attack game 1. We will show that either the resulting contract balance is positive (the adversary lost the game), or the adversary has been able to either break the binding property of the authenticated dictionary scheme or found a collision of the hash function H. Let $B_* = (B_i)_{i \in [n]}$ be the contract state after the attack game🗗 , let $I \subseteq [n]$ be the indices of the withdrawal blocks in B_*🗗 and let $(\pi_i)_{i \in I}$ be the balance proofs used in the withdrawal requests🗗 . The resulting contract balance can be computed by adding all deposited amounts and subtracting all withdrawn amounts🗗 :

$$contractBalance = v_{deposited} - v_{withdrawn},$$

where

$$v_{deposited} = \sum_{\substack{i \in [n] \\ B_i \in \mathcal{B}_{deposit} \\ B_i = (r,v)}} v$$

and

$$v_{withdrawn} = \sum_{\substack{i \in I \\ k \in \mathcal{K}_1}} \mathsf{Bal}(\pi_i, (B_j)_{j \in [i-1]})_k.$$

We now have two possibilities, either the balance proofs $(\pi_i)_{i \in I}$ have a join in Π or they don't🗗 . Suppose they have a join $\pi \in \Pi$. Then we have

$$0 \leq -\mathsf{Bal}(\pi, B_*)_{\mathsf{Source}} \qquad \text{(lemma 3)}$$
$$= v_{deposited} - \sum_{\substack{i \in I \\ k \in \mathcal{K}_1}} \mathsf{Bal}(\pi_i, (B_j)_{j \in [i-1]})_k \wedge \mathsf{Bal}(\pi, (B_j)_{j \in [i-1]})_k \qquad \text{(lemma 5)}$$
$$= v_{deposited} - \sum_{\substack{i \in I \\ k \in \mathcal{K}_1}} \mathsf{Bal}(\pi_i, (B_j)_{j \in [i-1]})_k \qquad \text{(Follows from Lemma 4 since } \pi_i \leq \pi\text{)}$$
$$= contractBalance$$

which shows that the contract balance is positive🗗 . Now, suppose the balance proofs $(\pi_i)_{i \in I}$ do not have a join in Π. Let i_k be the $k'th$ index in I (so that $I = \{i_1, i_2, \ldots, i_m\}$, where $m = |I|$). Then, let $(\pi'_k)_{k \in [m]}$ be the balance proofs defined recursively as

$$\pi_k = \begin{cases} \bot, & \text{if } k = 0 \\ \mathsf{Merge}(\pi'_{k-1}, \pi_{i_k}), & \text{if } k \geq 1. \end{cases}$$

🗗 🗗 . Clearly, these merged balance proofs are valid, since each of the original balance proofs are valid (otherwise they wouldn't be accepted by the rollup contract), and since the merge of two valid balance proofs is again valid. Now, we argue that there must be an index $k \in \{1, \ldots, m\}$ such that π'_k is *not* the join of π'_{k-1} and π_{i_k} in Π, since if not, the final merged balance proof π'_m would be a join of $(\pi_i)_{i \in I}$ (by Proposition 6), which we have assumed not to exist🗗 .

It then follows from Proposition 6 that there is a key $(C, s) \in \mathsf{AD}.\mathcal{C} \times \mathcal{K}_2$ such that $\pi'_{k-1}(C,s) \not\simeq \pi_{i_k}(C,s)$🗗 . Letting $((\pi, salt), t) = \pi'_{k-1}(C,s)$ and $((\pi', salt'), t') = \pi_{i_k}(C,s)$, this implies $t \neq t'$🗗 . Also, since both balance proofs are valid, as remarked earlier, we have🗗

$$\mathsf{AD.Verify}(\pi, s, \mathsf{H}(t, salt), C)$$

and⊡
$$\mathsf{AD.Verify}(\pi', s, \mathsf{H}(t', salt'), C).$$

It follows that that either $\mathsf{H}(t, salt) = \mathsf{H}(t', salt')$, meaning that we have found a hash collision⊡ , or $\mathsf{H}(t, salt) \neq \mathsf{H}(t', salt')$, which means we have broken the binding property of the authenticated dictionary scheme⊡ .

D Discussion

D.1 Tracing the Path to Intmax2

Plasma Prime [19] is the starting point for the path that lead to Intmax2. Plasma Prime incorporates RSA accumulators and is based on the UTXO model, where each unspent output represents ownership of a specific segment. The concept of range chunking is also introduced, and is used to compress transaction history to simplify block verification. This design also features the use of a SumMerkleTree for efficient overlap verification between transaction segments and inclusion proof generation.

Springrollup [9] is a Layer 2 solution that introduces a new type of zk-rollup, that aims to use less on-chain data and enhance privacy. The rollup state is divided into on-chain and off-chain available states, with the design ensuring users' funds remain safe even if the off-chain state is withheld by the operator. The operator can modify the rollup state by posting a rollup block to the L1 contract, which includes the new merkle state root, a diff between the old and new on-chain states, and a zk-proof of valid operations. The system also includes a frozen mode for situations where the operator doesn't post a new rollup block within 3 d.

Intmax [14] introduces a design where the aggregator maintains a global state that is used when the aggregator makes new rollup blocks. This state is not necessarily known by anyone other than the aggregator, and can be withheld by the aggregator. This means that to allow multiple aggregators for the rollup, each aggregator must be trusted to provide the updated rollup state off-chain to the next aggregator in order to keep the rollup alive. This results in two things: First, since each aggregator needs to build upon the previous block, this method requires the complexity of a leader selection method to determine which aggregator can create the next block. Second, and more importantly, the rollup will halt if one of the aggregators fails to provide the data to the next aggregator, and all users would need to exit the rollup. This means that all aggregators need to be trusted in order to guarantee liveliness.

Intmax2 (this work), solves these problems by modifying the protocol so that block production becomes stateless, meaning that new blocks can be added to the rollup without having to know the previous blocks at all, allowing aggregating to become decentralized.

D.2 Liveness

We highlight that if a user receives a transaction and then remains offline for an extended period of time, the user is still able to perform withdrawals at a future point in time when they are online again. While it is recommended that a user continuously performs the update of the recursive zero-knowledge balance proof that allows for the withdrawal of funds, the user can remain offline for a certain time period and then, when back online, can perform a synchronization process and calculate the corresponding recursive zero knowledge proof (e.g., [18]).

D.3 Privacy of Intmax2

Our proposed solution does not post any transaction data on the underlying layer 1. Also, since aggregators do not need to verify transactions, the transaction data can also be hidden from the aggregators. As a result, the details of user transactions are only revealed to the recipients. As the importance of privacy on blockchains continues to grow, our proposed solution offers a promising path towards a privacy-focused future.

D.4 Delegating Zero-Knowledge Proof Generation

The emergence of new research on delegating the generation of zero-knowledge proofs [11], brings exciting prospects for the wider adoption of these technologies, particularly among light clients like mobile phones. This development holds great promise in overcoming the computational limitations of resource-constrained devices and enabling them to actively engage in zero-knowledge proof protocols. By delegating the generation of zero-knowledge proofs to more powerful devices or servers, the burden of computationally intensive tasks can be alleviated, paving the way for enhanced participation and utilization of zero-knowledge proofs.

As the research continues to evolve and mature, we anticipate a future where zero-knowledge proofs become more accessible and seamlessly integrated into various domains, empowering users with enhanced security and privacy guarantees. This development holds immense potential for bringing zero-knowledge proofs to the masses and unlocking their benefits for various applications.

References

1. Blocks: Block time. Ethereum Development Documentation. https://ethereum.org/en/developers/docs/blocks/#block-time, Accessed 20 July 20 2025
2. Nethermind formal verification team. https://www.nethermind.io/formal-verification
3. Ben-Sasson, E., Bentov, I., Horesh, Y., Riabzev, M.: Scalable, transparent, and post-quantum secure computational integrity. Cryptology ePrint Archive, Paper 2018/046 (2018). https://eprint.iacr.org/2018/046
4. Boneh, D., Drijvers, M., Neven, G.: Compact multi-signatures for smaller blockchains. In: Peyrin, T., Galbraith, S. (eds.) ASIACRYPT 2018. LNCS, vol. 11273, pp. 435–464. Springer, Cham (2018). https://doi.org/10.1007/978-3-030-03329-3_15
5. Bünz, B., Fisch, B., Szepieniec, A.: Transparent snarks from dark compilers. Cryptology ePrint Archive, Paper 2019/1229 (2019). https://eprint.iacr.org/2019/1229
6. Chiesa, A., Hu, Y., Maller, M., Mishra, P., Vesely, P., Ward, N.: Marlin: Preprocessing zksnarks with universal and updatable srs. Cryptology ePrint Archive, Paper 2019/1047 (2019). https://eprint.iacr.org/2019/1047
7. Chiesa, A., Ojha, D., Spooner, N.: Fractal: Post-quantum and transparent recursive proofs from holography. Cryptology ePrint Archive, Paper 2019/1076 (2019). https://eprint.iacr.org/2019/1076
8. Dahlberg, R., Pulls, T., Peeters, R.: Efficient sparse merkle trees. In: Brumley, B.B., Röning, J. (eds.) NordSec 2016. LNCS, vol. 10014, pp. 199–215. Springer, Cham (2016). https://doi.org/10.1007/978-3-319-47560-8_13
9. Dompeldorius, A.: Springrollup. https://github.com/adompeldorius/springrollup (2021), Accessed 20 July 20 2025
10. Gabizon, A., Williamson, Z.J., Ciobotaru, O.: Plonk: Permutations over lagrange-bases for oecumenical noninteractive arguments of knowledge. Cryptology ePrint Archive, Paper 2019/953 (2019). https://eprint.iacr.org/2019/953
11. Garg, S., Goel, A., Jain, A., Policharla, G.V., Sekar, S.: zkSaaS: zero-knowledge snarks as a service. Cryptology ePrint Archive, Paper 2023/905 (2023). https://eprint.iacr.org/2023/905
12. Goldwasser, S., Micali, S., Rackoff, C.: The knowledge complexity of interactive proof-systems. In: Proceedings of the Seventeenth Annual ACM Symposium on Theory of Computing, STOC 1985, pp. 291–304. Association for Computing Machinery, New York (1985). https://doi.org/10.1145/22145.22178
13. Groth, J.: On the size of pairing-based non-interactive arguments. Cryptology ePrint Archive, Paper 2016/260 (2016). https://eprint.iacr.org/2016/260
14. Hioki, L.: Intmax: Trustless and near-zero gas cost token transfer payment system. https://ethresear.ch/t/intmax-trustless-and-near-zero-gas-cost-token-transfer-payment-system/13904, Accessed: 20 July 2025
15. Mac Lane, S.: Categories for the working mathematician, vol. 5. Springer Science & Business Media (2013)
16. Maller, M., Bowe, S., Kohlweiss, M., Meiklejohn, S.: Sonic: Zero-knowledge snarks from linear-size universal and updateable structured reference strings. Cryptology ePrint Archive, Paper 2019/099 (2019). https://eprint.iacr.org/2019/099
17. Moura, L., Ullrich, S.: The lean 4 theorem prover and programming language. In: Platzer, A., Sutcliffe, G. (eds.) CADE 2021. LNCS (LNAI), vol. 12699, pp. 625–635. Springer, Cham (2021). https://doi.org/10.1007/978-3-030-79876-5_37

18. Nguyen, W., Boneh, D., Setty, S.: Revisiting the nova proof system on a cycle of curves. Cryptology ePrint Archive, Paper 2023/969 (2023). https://eprint.iacr.org/2023/969
19. team, B.F.: Plasma prime design proposal. https://ethresear.ch/t/plasma-prime-design-proposal/4222, Accessed 20 July 2025
20. (@vbuterin), V.B., (@dankrad), D.F., (@protolambda), D.L., (@asn d6), G.K., (@lightclient), M.G., (@Inphi), M.T., (@adietrichs), A.D.: Eip-4844: Shard blob transactions [draft]. Ethereum Improvement Proposals, no. 4844 (2022). https://eips.ethereum.org/EIPS/eip-4844

Quest Love: A First Look at Blockchain Loyalty Programs

Joseph Al-Chami[1] and Jeremy Clark[2]

[1] Montreal, Canada
alchamijoseph@gmail.com
[2] Concordia University, Montreal, Canada
j.clark@concordia.ca

Abstract. Blockchain ecosystems—such as those built around chains, layers, and services—try to engage users for a variety of reasons: user education, growing and protecting their market share, climbing metric-measuring leaderboards with competing systems, demonstrating usage to investors, and identifying worthy recipients for newly created tokens (airdrops). A popular approach is offering user quests: small tasks that can be completed by a user, exposing them to a common task they might want to do in the future, and rewarding them for completion. In this paper, we analyze a proprietary dataset from one deployed quest system that offered 43 unique quests over 10 months with 80M completions. We offer insights about the factors that correlate with task completion: amount of reward, monetary value of reward, difficulty, and cost. We also discuss the role of farming and bots, and the factors that complicate distinguishing real users from automated scripts.

1 Introductory Remarks

Blockchain projects understand that even the best technical ideas and code may struggle to have an impact without user adoption of the platform. There is no clear method for reaching pseudonymous users, who rarely seek out new blockchain platforms, and there's no prominent 'DApp store.'

One approach for introducing users to a new blockchain (including layer 1 chains, sidechains, and layer 2 solutions) is showcasing its features and partners through gamification. A set of *quests* or *tasks* or *boosts* are created that offer a *bounty* or *reward* to users for performing a specific action on the blockchain, such as transferring a token or using a specific DeFi service. The reward could be a collectible badge (often as an NFT), points on a leaderboard (often referred to as XP, inspired by games like Fortnite and platforms like Duolingo), or an airdrop of tokens with some monetary value [9,12,17]. Most projects favour the term 'quests' over 'tasks' to avoid associations with employment. The term quest highlights the user's journey toward achievement and mastery, creating a more

---

J. Al-Chami—Independent Researcher

legally favourable framing rooted in gamification. Despite the aspirational tone, these actions remain structured and transactional, serving both users' reward-driven motivations and projects' growth and engagement objectives.

A few examples of quest initiatives include Arbitrum's Odyssey 2.0, Avalanche's Coachella Quests, Base's Builder Quests, Binance's BSC GameFi Quest and Polygon's Wallet Suite Quest. Platforms like Galxe, Layer3, Boost, DeBank, and Zealy have emerged as centralized hubs offering users a variety of quests from multiple projects and have adopted the description: the loyalty layer.

In this measurements paper, we study one quest system over time to understand how the completion-rate of quests is correlated with factors such as difficulty, cost, reward amount, and reward type (monetary or non-monetary value). From our data, we are not able to directly classify users between humans and bots, however we do offer some insights and discussion points about the influence of automated task-completion. To inform this discussion, we identify key stakeholders involved (such as blockchain platforms, blockchain-based services, investors, activity-monitoring services, users, and bots) and analyze their preferences and incentives. We maintain a neutral position on whether quests are useful or not—we study them because they are commonly used (perhaps poised for broader adoption) and we failed to find another detailed study on the parameters that correlate with task completion.

1.1 Research Questions

Our paper sheds light on the following research question (RQ) and two discussion questions (DQs). DQs have less (or no) empirical basis and are instead based on insights or discussion points.

- **RQ1:** What factors are correlated with quest completion rates? We analyze (a) reward amount, (b) task difficulty, (c) cost, (d) reserve requirements, and (e) rewards with monetary value.
- **DQ1:** To what extent can the design of the quest help distinguish genuine users from automated bots and farming?
- **DQ2:** Who are the stakeholders in quest systems? What can we learn from their preferences?

1.2 Related Work

We are not aware of other research papers on quest systems for blockchain projects. Brand loyalty programs [6] have been studied deeply, and more recently gamification of learning tasks [10]. Experience points in games have been criticized [3]. For loyalty programs, Wulf *et al.* outline several drivers of participation [16]. Relevant to our study are: users engage when costs are zero as opposed to non-zero, they are asked to make minimal efforts as opposed to extended efforts, and when rewards are 'hard' (*e.g.*, a discount) as opposed to 'soft' (*e.g.*, product updates).

On the blockchain side, the relationship between new tokens and user adoption has been studied [2]. One particular (and recent) focus is on airdrops [9, 12, 17] where a large quantity (majority to totality) of tokens are distributed to users for the first time. This literature finds a positive impact of airdrops on token value, that retaining user engagement after an airdrop is difficult, and evidence of artificial engagement to 'farm' airdropped tokens (including detection algorithms [7, 18]). In our dataset, the quest system is run both before and after an airdrop. In discussing the role of farming and bots, we use a persuasion model [8] which suggests certain deterrents to engagement: time, money, physical effort, brain cycles, social deviance, and non-routine. We examine the relationship between quest difficulty (time, brain cycles, and non-routine) and cost (money) with completion, assuming most quests have similar levels of physical effort (minimal) and social deviance (legal or unregulated in most jurisdictions).

1.3 Dataset and Limitations

Reproducibility. For our paper, we study a quest system built and maintained by a company offering a new EVM-compatible, proof of stake blockchain. The quests themselves were co-designed with various services (DApps) running on the company's blockchain. The choice to use proprietary data has pros and cons.

The disadvantage is that we offered the company final say over being named or identifiable in our paper; they declined after our study was complete. Thus we only provide our dataset after processing and de-identifying.[1] Our statistics and figures can be replicable from the data and new insights could be developed by other researchers, however the accuracy of the data cannot be independently verified against on-chain data or website archives.

The advantage of engaging with a company is that we were able to inform the quest design to some extent. For example, we were able to suggest the addition of reserve requirements (Sect. 2.4) to quests and rewards with monetary value (Sect. 2.5), and ensure they were added/removed from tasks that otherwise were unchanged (isolating two main variables: the requested feature and the epoch). To control for different completion rates across epochs, we also ensured some tasks were offered across multiple epochs without change.

Representativeness. Our dataset originates from a single platform, which means we cannot assert broad generalizability. However, the platform's quests and bot-control measures appear standard and comparable to other blockchain quest systems we examined. Our data covers both pre- and post-airdrop periods, enabling us to observe user behaviour changes around significant events. It's important to note that our findings may become less representative over time due to the increasing ease with which non-experts can create bots, particularly as AI-driven agents [1,15] become more prevalent.

Ground Truth on Bots. We lack ground truth distinguishing genuine users from Sybil accounts, whether manual (farming) or automated (bots/scripts). Thus, our data reports only unique address completions, and interpretations should be made cautiously of this fact. Nevertheless, understanding factors correlated

---

[1] Available on GitHub: https://github.com/MadibaGroup/2025-Quests.

with quest completion rates remains valuable for designing effective blockchain engagement strategies, even without explicit bot classification.

1.4 Data Analysis

The data we used includes the quest system's website interface where each quest corresponds to specific actions executed on-chain, defined by interactions with smart contracts. Upon quest completion, the loyalty program verifies the user's on-chain transaction to confirm that all quest requirements are met. Once verified, the program stores the details in the company's database—including transaction hash, user address, and contract address. This information is merged with additional off-chain data such as the points awarded for quest completion and the epoch, a time metric controlled by the loyalty program rather than the blockchain. We were provided SQL access to this raw data and exported CSV files (anonymized and available on our repository) for analysis. The statistics we compute (such as Spearman correlation) are documented in our repository. We skip the details in the paper as the techniques themselves not novel or innovative.

1.5 Key Events in Dataset

Our research analyzes data spanning the entirety of 2024. New quests are offered for an epoch, which was initially a one day period and transitioned (at epoch 10) to one week. Our data is organized by epoch 5–42 (the company's backend database starts at epoch 5). Over this period, 43 unique quests were offered. Some quests were offered in multiple epochs and could be completed multiple times. 1.2M unique addresses completed at least one quest. Across the period, 80M quests were completed.

As seen in Fig. 1, overall participation seems to be influenced by various public announcements. When a blockchain does not offer a token but does offer quests, speculative users might assume that an airdrop of tokens is on the blockchain's future roadmap and quest completion points might factor into who receives airdropped tokens. At epoch 21, the project announces an airdrop and that a snapshot of user activity had been captured as a basis for the airdrop. Since the snapshot is taken, it is too late to complete quests for the purposes of gaining in airdropped tokens (unless you speculate that the project will do a second snapshot or a second airdrop). Participation dropped 29.5% immediately after the snapshot announcement. By epoch 23, a further 45.7% drop occurred, totalling a 61.7% decline over two weeks. At epoch 28, a request for proposals (RFP) was announced to ask ecosystem apps and partners to submit how they want to do airdrop allocation, which further cements the fact that quest completions after the snapshot will not be considered. A 22.9% drop in participation follows the RFP. At epoch 30, the RFP closed and the airdrop itself starts, which sees another 42% decline in quest completions. In summary, from epoch 21 to epoch 32, quest completions declined 93.5%.

In epoch 36, a new program was launched where certain quests would receive token rewards (which have monetary value), as opposed to just receiving XP

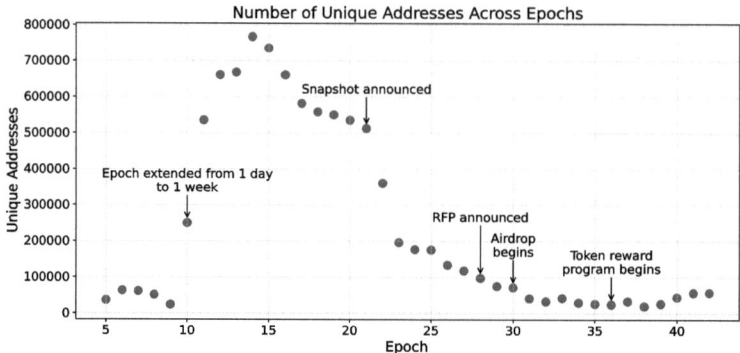

Fig. 1. Total completions of all quests offered in each epoch. Overlay of public announcements that may impact user participation.

points. We will study this further later but for now, we note that this leads an increase in participation: 34% increase in epoch 37 and 128.7 % by epoch 42. The reward program kept evolving and increasing rewards over the following epochs. By epoch 50 the cumulative effect of this token program was 251.8%.

Retention rate can be computed as $RR = \frac{(E-N)}{S} \cdot 100$ for users at the start (S), end (E), and newly acquired users (N). Between epochs 21 and 35, RR was -0.183%. After token rewards were introduced (epoch 42), RR rose slightly to just 0.59%. Transaction volume dropped sharply from 11,301,078 at peak participation to just 572,595 by epoch 39 (5% of peak volume). Taken together, retention is extremely low and incentive-driven (reacting to monetary rewards). This supports the idea that user engagement was transactional and profit-driven rather than loyalty-driven.

2 RQ1: Task Completion Factors

2.1 Reward Amounts in Points

Points have long been a key element in gamification systems [10], primarily used to incentivize specific behaviours or actions, such as educational tasks, objectives in a game, or fostering loyalty through purchases at a business. For quests, points are usually presented in leaderboards—a public, ordered ranking of users and their points, which can boost competition, and result in users striving not merely to collect points but to climb the ranks. Leaderboards have a downside too. Newcomers might feel deterred by the seemingly insurmountable gap between themselves and top-ranked users, and excessive focus on ranking can foster cheating or the transacting of user profiles (with their points).

To what extent do points motivate users? Consider Fig. 2 where it shows a dot for each quest offered in each epoch (x-axis) and the number of times it was completed (y-axis). The shape of the curve follows the overall trend (Fig. 1). The dots in Fig. 2 are colour-coded for how many points the user receives for completing

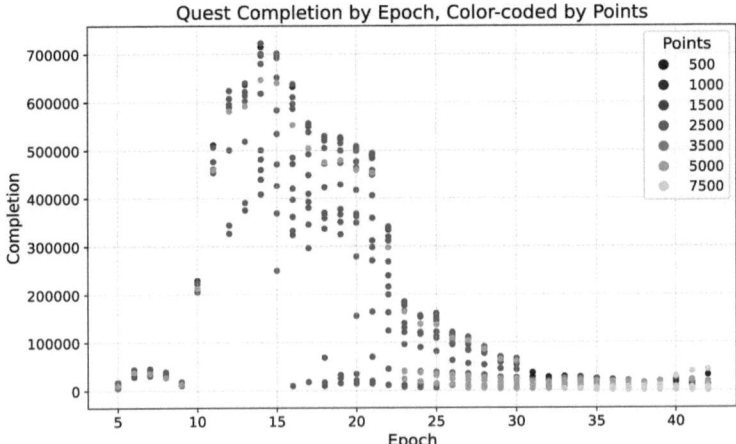

Fig. 2. Reward amount (in non-monetary points) of different quests offered from Epoch 5–42. Completion rates do not correlate with points, indicating other contributing factors.

the quest. A simple hypothesis is that quest completions would correlate positively with the number of points. Using the Spearman correlation [14], we found that correlations across epochs ranged from -0.115 to -0.870, with no epoch showing a significant positive monotonic relationship. In other words, the rank ordering of points and completions does not reveal any consistent patterns—for instance, higher points do not reliably correspond to more completions.

Finally, we note that in the later epochs, a strong negative monotonic relationship emerged, indicating that higher-point quests were completed less frequently. This was an intentional design decision, as more challenging quests were assigned higher point rewards to incentivize completion. As the data suggests, higher point rewards alone were not associated with increased engagement for these harder quests. Instead, quest difficulty, and other factors that act as deterrents, are more strongly associated with variations in task completion. This finding highlights the need to consider additional factors to better understand the predictors of task completion.

2.2 Task Difficulty

The first research question addresses points, which pull users toward certain quests. On the other side, frictions or deterrents may push users away from certain quests. We willl address three of these: difficulty, cost, and minimum token requirements (or thresholds), starting with task difficulty. We classify all quests based on (i) completion time and (ii) external dependencies that are out of the user's direct control, such as waiting for a response from another system, interacting with other users, or relying on network availability. Completion time was measured by lead researcher who completed each quest modelling average

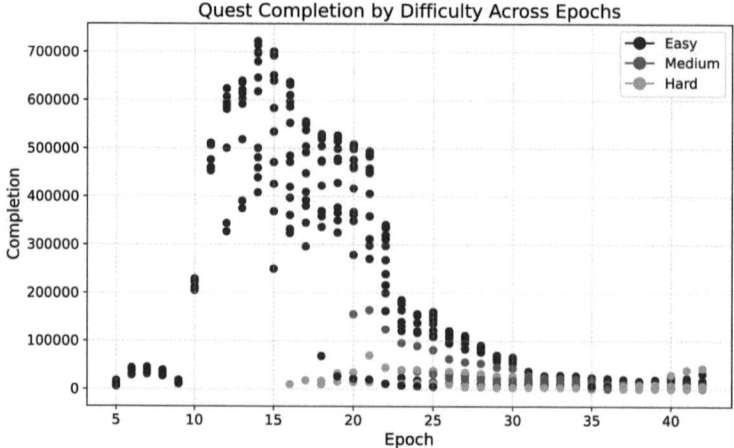

Fig. 3. Quest difficulty is strongly associated with completion rates, with easy quests (purple) completed most often and difficult quests (orange) completed least often. Variance in the right tail (epochs 40+) correspond to offering medium quests (pink) with tokens of monetary value. (Color figure online)

user behaviour; we felt this was objective enough but more robust followup studies might take the agreement of several researchers independently assessing difficulty.

- Easy: quest takes less than 1 min and has no external dependencies.
- Medium: quest takes 1–2 min and/or has external dependencies but dependencies require minimal effort to resolve.
- Hard: quest takes longer than 2 min and/or has significant external dependencies.

An example of an easily resolved external dependency would be finding another player for a game where many players are available at all times. By contrast, if players were rarely available, the quest would be ranked hard instead of medium. If a quest falls between two levels, we will typically classify it as the easier of the two.

As evident from Fig. 3, difficulty is strongly associated with task completion. Using Spearman correlation (with reversed difficulty mapping), we found that correlations across epochs ranged from 0.121 to 0.663, mostly indicating a positive monotonic relationship. Easier tasks consistently had higher completion rates.

Nevertheless, in certain epochs, the positive correlation was not as strong. As shown in Fig. 3, some medium or hard quests were completed more frequently than easier tasks, suggesting that other deterrents or negative incentives may be more strongly associated with quest completion than difficulty alone. This observation is further explored by analyzing factors such as cost and thresholds in subsequent sections.

2.3 Cost

All quests involving an on-chain transaction will have non-zero cost to complete, as the user needs to pay the transaction fee. The more complex the task, the larger the gas fee could be. For example, if a quest involves using a DeFi service, the service itself may charge fees on top of the gas costs. Quests that involve bridging assets between (layer 1) Ethereum and the blockchain project seemed particularly disliked, likely due to gas fees being high on Ethereum.

In Fig. 4, we show a selection of quests from epochs 37–46 (later quests demonstrated more variety in complexity) and coded their cost into three colours: purple is less than $0.10 USD, pink is less than $1.00 USD (and more than purple), and orange is $1.00 USD and more (no quest was greater than $10 USD but some cost greater than $5.00 USD). Quest costs in USD were computed using token exchange rates at the time of each transaction, based on price data provided by CoinGecko, aligning precisely with the prices displayed to users on the quest platform UI. The analysis of quest completion data revealed a clear trend: quests with a cost under $0.10 USD are consistently completed by a larger number of users across all epochs, while those costing between $1 and $10 USD see minimal engagement. This pattern suggests that cost is strongly associated with lower engagement in high-cost quests. Given this observed relationship, quest designers may benefit from considering alternative incentives or cost structures.

Using the Spearman correlation, we found that correlations across epochs ranged from -0.843 to -0.896, consistently showing the strongest monotonic relationship among all research questions. As shown in Fig. 4, the rank ordering of cost and completions reveals a clear pattern—less costly quests (e.g., purple, costing less than $0.10) are completed far more frequently than higher-cost quests

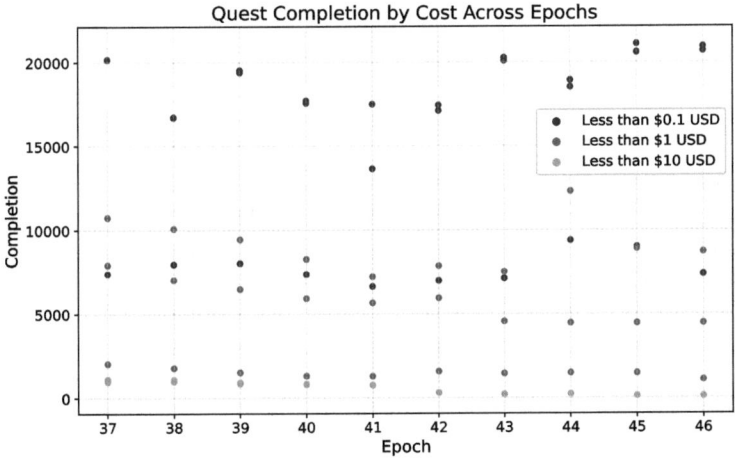

Fig. 4. Quest cost is strongly associated with completion rates, with cheaper quests (purple) completed most often and more expensive quests (orange) completed least often. (Color figure online)

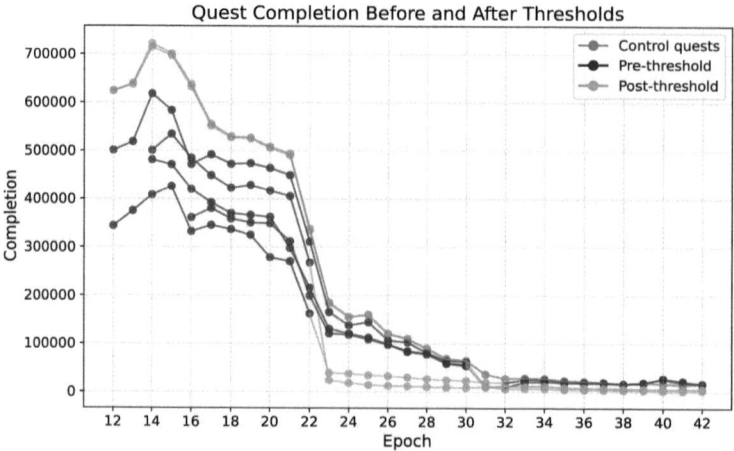

Fig. 5. The implementation of a minimum threshold of tokens for quest completion is associated with an immediate decline in completions for quests that previously ran without thresholds (orange segment compared to the purple segment). The grey lines represent highly completed tasks as a control group. (Color figure online)

(e.g., orange, costing up to $10). This finding reinforces the idea that cost is strongly associated with lower task completion.

Since cost showed the strongest correlation, we infer that users are not completing quests randomly, nor are they primarily motivated by mastery or loyalty. Instead, their behavior suggests a tendency to minimize cost, aligning with patterns commonly associated with Sybils or automated bots. This observation led us to the next research question, where thresholds were introduced to user wallets to investigate their association with completion rates and assess whether financial deterrents influence engagement in a more structured manner.

2.4 Thresholds

We consider one last complication for users: quests that can only be completed by accounts with a minimum threshold of tokens. Thresholds are used to combat farming and bots, which we discussed further in the next section. For now, we simply measure their correlation with quest completion.

Consider Fig. 5. It shows 5 quests (purple lines) that ran for multiple epochs without a threshold, and then a threshold was applied to them (purple lines turn orange). In a few cases, the threshold was removed and the line goes back to purple. As a control group of quests for comparison, the grey line shows 5 highly completed quests (all simple token transfers). Throughout all epochs, these tasks had no threshold requirements for completion, and no thresholds were added at any point during the measurement. Most thresholds were in the native token on the blockchain project, and the amount of tokens required were worth between

$1 and $10 USD. Some thresholds were in small amounts of ETH (0.002) or BTC (0.000125).

As apparent from the figure, the implementation of a threshold is associated with an immediate decline in quest completion. The purple lines follow the same trend as the grey (control) lines (dampened by not being easy tasks) until the threshold is implemented, and then plummet. One might hypothesize that bots and farmers would take a few epochs to update their scripts or acquire threshold tokens, but the association appears sticky with no future uptick. When the threshold is removed, the quests' completion rates return to levels similar to those observed in the control group.

For example, one quest was completed 268,104 times in epoch 22, just before a threshold of approximately $10 USD was introduced at epoch 23. Following the enforcement of the threshold, completions dropped dramatically to 23,923—a 91% decrease. When the threshold was removed at epoch 33, the quest saw a significant rebound, with completions more than doubling, increasing by 112.8%.

Similarly, another quest, which had a threshold of approximately $5 USD enforced at epoch 23, experienced a 75.8% drop in completions. After the threshold was removed at epoch 33, completions increased by 33.4%.

These examples highlight a substantial association between thresholds and lower user participation, as well as an association between the removal of thresholds and a return to higher completion rates.

2.5 Rewards with Monetary Value

Consider Fig. 6 which depicts 5 quests by colour, each offered over epochs 43–49 (except the yellow quest, which was first offered in epoch 46). For most epochs, the completion award was non-monetary (loyalty or experience) points, as we have analyzed in the previous section. In contrast, for one epoch (shown with a star), alongside the usual point rewards, specific quests were selected for a token reward (in the native token of the blockchain project) which had a small monetary value of $0.10 USD. The grey line shows the completion rate of the control quest offered across the same epochs.

This was not a perfect experiment for assessing the association of monetary rewards with quest completion, as the rewards were capped at $5000 USD, allowing a maximum of 50,000 users to claim rewards before they ran out. Further, if two quests offered monetary rewards in the same epoch, they would compete against each other until the tokens were depleted (see epoch 46 in Fig. 6).

Despite these defects in the data, the results are insightful: even with a minimal reward, completion rates surged. The highest increase was over 12x for a quest typically completed by around 3,500 users. With the token reward, this quest (purple in Fig. 6) saw 44,196 completions. Directly after the token reward for this quest was removed, the completion rate dropped back to its original levels before the reward was introduced. Note that in the literature on loyality programs, users prefer monetary rewards as opposed to non-monetary [13].

These data reveal that the introduction of a token reward is associated with a spike in completions, while the removal of the reward corresponds with a

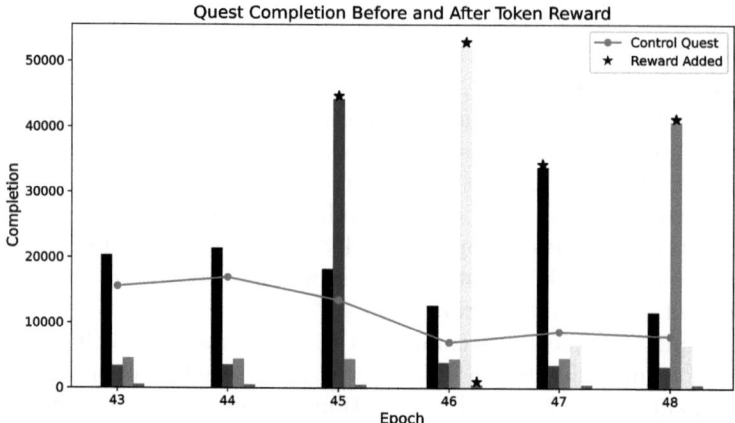

Fig. 6. Five quests (by colour) with rewards in non-monetary points (bars without stars) and token rewards for one epoch (bars with stars). The grey line shows an average of task completion for the other quests over the same epochs. The chart shows that offering tokens (with a monetary value) as rewards is associated with higher quest completion. (Color figure online)

decline back to earlier levels. These spikes suggest that token rewards do not foster loyalty or habitual engagement but rather create a purely transactional relationship. Users appear to compare the cost to the reward and only engage when there is a clear opportunity for profit.

In epoch 46, two quests with token rewards showed different outcomes. While the yellow quest (which had a low cost) saw a significant increase in completions, the red quest (with a cost higher than the reward) experienced no increase at all. If users were engaging with the platform out of loyalty or mastery, they would have completed the red quest as well as the yellow quest. However, this did not happen: users who claimed the reward for the yellow quest did not complete the red quest, leaving the reward for the red quest unclaimed.

3 Discussion

3.1 DQ1: Farming and Bots

We currently lack data revealing how many task completions come from genuine users as opposed to farmers (humans and bots). The Fogg behavior model [8] (B=MAP) states that a behaviour requires motivation (M), ability (A), and a prompt (P). If any element is missing, the behaviour likely will not occur. Under this model, humans and bots differ: even tiny rewards can motivate (M) bots at scale (picking up every penny), while humans aware of the tasks will likely not change (either continuing completion due to loyalty or continuing to ignore them). Bots also detect prompts (P) faster than humans, including generalized MEV bots that monitoring mempools and front-run profitable transactions [5].

This ability (A) to react instantly sets bots apart. Both farmers and bots operating from sybil addresses split tokens across many newly created addresses, each with minimal capital to cover fees, while genuine users often keep higher balances.

Putting this together, we suggest three heuristics that may help distinguish genuine users from bots: (1) If a quest alternates between unprofitable and profitable, bots will be sensitive to the exact moment it becomes marginally profitable and act; (2) if a quest requires a threshold (minimal amount of tokens), bots will be sensitive to ensuring the address meets but does not exceed the threshold amount; and (3) if a (profitable) quest is announced (especially unexpectedly), bots will be the quickest to react. We emphasize that if these heuristics were deployed in a way that harmed bots (*e.g.*, banning rather than passive measurement), bots can adjust their behaviour to evade detection, resulting in a 'cat and mouse' game between farmers and quest creators. That said, we suggest new quest designs that might help identify and quantify farming activity.

The first design observes that if costs (*i.e.*, gas fees, service fees, buying a token or NFT as part of the quest, *etc.*.) are slightly higher than rewards (*i.e.*, tokens of monetary value received for quest completion), genuine users might be happy they are at least receiving a subsidy for a quest they would complete anyways (*cf.* [11]), while bots will avoid unprofitable tasks. When benefits are slightly higher than costs, bots will engage (including general-purpose Maximal Extractable Value (MEV) bots [5] that agnostic about the quest system). For many quest designs, profitability could vary due to external factors, such as fluctuations in gas or token values, creating the conditions for a 'natural experiment.' New engagement when quests become slightly profitable could be largely attributed to bots.

The second idea corresponds to the use of thresholds. If a quest can only be completed by addresses holding at least X tokens for a certain period of time (days or weeks), bot farms need to divvy their tokens between their addresses. The transaction trace of this unusual activity could augment other patterns used by exiting farming-detection algorithms [7,18].

A final idea builds on the speed at which bots react. In the quest system we studied, a smart contract was randomly replenished with a fixed daily reward pool of $500. Pre-enrolled participants with sufficient loyalty points could claim a nominal reward ($0.01 or $0.025, depending on tier) until the pool was depleted. Looking at Table 1, we see that depletion happened quicker each day. We also see that refill times were not always predictable. On Day 7, for instance, despite a one-hour delay in the refill time, approximately 1,500 claims were made within 2 min. The following day, a more drastic delay of 3 h saw claims drop to 300, likely due to the implementation of rate-limiting and a mandatory wait period between claims. Notably, this led to a temporary spike in the time required to deplete all rewards, which rose to 2 h 41 m. By Day 9, however, the refill occurred 4.5 h earlier, and bots had clearly adapted, with 1,500 claims occurring within 2 min and the time to deplete rewards dropping to 27 min. Finally, following the introduction of an automated daily refill schedule on Days 10 and 11, the system

Table 1. Daily Refill Times and Depletion Data.

Day	Refill Time	Immediate Claims (within 2 min)	Duration to Deplete Rewards
1	13:00:00	–	12 h
2	12:02:17	200	1 h 50 m
3	13:25:45	500	1 h 33 m
4	12:09:01	1500	58 m
5	12:45:58	350	1 h 30 m
6	12:27:53	200	1 h 40 m
7	13:30:17	1500	28 m
8	16:30:07	300	2 h 41 m
9	11:59:57	1500	27 m
10	11:59:57	>1500	<30 m
11	11:59:57	>1500	<30 m

reached its operational minimum, with rewards being depleted in under 30 min and claims stabilizing at 1,500 within the first 2 min.

Although these observations are suggestive, they are not conclusive for two reasons: (1) a backend system (using Cloudflare) attempted to block or rate-limit repeated bot requests, requiring multiple submissions for a single on-chain claim to succeed, and (2) the smart contract batched multiple claims into a single transaction, potentially delaying some submissions that had occurred earlier. A more direct on-chain approach—where each wallet claim corresponds to an individual transaction—would likely yield clearer data.

3.2 DQ2: Stakeholder Analysis

A deeper question is what stakeholders actually prioritize. Is it the elimination of bots, metric boosts, revenue, other things? We conduct a *stakeholder analysis*. Our stakeholder analysis (Table 2) is based on our assessment as researchers of the preferences and incentives of different groups, rather than empirical data collected through surveys or interviews. This approach follows the methodology used by Clark et al. [4] for secure email systems. For space constraints, the full explanation of Table 2 is in the full version of the paper.[2]

We highlight the column resilient to farming as the most contentious. DApps favor platforms with large genuine user bases, supporting anti-farming measures. Project-based stakeholders often tolerate farming or turn a blind eye. Investors accept inflated metrics when selling but seek real user data when buying, creating internal conflict. Developer teams face the same tension—wanting ground truth when selecting projects but valuing vanity metrics once committed.

---

[2] Appendix, Full version: https://arxiv.org/abs/2501.18810.

Table 2. A set of stakeholder groups and potential deliverables from a quest platform. Each cell indicates the priority of the stakeholder for the deliverable: empty means the priority is ambivalent to moderately favourable, ⇑ means it is high priority, ⇓ means the stakeholder opposes the deliverable, and ○ indicates conflicting priorities within the stakeholder group.

Stakeholder	Enhances activity	Enhances education	Enhances lock-in	Resilient to farming	Revenue for project	Revenue for third parties	Revenue for user
Project: Developers	⇑	⇑	⇑	○	⇑		
Project: Executives	⇑	⇑	⇑	⇓	⇑	⇑	○
Project: Investors	⇑	⇑	⇑	○	⇑		⇑
Project: Token Holders	⇑		⇑	⇓	⇑		
Users: Transactional							⇑
Users: Exploratory		⇑					
Users: Loyal	⇑	⇑	⇑	⇑			
Third Party: DApps	⇑	⇑	⇑	⇑		⇑	
Third Party: Quest Platforms	⇑	⇓					⇑
Third Party: Metric Platforms				⇑			

4 Concluding Remarks

Many teams (based on personal conservations and social media) sense that their platform has attracted a significant number of bots. In some instances, these teams recognize that their applications or quest systems have effectively become 'farming machines' for bots. Farming is a kind of "Midas touch' for projects, immediately boosting metrics and engagement. But ultimately, it forces teams into an uncomfortable dilemma: either admit that much of their previous participation came from bots—risking tension with partners, genuine users, and investors—or remain silent and appear to lose the bulk of their user base.

Acknowledgements. The authors thank the reviewers, shepherd, and workshop chairs for pointing out many issues that greatly improved the paper and its results. J. Clark acknowledges support for this research project from NSERC, Raymond Chabot Grant Thornton, and Autorité des Marchés Financiers.

Disclosure of Interests. The authors declare that they have no competing interests.

A Further Stakeholder Analysis

Table 2 provides, as rows, a set of stakeholder groups and, as columns, a set of possible deliverables a quest system might provide. Deliverables are phrased to be generally favourable, so most stakeholder groups will default to being moderately in favour or, at worst, ambivalent (empty cell). Cells showcase when there is strong support, strong opposition, or internal conflict over a priority. This table helps us locate tensions between stakeholder groups. The first column describes the main function of a quest system: to enhance genuine user activity, a goal no stakeholder group opposes. Quest completions are not 'genuine' in the sense of economic activity—quests are completed for the sake of the quest, which is superficial. However we use 'genuine' to distinguish from attempts to game the quest system (which we will turn to in column 4). In the second column, again no stakeholder group opposes quests with educational value for users, while such quests are strongly preferred by exploratory users.

As of writing, the blockchain space is fragmented with many competing L1s, L2s, and services for common on-chain tasks (*e.g.,* DEXes, lending protocols, leveraged trading, *etc.*.). Market share and user retention is a basic business goal of projects and their loyal users. Projects offering quests will typically only include tasks that engage with their own platform, while quest platforms (the 'loyalty layer') offer a single hub for quests across multiple projects. Their niche is based on quests being spread across competitors. Occasionally projects will join quest platforms and then poach users for their own internal quest systems—called a 'vampire attack.'

The most contentious deliverable is the elimination of farming—bots, sybils, and other methods used by transactional users to automate task completion. The basic tension is that inflated completion metrics (*e.g.,* monthly active users (MAU)) paint the picture of a fast-growing, robust user base, but its illusionary nature ('vanity metrics') could compromise credibility or collapse if transactional users exhaust the opportunities and move on to newer projects. Anti-farming measures are supported by DApps choosing a project to deploy on, favouring platforms with large genuine user bases. Joining them are metric platforms, which provide rankings of most popular projects, will lose credibility and relevance if it is easy for projects to use quests to game their metrics and climb the leaderboard. Loyal users receive more recognition when their contributions are not drowned out by a sea of fake engagement.

We expect project-based stakeholders to tacitly support farming (or at least turn a blind eye). Investors understand this when they are in a position of selling or exiting, however they want a real picture of the user base when buying into a project—thus are in internal conflict. Developer teams are similar, wanting ground truth when choosing between projects to work on and wanting success once in a team.

When it comes to the final three columns, which emphasize the main groups that might make revenue from quests, there are no big surprises. No one opposes stakeholder capturing some revenue and stakeholder groups are self-interested, prioritizing revenue to themselves. In our evaluation, we assume revenues are non-zero sum—that is, revenue to one stakeholder group does not siphon profit from the others.

References

1. Ante, L.: Autonomous AI agents in decentralized finance: market dynamics, application areas, and theoretical implications. Application Areas, and Theoretical Implications (2024)
2. Bakos, Y., Halaburda, H.: The role of cryptographic tokens and ICOs in fostering platform adoption. Tech. rep., CESifo Working Paper (2019)
3. Bogost, I.: Exploitationware. In: Rhetoric/Composition/Play Through Video Games: Reshaping Theory and Practice of Writing, pp. 139–147. Springer (2013)
4. Clark, J., van Oorschot, P.C., Ruoti, S., Seamons, K., Zappala, D.: SoK: securing email—a stakeholder-based analysis. In: Financial Cryptography (2021)
5. Daian, P., et al.: Flash boys 2.0: frontrunning in decentralized exchanges, miner extractable value, and consensus instability. In: IEEE Symposium on Security and Privacy (2020)
6. Dowling, G.R., Uncles, M.: Do customer loyalty programs really work? MIT Sloan Management Review (1997)
7. Fan, S., Min, T., Wu, X., Cai, W.: Altruistic and profit-oriented: making sense of roles in web3 community from airdrop perspective. In: CHI (2023)
8. Fogg, B.: A behavior model for persuasive design. In: ACM Persuasive (2009)
9. Fröwis, M., Böhme, R.: The operational cost of ethereum airdrops. In: CBT (2019)
10. Hamari, J., Koivisto, J., Sarsa, H.: Does gamification work?–a literature review of empirical studies on gamification. In: HICSS (2014)
11. Lara, P.R., De Madariaga, J.G.: The importance of rewards in the management of multisponsor loyalty programmes. J. Database Market. Cust. Strat. Manage. **15**, 37–48 (2007)
12. Messias, J., Yaish, A., Livshits, B.: Airdrops: giving money away is harder than it seems. Tech. rep., arXiv (2024)
13. Ruzeviciute, R., Kamleitner, B.: Attracting new customers to loyalty programs: the effectiveness of monetary versus nonmonetary loyalty programs. J. Consum. Behav. **16**(6), e113–e124 (2017)
14. Spearman, C.: The proof and measurement of association between two things. Am. J. Psychol. **15**(1), 72–101 (1904)
15. Walters, S., et al.: Eliza: a web3 friendly AI agent operating system. Tech. rep. arXiv:2501.06781 (2025)
16. Wulf, K.D., Odekerken-Schröder, G., Canniére, M.H.d., Van Oppen, C.: What drives consumer participation to loyalty programs? A conjoint analytical approach. J. Relation. Market. **2**(1–2), 69–83 (2003)
17. Yaish, A., Livshits, B.: Tierdrop: harnessing airdrop farmers for user growth. Tech. rep., arXiv (2024)
18. Zhou, C., Chen, H., Wu, H., Zhang, J., Cai, W.: Artemis: detecting airdrop hunters in NFT markets with a graph learning system. In: WWW (2024)

SoK: Designing a Curriculum for Open Finance

Daniel Broby[✉] [iD] and Eduardo T. Valencia Jr.

Asian Institute of Management, Makati, Philippines
{dbroby,etvalencia}@aim.edu

Abstract. This thought piece explores the role of higher education in promoting FinTech innovation and addressing the skills gap within Open Finance. This field extends beyond traditional banking by leveraging third-party permissioned data-sharing principles to include areas such as insurance, pensions, and investments. A transdisciplinary curriculum in Open Finance can provide computer scientists with both technical and contextual skills. Key areas of focus include data management, API development, machine learning, and data privacy. By aligning educational content with industry needs and technological advancements, our insights underscore how academia can collaborate with industry to prepare graduates for the future. In adopting it, universities can drive innovation and influence the evolving FinTech ecosystem.

Keywords: Open Finance · Open Banking · Financial Technology · third-party data · application programming interface · account information service providers · payment initiation service providers · transdisciplinary curriculum design and development · enquiry-based learning

1 Introduction

This thought piece examines the relevant components universities should consider when designing degree programmes focused on Open Finance. It builds on a white paper detailing a master's-level syllabus by Broby and Murphy (2024), and an approach to the curriculum in FinTech by Karkkainen et al. (2018). We adopt a Systematization of Knowledge (SoK) approach, incorporating a transdisciplinary content approach. By combining domain-specific content with practical FinTech skills, we suggest universities can develop a course that prepares graduates to navigate the evolving job market in Open Finance.

Open Finance describes the extension of "Open Banking" to pensions, investments and savings (Brodsky and Oakes (2017)). It relies on third party permission to access data. Our key premise reflects this requirement. Namely, that university programmes directed at Open Finance should integrate finance, technology, and data science (Broby (2024)). This integration will equip students with industry-relevant competencies. Additionally, students must develop an understanding of the regulatory, technical, and ethical issues inherent in this nascent industry. The need for such a focus is underscored by the Higher Education Funding Council for England (HEFCE), which advocates for STEM curricula that include transferable skills. We therefore discuss the practical implications for this in curricula development.

The term "Open Finance" expands upon Open Banking. It is a concept introduced in the UK in 2018 as a result of the EU Directive on Payment Services (PSD2) (Pascalis (2022)). Initially, it was set up as an initiative designed to improve competition and customer experience in retail banking, Open Banking has since extended to other financial sectors. This evolution is particularly relevant in Southeast Asia, where the authors are based. The region's diverse financial ecosystems are emerging rapidly, supported by a significant population increasingly favoring digital financial services.

It is widely accepted that permissioned access to financial data signifies a transformative shift. One that builds on the foundational principles of the Open Banking initiative. That said, it goes further and also encompasses a broad spectrum of financial products, including pensions, investments, insurance, and savings. The concept is grounded in data science. By facilitating third-party access to financial data with explicit consumer consent, Open Finance creates opportunities for product innovation. However, as its adoption expands, there is a need to address the associated educational requirements. Universities must adapt their curricula to equip graduates with the requisite skills and interdisciplinary knowledge required.

The highlighted potential lies in the capacity to utilise large-scale data. This is based on its volume, velocity, and variety. Using such data, emerging entities, such as Account Information Service Providers (AISPs) and Payment Initiation Service Providers (PISPs), are disrupting personalised financial advice, automated savings and investment mechanisms, and customised credit assessment (Hussain and Prieto (2016); Zachariadis and Ozcan (2017)). To align with these developments, we therefore suggest that degree programmes tailored to Open Finance must prioritise the cultivation of domain-level expertise. They should emphasise the technical and analytical skills required, alongside an understanding of regulatory and ethical dimensions.

We therefore argue that the core components should include advanced technical skills. In this respect, we mean programming and data analytics. We suggest that this should be combined with a deep comprehension of financial systems, and the ability to innovate and thrive in professional environments. We also believe that work-integrated learning and interdisciplinary pedagogical approaches are essential. These ensure that students can acquire practical experience while mastering theoretical foundations. We caveat our remarks by acknowledging that there are various job descriptors in the field. For the sake of clarity, we expand on the skills required for managers and senior level industry personnel, those typically taught by business schools.

In summary, our thought piece on curriculum design offers a contribution to the academic and professional backdrop of Open Finance. It is written to promote discussion. It suggests addressing gaps in current educational provision. It also suggests universities respond to demand for skilled professionals equipped to advance this specialisation. We caution that the curriculum will have to adapt. As the sector evolves, firms will require a workforce adept at addressing challenges in information technology, data analytics, artificial intelligence, and financial acumen. Universities must thus align their educational offerings with these emerging industry demands to support the sector's growth effectively.

2 Identification of Skill Gaps

We were motivated to prepare this curriculum in order to address a clear skills gap, particularly in futures related skills. We recognise that delivering such educational content requires a focus on the intersection of financial knowledge, programming, and practical problem-solving abilities. Higher education traditionally struggles with this. We suggest that universities must embrace this challenge by designing programmes that blend theoretical understanding with hands-on application (Curran and Muphy (2019); Murphy and Curran (2018)). Central to this could be the Barnett and Coate (2005) curricular domain model. This focuses on what students need to know (Knowledge Domain), do (Skills Domain), and become (Attributes Domain).

We believe that the data-driven nature of Open Finance necessitates cognitive skills such as the ability to analyse and interpret complex datasets. Students must develop metacognitive skills, including critical thinking and a capacity for self-directed learning, to stay adaptable in a rapidly changing field. Practical skills should enable graduates to communicate insights derived from data effectively, both to technical and non-technical stakeholders. Collaborative abilities, essential in multidisciplinary environments, are also critical, aligning with the principles of teamwork emphasised in business education McKenna, Cotton, and Van Auken (1995).

To comprehensively address the educational requirements for Open Finance from a computing science perspective, we propose a structured taxonomy. We produce one summarised in Table 1. This taxonomy divides essential concepts, theories, and competencies into five core domains: foundational concepts, key theories, data processing, emerging technologies, and software tools. Each domain encompasses specific sub-categories that reflect both theoretical underpinnings and practical applications. Integrating these elements, the taxonomy serves as a bridge between academic knowledge and real-world implementation, equipping graduates with a balanced and industry-relevant skill set.

The concept is multidisciplinary. Any curriculum addressing Open Finance must therefore be holistic, accommodating the complexity introduced by permissioned access to data. This necessitates the inclusion of modules on programming, communication, leadership, and problem-solving to supplement traditional finance modules. For example, while traditional finance programmes often emphasise topics such as the pricing of derivatives, Open Finance curricula should prioritise areas like banking risk, data governance, and regulatory compliance. To support this, we suggest programming courses could incorporate case studies tailored to Open Finance, such as developing algorithms for credit scoring or fraud detection.

Curriculum development in this context should adhere to established educational norms, drawing on frameworks like those proposed by Acemoglu and Autor (2011). They distinguish between skills and tasks. Their emphasis on task-focused pedagogy is particularly relevant in the context of FinTech related technological advancements. In line with this principle, we advocate for assessment strategies that prioritise applied tasks, enabling students to efficiently execute real-world workplace functions. For instance, assessments could involve analysing business opportunities within Open Finance ecosystems or designing scenarios to explore potential market and regulatory developments.

To adequately prepare students for the dynamic nature of Open Finance, we suggest the curriculum should integrate a comprehensive range of topics (see Table 2),

Table 1. Taxonomy for Open Finance Education

Category	Subcategory	Examples and Applications
Foundational Concepts	Data Structures and Algorithms	Hash tables, trees, graph theory for modelling financial networks
	Databases	Relational (SQL) and nonrelational (NoSQL) databases for storing financial data
	Computer Networks	Internet protocols (TCP/IP, HTTPS) and secure data transfer via APIs
	Software Engineering Principles	Agile methodologies, modular design, and version control in financial software systems
Key Theories	Distributed Systems	CAP theorem, consensus algorithms (e.g., Paxos, Raft)
	Cryptography	Public-key infrastructure (PKI), hashing, digital signatures
	Machine Learning	Supervised/unsupervised learning, deep learning, and neural networks
	Human-Computer Interaction (HCI)	Usability principles, user interface (UI) and user experience (UX) design
Data Processing	Big Data Processing	MapReduce, Spark, and distributed storage systems (e.g., HDFS)
	API Development	RESTful APIs, GraphQL, and API versioning
	Data Privacy and Security	Anonymisation techniques, encryption standards (AES, RSA), GDPR compliance

(*continued*)

Table 1. (*continued*)

Category	Subcategory	Examples and Applications
	Cloud Computing	Virtualisation, containerisation (e.g., Docker, Kubernetes), and serverless architectures
Emerging Technologies	Blockchain and Decentralised Finance	Distributed ledgers, smart contracts, consensus mechanisms (e.g., PoW, PoS)
	Artificial Intelligence	Explainable AI, AI ethics, and AI for credit scoring and fraud detection
	Edge Computing	IoT-based financial services, latency reduction
	Quantum Computing	Potential applications in cryptography and portfolio optimisation
Software and Tools	Programming Languages	Python (pandas, NumPy), R, JavaScript (Node.js), Solidity for smart contracts
	Development Frameworks	Django, Flask for back-end; React.js for front-end
	Version Control Systems	Git, GitHub, GitLab
	Testing and Debugging Tools	Unit testing (JUnit, PyTest), debugging tools and continuous integration (CI)

combining historical context with practical skill development. Understanding the technical and regulatory evolution of Open Banking will provide students with the ability to anticipate trends and adapt to the changing financial ecosystem. This foundational knowledge should be complemented by practical strategies for creating personalised financial services using Open Finance protocols.

While the topic is inherently data-centric, it is essential to recognise that the financial component remains central. An application of quantitative methods is therefore imperative, equipping students with the tools to model and assess risks across areas such as credit, insurance, investment, and interest rates. These analytical capabilities can be further enhanced through statistical techniques designed for behavioural modelling, customer segmentation, and valuation frameworks. When integrated with qualitative research, these methods enable students to derive comprehensive insights from financial data and formulate actionable conclusions.

Table 2. Key Concepts for an Open Finance Curriculum

Category	Key Concepts	Educational Strategies	Applications in Open Finance
Knowledge	Open Finance principles Financial systems basics (banking, insurance) Data privacy and regulatory frameworks API development and machine learning Ethical use of data and sustainability	Lectures, reading materials, and guest seminars Case studies on real-world financial ecosystems Comparative studies of GDPR, CCPA, PSD2 Technical coding labs and projects Discussion forums, ethical dilemmas, and reflective essays	Understanding third-party data sharing in finance (e.g., AISPs, PISPs) Analysing the evolution of Open Banking to Open Finance Compliance strategies for Open Finance solutions Designing algorithms for credit scoring and fraud detection Implementing responsible innovation aligned with societal goals
Skills	Programming (Python, R, SQL) Data analysis and visualisation Problem-solving and innovation Communication (technical and non-technical)	Hands-on coding workshops Data-driven assignments and group projects Hackathons, design thinking workshops Presentations and report-writing exercises	API creation, data cleaning, and managing structured/unstructured data Building customer segmentation models and financial risk assessments Developing solutions for integrating APIs in financial ecosystems Translating complex datasets into actionable insights for stakeholders
Attributes	Adaptability and self-directed learning Collaboration and teamwork Leadership and consulting	Self-paced modules, MOOCs Group assignments and interdisciplinary projects Role-playing exercises, mentoring	Staying updated with advancements like blockchain and DeFi Working with cross-functional teams in industry settings Guiding digital transformation projects in financial services

(*continued*)

Table 2. (*continued*)

Category	Key Concepts	Educational Strategies	Applications in Open Finance
Integration	Capstone projects	Real-world industry collaborations Work placements Internships and shadowing programmes	Integrating all knowledge, skills, and attributes into practical Open Finance applications Solving real-world challenges like managing data security or developing financial forecasts

As part of the broad financial knowledge, students should gain the ability to navigate profit and loss statements, and balance sheets, and understand distinctions among sectors such as retail banking, insurance, and asset management. These skills should be reinforced by insights into how financial intermediaries leverage data to enhance decision-making processes. By combining technical expertise with a robust financial framework, students will be well-equipped to thrive in the emerging Open Finance landscape. Furthermore, recognizing the trend towards greater social awareness, financial literacy should be a core component.

It goes without saying that a well-structured curriculum must balance technical rigour with strategic and contextual understanding. This ensures that graduates are not only adept at managing and analysing financial data but are also equipped to innovate and adapt in a rapidly evolving field. By blending historical, technical, and practical elements, the programme can prepare students to meet the challenges of Open Finance from a multidisciplinary perspective.

Any transdisciplinary approach, such as this, should be rooted in research-based teaching methodologies. As Healey (2005) argue, such an approach fosters innovation and inquiry, which are essential in emergent fields like Open Finance. Traditional instructional methods may not fully address the unique challenges of this domain. We recommend that approaches encouraging innovation, such as problem-based learning, be incorporated (Khuan et al. (2024)).

Additionally, we suggest that curricula should emphasise creative problem-solving, independent research, and the acquisition of new knowledge. This aligns with Barnett (2009), who emphasises the importance of nurturing holistic development. Such an approach ensures that graduates possess not only technical and analytical expertise but also the interpersonal skills required to succeed in a dynamic industry. By allowing room for exploration and adaptability, the proposed programme can address both the current demands and future developments in Open Finance education (Null (2016)). This includes work-integration, such as industry projects and internships, in order to bridge the gap between theoretical knowledge and practical application (Fichman, Dos Santos, and Zheng (2014)).

Hopefully, we have made it clear that Open Finance occupies a unique position between computer science and finance. Traditionally, computer science faculties focus on data science, while finance is housed within business schools. This disciplinary divide necessitates a hybrid approach to Open Finance education. Course content should integrate structured financial datasets with advanced data analytics techniques. Incorporating these elements ensures that students are not only proficient in understanding technological innovations but are also capable of applying them within financial contexts.

3 Proposed Curriculum Framework

Designing a focused curriculum for computer scientists and data scientists requires the integration of advanced computing skills with foundational financial knowledge. Guided by the Barnett and Coate (2005) Curricular Domains Model, we now turn to the curriculum framework. Designing an Open Finance-focused curriculum for computer scientists and data scientists requires the integration of advanced computing skills with foundational financial knowledge.

As is evident from our observations, a comprehensive approach should integrate both core and specialist components. Core modules focus on fundamental skills, including programming in Python, R, and SQL, applied machine learning, and fundamental financial principles. These courses provide essential technical capabilities while fostering a contextual understanding of financial systems. This foundation enables students to manage complex datasets, develop APIs, and apply statistical methods to financial data. For example, programming modules extend beyond basic coding to teach students how to interact with APIs and process both structured and unstructured data skills that are indispensable in Open Finance.

We do not wish to be too prescriptive. This is, after all, a thought piece. Specialist modules can be used to address the interdisciplinary demands of Open Finance, encompassing topics such as API development, data privacy, and financial risk modeling. These modules highlight the intersection of technical standards, regulatory frameworks, and ethical considerations. Optional modules provide flexibility, allowing students to customise their learning pathways based on personal interests or career goals. Topics such as digital transformation, sustainability in FinTech, and modern banking practices enable exploration of emerging trends, aligning the curriculum with the dynamic and evolving landscape of Open Finance.

Data privacy and security are key. Students need to engage with the entire data lifecycle, including encryption, anonymisation, and storage strategies. These skills ensure the safeguarding of sensitive information while enabling innovation. Furthermore, integrating topics such as advanced machine learning techniques, deep learning and big data analytics equips graduates to harness cutting-edge technologies for customer insights, fraud detection, and financial forecasting. Familiarity with data protection laws such as the General Data Protection Regulation (GDPR), the California Consumer Privacy Act (CCPA), the Health Insurance Portability and Accountability Act (HIPAA), the Children's Online Privacy Protection Act (COPPA), the Gramm-Leach-Bliley Act (GLBA), and various US state-level laws like the Virginia Consumer Data Protection Act (VCDPA) is crucial. These regulations collectively establish frameworks for safeguarding personal information, granting individuals rights over their data, and imposing compliance obligations on organisations to ensure transparency, accountability, and security in data handling practices equips students to navigate the complexities of handling sensitive financial data, while expertise in API development ensures interoperability across diverse financial systems.

We would also suggest that practical application is integral to a successful programme. In this respect, projects and industry placements should be devised to provide real-world learning experiences. This would enable students to develop Open Finance related problem-solving, critical thinking and decision-making skills. These opportunities allow students to tackle industry-relevant challenges, such as integrating APIs or performing financial data analysis. Additionally, case studies and project-based tasks further enhance their ability to apply technical skills within broader financial and regulatory landscapes, ensuring that graduates are well-prepared to meet the demands of the Open Finance industry.

In summary, a balance between theoretical and practical components is required in order to equip students with the technical, analytical, and strategic competencies necessary.

4 Recommended Assessment

As this is a practical and science-based discipline, we further recommend overhauling the assessment strategy to better align with the practical and theoretical blend of the curriculum's learning outcomes. Given the applied nature of the subject matter, traditional examinations are not the most effective method for assessment. Instead, we propose adopting a 100% coursework-based approach, which has been gaining traction in the industry. This method enhances relevance and authenticity by incorporating live cases, real-world problems, actual datasets, and simulations into the learning process. Focusing the assessment in this way aligns with the sector's shift from an assessment of learning approach to one that also emphasises "assessment for learning" and "assessment as learning" (O'Neill, McEvoy, and Maguire (2020)). In this context, the assessment framework should support the development of all three curricular domains: skills, attributes, and knowledge creation. Applied, authentic assessments that address real-world challenges are particularly effective in fostering both skills and attribute domains of the curriculum.

A robust assessment should ensure students meet the technological, analytical, and leadership demands of the industry. Graduates develop the ability to design and implement technical solutions for managing third-party data access while applying advanced analytical methods to financial datasets. Through the integration of statistical, mathematical, and data-driven approaches, students learn to extract actionable insights that enhance financial decision-making processes. Key to this development is the ability to produce well-substantiated reports and communicate findings orally and in writing.

The assessment should also prepare graduates to explore and critically evaluate financial datasets, applying their skills to identify innovative applications for financial data. Leadership capabilities are nurtured through modules focused on communication, consultancy, and managing disruptive innovation, empowering students to play pivotal roles in guiding digital transformation initiatives. Additionally, students gain a nuanced understanding of the broader context of digital innovation, enabling them to navigate its implications for both the finance and technology sectors.

With the rise of generative AI, it is important to assess critical judgment and analytical rigour. The curriculum should enable students to assess financial theories and data methodologies, identifying and questioning the assumptions that underpin their analyses. This ability to critically evaluate data and recognise its limitations is crucial for maintaining the integrity of Open Finance initiatives. Collectively, these competencies ensure graduates are prepared to excel in an industry characterised by rapid technological advancements, complex regulatory environments, and evolving consumer expectations. With the rise of generative AI, it is important to assess critical judgment and analytical rigour. The curriculum should enable students to assess financial theories and data methodologies, identifying and questioning the assumptions that underpin their analyses. This ability to critically evaluate data and recognise its limitations is crucial for maintaining the integrity of Open Finance initiatives. Collectively, these competencies ensure graduates are prepared to excel in an industry characterised by rapid technological advancements, complex regulatory environments, and evolving consumer expectations.

5 Scope

Another consideration in designing an Open Finance curriculum is defining its scope. While programming skills, data cleaning, and API usage are essential, the curriculum should not attempt to replicate the depth of specialised degrees in data science or finance. Instead, a focused approach ensures that graduates acquire the unique competencies required for Open Finance without overextending into areas better suited to other disciplines. We think that it is important for graduates to demonstrate a solid conceptual understanding of Open Finance. This includes a mastery of the data tools and techniques required to succeed in this nascent industry. Additionally, we emphasise the importance of fostering an understanding of the ethical use of data, particularly as it relates to societal and individual impacts. This ethical dimension is integral to ensuring that graduates contribute responsibly to the development and sustainability of the Open Finance ecosystem. We present an illustration of how the final set-up could look like in Fig. 1.

Note in the figure the final row on skills development. The integration of practical, real-world experiences is vital for enhancing learning outcomes. Case studies, project-based tasks, and work placements foster critical thinking and problem-solving while bridging the gap between theoretical knowledge and application. These experiential learning components allow students to engage directly with current industry challenges, including API integration, managing large-scale datasets, and navigating complex regulatory environments.

The dynamic nature of Open Finance requires ongoing curriculum updates. Advances in machine learning, data encryption, anonymisation techniques, and cloud-based solutions necessitate that students remain current with technological innovations. For instance, understanding the risks and opportunities of cloud storage, particularly regarding data security and resilience in decentralised environments, is increasingly relevant. To address emerging trends, additional curriculum components should be incorporated to equip students for innovation in the financial technology sector. Algorithm design and

Sem	Progressive Skills Development	Level 7 Exit Points	Module Titles and Credits			
S1	Develop	Cert	X 20 Principles of Finance	X 20 Introductory programming and Database Structure	X 10 Open finance in practice	X10 Contemporary Challenges – Regulatory Societal and Industry
S2	Practice	Diploma	X20 Phyton and R	X 20 API Development	X10 Open Finance Management and Strategy Challenges	X 10 Fundamental of banking
S3	Master	Masters	X60 Third Party data Work-based Project			
	Skills Development		Exploring Statistics and predictive analytics	Quantitative Research Methods	Reflective Account of WB practice	

Fig. 1. A 180 credit one year Master's degree programme. The course includes compulsory elements such as programming, finance and an Application Programming Interface module. Semesters are denoted by S*.Broby and Murphy (2024).

optimisation are critical for solving complex problems such as risk assessment and portfolio management. Knowledge of distributed systems and cloud computing is equally important, given the reliance on decentralised storage and computational resources to ensure scalability, resilience, and efficiency in managing financial data.

We acknowledge that developing a comprehensive programme requires significant investment in time and resources. Institutions must balance the need for careful preparation with the urgency of meeting industry demands. While adoption rates may vary, aligning education with the evolving requirements of Open Finance ensures graduates are well-prepared for this transformative field.

We would argue that sustainability must also form a part of Open Finance education. Universities must explore how Open Finance aligns with broader environmental, social, and economic goals, reflecting the growing demand for responsible innovation. By incorporating sustainability themes, students can contribute to developing systems that balance technological progress with societal impact. Also, data ethics and responsible AI are increasingly shaping the financial technology sector, including Open Finance. Ethical considerations, such as bias mitigation and algorithm accountability, are essential to fostering trust in financial systems. Blockchain and decentralised finance technologies add another dimension, introducing possibilities for identity verification, secure transactions, and process automation through smart contracts, making them vital topics in the curriculum. Human-computer interaction should also be included. Designing user-friendly interfaces for financial products enhances accessibility and builds consumer trust. A practical understanding of security protocols is indispensable, especially with the increased reliance on cloud-based and distributed data architectures. Financial datasets often contain sensitive information, and ensuring their security is foundational to maintaining system integrity.

The curriculum should also incorporate advanced analytics and decision science. Techniques such as machine learning, statistical modeling, and prescriptive analytics are essential for deriving actionable insights from complex financial data. Additionally, a focus on open standards and interoperability equips graduates to design systems that enable seamless data exchange between diverse financial platforms. Optional modules on economic and behavioural models further enrich the curriculum, enabling students to understand market dynamics and consumer decision-making.

Finally, hands-on experiences through the capstone project or multi-semester collaborations with industry partners will bridge the gap between theoretical knowledge and its practical application. These projects should challenge students to address real world issues, such as building scalable financial systems or implementing innovative Open Finance use cases. By integrating these elements, the curriculum ensures graduates are well-rounded, industry-ready, and equipped to lead in the evolving field of financial technology.

6 Conclusion

Our thought piece on Open Finance is presented as a Statement of Knowledge. It has outlined areas where universities can focus to improve graduate outcomes and address existing skills gaps. Presented in a systematic knowledge framework, it emphasises the critical role of computer science in advancing the field.

Open Finance employs a lot of data scientists. The skills we identify are different. In order for graduates to be employable and differentiated from existing courses, the curriculum must address transferable and financial skills. Kemp and Seagraves (1995) highlight these as critical for employability. They include problem-solving, adaptability, and effective communication within multidisciplinary teams. Incorporating guest lectures from industry professionals offers students valuable perspectives on emerging technologies and practical challenges, further enriching their educational experience.

Integrating financial insights with technical expertise offers the most effective pathway for preparing a workforce capable of addressing the challenges and opportunities presented by Open Finance. Therefore, we propose that core area, such as data management, API development, machine learning, and data privacy, receive focused attention. This ensures that educational programmes align with the evolving demands of the Open Finance industry and adequately prepare graduates.

Our observations underscore the importance of equipping graduates with both foundational knowledge and practical skills to navigate the dynamic and rapidly evolving landscape. The incorporation of sustainability, real-world applications, and ethical considerations into curricula. This ensures that Open Finance can contribute positively to industry innovation and broader societal outcomes.

In conclusion, we recommend that universities refine their educational offerings to adapt to technological advancements and regulatory changes, ensuring that curricula remain relevant, forward-looking, and impactful. As Open Finance evolves, collaboration between academia, industry, and policymakers will be crucial for shaping a comprehensive educational framework. Such a framework will support innovation, uphold ethical standards, and drive sustainable economic growth.

Acknowledgments. This study was funded by X (grant number Y).

Disclosure of Interests. The authors have no competing interests.

References

Acemoglu, D., Autor, D.: Skills, tasks and technologies: Implications for employment and earnings. In: Handbook of Labor Economics, vol. 4, pp. 1043–1171. Elsevier (2011)

Barnett, R., Coate, K.: Engaging the Curriculum in Higher Education. Society for Research into Higher Education & Open University, Berkshire (2005)

Barnett, R.: Knowing and becoming in the higher education curriculum. Stud. High. Educ. **34**(4), 429–440 (2009)

Broby, D.: Contemporary issues in financial technology: the role of the internet. In: Proceedings of the 6th International Conference on Advanced Research Methods and Analytics (CARMA 2024), Valencia, 26–28 June. https://doi.org/10.4995/CARMA2024.2024.17250

Broby, D., Murphy, C.: A curriculum for the body of knowledge in open finance (2024)

Brodsky, L., Oakes, L.: Data sharing and open banking, pp. 1097–1105. McKinsey & Company (2017)

Curran, R., Murphy, C.: Empowering curriculum leaders to innovate: an overview and evaluation of an Integrated Curriculum Design Framework. In: Staff and Educational Development Association (SEDA) Spring Teaching, Learning and Assessment Conference: Collaboration to Support the Student Experience and Progression. Staff and Educational Development Association (2019)

Fichman, R.G., Dos Santos, B.L., Zheng, Z.: Digital innovation as a fundamental and powerful concept in the information systems curriculum. MIS Q. **38**(2), 329-A15 (2014)

Healey, M.: Linking research and teaching: disciplinary spaces. In: Reshaping the University: New Relationships Between Research, Scholarship and Teaching, vol. 30, p. 42 (2005)

Hussain, K., Prieto, E.: Big data in the finance and insurance sectors. In: New horizons for a data-driven economy, 209–223. Springer, Cham (2016). https://doi.org/10.1007/978-3-319-21569-3_12

Karkkainen, T., Panos, G.A., Broby, D., Bracciali, A.: On the educational curriculum in finance and technology. In: Internet Science: INSCI 2017 International Workshops, IFIN, DATA ECONOMY, DSI, and CONVERSATIONS, Thessaloniki, Greece, November 22, 2017, Revised Selected Papers, vol. 4, pp. 7–20. Springer (2018). https://doi.org/10.1007/978-3-319-77547-0_1

Kemp, I.J., Seagraves, L.: Transferable skills—can higher education deliver? Stud. High. Educ. **20**(3), 315–328 (1995)

Khuan, H., Judijanto, L., Rachmawati, T., Tanjung, T., Vandika, A.Y.: Bibliometric analysis on the use of artificial intelligence in improving the efficiency of banking financial processes in southeast Asian countries. West Sci. Interdisc. Stud. **2**, 129–137 (2024)

McKenna, J.F., Cotton, C.C., Van Auken, S.: Business school emphasis on teaching, research and service to industry: Does where you sit determine where you stand. J. Organ. Change Manage. (1995)

Murphy, C., Curran, R.: Integrated Curriculum Design Framework. Ulster University (2018). https://www.ulster.ac.uk/cherp/academic-development/icdf

Null, W.: Curriculum: From Theory to Practice. Rowman & Littlefield (2016)

O'Neill, G., McEvoy, E., Maguire, T.: Developing a national understanding of assessment and feedback in Irish higher education. Irish Educ. Stud. **39**(4), 495–510 (2020)

Pascalis, F.D.: The journey to open finance: learning from the open banking movement. Eur. Bus. Law Rev. **33**, 397–420 (2022)

Zachariadis, M., Ozcan, P.: The API economy and digital transformation in financial services: the case of open banking (2017)

3+ Seat Risk-Limiting Audits for Single Transferable Vote Elections

Michelle Blom[1]($\boxtimes$), Alexander Ek[2], Peter J. Stuckey[3], Vanessa Teague[4], and Damjan Vukcevic[2]

[1] School of Computing and Information Systems, University of Melbourne, Parkville, Australia
michelle.blom@unimelb.edu.au
[2] Department of Econometrics and Business Statistics, Monash University, Clayton, Australia
[3] Department of Data Science and AI, Monash University, Clayton, Australia
[4] Thinking Cybersecurity Pty. Ltd., Melbourne, Australia

Abstract. Constructing efficient risk-limiting audits (RLAs) for multi-winner single transferable vote (STV) elections is a challenging problem. An STV RLA is designed to statistically verify that the reported winners of an election did indeed win according to the voters' expressed preferences and not due to mistabulation or interference, while limiting the risk of accepting an incorrect outcome to a desired threshold (the risk limit). Existing methods have shown that it is possible to form RLAs for two-seat STV elections in the context where the first seat has been awarded to a candidate in the first round of tabulation. This is called the *first winner criterion*. We present an assertion-based approach to conducting full or partial RLAs for STV elections with three or more seats, in which the first winner criterion is satisfied. Although the chance of forming a full audit that verifies all winners drops substantially as the number of seats increases, we show that we can quite often form partial audits that verify most, and sometimes all, of the reported winners. We evaluate our method on a dataset of over 500 three- and four-seat STV elections from the 2017 and 2022 local council elections in Scotland.

1 Introduction

The single transferable vote (STV) is a multi-winner proportional ranked-choice election system. Voters cast a ballot in which they rank available candidates in order of preference. Depending on the jurisdiction, votes may be partial, expressing a ranking over only a subset of candidates, or total, in which all candidates are ranked. In general, candidates are awarded a seat when they amass more than a certain share of the total vote, called a *quota*. This quota will depend on the number of available seats and the total number of valid ballots cast. Tabulation is complex, as while each cast ballot starts with a value of 1, this value changes as tabulation proceeds. This complexity makes auditing STV elections hard. In this paper, we build upon earlier work on 2-seat STV risk-limiting audits (RLAs) [1,2], presenting a generalisation of the prior method to N-seat RLAs.

STV tabulation proceeds in rounds of candidate election and elimination. Initially, each candidate is given all of the ballots on which they have been ranked first. Candidates are elected when their tally reaches or exceeds the election's quota. Where multiple candidates reach a quota in the same round, they are elected in order of their tallies, highest first. The ballots in a seated candidates' tally pile are subsequently re-weighted, and given to the next most preferred eligible candidate in their rankings. This re-weighting is designed to remove a quota's worth of votes from the system, and can be accomplished in myriad ways. In this paper, we consider the variant of STV that uses the Weighted Inclusive Gregory method. The current value of each ballot in the winner's tally pile is multiplied by a *transfer value* equal to the difference between their total tally and the quota (their *surplus*) divided by their total tally. In any round where no candidate has a quota, the candidate with the smallest tally is eliminated, with their ballots given, at their current value, to candidates preferenced further down the list. This variant of STV is used in the United States and Scotland.

Blom et al. [1] presented a first approach for constructing an assertion-based STV RLA in the 2-seat context. Two cases were considered separately: (i) where a candidate was awarded a seat in the first round of tabulation, on the basis of their first preference tally (the *first winner* criterion), and (ii) where a candidate was eliminated in the first round. Case (i) was found to be more straightforward to audit. The audit consisted of assertions to verify that: the candidate who won in the first found did indeed have a quota's worth of votes, and that the second winner could not possibly lose to all the reported losers. A method designed to tackle the second case was presented, but found to be impractical in general.

In follow-up work, Blom et al. [2] showed how 2-seat STV RLAs, where the first winner criterion was satisfied, could be made more efficient by substantially reducing the number of ballots to be sampled in the audit. Previously, assertions were formed to establish an upper bound on the first winner's transfer value. This upper bound was then used to help form assertions to show that the second winner beat all of the reported losers. These assertions compared the minimum possible tally of the second winner against the maximum possible tally of the reported losers. This kind of assertion could only be formed when the minimum tally of the winner was greater than the maximum tally of the loser. The transfer value upper bound was used to reduce these maximum tallies. Blom et al. [2] extended this earlier work by adding assertions to establish a lower bound on the first winner's transfer value. This bound was used to increase the winner's minimum possible tally in these minimum-maximum tally comparisons. The result was both assertions that are more efficient to audit, and an increase in the number of assertions that could be formed. This work additionally introduced the concept of a *partial* audit, where all winners were not verified, but some candidates are shown to have definitely lost, and some to have definitely won.

The approach we present in this paper is restricted to the context where *at least one candidate has been seated in the first round* of tabulation. Our method forms either a full RLA, where all winners can be verified, or a partial RLA, in which we verify only a subset. One new assertion type is presented to help form these audits. We evaluate this approach on a data set of 513 three- or four-seat Scottish local council STV elections, all satisfying the first winner criterion. Of the 252 three-seat contests, we can verify all winners in 58% of instances, two of the three winners in 29%, one winner in 11%, and no winners in 2%. Of the 261 four-seat contests, we verify all four winners in 32% of instances, three winners in 30%, two winners in 26%, one winner in 10%, and no winners in 2%.

2 Single Transferable Vote

STV tabulation proceeds in rounds of candidate election and elimination. As candidates are elected or eliminated, the ballots in their tally piles are re-distributed to the next most preferred *eligible* candidate. Candidates are eligible to receive votes in a round iff: they have not yet been elected or eliminated, and they did not already have a quota at the start of the round.[1] Tabulation stops when all seats have been filled, or the number of candidates remaining equals the number of unfilled seats, at which point all remaining candidates are elected to a seat.

Table 1 presents an example 3-seat STV election with five candidates, A to E, tabulated using the Weighted Inclusive Gregory Method. The quota is 308 votes. The first preference tallies of A to E are 250, 120, 400, 350 and 110 votes, respectively. Candidates C and E have a quota on first preferences. Candidate C has the largest surplus, at 202 votes, and is elected first. Their transfer value is $\tau_1 = 208/510 = 0.396$. The 400 $[C, D]$ ballots are each re-weighted to 0.396, and 158.4 votes are added to D's tally. The 110 $[C, E, D]$ ballots are also re-valued to 0.396, and are given to D, skipping E as E already has a quota. Candidate E is then elected. Their transfer value would be $\tau_2 = 42/350 = 0.12$, but all of the ballots in their tally pile exhaust, with no later eligible preferences. In the third round, no candidate has a quota's worth of votes, and the candidate with the smallest tally, B, is eliminated. The 120 $[B, A, C]$ ballots go to A, each retaining their current value of 1. At the start of the fourth round, candidate A has reached a quota, at 370 votes, and is elected to the third and final seat.

3 Assertion-Based RLAs

An assertion-based RLA is an RLA in which we statistically test a set of statements about a contest, called assertions. An *assertion* is a statement about the full set of ballots cast in an election, typically expressed as an inequality comparing the number of votes in one category against the number of votes in another. To construct an audit in the SHANGRLA framework [4], we need to

---

[1] If a candidate reaches a quota mid-transfer, the transfer does not stop. The candidate will continue to receive all votes in the transfer designated for them.

Table 1. 3-seat STV election, quota 308 votes, stating (a) the number of ballots cast with each listed ranking over candidates A to E, and (b) the tallies for each candidate after each round, and when a quota is reached (in bold).

Ranking	Count
[A]	250
[B,A,C]	120
[C,D]	400
[E]	350
[C,E,D]	110

(a)

N: 3	Q: 308			
Cand.	Round 1	Round 2	Round 3	Round 4
	C elected	E elected	B elim.	A elected
	$\tau_1 = 0.396$	$\tau_2 = 0.12$		
A	250	250	250	**370**
B	120	120	120	–
C	**510**	–	–	–
D	0	201.96	201.96	201.96
E	350	**350**	–	–

(b)

design a set of assertions such that, if they are all true, they imply that the reported winner(s) really won the election. In general, any linear combination of tallies (counts of different types of ballots) can be converted into a SHANGRLA assertion [3].

4 Preliminaries and Notation

We define an STV election as per prior work [1,2]. A ballot b is a sequence of candidates π, listed in order of preference (most popular first), without duplicates but without necessarily including all candidates. We use list notation (e.g., $\pi = [c_1, c_2, c_3, c_4]$) and $\text{first}(\pi) = \pi(1)$ to denote the first candidate in sequence π.

Definition 1 (STV Election). *An STV election E is a tuple $E = (\mathcal{C}, \mathcal{B}, Q, N)$ where $\mathcal{C}$ is a set of candidates, $\mathcal{B}$ the multiset of ballots cast,[2] Q the election quota (the number of votes a candidate must attain to win a seat—usually the Droop quota—Equation 1), and N the number of seats to be filled.*

$$Q = \left\lfloor \frac{|\mathcal{B}|}{N+1} \right\rfloor + 1 \tag{1}$$

We use the concept of projection of one set onto another to reason about who a ballot belongs to when we assume that only a subset of candidates are 'still standing' (i.e., they have not yet been eliminated or elected to a seat).

Definition 2. (Projection $\sigma_S(\pi)$). *We define the projection of a sequence π onto a set $\mathcal{S}$ as the result of filtering all elements from π that are not in $\mathcal{S}$. (The elements keep their relative order in π.) For example: $\sigma_{\{c_2,c_3\}}([c_1, c_2, c_4, c_3]) = [c_2, c_3]$ and $\sigma_{\{c_2,c_3,c_4,c_5\}}([c_6, c_4, c_7, c_2, c_1]) = [c_4, c_2]$.*

---
[2] A multiset allows for the inclusion of duplicate items.

We use notation $t_{c,r}$ to denote the *tally* of candidate c in round r. The tally of each candidate in the first round is comprised of all the ballots on which they are ranked first (also referred to as their first preference tally). Note that, unlike in most elections, tallies are not necessarily integers.

The cost of auditing a given assertion refers to the estimated number of ballots we expect will need to be sampled in order to verify it–it's *approximate sample number* (ASN). The estimated cost of an audit as a whole, consisting of a set of assertions, is the maximum of the expected costs of its assertions.

We use $\mathcal{A}$ to denote a set of assertions, a to denote a single assertion, $ASN(a)$ to denote the expected sample size required to audit a, and $ASN(\mathcal{A})$ to denote the maximum ASN across all assertions in $\mathcal{A}$. We use the notation M to denote the maximum sample size that we would consider to be *auditable*. Throughout this paper, we consider an assertion a to be *auditable* if its ASN is less than or equal to a defined threshold, M (i.e., $ASN(a) \leq M$).

For an N-seat STV election E using the Droop quota (Eq. 1), the maximum theoretical transfer value computable for any winning candidate is known to be $\tau_{max} = N/(N+1)$. For a three-seat contest, for example, $\tau_{max} = 0.75$. The maximum transfer value arises when a candidate achieves the maximum possible vote (i.e., all the votes). It is clear that this is no more than $(N+1)Q$. This gives a transfer value of $\tau_{max} = ((N+1)Q - Q)/((N+1)Q) = N/(N+1)$.

5 Assertions

Existing Assertions. The following five assertion types are re-used from prior work [1,2], although with some slight changes, as noted.

IQ(c). Candidate c's first-preference tally is at least a quota: $t_{c,1} \geq Q$.
In the context where candidate c has been elected on their first preferences:
UT$(c, \overline{\tau}_c)$. Candidate c's transfer value is less than $\overline{\tau}_c$: $t_{c,1} < Q/(1 - \overline{\tau}_c)$.
LT$(c, \underline{\tau}_c)$. Candidate c's transfer value is greater than $\underline{\tau}_c$: $t_{c,1} > Q/(1 - \underline{\tau}_c)$.
In the context where candidates W have been *elected on their first preferences* with lower and upper bounds on their transfer values, $\underline{\tau}$ and $\overline{\tau}$:
AG$^*(w, l, W, \underline{\tau}, \overline{\tau})$. The minimum tally of candidate w is greater than the maximum tally of l. Thus, w will always have higher tally than l. The contributions of ballot $b \in \mathcal{B}$ to w's minimum tally, and l's maximum tally, are:

$$C^{AG^*}_{min}(b, w, W, \underline{\tau}, \overline{\tau}) = \begin{cases} 1 & \text{first}(b) = w \\ \underline{\tau}_{\text{first}(b)} & \text{first}(\sigma_{C-W}(b)) = w \\ 0 & \text{otherwise} \end{cases}$$

$$C^{AG^*}_{max}(b, l, W, \underline{\tau}, \overline{\tau}) = \begin{cases} 0 & l \text{ does not occur in } b \\ 0 & w \text{ appears before } l \text{ in } b \\ \overline{\tau}_{\text{first}(b)} & \text{first}(b) \in W \\ 1 & \text{otherwise} \end{cases}$$

We say that $\mathsf{AG}^*(w, l, W, \underline{\tau}, \overline{\tau})$ iff $t1_w^{min} > t1_l^{max}$, where

$$t1_w^{min} = \sum_{b \in \mathcal{B}} C^{AG^*}_{min}(b, w, W, \underline{\tau}, \overline{\tau}) \quad \text{and} \quad t1_l^{max} = \sum_{b \in \mathcal{B}} C^{AG^*}_{max}(b, l, W, \underline{\tau}, \overline{\tau})$$

$\mathsf{NL}^*(w, l, W, \underline{\tau}, \overline{\tau}, O^*)$. Candidate w will always have a higher tally than l given that O^* is the set of candidates $o \in \mathcal{C}$ for which $\mathsf{AG}^*(w, o, W, \underline{\tau}, \overline{\tau})$ holds. The assertion holds if the minimum tally of w, in this context, is greater than the maximum of l. We define w's minimum tally at a point at which they could be eliminated, where O^* must already be eliminated. The contribution of $b \in \mathcal{B}$ to the minimum tally of w, and the maximum tally of l, is:

$$C_{min}^{\mathsf{NL}^*}(b, w, W, \underline{\tau}, \overline{\tau}, O^*) = \begin{cases} 1 & \text{first}(\sigma_{\mathcal{C}-O^*}(b)) = w \\ \underline{\tau}_{\text{first}(b)} & \text{first}(\sigma_{\mathcal{C}-W}(b)) = w \\ 0 & \text{otherwise} \end{cases}$$

$$C_{max}^{\mathsf{NL}^*}(b, l, W, \underline{\tau}, \overline{\tau}) = \begin{cases} 0 & l \text{ does not occur in } b \\ 0 & w \text{ appears before } l \text{ in } b \\ \overline{\tau}_{\text{first}(b)} & \text{first}(b) \in W \\ 1 & \text{otherwise} \end{cases}$$

We say that $\mathsf{NL}^*(w, l, W, \underline{\tau}, \overline{\tau}, O^*)$ iff $t2_w^{min} > t2_l^{max}$, where:

$$t2_w^{min} = \sum_{b \in \mathcal{B}} C_{min}^{\mathsf{NL}^*}(b, w, W, \underline{\tau}, \overline{\tau}, O^*) \quad \text{and} \quad t2_l^{max} = \sum_{b \in \mathcal{B}} C_{max}^{\mathsf{NL}^*}(b, l, W, \underline{\tau}, \overline{\tau})$$

In earlier work [2], AG^*'s and NL^*'s were defined in the context where we assume W have already been seated, but not necessarily on their first preferences. In this paper, we use the stricter assumption that W were seated on first preferences as (i) this is the only context in which we form the assertions, and (ii) the stricter assumption allows us to provide more straightforward definitions of how each ballot contributes to the minimum and maximum tallies of candidates.

New Assertions. With W, $\underline{\tau}$ and $\overline{\tau}$ defined as above:
$\mathsf{IQX}(w, W, \underline{\tau}, \overline{\tau}, O^*)$. The total of candidate w's first preference tally, in addition to any votes that would flow to them upon the election of candidates in W and elimination of all candidates O^*, where O^* is the set of candidates $o \in \mathcal{C}$ for which $\mathsf{AG}^*(w, o, W, \underline{\tau}, \overline{\tau})$ holds, is at least a quota. If true, w is guaranteed to be awarded a seat. We define w's IQX tally as:

$$T_w^{\mathsf{IQX}} = \sum_{b \in \mathcal{B}} C^{\mathsf{IQX}}(b, w, W, \underline{\tau}, \overline{\tau}, O^*)$$

$$C^{\mathsf{IQX}}(b, w, W, \underline{\tau}, \overline{\tau}) = \begin{cases} 1 & \text{first}(\sigma_{\mathcal{C}-O^*}(b)) = w \\ \underline{\tau}_{\text{first}(b)} & \text{first}(b) \in W \text{ and } \text{first}(\sigma_{\mathcal{C}-W}(b)) = w \\ 0 & \text{otherwise} \end{cases}$$

6 Overview: Two Audit Options

Our approach considers two alternate ways of forming an RLA for a 3+ seat STV election: an audit that consists only of IQX assertions; and an audit formed by a dual-loop heuristic. In this section, we describe the straight IQX audit and give an overview of the dual-loop heuristic (presented in greater detail in Sect. 7).

Consider an STV election $E = (\mathcal{C}, \mathcal{B}, Q, N)$ with reported winners $\mathcal{W}$ and losers $\mathcal{L}$. Let $\mathcal{W}_0$ denote the subset of reported winners that, in the reported election outcome, have won on first preferences. This is distinct from the notation W, which in the context of an assertion denotes the subset of candidates that we *assume* have been seated on first preferences ($W \subseteq \mathcal{W}_0$).

Let $\mathcal{A}_{E,\mathsf{IQX}}$ and $\mathcal{A}_{E,DL}$ denote the set of assertions forming, respectively, a straight IQX audit and a dual-loop audit. If we can form a full audit via either approach, we choose the audit with the least expected cost, and the best partial audit formed by the dual-loop method, otherwise.

Option 1: Straight IQX. Audit. We consider a context where we *do not* make assumptions about who has won on first preferences, and compute the set of all auditable AG* relationships we can form between reported winners and losers.

$$\mathcal{A}_{\mathsf{AG}} \leftarrow [\mathsf{AG}^*(w, l, W = \emptyset, \underline{\tau} = \emptyset, \overline{\tau} = \emptyset) | \forall w \in \mathcal{W}, l \in \mathcal{L}]$$

We then compute the set of all auditable IQX relationships we can form for reported winners in this same context, where, for a given $w \in \mathcal{W}$, O^* is the set of candidates $o \in \mathcal{C}$ for which $\mathsf{AG}^*(w, o, \emptyset, \emptyset, \emptyset) \in \mathcal{A}_{\mathsf{AG}}$.

$$\mathcal{A}_{\mathsf{IQX}} \leftarrow [\mathsf{IQX}(w, W = \emptyset, \underline{\tau} = \emptyset, \overline{\tau} = \emptyset, O^*) | \forall w \in \mathcal{W}]$$

If we can form an auditable IQX assertion for each reported winner, we can form a complete audit with just these assertions and any AG* relationships used to form them. Let $\mathcal{A}_{E,\mathsf{IQX}}$ denote this set of assertions.

Option 2: Dual-Loop Audit. If the straight IQX audit is not possible ($\mathcal{A}_{E,\mathsf{IQX}} = \emptyset$), or we want to try and find an audit with a smaller sample size, we shift our context to one where we do assume that at least one of our reported winners have won on their first preferences. Figure 1 provides an outline of the 'outer' loop of the dual-loop method. We describe this algorithm in detail, below.

We first create the set of all auditable IQ assertions we can form for winners in $\mathcal{W}_0$ (step 1), forming the set $\mathcal{A}_{\mathsf{IQ}}$. If $\mathcal{A}_{\mathsf{IQ}} = \emptyset$ then we report that an audit is not possible by the dual-loop method (step 4). We need to verify at least one reported winner with an IQ assertion to proceed with this second audit type.

If $|\mathcal{A}_{\mathsf{IQ}}| = |\mathcal{W}|$ then we use this set of assertions, $\mathcal{A}_{E,DL} = \mathcal{A}_{\mathsf{IQ}}$, to form our audit (step 5). If $|\mathcal{A}_{\mathsf{IQ}}| < |\mathcal{W}|$, we have a set of reported winners $\mathcal{W}' \subseteq \mathcal{W}_0$ whose win on first preferences we can verify, and a set of other winners $\mathcal{R} = \mathcal{W} \setminus \mathcal{W}'$ (steps 6–7). We then need to verify that each $r \in \mathcal{R}$ deserved to win.

This is accomplished with a heuristic, similar to that of [2], with an outer and inner loop. The outer loop performs a neighbourhood search over transfer value lower bounds for the candidates in $\mathcal{W}'$, while the inner loop performs a neighbourhood search over transfer value upper bounds. In the 3+ seat context, these loops will need to search through spaces of upper and lower bound vectors. For a given pair of lower and upper bound vectors, our heuristic attempts to find a candidate full audit that verifies each $w \in \mathcal{W}$, and if this is not possible, establish a candidate partial audit that verifies some but not all of these winners.

The heuristic keeps track of the best (cheapest) full audit we can form, and the partial audit that verifies the most winners with the least expected cost.

Outer Loop. Given a set of verified winners on first preferences, W', and the IQ assertions used to verify them, the loop searches for the best full and partial audit that it can find (steps 9–21 of Fig. 1). It performs a neighbourhood search over candidate transfer value lower bound vectors, starting from 0 and gradually increasing these bounds in small increments $\delta \ll 1$, executing an inner loop for each of these vectors (step 14), and replacing $\mathcal{A}_{full}$ and $\mathcal{A}_{partial}$ when a better full and partial audit is found (steps 15–18).

Inner Loop. Given a vector of lower bounds on first winner transfer values, $\underline{\tau}$, performs a neighbourhood search over the space of transfer value upper bound vectors (Fig. 3), starting their reported values and gradually increasing these bounds in small increments $\delta \ll 1$. For each candidate $\overline{\tau}$, together with $\underline{\tau}$, a procedure CONSTRUCTAUDIT returns a candidate full audit, $\mathcal{A}'_{full}$, and partial audit, $\mathcal{A}'_{partial}$. We use the same increment size δ for both loops, however different parameters could be used. A smaller δ can allow us to find cheaper audits, at the cost of increasing the heuristic's run time. Note that the ordering of the two loops is arbitrary, the heuristic could be equivalently re-framed with the outer loop searching over upper bounds, and the inner over lower bounds.

Audit Formation. A procedure CONSTRUCTAUDIT that, given a pair of lower and upper bound vectors on first winner transfer values, $\underline{\tau}$ and $\overline{\tau}$, returns a candidate full audit, $\mathcal{A}'_{full}$, and partial audit, $\mathcal{A}'_{partial}$ (Fig. 2). If the procedure could not form all the assertions necessary to verify both the validity of the given lower and upper bounds, and each reported winner, then $\mathcal{A}'_{full} = \emptyset$ and $ASN(\mathcal{A}'_{full}) = \infty$. The partial audit will, at least, verify the set of first winners in W', with the assertion set $\mathcal{A}_{IQ}$. If $\mathcal{A}'_{full} \neq \emptyset$, then $\mathcal{A}'_{partial} \equiv \mathcal{A}'_{full}$.

7 Dual-Loop Audits: The Details

In this section, we describe the three core components of the dual-loop method in more detail: the outer loop; the inner loop; and the procedure for constructing an audit given a candidate transfer value lower and upper bound vector.

Constructing an Audit. Figure 2 outlines the steps performed when constructing a full and partial audit given: a set of winners assumed to have won on first preferences, W'; a vector of lower and upper bounds on transfer values for each candidate in W', $\underline{\tau}$ and $\overline{\tau}$; a set of assertions verifying that candidates W' won on first preferences, $\mathcal{A}_{IQ}$; and reported winners $\mathcal{R}$ that need to be verified.

CONSTRUCTAUDIT first initialises its candidate full and partial audit to an empty set and the set of auditable IQ assertions, $\mathcal{A}_{IQ}$, respectively (step 1). It then attempts to verify the set of transfer value lower bounds, $\underline{\tau}$, by forming all of the auditable LT assertions it can form for each $w \in W'$ (step 2), $\mathcal{A}_{LT}$. If $|\mathcal{A}_{LT}| < |W'|$, then we can't validate the given set of transfer value lower bounds, and return the empty $\mathcal{A}'_{full}$ and unchanged $\mathcal{A}'_{partial}$ (step 3). We follow the same process to verify the set of transfer value upper bounds, $\overline{\tau}$, in steps 4–5.

Now that we have validated a set of lower and upper bounds on first winner transfer values, we use these bounds to help us verify our other winners $\mathcal{R}$. For

DUALLOOPAUDIT($E = (\mathcal{C}, \mathcal{B}, Q, N)$, $\mathcal{W}$, $\mathcal{L}$, $\boldsymbol{\tau}^R$, δ):
1    $\mathcal{W}_0 \leftarrow$ Subset of $\mathcal{W}$ that have won on first preferences
2    $\mathcal{A}_{E,DL} \leftarrow \emptyset$ ▷ Our (eventual) dual-loop audit
3    $\mathcal{A}_{\text{IQ}} \leftarrow [\text{IQ}(w) | \forall w \in \mathcal{W}_0]$ ▷ Compute <u>auditable</u> IQ assertions for winners in $\mathcal{W}_0$
4   **if** $\mathcal{A}_{\text{IQ}} \equiv \emptyset$ **then return** $\emptyset$ ▷ A dual-loop audit is not possible
5   **else if** $|\mathcal{A}_{\text{IQ}}| \equiv |\mathcal{W}|$ **then** $\mathcal{A}_{E,DL} \leftarrow \mathcal{A}_{\text{IQ}}$ ▷ Our IQ assertions form a full audit
    else then
6        $W' \leftarrow [w | \forall w \in \mathcal{W}_0 \,.\, \text{IQ}(w) \in \mathcal{A}_{\text{IQ}}]$
7        $\mathcal{R} \leftarrow \mathcal{W} \setminus W'$ ▷ Compute set of unverified winners $\mathcal{R}$
8        $\mathcal{A}_{full}, \mathcal{A}_{partial} \leftarrow \emptyset, \mathcal{A}_{\text{IQ}}$ ▷ Initialise full and partial audits
        ▷ Initialise neighbourhood of transfer value lower bounds for candidates in W'
9        $\underline{\boldsymbol{\tau}}_0 \leftarrow [\tau_w^R - \delta | \forall w \in W']$
10    $\underline{\boldsymbol{N}} \leftarrow [\underline{\boldsymbol{\tau}}_0]$
11   **while** $\underline{\boldsymbol{N}} \neq \emptyset$ **do**
        ▷ Initialise 'best' lower bound vector to the first in our neighbourhood
12        $\underline{\boldsymbol{\tau}}_{best} \leftarrow \underline{\boldsymbol{N}}[0]$
        ▷ Consider each candidate transfer value lower bound vectors in our neighbourhood, and run the INNERLOOP (Figure 3) to find a full and partial audits. Keep track of the best found full and partial audit.
13   **for** $\underline{\boldsymbol{\tau}} \in \underline{\boldsymbol{N}}$ **do**
14            $\mathcal{A}'_{full}, \mathcal{A}'_{partial} \leftarrow$ INNERLOOP($E, \mathcal{W}, \boldsymbol{\tau}^R, \underline{\boldsymbol{\tau}}, \mathcal{R}, W', \mathcal{A}_{\text{IQ}}, \delta$)
15   **if** $ASN(\mathcal{A}'_{full}) < ASN(\mathcal{A}_{full})$ **then**
16                $\mathcal{A}_{full}, \mathcal{A}_{partial}, \underline{\boldsymbol{\tau}}_{best} \leftarrow \mathcal{A}'_{full}, \mathcal{A}'_{full}, \underline{\boldsymbol{\tau}}$
17   **else if** $\mathcal{A}'_{partial} \succ \mathcal{A}_{partial}$ **then**
18                $\mathcal{A}_{partial}, \underline{\boldsymbol{\tau}}_{best} \leftarrow \mathcal{A}'_{partial}, \underline{\boldsymbol{\tau}}$
        ▷ Find new candidate lower bound vectors around $\underline{\boldsymbol{\tau}}_{best}$, if possible
19        $\underline{\boldsymbol{N}} \leftarrow$ NEIGHBOURS$_{LB}(\underline{\boldsymbol{\tau}}_{best})$
        ▷ If the assertions used to validate the transfer value lower bounds are not the most expensive of those in $\mathcal{A}_{partial}$ then continuing to explore further lower bound vectors will not improve either $\mathcal{A}_{full}$ or $\mathcal{A}_{partial}$
20   **if** LT assertions are not the most expensive in $\mathcal{A}_{partial}$ **then break**
    ▷ If we have found a full audit, return it as our dual-loop audit, otherwise return the best partial audit.
21   **if** $\mathcal{A}_{full} \neq \emptyset$ **then** $\mathcal{A}_{E,DL} \leftarrow \mathcal{A}_{full}$ **else** $\mathcal{A}_{E,DL} \leftarrow \mathcal{A}_{partial}$
22 **return** $\mathcal{A}_{E,DL}$

Fig. 1. Outline of the outer-loop of the Dual-Loop STV Audit method for an STV election $E = (\mathcal{C}, \mathcal{B}, Q, N)$, with reported winners $\mathcal{W}$, reported losers $\mathcal{L}$, and reported transfer values τ_w^R for each winner $w \in \mathcal{W}$, $\boldsymbol{\tau}^R = [\tau_w^R | \forall w \in \mathcal{W}]$. This outer-loop calls a procedure that takes a candidate transfer value lower bound vector and generates new candidates in its neighbourhood, NEIGHBOURS$_{LB}$.

CONSTRUCTAUDIT($E = (\mathcal{C}, \mathcal{B}, Q, N)$, $\mathcal{L}$, $\underline{\tau}$, $\overline{\tau}$, W', $\mathcal{A}_{\text{IQ}}$, $\mathcal{R}$):
1   $\mathcal{A}'_{full}, \mathcal{A}'_{partial} \leftarrow \emptyset, \mathcal{A}_{\text{IQ}}$ ▷ Initialise a candidate full and partial audit

▷ Compute <u>auditable</u> LT assertions to validate transfer value lower bounds in $\underline{\tau}$
2   $\mathcal{A}_{\text{LT}} \leftarrow [\text{LT}(w, \underline{\tau}_w) | \forall w \in W']$

▷ If we cannot verify all lower bounds in $\underline{\tau}$, then we cannot form a full audit and our partial audit verifies only those winners for which we formed IQ assertions.
3   **if** $|\mathcal{A}_{\text{LT}}| < |W'|$ **then return** $\emptyset, \mathcal{A}'_{partial}$

▷ Compute auditable UT assertions to validate transfer value upper bounds in $\overline{\tau}$
4   $\mathcal{A}_{\text{UT}} \leftarrow [\text{UT}(w, \overline{\tau}_w) | \forall w \in W']$

▷ If we cannot verify all upper bounds in $\overline{\tau}$, then we cannot form a full audit and our partial audit verifies only those winners for which we formed IQ assertions.
5   **if** $|\mathcal{A}_{\text{UT}}| < |W'|$ **then return** $\emptyset, \mathcal{A}'_{partial}$

▷ Consider three approaches for verifying each unverified winner $r \in \mathcal{R}$
6   $\mathcal{A}_\mathcal{R} \leftarrow \emptyset$, Verified $\leftarrow 0$
7   **for each** $r \in \mathcal{R}$ **do**
8      $\mathcal{A}_{\text{AG}^*}, \mathcal{A}_{Vo1} \leftarrow \text{AUDITBYAG}^*(E, \mathcal{L}, W', \underline{\tau}, \overline{\tau}, r)$
9      $\mathcal{A}_{Vo2} \leftarrow \text{AUDITBYNL}^*(E, \mathcal{L}, W', \underline{\tau}, \overline{\tau}, r, \mathcal{A}_{\text{AG}^*})$
10     $\mathcal{A}_{Vo3} \leftarrow \text{AUDITBYIQX}(E, W', \underline{\tau}, \overline{\tau}, r, \mathcal{A}_{\text{AG}^*})$
11   **if** at least one $\mathcal{A}_{Voi} \neq \emptyset$ **then**
12        $\mathcal{A}_r \leftarrow$ Cheapest of the assertion sets $\mathcal{A}_{Vo1}, \mathcal{A}_{Vo2}$, and $\mathcal{A}_{Vo3}$
13        $\mathcal{A}_\mathcal{R} \leftarrow \mathcal{A}_\mathcal{R} \cup \mathcal{A}_r$
14   Verified $\leftarrow$ Verified $+ 1$

15 **if** Verified > 0 **then**
16     $\mathcal{A}'_{partial} \leftarrow \mathcal{A}_{\text{IQ}} \cup \mathcal{A}_{\text{LT}} \cup \mathcal{A}_{\text{UT}} \cup \mathcal{A}_\mathcal{R}$
17   **if** Verified $\equiv |\mathcal{R}|$ **then** $\mathcal{A}'_{full} \leftarrow \mathcal{A}'_{partial}$

18 **return** $\mathcal{A}'_{full}, \mathcal{A}'_{partial}$

Fig. 2. Construction of a candidate full and/or partial audit for an STV election $E = (\mathcal{C}, \mathcal{B}, Q, N)$ given: reported losers $\mathcal{L}$; assumed winners on first preferences W'; assumed lower and upper bounds on the transfer values of candidates in W', $\underline{\tau}$ and $\overline{\tau}$; assertions used to verify that the candidates in W' won on first preferences, $\mathcal{A}_{\text{IQ}}$; and the set of currently unverified winners, $\mathcal{R}$.

a given $r \in \mathcal{R}$, we consider three ways of verifying them. Let $\mathcal{A}_{Voi}$ denote the set of assertions formed by i'th verification approach.

Vo1 (Step 8). We compute all possible auditable AG* relationships between reported winner r and each reported loser $l \in \mathcal{L}$.

$$\mathcal{A}_{\text{AG}^*} \leftarrow [\text{AG}^*(r, l, W', \underline{\tau}, \overline{\tau}) | \forall l \in \mathcal{L}]$$

If $|\mathcal{A}_{\text{AG}^*}| \equiv |\mathcal{L}|$, we verify r with $\mathcal{A}_{Vo1} = \mathcal{A}_{\text{AG}^*}$. Otherwise, $\mathcal{A}_{Vo1} = \emptyset$.

Vo2 (Step 9). We compute all possible auditable NL* relationships between reported winner r and each reported loser $l \in \mathcal{L}$, reusing $\mathcal{A}_{\text{AG}^*}$.

$$\mathcal{A}_{\text{NL}^*} \leftarrow [\text{NL}^*(r, l, W', \underline{\tau}, \overline{\tau}, O^*) | \forall l \in \mathcal{L}]$$

Here, O^* denotes the set of candidates o for which $\mathsf{AG}^*(r, o, W', \underline{\tau}, \overline{\tau}) \in \mathcal{A}_{\mathsf{AG}^*}$. If $|\mathcal{A}_{\mathsf{NL}^*}| \equiv |\mathcal{L}|$, we verify r as a winner with assertions $\mathcal{A}_{Vo2} = \mathcal{A}_{\mathsf{NL}^*} \cup \mathcal{A}_{\mathsf{AG}^*}$. Otherwise, if we have been able to form *some* NL^* assertions between r and a subset of the losers $L \subset \mathcal{L}$, we may be able to use these to help us form NL^* assertions between r and the losers in $\mathcal{L} \setminus L$. We iterate this verification method until we reach a fixed point. The first iteration of this loop forms the assertions:

$$\mathcal{A}_{\mathsf{NL}^*,0} \leftarrow [\mathsf{NL}^*(r, l, W', \underline{\tau}, \overline{\tau}, O^*) | \forall l \in \mathcal{L}]$$

Let L_0 denote the set of losers l for which $\mathsf{NL}^*(r, l, \ldots) \in \mathcal{A}_{\mathsf{NL}^*,0}$. The ith iteration of the loop forms the assertions:

$$\mathcal{A}_{\mathsf{NL}^*,i} \leftarrow \mathcal{A}_{\mathsf{NL}^*,i-1} \cup [\mathsf{NL}^*(r, l, W', \underline{\tau}, \overline{\tau}, O_i^*) | \forall l \in \mathcal{L} \setminus L_i]$$

Here, O_i^* denotes the set of candidates o for which *either* $\mathsf{AG}^*(r, o, W', \underline{\tau}, \overline{\tau}) \in \mathcal{A}_{\mathsf{AG}^*}$ or $\mathsf{NL}^*(r, o, W', \underline{\tau}, \overline{\tau}, \_) \in \mathcal{A}_{\mathsf{NL}^*,i-1}$.

We terminate this process when $\mathcal{A}_{\mathsf{NL}^*,i} \equiv \mathcal{A}_{\mathsf{NL}^*,i-1}$. If $|\mathcal{A}_{\mathsf{NL}^*,i}| \equiv |\mathcal{L}|$, we verify r as a winner with assertions $\mathcal{A}_{Vo2} = \mathcal{A}_{\mathsf{NL}^*,i} \cup \mathcal{A}_{\mathsf{AG}^*}$. Otherwise, $\mathcal{A}_{Vo2} = \emptyset$.

Vo3 (Step 10). If $a = \mathsf{IQX}(r, W', \underline{\tau}, \overline{\tau}, O^*)$, where O^* is, as previously, the set of candidates o for which $\mathsf{AG}^*(r, o, \underline{\tau}, \overline{\tau}) \in \mathcal{A}_{\mathsf{AG}^*}$, can be formed and is auditable, we verify r as a winner with assertions $\mathcal{A}_{Vo3} = \{a\} \cup \mathcal{A}_{\mathsf{AG}^*}$.

If none of these methods are successful, we move on to consider the next unverified winner in r. Otherwise, we use the set of assertions $\mathcal{A}_{Voi}$ with the smallest ASN to verify winner r (step 12). For all $r \in \mathcal{R}$ that we can verify using one of these three verification methods, we combine each $\mathcal{A}_r$ to form the set $\mathcal{A}_{\mathcal{R}}$ (step 13). If $\mathcal{A}_{\mathcal{R}} \neq \emptyset$, we form a new partial audit (step 16). If we have verified all winners in $\mathcal{R}$, this audit is a full RLA, and we set $\mathcal{A}'_{full} \equiv \mathcal{A}'_{partial}$ (step 17). We return, for the given lower and upper bounds on first winner transfer values, $\underline{\tau}$ and $\overline{\tau}$, these full and partial audits in step 18.

Note that we do not need to form an LT assertion for a candidate if the assumed lower bound on their transfer value is 0, or a UT assertion when the assumed transfer value upper bound is the theoretical maximum, τ_{max}.

Inner Loop. Given a vector of lower bounds on verified first winner transfer values, $\underline{\tau}$, the inner loop will start with a neighbourhood $\overline{N}$ containing just one upper bound vector, $\overline{N} = [\overline{\tau}_0]$, where the upper bound for winner $w \in W'$ in $\overline{\tau}_0$ is set to their reported transfer value plus $\delta \ll 1$. For each neighbourhood $\overline{N}$ that the inner loop considers, each upper bound vector in $\overline{N}$, $\overline{\tau}_i$, is considered in turn. The CONSTRUCTAUDIT procedure is called for the pair of vectors $\underline{\tau}$ and $\overline{\tau}_i$, finding a candidate full and partial audit, $\mathcal{A}'_{full}$ and $\mathcal{A}'_{partial}$.

Updating our Running Full and Partial Audits. If $ASN(\mathcal{A}'_{full}) < ASN(\mathcal{A}_{full})$, then we have found a better full audit and we replace $\mathcal{A}_{full}$ and $\mathcal{A}_{partial}$ with $\mathcal{A}'_{full}$. If $\mathcal{A}'_{full} = \emptyset$, and $\mathcal{A}'_{partial}$ either (i) verifies *more* winners than $\mathcal{A}_{partial}$, or (ii) verifies the same number of winners but at a cheaper cost, $ASN(\mathcal{A}'_{partial}) < ASN(\mathcal{A}_{partial})$, then we replace the current $\mathcal{A}_{partial}$ with $\mathcal{A}'_{partial}$.

Terminating the Inner Loop. Recall that the inner loop searches for audits or improved audits by iterating over possible upper bound transfer value vectors for candidates seated on their first preferences. These candidate upper bounds are

INNERLOOP($E = (\mathcal{C}, \mathcal{B}, Q, N)$, $\mathcal{W}$, $\mathcal{L}$, $\boldsymbol{\tau^R}$, $\underline{\boldsymbol{\tau}}$, $\mathcal{R}$, W, $\mathcal{A}_{\text{IQ}}$, δ):
1. $\mathcal{A}'_{full}, \mathcal{A}'_{partial} \leftarrow \emptyset, \mathcal{A}_{\text{IQ}}$ ▷ Initialise full and partial audits

     ▷ Initialise neighbourhood of transfer value upper bounds for candidates in W'
2. $\overline{\boldsymbol{\tau}_0} \leftarrow [\tau_w^R + \delta | \forall w \in W']$
3. $\overline{\boldsymbol{N}} \leftarrow [\overline{\boldsymbol{\tau}_0}]$
4.   **while** $\overline{\boldsymbol{N}} \neq \emptyset$ **do**

       ▷ Initialise 'best' upper bound vector to the first in our neighbourhood
5. $\overline{\boldsymbol{\tau}}_{best} \leftarrow \overline{\boldsymbol{N}}[0]$

       ▷ Consider each candidate transfer value upper bound vector in our neighbourhood, and run CONSTRUCTAUDIT (Figure 2) to find a full and partial audits. Keep track of the best found full and partial audit.
6.   **for** $\overline{\boldsymbol{\tau}} \in \overline{\boldsymbol{N}}$ **do**
7. $\mathcal{A}''_{full}, \mathcal{A}''_{partial} \leftarrow$ CONSTRUCTAUDIT(E, $\mathcal{L}$, $\underline{\boldsymbol{\tau}}$, $\overline{\boldsymbol{\tau}}$, W', $\mathcal{A}_{\text{IQ}}$, $\mathcal{R}$)
8.   **if** $ASN(\mathcal{A}''_{full}) < ASN(\mathcal{A}'_{full})$ **then**
9. $\mathcal{A}'_{full}, \mathcal{A}'_{partial}, \overline{\boldsymbol{\tau}}_{best} \leftarrow \mathcal{A}''_{full}, \mathcal{A}''_{full}, \overline{\boldsymbol{\tau}}$
10.   **else if** $\mathcal{A}''_{partial} \succ \mathcal{A}'_{partial}$ **then**
11. $\mathcal{A}'_{partial}, \overline{\boldsymbol{\tau}}_{best} \leftarrow \mathcal{A}''_{partial}, \overline{\boldsymbol{\tau}}$

       ▷ Find new candidate upper bound vectors around $\overline{\boldsymbol{\tau}}_{best}$, if possible
12.   **if** $\overline{\boldsymbol{\tau}}_{best} \neq \emptyset$ **then** $\overline{\boldsymbol{N}} \leftarrow$ NEIGHBOURS$_{UB}(\overline{\boldsymbol{\tau}}_{best})$ **else** $\overline{\boldsymbol{N}} \leftarrow \emptyset$

       ▷ If the assertions used to validate the transfer value upper bounds are not the most expensive of those in $\mathcal{A}'_{partial}$ then continuing to explore further upper bound vectors will not improve either $\mathcal{A}'_{full}$ or $\mathcal{A}'_{partial}$
13.   **if** UT assertions are not the most expensive in $\mathcal{A}'_{partial}$ **then break**
14.   **return** $\mathcal{A}'_{full}, \mathcal{A}'_{partial}$

Fig. 3. Inner-loop of the Dual-Loop audit method for an STV election $E = (\mathcal{C}, \mathcal{B}, Q, N)$, with: reported winners and losers $\mathcal{W}$, $\mathcal{L}$; reported transfer values τ_w^R for each $w \in \mathcal{W}$, $\boldsymbol{\tau}^R = [\tau_w^R | \forall w \in \mathcal{W}]$; assumed winners on first preferences W'; assumed lower bounds on transfer values for W', $\underline{\boldsymbol{\tau}}$; assertions used to verify that the candidates in W' won on first preferences, $\mathcal{A}_{\text{IQ}}$; and the set of unverified winners, $\mathcal{R}$. The inner-loop calls a procedure that takes a candidate transfer value upper bound vector and generates new candidates, NEIGHBOURS$_{UB}$.

gradually increased over the course of the loop. Increasing these upper bounds makes our UT assertions easier to form (with smaller ASNs), or possible to form, but makes verifying each reported winner in $\mathcal{R}$ with AG*, NL*, and IQX assertions more difficult. If we can form all required UT assertions, and their cost is not the dominant cost in our best partial audit, then we can break out of the inner loop. Searching further will only result in cheaper UT assertions at the expense of increasing the cost of the AG*, NL*, and IQX needed to verify our winners.

Generating a New Neighbourhood. If, after considering each upper bound vector in $\overline{N}$, our termination condition has not been satisfied, we take the upper bound vector used to form the current best full or partial audit, or the first upper bound vector in $\overline{N}$, $\overline{\tau}$, and generate a new neighbourhood of upper bound vectors. This neighbourhood consists of up to $|W'|$ new vectors, one for each $w \in W'$ where $\overline{\tau}_w < \tau_{max}$, where we replace $\overline{\tau}_w$ with $\min(\tau_{max}, \overline{\tau}_w + \delta)$. The inner loop then explores this new neighbourhood as described above. The inner loop also terminates when we cannot form a new neighbourhood, i.e., all transfer value upper bounds are at their maximum theoretical value τ_{max}.

Outer Loop. Steps 9–21 of Fig. 1 represent the outer loop of the dual-loop method. The outer loop starts with a neighbourhood of candidate transfer value lower bounds for winners on first preferences, $\underline{N}$, initialised to $[\underline{\tau}_0]$, where the lower bound for winner $w \in W'$ in $\underline{\tau}_0$ is set to their reported transfer value minus $\delta \ll 1$ (steps 9–10). The outer loop considers each candidate lower bound vector in $\underline{N}$, and executes the inner loop (steps 13–18). The inner loop returns a candidate full and partial audit for a given lower bound vector (step 14). We keep track of the best found full and partial audit as we explore candidate lower bound vectors (steps 15–18), and the 'best' transfer value lower bound vector in the current neighbourhood, $\underline{\tau}_{best}$ (steps 16 and 18). Once we have explored the current neighbourhood, we generate a new one, if possible, from $\underline{\tau}_{best}$ (step 19).

Terminating the Outer Loop. Candidate transfer value lower bounds are reduced over the course of the outer loop. Decreasing these bounds makes our LT assertions easier to form (with smaller ASNs), but makes verifying each reported winner in $\mathcal{R}$ with AG*, NL*, and IQX assertions more difficult. If we can form all required LT assertions, and their cost is not the dominant cost in our best partial audit, then we can break out of the outer loop (step 20). Searching further will only result in cheaper LT assertions at the expense of increasing the cost of the AG*, NL*, and IQX needed to verify our winners.

Generating a New Neighbourhood. (NEIGHBOURS$_{LB}$). If, after considering each lower bound vector in $\underline{N}$, our termination condition is unsatisfied, we take one of the vectors in our neighbourhood, $\underline{\tau}_{best}$, and generate a new neighbourhood of lower bound vectors (step 19). The new neighbourhood consists of up to $|W'|$ new vectors, one for each $w \in W'$ where $\underline{\tau}_w > 0$, in which we replace $\underline{\tau}_w$ with $\underline{\tau}_w - \delta$, if $\underline{\tau}_w > \delta$, and 0 otherwise. The outer loop terminates if we cannot form a new neighbourhood, i.e., all transfer value lower bounds in $\underline{\tau}_{best}$ are 0.

8 Results

We used data from 513 three- or four-seat STV elections from local council elections in Scotland in 2017 and 2022. Scotland uses the Weighted Inclusive Gregory method at the local council level. Each election in this data set satisfies the 'first winner' criterion, and involves 3 to 13 candidates.[3] For each of these

---

[3] It is not possible to say how often the first winner criterion would be satisfied by STV elections in general, however it becomes more likely with an increased number of seats, smaller quotas, and the presence of at least one dominant candidate.

Table 2. Across 252 3-seat and 261 4-seat STV contests, we report: the number and percentage of instances where we verify no or only 1 to 4 winners within an ASN of 2500 ballots; and the average and range of ASNs for these audits.

Winners verified	3 seats		4 seats	
	Instances (/252)	ASN Avg (Min, Max)	Instances (/261)	ASN Avg (Min, Max)
None	5 (2%)		4 (2%)	
1	28 (11%)	74 (14, 289)	25 (10%)	98 (16, 457)
2	73 (29%)	281 (27, 2036)	69 (26%)	331 (36, 1677)
3	146 (58%)	379 (35, 1790)	79 (30%)	406 (54, 2033)
4			84 (32%)	635 (71, 2339)

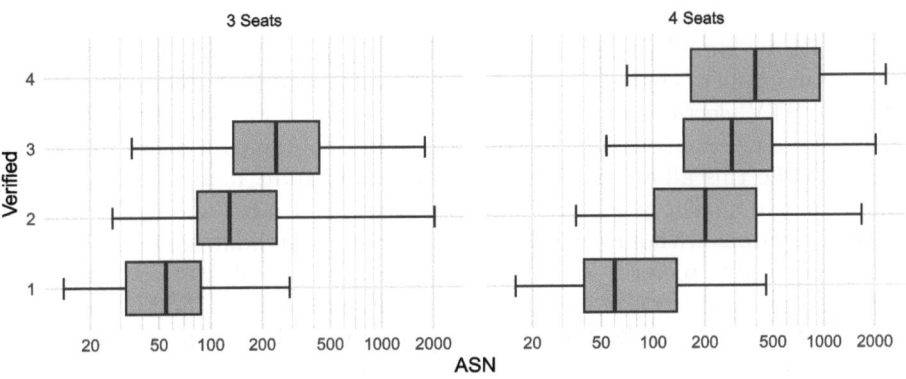

Fig. 4. Side-by-side box plots showing the spread of ASNs (x-axes in log scale) of *formed* audits that verify varying numbers of winners for our data set of 252 3-seat (left) and 261 4-seat (right) STV contests. For each box plot: the vertical line in the middle of each 'box' shows the median ASN for each group, the edges of the boxes are the first and third quartiles, and the 'whiskers' extending out of each box show the minimum and maximum ASN.

contests, we applied the method described in Sect. 6 and Sect. 7 to form a set of assertions, designed to verify as many reported winners as possible.

We computed ASN estimates via simulation for each assertion. The simulation considered incrementally larger sample sizes, randomly generating 1-vote overstatements (errors that overstate the margin of the assertion by one) at a defined rate, until the risk value of the audit fell below the desired limit. This simulation was repeated, and the average sample size needed to meet the risk limit, rounded up, formed the ASN for the assertion. For sample size estimations, we used a risk limit of 5%, an expected error rate of 2 overstatements per 1000 ballots, 20 simulations, $\delta = 0.005$, and the ALPHA risk function [4].

Across the 252 3-seat and 261 4-seat contests in our data set, Table 2 reports the number, and percentage, of instances in which we *can form an audit* that verifies a specific number of winners, from 0 to 4, alongside the average, minimum, and maximum ASNs for these audits. For this paper, we considered a contest to be auditable if its ASN was $M = 2500$ ballots or less. The average number of ballots cast in the Scottish elections in our dataset is just under 5500. Our choice of M in this case was designed to give us a sense of how many elections we could audit with a reasonably modest sample size. In place of a fixed M, we could alternately set M to a defined percentage of the number of ballots cast. Figure 4 presents two side-by-side box plots visualising the distribution of ASNs across audits that verify 1 to 3 winners in 3-seat contests (left) and 1 to 4 winners in 4-seat contests (right). All code used to form these audits can be found at: https://github.com/michelleblom/stv-rla.

9 Conclusion

Finding RLAs for STV elections is challenging, since the election process is complex and ballots change in value during tabulation. Previous methods were limited to STV elections of 2 candidates. In this paper we extend this to "arbitrarily" large elections, as long as some candidates obtained a quota in the first round. While this allows us to, at least partially, audit many elections, there remains much further work. To date, we have been most successful in tackling STV elections with a relatively small number of candidates. On the Scottish dataset, our ability to verify all winners reduces as the number of seats increases. In general, elections with more seats involve more candidates, and more surplus transfers, which can make them harder to audit with current methods. The heuristic presented in this paper could be improved by taking a more nuanced view when forming partial audits by identifying the relative cost of auditing each winner.

Acknowledgements. This work was supported by the Australian Research Council (Discovery Project DP220101012, OPTIMA ITTC IC200100009).

References

1. Blom, M., Stuckey, P.J., Teague, V., Vukcevic, D.: A first approach to risk-limiting audits for single transferable vote elections. In: Workshop on Advances in Secure Elections VOTING'22 (2022)
2. Blom, M., Stuckey, P.J., Teague, V., Vukcevic, D.: RLAs for 2-seat STV elections: revisited. In: Workshop on Advances in Secure Elections VOTING'24 (2024)
3. Blom, M., et al.: Assertion-based approaches to auditing complex elections, with application to party-list proportional elections. In: Electronic Voting. E-Vote-ID 2021, pp. 47–62. LNCS 12900, Springer (2021)
4. Stark, P.B.: Sets of half-average nulls generate risk-limiting audits: SHANGRLA. In: Bernhard, M., et al. (eds.) FC 2020. LNCS, vol. 12063, pp. 319–336. Springer, Cham (2020). https://doi.org/10.1007/978-3-030-54455-3_23

Doing More with Less: Mismatch-Based Risk-Limiting Audits

Alexander Ek[1], Michelle Blom[2], Philip B. Stark[3], Peter J. Stuckey[4], Vanessa J. Teague[5], and Damjan Vukcevic[1]($\boxtimes$)

[1] Department of Econometrics and Business Statistics, Monash University, Clayton, Australia
damjan.vukcevic@monash.edu
[2] Department of Computing and Information Systems, University of Melbourne, Parkville, Australia
[3] Department of Statistics, University of California, Berkeley, CA, USA
[4] Department of Data Science and AI, Monash University, Clayton, Australia
[5] Australian National University and Thinking Cybersecurity Pty Ltd., Melbourne, Australia

Abstract. One approach to risk-limiting audits (RLAs) compares randomly selected cast vote records (CVRs) to votes read by human auditors from the corresponding ballot cards. Historically, such methods reduce audit sample sizes by considering *how* each sampled CVR differs from the corresponding true vote, not merely *whether* they differ. Here we investigate the latter approach, auditing by testing whether the total number of mismatches in the full set of CVRs exceeds the minimum number of CVR errors required for the reported outcome to be wrong (the "CVR margin"). This strategy makes it possible to audit more social choice functions and simplifies RLAs conceptually, which makes it easier to explain than some other RLA approaches. The cost is larger sample sizes. "Mismatch-based RLAs" only require a lower bound on the CVR margin, which for some social choice functions is easier to calculate than the effect of particular errors. When the population rate of mismatches is low and the lower bound on the CVR margin is close to the true CVR margin, the increase in sample size is small. However, the increase may be very large when errors include errors that, if corrected, would widen the CVR margin rather than narrow it; errors affect the margin between candidates other than the reported winner with the fewest votes and the reported loser with the most votes; or errors that affect different margins.

Keywords: Single transferable vote · Risk-limiting audit · Margin of victory · Mismatch-based audit

---

This work was supported by the Australian Research Council (Discovery Project DP220101012, OPTIMA ITTC IC200100009) and the U.S. National Science Foundation (SaTC 2228884).

1 Introduction

Growing international skepticism of election outcomes emphasizes the need for "evidence-based elections," which provide affirmative evidence that the reported winners really won [1,16]. Risk-limiting audits (RLAs) using a demonstrably trustworthy record of the votes are a key component of evidence-based elections. RLAs limit the probability (risk) that an incorrect reported outcome will become final by manually reading the votes from randomly sampled records until either the sample provides sufficiently strong statistical evidence that the reported winners really won or there has been a full manual tabulation of the trustworthy vote record to determine the correct winner. RLAs are now mandatory or authorized in about fifteen U.S. states.

RLAs can be conducted using different sampling designs and different data, depending on local laws, logistical constraints, and the capability of election technology [20]. A particularly efficient approach to RLAs, *card-level comparison*, involves comparing a human reading of the votes on validly cast ballot cards selected at random to the voting system's record of the votes on each selected card, the *cast vote record* (CVR) for that card. Methods for card-level comparison RLAs have been developed for many social choice functions (the rules for determining who won and how voters can express their preferences), including first-past-the-post [14,17,18], supermajority [17,18], instant-runoff voting (IRV) [7,11], D'Hondt [21], Hamiltonian elections [6], and approval, Borda, STAR-Voting, and arbitrary scoring rules [18].

There is so far no efficient RLA method for some social choice functions, such as single transferable vote (STV) with more than two seats [4] and certain Condorcet elections [9].[1] For some of these, it is possible to compute a *lower bound* on the *CVR margin*—the minimum number of CVRs that must differ from the votes on their corresponding ballot cards for the reported election outcome to be incorrect. This lower bound enables a straightforward audit: check (statistically) whether the number of mismatches between CVRs and their corresponding ballots is below this lower bound. If so, the reported election outcome is correct. Here we define a *mismatch-based RLA*, which involves testing (the complement of) this assertion, at significance level α. This method is statistically rigorous and broadly applicable. It produces a card-level comparison RLA whenever a lower bound on the CVR margin can be computed, including social choice functions for which computing the CVR margin is challenging but computing a lower bound is tractable. For example, computing the CVR margin for IRV is NP-hard [22] (but usually feasible in practice [10]); similarly, for STV there exist methods for calculating lower bounds [5,8] for elections where no efficient RLA approach is known.

Mismatch-based RLAs make worst-case assumptions about every CVR error. For instance, in a plurality contest, they treat the following errors as equivalent:

---

[1] A full manual re-tabulation of the votes is an RLA for any social choice function, but it is inefficient.

- an error that changes a vote for the reported runner-up into a vote for the reported winner (the most serious error possible)
- an error that changes an invalid vote into a vote for the reported winner (a less serious error)
- an error that turns a vote for the candidate reported to have the fewest votes into a vote for another losing candidate (an error that might not be consequential for the outcome)
- an error that changes a vote for the reported winner into a vote for the reported runner-up (an error that adds evidence that the outcome is correct).

This pessimism generally results in larger sample sizes than an audit that considers the effect of each error—possibly requiring a full hand count when a relatively small sample would suffice for a more nuanced method. Using a lower bound on the CVR margin (rather than the exact margin) exacerbates this conservatism, depending on how much slack the bound has.

Mismatch-based RLAs require a CVR for each ballot card, "linked" to the card it purports to represent, in order to compute mismatches. Not every voting system can provide CVRs linked to physical cards.[2] Thus mismatch-based RLAs may not help unless a jurisdiction uses central-count optical scan systems or is willing to rescan precinct-tabulated cards. Ballot-polling or batch-comparison audits are simply not possible using a mismatch-based approach.

Here we examine the impact of the pessimistic treatment of mismatches using simulated audits of IRV and two-candidate plurality contests, for which there are tailored RLA methods [7,11]. We find scenarios where the workload is about the same, and others where mismatch-based RLAs require much larger samples. Mismatch-based auditing is perhaps most useful for social choice functions such as STV, for which no better RLA method exists.

Our contribution is to explain the details of mismatch-based RLAs and identify scenarios in which they are helpful. We also quantify their performance, using simulations to show when they perform well and when they require much larger samples than more precise methods. Although the idea of mismatch-based RLAs is not new, we are not aware of any work that fleshes out the details [or] examines their performance.

The paper is organized as follows. Section 2 provides definitions and notation. Section 3 defines and constructs mismatch-based RLAs and contrasts them with card-level comparison audits. Section 4 explores the relative efficiency of mismatch-based RLAs for various social choice functions using simulation. Section 5 discusses the implications and directions for future work.

2 Terminology, Definitions, and Assumptions

We consider one contest at a time, but generalizing to an arbitrary number of contests is straightforward [12,14]. A *ballot card* is a piece of paper. (A *ballot*

---

[2] Moreover, methods such as ONEAudit [20] that create CVRs and associate them to cards do not "play nice" with this approach because the CVRs they produce have offsetting errors but possibly a high mismatch rate.

comprises one or more ballot cards.) There are N validly cast ballot cards, each containing the contest in question. A *vote* is a value derived from the marks a voter makes on a ballot card. Depending on the social choice function, law, and regulation, some ways of marking (or failing to mark) ballots produce "invalid votes" or "non-votes," which the social choice function ignores; we call all of these *null votes*.

We are able to draw ballot cards at random from the full set of N cards. Each card is uniquely identifiable in some way, e.g., by its physical location or through an identifying mark printed on the card; there is a canonical ordering so that it makes sense to talk about the ith ballot card. Let $[N] := \{1,\ldots,N\}$.

The vote on the ith card is b_i. The set of possible values of b_i is $\mathcal{V}$, which includes valid and null votes. The N-tuple of votes on the N cards is $\mathcal{B} = (b_1, b_2, \ldots, b_N)$. If we select the ith card for audit, we observe b_i. For each $i \in [N]$, we also have a cast vote record c_i, committed to before the audit starts. The N-tuple of N cast vote records is $\mathcal{C} = (c_1, c_2, \ldots, c_N)$. A mismatch-based audit involves comparing b_i to c_i for a sequence of random draws from $[N]$.

Many of these assumptions can be relaxed at the cost of some bookkeeping: methods by Stark [15, 18, 20] can deal with situations where:

- the exact number N of cards is unknown but an upper bound is available
- the contest is not on every ballot card
- the election official cannot account for all N cards
- a particular card is selected for audit but cannot be found
- the number of cast vote records is not the same as the number of cards
- the voting system cannot report a CVR linked to some cards.

The set of possible election outcomes is $\mathcal{O}$. (Typically an outcome is a candidate, a party, an allocation of seats, or the "yes" or "no" position on some measure.) The social choice function for the contest is $\mathbb{S}(\cdot)$, a mapping from a tuple of elements of $\mathcal{V}$ (a tuple of votes), to an element of $\mathcal{O}$ (an outcome). The social choice function is assumed to depend on the tuple of votes only though the multiset of votes—not, for example, on the order in which votes are cast or tabulated, nor on auxiliary randomness to break ties. The *correct outcome* of the contest is $\mathbb{S}(\mathcal{B}) \in \mathcal{O}$, the outcome that results from applying the social choice function to $\mathcal{B}$, the actual votes on the ballot cards. The *reported outcome* is $\mathbb{S}(\mathcal{C}) \in \mathcal{O}$, the output of applying the social choice function to the CVRs $\mathcal{C}$.

A common definition of *margin of victory* for plurality contests is the difference between the number of votes reported to have been received by the winner and by the runner-up, which we call the *vote margin*.

A more general notion of margin, applicable to any social choice function if CVRs are available, is the minimum number of CVRs with a vote that differs from the vote on the corresponding card if the reported outcome is wrong. This minimum, the *CVR margin*, is taken over all possible true votes and all subsets of the CVRs:

$$V(\mathcal{C}) := \min_{\mathcal{X}=(x_1,\ldots,x_N) \in \mathcal{V}^N} \min_{\mathcal{I} \subset [N]} \{|\mathcal{I}| : \mathbb{S}(\mathcal{C}) \neq \mathbb{S}(\mathcal{X}) \text{ and } (c_i = x_i, \forall i \in [N] \setminus \mathcal{I})\}. \tag{1}$$

Equivalently, $V(\mathcal{C})$ is the smallest radius of any Hamming-distance ball centered at $\mathcal{C}$ whose image under $\mathbb{S}(\cdot)$ contains at least two elements of $\mathcal{O}$:

$$V(\mathcal{C}) := \min\{n : \#\mathbb{S}(\mathbb{B}(\mathcal{C},n)) > 1\}, \tag{2}$$

where $\mathbb{B}(\mathcal{C}, n)$ is the Hamming ball of radius n centered at $\mathcal{C}$:

$$\mathbb{B}(\mathcal{C}, n) := \{\mathcal{D} = (d_1, \ldots, d_N) \in \mathcal{V}^N \text{ s.t. } \#\{i : c_i \neq d_i\} \leqslant n\}. \tag{3}$$

This abstract definition is natural for audits that check whether $c_i = b_i$ for randomly selected values of i.

This definition tacitly assumes there is a CVR for every card. It can be modified to account for differences in the number of cards and CVRs; alternatively, the number of CVRs and (an upper bound on) the number of cards can be forced to be equal using methods by Stark [15, 18] to create CVRs (with null votes) or delete CVRs (without changing the reported outcome) before calculating the CVR margin using this definition.

The related normalized measure is the *CVR margin proportion*, the CVR margin divided by the number of cards

$$v = v(\mathcal{C}) := \frac{V(\mathcal{C})}{N}. \tag{4}$$

This is similar to *diluted margin* defined by Stark [14], but the numerator uses the CVR margin rather than the vote margin.

In a plurality election, the vote margin is twice the CVR margin because a change to a CVR can change the vote margin by up to two votes: changing votes for the reported winner in (vote margin)/2 CVRs into votes for the reported runner-up yields a tie or a win for the runner-up. In an IRV election, finding the CVR margin is more complicated.

Example 1. Consider an IRV election with candidates $\mathcal{O} = \{\text{Ali}, \text{Bob}, \text{Cal}, \text{Dee}\}$. Suppose $N = 60$ cards were cast. Of the 60 CVRs, 20 are (Ali), 15 are (Dee, Ali, Bob), 9 are (Cal, Dee), 6 are (Bob, Cal, Dee), 6 are (Ali, Cal), and 4 are (Bob, Cal). The tally proceeds as shown in Table 1a: first Cal is eliminated and 9 votes flow to Dee; next Bob is eliminated and 6 votes flow to Dee and 4 CVRs are exhausted; finally Ali is eliminated and Dee wins. The CVR margin is $V = 1$: changing one CVR from (Bob, Cal, Dee) to (Cal, Dee) changes the winner to Ali, as illustrated in Table 1b. The CVR margin proportion is $v = 1/60$.

The *last-round CVR margin* (the minimum number of CVRs that need to be changed in order to alter the outcome in the final round of the count) is 2, since Dee beats Ali by 4 votes: the CVR margin of an IRV election can be smaller than the last-round CVR margin. □

3 Risk-Limiting Audits Using Mismatches

Suppose we have a set of CVRs $\mathcal{C}$ and we can compute a number $V^- \leqslant V(\mathcal{C})$, a lower bound for the CVR margin. Define $v^- := V^-/N \leqslant v$. Let $M = M(\mathcal{C}) :=$

Table 1. IRV election from Example 1.

(a) Original election				(b) Election with one vote changed			
Cand.	Round 1	Round 2	Round 3	Cand.	Round 1	Round 2	Round 3
Ali	26	26	26	Ali	26	26	41
Bob	10	10	—	Bob	9	—	—
Cal	9	—	—	Cal	10	19	19
Dee	15	24	30	Dee	15	15	—

$\#\{i \in [N] : b_i \neq c_i\}$ be the number of CVRs with votes that do not match the votes on the corresponding card, and let $m = m(\mathcal{C}) := M(\mathcal{C})/N$ be the *mismatch rate*. We can perform an RLA by testing (at significance level α) whether $M \geq V^-$, or equivalently, whether $m \geq v^-$. Rejecting that hypothesis amounts to strong evidence that $\mathbb{S}(\mathcal{B}) = \mathbb{S}(\mathcal{C})$, i.e., that the reported outcome is correct.

We now develop a test of whether $M \geq V^-$ using the SHANGRLA [18] framework, which characterizes the correctness of outcomes in terms of the means of bounded, nonnegative functions on votes called *assorters*. An assorter uses the votes on a card and other information (for instance, a list of CVRs) to assign a bounded, nonnegative number to that card.

For a broad variety of social choice functions, the reported winners really won if the mean of each of the lists that result from applying each assorter in a collection of assorters to the true votes $\mathcal{B}$ is greater than $1/2$. (For IRV, there are many collections that suffice; the outcome is correct if the means of all assorters in any of those collections are all greater than $1/2$ [11].)

Testing whether the mean of an assorter is greater than $1/2$ can be done in various ways [18–20]; the most relevant for the current work is a card-level comparison audit, which is the most efficient method when accurate comparison values for each card are available. We first briefly review comparison audits in general.

Given an assorter A with upper bound u, we can compare the assorter values for the votes to a corresponding set of known "reference values" $x = (x_1, \ldots, x_N)$. If CVRs $\mathcal{C} = (c_1, \ldots, c_N)$ are available, the reference values might be, for instance, $(x_1, \ldots, x_N) = (A(c_1), \ldots, A(c_N))$, but other choices are possible [20]. Let $\bar{A} := N^{-1} \sum_i A(b_i)$ and $\bar{x} := N^{-1} \sum_i x_i$. The *assorter margin* of x is $\nu = \nu(x) := 2\bar{x} - 1$, twice the amount by which the mean of the values of x exceeds $1/2$. Then

$$\bar{x} - \bar{A} < \bar{x} - 1/2 = \nu/2 \qquad (5)$$

iff $\bar{A} > 1/2$. Comparison audits work by testing whether $\overline{(x-A)} := N^{-1} \sum_i (x_i - A(b_i)) \leq \nu/2$, as follows: Define the *overstatement assorter*

$$B(b_i) := \frac{u + A(b_i) - x_i}{2u - \nu} \in [0, 2u/(2u - \nu)], \qquad (6)$$

and $\bar{B} := N^{-1} \sum_i B(b_i)$. Then $\bar{A} > 1/2$ iff $\bar{B} > 1/2$.

If $A(b_i) = x_i$, the reference value for card i matches the true value of the assorter. If $A(b_i) \neq x_i$, there is a *mismatch* or *discrepancy*. If $A(b_i) > x_i$, the discrepancy is an *understatement*: correcting it widens the margin, so discovering the error adds to the evidence that the reported outcome is correct. If $A(b_i) < x_i$, the discrepancy is an *overstatement*: correcting it narrows the margin, so it reduces the evidence that the reported outcome is correct.

For card-level comparison audits, $x_i = A(c_i)$, so the possible values of x_i are the same as the possible values of $A(b_i)$. For plurality (including multi-winner plurality), approval, and some other social choice functions (including assorters used to audit IRV), the possible values of $A(b_i)$ are 0, 1/2, and 1, so $u = 1$. Thus for card-level comparison audits of such social choice functions, the possible values of the numerator of $B(b_i)$, $u + A(b_i) - x_i$ (i.e., $u + A(b_i) - A(c_i)$), are 0, 1/2, 1, 3/2, and 2.

In a two-candidate plurality contest, Ali vs. Bob, where Ali is the reported winner, correctness of the outcome is determined by a single assorter A:

$$A(b_i) = \begin{cases} 1, & b_i = \text{Ali} \\ 1/2, & b_i = \text{null vote} \\ 0, & b_i = \text{Bob}. \end{cases} \quad (7)$$

Ali got more votes than Bob iff $\bar{A} > 1/2$. For this assorter, $u = 1$, and the numerator of Eq. 6 takes the following values:

$$u + A(b_i) - x_i = \begin{cases} 0, & b_i = \text{Bob}, c_i = \text{Ali} & \text{(2-vote overstatement)} \\ 1/2, & b_i = \text{Bob}, c_i = \text{null vote} & \text{(1-vote overstatement)} \\ 1/2, & b_i = \text{null vote}, c_i = \text{Ali} & \text{(1-vote overstatement)} \\ 1, & b_i = c_i & \text{(match)} \\ 3/2, & b_i = \text{null vote}, c_i = \text{Bob} & \text{(1-vote understatement)} \\ 3/2, & b_i = \text{Ali}, c_i = \text{null vote} & \text{(1-vote understatement)} \\ 2, & b_i = \text{Ali}, c_i = \text{Bob} & \text{(2-vote understatement)}. \end{cases} \quad (8)$$

We now derive an assorter for mismatch-based RLAs. Let v' be any nonnegative number less than or equal to v. Define the *mismatch assorter*:

$$C(b_i) := \frac{1 - 1_{b_i \neq c_i}}{2 - 2v'} \in \{0, 1/(2 - 2v')\}. \quad (9)$$

If $\bar{C} := N^{-1} \sum_i C(b_i) > 1/2$, then $m < v' \leq v$, $M(\mathcal{C}) < V$, and the reported outcome is correct. Note that this assorter requires that CVRs are "linked" to cards, in order to determine whether $b_i \neq c_i$.

The mismatch assorter is a special case of a supermajority assorter [18, §2.3]: the outcome is correct if the fraction of matching CVRs is greater than 100% minus the CVR margin proportion. (It is simpler than a supermajority assorter in that it does not take the value 1/2.) The mismatch assorter is structurally similar to an overstatement assorter, with $u = 1$ and $v' = \nu/2$ (recall that for plurality contests, the vote margin is twice the CVR margin; SHANGRLA in effect reduces elections to a collection of two-candidate plurality contests). However, the largest value $C(b_i)$ can attain is $1/(2-2v')$, while $B(b_i) \leq 2u/(2u - \nu)$; this has implications discussed below.

4 Results

4.1 Algorithms and Parameter Settings

Testing the hypothesis $\bar{C} \leqslant 1/2$ yields a mismatch-based RLA with risk limit no greater than the significance level of the test. There are many ways to perform that test. Here we use a sequential random sample of values of $C(b_i)$ without replacement and the ALPHA test supermartingale [19].

We investigated the performance of mismatch-based audits using simulations based on the current implementation of SHANGRLA[3] with minor modifications. The ALPHA test in SHANGRLA is parametrized by a function η_j that can be thought of as an estimator of the mean of the values of the assorter that remain just before the jth random draw. Using the true mean minimizes the expected sample size when the assorter has only two possible values, as is the case for C_i; it yields Wald's sequential probability ratio test [19]. Of course, the true mean is unknown: the default function η_j in the current implementation is a truncated shrinkage estimator with several tuning parameters, including an initial guess η_0, a weight d for the initial guess relative to the sample, and a "guardrail" parameter c that controls how quickly η_j can approach $1/2$ as the sample grows.

For the mismatch assorter we used $d = 100$ (the default), and $\eta_0 = 0.999/(2 - 2v)$, corresponding to an assumed rate of 10^{-3} erroneous CVRs. Because the truncated shrinkage estimator produced values of η_j that were larger than optimal for mismatch-based audits, we added a constraint to keep η_j from approaching its upper bound too quickly (the mirror image of the "guardrail" that keeps η_j above $1/2$) and used a smaller value of c. For card-level comparison audits (overstatement assorters), we used the COBRA estimator η_j [13], which is parametrized by an assumed rate of 2-vote overstatements; we used 10^{-5}. Differences between the functions used for η_j in the two types of audit may account for some of the observed performance differences. Code is available at: https://github.com/aekh/margin-audit.

4.2 Simulations

We ran several experiments to quantify the performance of mismatch-based RLAs and compared their performance to that of existing RLA methods. For each experimental condition, we created N-tuples of $\mathcal{C}$ of CVRs and $\mathcal{B}$ of votes, then conducted 1,000 independent audits using those pairs and summarized the performance of each method by the mean of the 1,000 sample sizes.

4.3 Performance of Mismatch-Based RLAs

The expected sample size of a mismatch-based RLA depends on: (i) the number of CVRs N, (ii) the CVR margin proportion v (or lower bound v^-), and (iii) the mismatch rate m. Table 2 shows the results for all combinations of the following: $N \in \{10^4, 5 \times 10^4, 10^5\}$; $v \in \{0.001, 0.002, 0.003, 0.006, 0.01, 0.02, 0.03, 0.06, 0.1\}$;

---
[3] https://github.com/pbstark/SHANGRLA, visited 23 January 2025.

Table 2. Performance of mismatch-based RLAs. The mean sample size (columns 3–8) for a given CVR margin proportion (v), number of CVRs (N) and mismatch rate (m). All entries show the mean sample size in 1,000 simulated audits. 'F' means every simulation required a full manual tabulation.

		Mismatch rate (m)					
v	N	None	0.0001	0.0003	0.001	0.003	0.01
0.001	10k	2,835	3,587	5,332	9,751	F	F
	50k	3,236	4,681	9,208	47,850	F	F
	100k	3,292	4,958	10,505	95,809	F	F
0.002	10k	1,509	1,757	2,382	5,629	9,947	F
	50k	1,612	1,958	2,894	10,649	49,649	F
	100k	1,626	2,010	3,030	12,654	99,410	F
0.003	10k	1,022	1,141	1,428	2,962	9,640	F
	50k	1,068	1,225	1,605	3,991	47,621	F
	100k	1,074	1,237	1,634	4,274	95,912	F
0.006	10k	515	550	626	985	3,106	9,962
	50k	526	562	652	1,069	4,369	49,678
	100k	527	572	658	1,068	4,733	99,552
0.01	10k	308	323	345	469	1,022	9,557
	50k	312	327	359	484	1,109	47,144
	100k	312	329	360	483	1,143	95,137
0.02	10k	152	156	162	190	294	1,321
	50k	153	157	163	194	296	1,570
	100k	153	158	164	193	295	1,583
0.03	10k	101	103	105	117	160	443
	50k	101	103	106	118	152	465
	100k	101	103	105	118	156	463
0.06	(all)	50	50	51	54	61	106
0.1	(all)	30	30	30	31	34	45

$m \in \{0, 0.0001, 0.0003, 0.001, 0.003, 0.01\}$. Unsurprisingly, when $m \gtrsim v$, a mismatch-based RLA usually requires a full manual tabulation.

4.4 Two-Candidate Plurality Contests

We examined the cost of mismatch-based audits compared to card-level comparison audits of a contest whose outcome is characterized by a single assorter, e.g., a two-candidate plurality contest. We ran experiments similar to those in Sect. 4.3, but also varied the nature of the discrepancies between b_i and c_i, since card-level comparison audits depend on the types of error as well as their rates. We considered four error models:

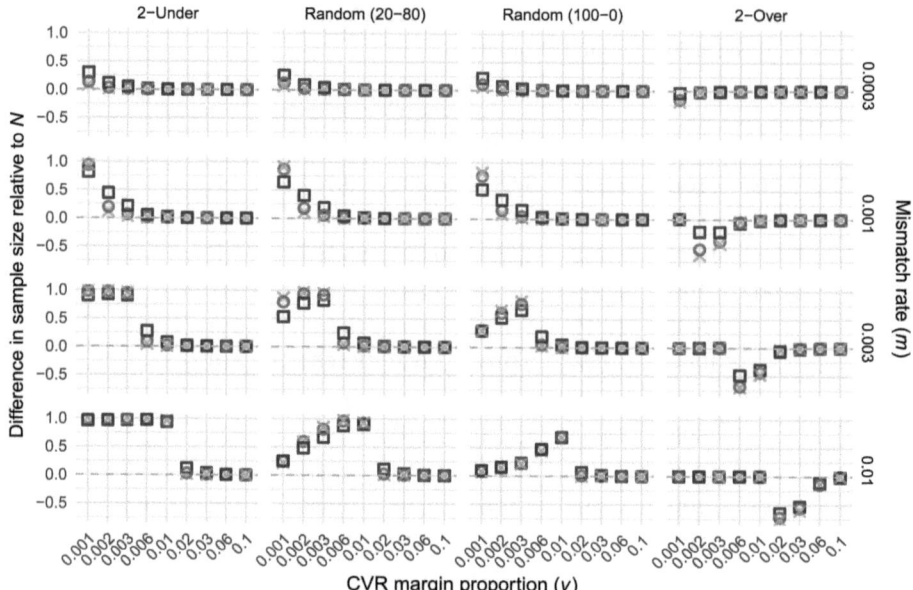

Fig. 1. Cost of mismatch-based RLAs versus card-level comparison RLAs for two-candidate plurality contests as a fraction of the number of cards. The difference in average sample size (mismatch-based audit sample size minus card comparison audit sample size) as a proportion of the total number of CVRs (y-axis), for various CVR margin proportions v (x-axis), number of CVRs N (point type and color; see legend), mismatch rates m (rows, as labeled on the right), and error models (columns, as labeled at the top). Along the y-axis, a value of 0 means the methods gave similar average sample sizes. Positive values mean the card-level comparison audit had smaller average sample size and vice versa for negative values. Values near 1 mean that the mismatch-based RLA required a full hand count when the card-comparison RLA generally terminated after examining only a small fraction of the cards.

2-Under. Every error is a 2-vote understatement. This is gives card-level comparison the greatest advantage.

2-Over. Every error is a 2-vote overstatement. This is the best case for a mismatch-based audit.

Random (100–0). Picking among votes other than b_i (including null votes) uniformly at random.

Random (20–80). Same as "Random (100–0)," but 80% of the CVRs have null votes, leading to a larger probability of having 1-vote over- and understatements. This scenario assesses the impact of a large number of invalid votes. For all other scenarios (above), every CVR had a valid vote.

The CVRs were constructed to attain the intended CVR margin proportion and mismatch rate. For example, in the "2-Under" scenario, the only mismatches involve CVRs with votes for the losing candidate.

Results are in Fig. 1. When the mismatch rate m is small compared to the CVR margin proportion v, the relative incremental cost of mismatch-based RLAs is low. As m approaches v, the incremental cost increases substantially, particularly when not every error is a two-vote overstatement. The incremental cost is greatest when $m \approx v$ but some CVR errors "cancel" (understatements and overstatements). Then a mismatch-based audit will typically lead to a full manual count, while a card-level comparison audit often certifies the election after examining only a fraction of the cards. Note that sometimes the mismatch-based audit leads to smaller average sample sizes than the card comparison audit, when the errors are the best case for the mismatch-based audit (which are very unlikely in practice, absent hacking, misconfiguration, or a serious malfunction). This is possible because we use different assorters and statistical tests for the two types of audit.

4.5 IRV Contests

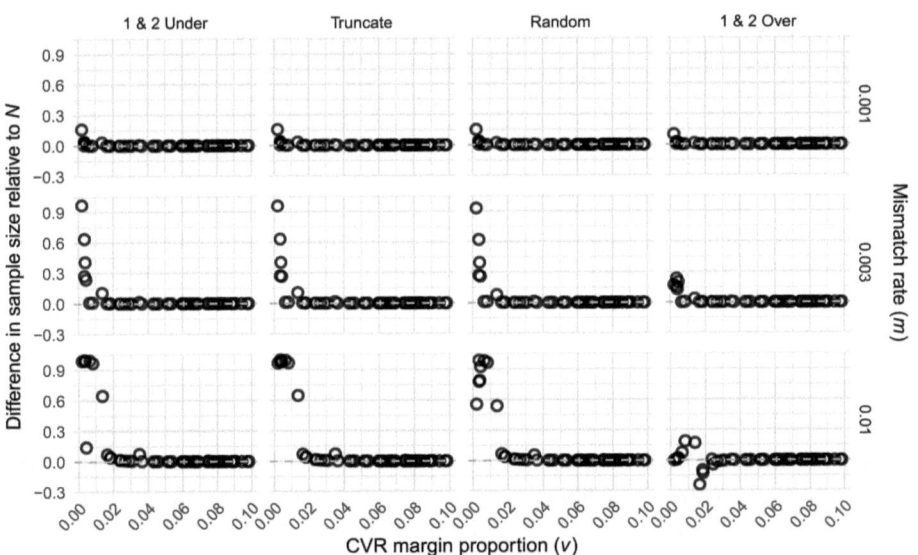

Fig. 2. Relative cost of mismatch-based RLAs versus RAIRE for IRV contests. Similar to Fig. 1, but for IRV rather than two-candidate plurality.

There are two methods for RLAs for IRV elections: RAIRE [7] and AWAIRE [11]. We compare the sample sizes of mismatch-based and RAIRE RLAs. CVR margins of IRV elections were found using the method of Blom et al. [10]. The simulated audits used the same election data as Blom et al. [7]: 93 New South Wales Legislative Assembly contests and 14 contests in the U.S.[4]

Results are in Fig. 2 for four kinds of error:

Under. Every error is a 2-vote (if possible) or a 1-vote (otherwise) understatement of the assorter with the smallest margin.

Over. Every error is a 2-vote (if possible) or a 1-vote (otherwise) overstatement of the assorter with the smallest margin.

Truncate. Truncate the preferences after a position selected uniformly at random between 0 and the number of preferences minus 1. If the original was a non-vote, randomly rank one candidate first.

Random. Replace a vote by randomly choosing ballot length (sampled from the CVRs), randomly choosing included candidates on the ballot (uniformly), and randomly permuting these candidates (uniformly), ensuring that the introduced ballot differs from the CVR.

Performance for IRV elections was similar to performance for two-candidate plurality elections: for mismatch rates much smaller than the CVR margin proportion there was essentially no extra cost for a mismatch-based audit. When errors cannot change the election result, a mismatch-based RLA may require a full hand count while RAIRE concludes the reported outcome is correct after a relatively small sample. When errors are only overstatements of the assorter with the smallest margin, the most favorable case for mismatch-based audits, mismatch-based RLAs are still generally less efficient than RAIRE.

4.6 STV Contests

Table 3. Mismatch RLA sample sizes (final 3 columns) in simulated audits of five STV contests in Scotland from 2022. The number of cards in each contest is N. The *best found lower bound* of the CVR margin is V^- (and $v^- = V^-/N$ the corresponding proportion).

Council	Ward	N	Cand.	Seats	V^- (v^-)	Mismatch rate (m)		
						None	0.0003	0.003
Glasgow	Greater Pollok	8,869	11	4	161 (1.82%)	168	178	349
Glasgow	East Centre	6,957	11	4	182 (2.62%)	115	120	191
Glasgow	Drumchapel/A	7,226	10	4	323 (4.47%)	67	68	91
Aberdeen	Torry Ferryhill	4,997	10	4	254 (5.08%)	59	60	79
Aberdeen	Lower Deeside	6,886	7	3	436 (6.33%)	47	48	58

While there is no RLA method for RLAs for STV contests with more than 2 seats [4], there are methods for computing lower bounds for the margin of STV

---

[4] https://github.com/michelleblom/margin-irv/ (visited 26 Jan 2025).

elections [8] that can handle many more seats. We simulated mismatch-based audits for several STV contests, with three choices for the mismatch rate. Our results are in Table 3.

We believe this is the first example of an efficient RLA for an STV election with more than 2 seats. We used the current best approach for computing lower bounds on CVR margins for STV [5].

CVR margins for STV are very hard to calculate and the best available lower bounds sometimes have considerable slack; indeed, the best known lower bound is 0 in some cases. For the STV contests we considered here, the lower bounds are a substantial fraction of the number of cards cast, so mismatch-based audit sample sizes are small.

5 Discussion and Conclusion

Although they are typically less efficient than more specialized card-level comparison RLAs, mismatch-based RLAs have some advantages:

- They only need a lower bound on the CVR margin for the social choice function, which might be possible to compute for some social choice functions for which a more nuanced RLA method does not yet exist.
- It is easier to explain how a mismatch-based RLA works to a general audience than it is to explain, say, RAIRE or AWAIRE.

However, when the discrepancy rate is an appreciable fraction of the CVR margin, mismatch-based RLAs typically require examining many more ballots, including requiring a full hand count when a more specialized method would not. Mismatch-based RLAs require a computing (a lower bound on) the CVR margin, which depends on the social choice function.

Differences in auditing strategies and differences in parameter settings in ALPHA affect audit sample sizes. COBRA, which we used for the card-level comparison audits, does not adapt to the data, so if m differs from the value assumed by COBRA (10^{-5} in our tests), it could have a disadvantage compared to the truncated shrinkage estimator used for the mismatch-based audit, which "learns" the error rate from the sample. That could explain the small number of situations where mismatch-based RLAs require smaller samples than card-level comparison RLAs: they correspond to using an assumed rate of 2-vote overstatements in COBRA that is orders of magnitude smaller than the actual rate of two-vote overstatements. Furthermore, the estimators for η_j that we used might not be optimally tuned in our applications; further refinements might improve performance.

Mismatch-based RLAs can use card-style information to audit a collection of contests simultaneously and efficiently [12]. The efficiency of mismatch-based RLAs might also be improved by distinguishing among broad classes of mismatches, for instance, mismatches where either the CVR or the ballot card has a null vote. For some social choice functions, it might take, say, k mismatches involving null votes to have the effect a single general mismatch could have. For instance, in a plurality contest, a mismatch involving a null vote can affect the reported margin by at most one vote, rather than two.

Mismatch-based RLAs require that the CVRs be available to compare to the sampled ballot cards. Publishing CVRs may have privacy implications. Mismatch-based RLAs are compatible with SOBA [2] and VAULT [3], which use cryptographic commitments to avoid revealing the full plaintext of CVRs other than those in the RLA sample.

References

1. Appel, A., Stark, P.: Evidence-based elections: create a meaningful paper trail, then audit. Georgetown Law Technol. Rev. **4**(2), 523–541 (2020), https://georgetownlawtechreview.org/wp-content/uploads/2020/07/4.2-p523-541-Appel-Stark.pdf
2. Benaloh, J., Jones, D., Lazarus, E., Lindeman, M., Stark, P.: SOBA: secrecy-preserving observable ballot-level audits. In: 2011 Electronic Voting Technology Workshop/Workshop on Trustworthy Elections (EVT/WOTE '11). USENIX (2011), arXiv:1105.5803
3. Benaloh, J., Stark, P.B., Teague, V.: VAULT: verifiable audits using limited transparency. E-Vote-ID 2019 (2019), https://www.stat.berkeley.edu/~stark/Preprints/vault19.pdf
4. Blom, M., , Stuckey, P.J., Teague, V., Vukcevic, D.: A first approach to risk-limiting audits for STV elections. In: Financial Cryptography and Data Security. FC 2022 International Workshops, pp. 366–380. LNCS 1312, Springer (2022), arXiv:2112.09921
5. Blom, M., Ek, A., Stuckey, P.J., Teague, V., Vukcevic, D.: Efficient lower bounding of single transferable vote election margins (2025), arXiv:2501.14847
6. Blom, M., Stark, P.B., Stuckey, P.J., Teague, V., Vukcevic, D.: Auditing Hamiltonian elections. In: Financial Cryptography and Data Security. FC 2021 International Workshops, pp. 235–250. LNCS 12676, Springer (2021), arXiv:2102.08510
7. Blom, M., Stuckey, P.J., Teague, V.: RAIRE: risk-limiting audits for IRV elections. arXiv:1903.08804 (2019), Preliminary version appeared in Electronic Voting (E-Vote-ID 2018), Springer LNCS 11143
8. Blom, M., Stuckey, P.J., Teague, V.: Towards computing the margin of victory in STV elections. INFORMS J. Comput. **31**(4), 636–653 (2019), arXiv:1703.03511
9. Blom, M., Stuckey, P.J., Teague, V., Vukevic, D.: Risk-limiting audits for Condorcet elections. In: Financial Cryptography and Data Security. FC 2023 International Workshops, pp. 79–94. LNCS 13953 (2023), arXiv:2303.10509
10. Blom, M., Teague, V., Stuckey, P.J., Tidhar, R.: Efficient computation of exact IRV margins. In: 22nd European Conference on Artificial Intelligence, pp. 480–488 (2016), arXiv:1508.04885
11. Ek, A., Stark, P.B., Stuckey, P.J., Vukcevic, D.: Adaptively weighted audits of instant-runoff voting elections: AWAIRE. In: E-Vote-ID 2023, pp. 35–51. LNCS 14230, Springer (2023), arXiv:2307.10972
12. Glazer, A., Spertus, J., Stark, P.: More style, less work: card-style data decrease risk-limiting audit sample sizes. Digit. Threats: Res. Pract. **2**, 1–15 (2021), arXiv:2012.03371

13. Spertus, J.V.: COBRA: comparison-optimal betting for risk-limiting audits. In: Financial Cryptography and Data Security. FC 2023 International Workshops, pp. 95–109. Springer (2023), arXiv:2304.01010
14. Stark, P.: Super-simple simultaneous single-ballot risk-limiting audits. In: 2010 Electronic Voting Technology Workshop/Workshop on Trustworthy Elections (EVT/WOTE 2010), USENIX (2010), http://www.usenix.org/events/evtwote10/tech/full_papers/Stark.pdf
15. Stark, P.: Non(c)esuch ballot-level risk-limiting audits for precinct-count voting systems. In: Computer Security. ESORICS 2022 International Workshops, pp. 541–554. LNCS 13785, Springer (2023), arXiv:2207.01362
16. Stark, P., Wagner, D.: Evidence-based elections. IEEE Secur. Priv. **10**, 33–41 (2012), https://www.stat.berkeley.edu/~stark/Preprints/evidenceVote12.pdf
17. Stark, P.B.: Conservative statistical post-election audits. Ann. Appl. Stat. **2**, 550–581 (2008), arXiv:0807.4005
18. Stark, P.B.: Sets of half-average nulls generate risk-limiting audits: SHANGRLA. In: Financial Cryptography and Data Security. FC 2020, pp. 319–336. LNCS 12063, Springer, August 2020, arXiv:1911.10035
19. Stark, P.B.: ALPHA: audit that learns from previously hand-audited ballots. Ann Appl. Stat. **17**(1), 641–679 (2023), arXiv:2201.02707
20. Stark, P.B.: Overstatement-net-equivalent risk-limiting audit: ONEAudit. In: Financial Cryptography and Data Security. FC 2023 Int'l Workshops, pp. 63–78. LNCS 13593, Springer (2024), arXiv:2303.03335
21. Stark, P.B., Teague, V.: Verifiable European elections: risk-limiting audits for D'Hondt and its relatives. USENIX J. Election Technol. Syst. (JETS) **3**(1), 18–39 (2014), https://www.usenix.org/jets/issues/0301/stark
22. Xia, L.: Computing the margin of victory for various voting rules. In: 13th ACM Conference on Electronic Commerce, EC 2012, pp. 982–999. ACM, New York, NY, USA (2012), https://doi.org/10.1145/2229012.2229086

Voting Without Self-voting

Peter B. Rønne

SnT, University of Luxembourg, Esch-sur-Alzette, Luxembourg
`peter.roenne@uni.lu`

Abstract. In an election, self-voting, i.e. candidates voting for themselves or their own proposals, might only capture an obvious inclination or a fear of loss of reputation, and hence may not be useful towards choosing the best candidate. In some contexts, e.g. for small scale boardroom elections, it can thus be sensible to prohibit self-voting, especially, this will prevent everybody pointing to themselves as the best choice. In the case of public elections this is easy to enforce, however, in standard secret ballot elections the no-self-voting condition is unchecked and relies on the honesty of the participants. More commonly, the constraint is simply not imposed in the first place due to lack of enforcement. A generalisation is where certain groups are not allowed to vote for their own candidate. In this case, preventing self-voting can also reduce the level of coercion, e.g., if team leaders demand, or more subtly simply expect, all their team members to vote for them in an election for the best team leader.

With the aid of secure e-voting, imposing the no-self-voting constraint becomes possible. We show how this constraint can be implemented efficiently, in the context of both centralised and decentralised voting. Especially, we show how to obtain a robust (i.e. allowing absentees) decentralised voting system preventing self-voting by using just standard linkable ring signatures and anonymous vote-casting channels.

1 Introduction

In elections, it is often the case that candidates are themselves part of the electorate. Sometimes *self-voting* is excluded in order to obtain an expressive result and avoiding everybody pointing to themselves as the best candidate. In general, we can envisage that for some voters, certain voting options are excluded. In the Eurovision Song Contest, as an example, countries are not allowed to vote for themselves. A more illustrative example is the Security Protocols Workshop where the best presentation is elected in a secret ballot but presenters are not allowed to vote for their own talk. Interestingly, prohibiting PhD students to vote for the talk of their supervisor, or vice versa, also helps to prevent implicit coercion threats, and hence to select a better winner.

Ideally, voting systems should fulfill at least two basic properties: 1) Verifiability: Allowing the detection of any vote fraud, including casting more or different votes than allowed, modifying or deleting the votes of other participants, and finally ensuring a correct tally of the votes; 2) Ballot Privacy: Protecting the privacy of the cast vote, besides the unavoidable privacy leakage from the actual result of the election. The challenge is to balance the levels of verifiability and privacy with good usability and efficiency. Disallowing self-voting adds yet another constraint that we need to be able to verify, and if done poorly can lead to privacy leaks.

In this paper, we show how to efficiently enforce the no-self-voting condition in different settings. For voting systems with central tally authorities, we show how to efficiently prove the correctness of cast ballots using a voter-side plaintext (in)equivalency test/proof. For these proofs, we carefully avoid pitfalls both in terms of soundness (see also discussion in [15]) and privacy (which does not seem to have been discussed earlier).

We also consider protocols in the decentralised setting (aka boardroom voting), i.e., in the case where we do not have or do not want to rely on a central authority trusted for privacy.

Decentralised voting systems come in (at least) two flavours. In systems like [9,10] cryptographic ballots are cast with a direct (authenticated) relation to the voter, and we can apply plaintext (in)equivalence proofs like in the central system case. However, if just a single voter fails to participate, we need to run recovery rounds until all anticipated voters participate (see [8] for a method to gain robustness but paying in terms of privacy and accuracy). The second type of decentralised scheme assumes anonymous channels to cast plaintext votes.[1] The advantage is that the protocol is robust, i.e. tolerates abstaining voters without having to redo the election. In this setting, we present a scheme which is simple, light-weight and fulfills both ballot-privacy, verifiability, and allows detection and removal of self-votes.

To achieve this we alter the known linkable ring signatures (LRS) decentralised voting protocol. We propose a new primitive called Conditional Linkable Ring Signatures to replace the LRS and detect self-votes. Importantly, we manage to achieve this without having to implement new zero-knowledge proofs, and build our scheme using two instantiations of the basic primitive of LRS.

In this short paper, we give possible solutions to prevent self-voting in paper-based voting (Sect. 2.1) and central-authority e-voting (Sect. 2.2) including an outlook towards coercion-resistant voting. We will also point out a privacy pitfall problem with plaintext-equivalence tests which relates to their general use in e-voting and beyond (Sect. 2.3). Finally, we discuss decentralised e-voting in Sect. 2.4, introduce the conditional linkable ring signatures and our decentralised scheme.

---

[1] Anonymous channels can be hard to implement in practice especially in a strong adversarial model, e.g. a malicious bulletin board seeing network metadata.

2 Proposals for No-Self-voting Solutions

2.1 Paper Ballots

In standard elections using paper ballots, where voters mark their choice among a number of candidates on the ballot, it seems hard to prevent self-voting. However, in some election systems, each candidate has their own ballot, and the voter makes their choice by casting their chosen candidate-ballot in the ballot box. Such systems have been used historically, but have privacy issues. Despite these, they are still in use, e.g. in Israel, see [1] which also discusses possible privacy attacks. However, in such a system we could hand out a selected range of ballots to each voter individually, preventing self-voting. The main difficulty here consists of verifying that only one vote is cast, and recollecting the non-cast ballots in a privacy-preserving way.

Advantages: Easy to implement for candidate-specific paper ballots.

Disadvantages: Hard to handle many candidates. Possibilities of privacy- and verifiability attacks.

2.2 E-Voting with Central Tally Authority

In the most common setup of e-voting we have a central authority responsible for the tally holding a key pair $(\mathsf{pk}, \mathsf{sk})$ for a public key encryption system. For better privacy, these keys might be distributed over several players which jointly will apply threshold verifiable decryption of the final election result, either after homomorphic aggregation of votes or using a mixnet for privacy. In this case, a voter will normally cast a ballot to the bulletin board as

$$\mathsf{ID}, \mathsf{Enc}(\mathsf{C}; r), \pi$$

where ID is the identity of the voter, C the choice of candidate, which is encrypted with randomness r. Finally, π is a zero-knowledge proof (ZKP) of correct encryption of a valid candidate which is also a proof of knowledge, and normally it ensures NM-CPA security of the ciphertext with the ZKP. To prevent self-voting, we want to prove that $\mathsf{ID} \neq \mathsf{C}$ (for some encoded version of ID).

There are several ways to ensure the absence of self-voting.

– We can adjust the proof π of correctness of C to ensure $\mathsf{C} \neq \mathsf{ID}$. If this is a simple OR proof over candidates, removing a candidate can even make the proof smaller. However, in some cases this is less efficient, e.g. π could be a range proof for the full candidate list which might be twice or more expensive to split; or in some cases there are no constraints on C over the message space, e.g., a write-in. Further, it can be easier for the implementation to have the same proof type π for all voters, and simply add a smaller ZKP for the exclusion of ID on top.
– The are methods for non-membership proofs, e.g., [4] gives efficient constructions but using the Groth-Sahai proof system in a bilinear group setting. Depending on the setting this can be good solution.

- The election authority could do standard Plaintext Equivalence Tests/Proofs (PETs) [15] on $\mathsf{Enc}(\mathsf{C};r)$ to prove that $\mathsf{C} \neq \mathsf{ID}$. However, this is not desirable. In particular, it will involve the secret election key which we prefer to keep inactive until the decryption of the final tally. Especially, if we want to verify ballots on the fly, this will be troublesome since PETs requires a threshold set of authorities to be available online in order to decrypt.

We here consider ElGamal encryption in a general DDH group, due to its extensive use in voting systems. We show how an encryptor can make an efficient plaintext (in)equivalence zero-knowledge proof using the knowledge of the encryption randomness, using straightforward known and very efficient techniques.[2] For generality, parallel to PETs, we show how to prove both equality and inequality, which can be useful in other settings.

Let $\mathbb{G}$ be a prime-order group with q being the order. Let g be a generator of $\mathbb{G}$ and $\mathsf{pk} = g^{\mathsf{sk}}$ the public election key. An ElGamal encryption of C is $\mathsf{Enc}(\mathsf{C};r) = (g^r, \mathsf{pk}^r \mathsf{C})$ where we abuse notation and use C both as the choice and the corresponding encoding as a group element. We have suppressed notation for group multiplications.

In our use case to prevent self-voting, we want a protocol to prove that the cast vote $\mathsf{Enc}(\mathsf{C};r_1)$ does not have the voter themself as chosen candidate. For generality, we present a more general proof of plaintext (in)equality test from a prover who is the encryptor of two ciphertexts.

The protocol for the proof of plaintext (in)equality of $\mathsf{Enc}(\mathsf{C};r_1) = (g^{r_1}, \mathsf{pk}^{r_1} \mathsf{C}_1)$ and $\mathsf{Enc}(\mathsf{C};r_2) = (g^{r_2}, \mathsf{pk}^{r_2} \mathsf{C}_2)$ between a prover P knowing r_1, r_2 (the voter) and a verfier V is now as follows[3]

1. P sends $\mathsf{Enc}(\mathsf{C}_1;r_1) = (g^{r_1}, \mathsf{pk}^{r_1} \mathsf{C}_1) := (a_1, b_1)$ and $\mathsf{Enc}(\mathsf{C}_2;r_2) = (g^{r_2}, \mathsf{pk}^{r_2} \mathsf{C}_2) := (a_2, b_2)$
2. P, V use the homomorphic property of ElGamal encryption to compute $(a_1/a_2, b_1/b_2) = \mathsf{Enc}(\mathsf{C}_1/\mathsf{C}_2; r_1 - r_2) := (d, e)$. The problem is now equivalent to showing whether $\mathsf{C}_1/\mathsf{C}_2 \stackrel{?}{=} 1$.
3. (a) In case of in-equivalence, P gives a ZKP $\pi_{\mathrm{non-eq}}$ of discrete log inequivalence which proves that $d = g^r = g^{r_1 - r_2}$ (including knowledge of r), but that $e \neq \mathsf{pk}^r$. This is done without proving knowledge of a discrete log of e (which could be unknown). We give references for this proof below.
   (b) In the case of equivalence, P gives a ZKP π_{eq} of discrete log equivalence which proves that $d = g^r = g^{r_1 - r_2}$ and $e = \mathsf{pk}^r = \mathsf{pk}^{r_1 - r_2}$. This can be done using a standard Chaum-Pedersen proof [7].
4. V verifies the correctness of π_{eq} or $\pi_{\mathrm{non-eq}}$ (unless proof was interactive).

Note that if the ZKP is non-interactive, then this protocol is also non-interactive. Whereas the Chaum-Pedersen proof is very well-known, the discrete

---

[2] Ref. [3] gives general constructions of PETs and PETs for encryptors, but due to their generality each proof iteration only has soundness 1/2 and will be less efficient.
[3] For our case, we can set $r_2 = 0$ but the general case is relevant in other contexts, e.g. when submitting ballots anonymously in JCJ [11].

log inequivalence proof is less known, but follows from [5, Sec. 5]. Both are very efficient, the size of the equality proof is just two group elements and the inequality has a size of three group elements [16]. Both can be made non-interactive using the strong Fiat-Shamir transformation [2].

Advantages: We only need to add a very small extra zero-knowledge proof to standard systems without changing other parts of the system. It also works easily if a group of voters has to be prevented from voting for a given candidate.

Disadvantages: If we need to exclude more than one candidate, the proof size will be linear in the number of excluded candidates.

2.3 Privacy Problems in Standard PETs

An important question is why did not follow the procedure of standard PETs by simply exponentiating $\mathsf{Enc}(\mathsf{C}_1/\mathsf{C}_2; r_1 - r_2)$ with r (for PETs this is done in a distributed way using several parties [15]) to get

$$(g^{r(r_1-r_2)}, \mathsf{pk}^{r(r_1-r_2)}(\mathsf{C}_1/\mathsf{C}_2)^r)$$

Then revealing $r(r_1 - r_2)$ to the verifier allows retrieving $(\mathsf{C}_1/\mathsf{C}_2)^r$ and checking whether this is 1 for equality or random for inequality. Following [15], the verifier should also check that $r(r_1 - r_2) \neq 0$ for soundness of the proof. However, this can actually result in privacy leaks of the encrypted candidate.

To see this, note that both here and for standard PETs [15], we reveal the terms

$$g^{r_1-r_2}, g^{r(r_1-r_2)}, (\mathsf{C}_1/\mathsf{C}_2)^r \tag{1}$$

which we cannot prove to be random to the adversary without further assumptions. In particular, if an active adversary happens to know $g^{r_1-r_2}$ beforehand when choosing the (encoding of) plaintexts, he could set $\mathsf{C}_1/\mathsf{C}_2 = g^{x(r_1-r_2)}$ for some x known to the adversary. Now, the plaintext equivalence proof between ciphertexts of resp. C_1 and C_2 would fail but would still reveal the choice of plaintexts by comparing the two last terms in Eq. 1, which would be $g^{r(r_1-r_2)}, g^{xr(r_1-r_2)}$ which can be checked by the adversary knowing x. In practice, one could imagine that this could happen if mixnets are prepared in advance for a fast online mixing phase, e.g., in JCJ where this is the bottleneck for the tally efficiency. Even if this attack seems theoretical, the privacy leak is important since it would make a proof of privacy of a scheme using such PETs troublesome.

We leave it as an open problem to avoid this privacy problem in general, but our solution above for the case where the encryptor makes the PET side-steps this problem.

Coercion-Resistant Voting: We finally comment on the possibilities in coercion-resistant voting. Here, the voter's submitted ciphertext should not be linkable to the voter. This makes the problem of avoiding self-voting harder.

In JCJ [11], one could imagine encoding candidate choices via the publicly encrypted credentials and then weed out self-votes using PETs. However, we leave it as an open problem to prevent self-voting efficiently while preserving coercion-resistance.

2.4 Decentralised Voting

Decentralised schemes like [9,10] have ballots which can be extended to ElGamal ciphertexts with a public key. This means, we can use the plaintext in-equivalence proof from Sect. 2.2 to prevent self-voting. However, these schemes are not robust - all eligible voters need to cast their vote to compute the election result. We now show how to get robust decentralised voting schemes without self-voting, and that this can be achieved without implementing new cryptographic primitives using only linkable signatures.

Linkable Ring Signatures. In the seminal paper [13] Linkable Ring Signatures (LRS) were introduced and shown to facilitate the construction of a robust decentralised voting protocol. We describe this approach here in an informal and abbreviated form. An LRS scheme contains four algorithms Gen, Sign, Ver, Link. Each user, U_i, holds a signing and public verification key pair $(\mathsf{sk}_i, \mathsf{pk}_i) \leftarrow$ Gen(1^k). Let L be a subset of the public keys, which is called the ring and provides an anonymity set. We need to use an enhanced version of LRS which in addition to the ring also has a label lbl, called *event-id* in [12]. U_i can then sign a message m as $\sigma \leftarrow$ Sign($\mathsf{sk}_i, m, (\mathsf{lbl}, L)$). These signatures are verified using Ver. Finally, the signatures can be pairwise checked if they are linked via Link. Signatures are linked iff they have the same signer, same ring and same label, formally Link(L, m, m', Sign($m, \mathsf{sk}_i, (\mathsf{lbl}, L)$), Sign($m', \mathsf{sk}_j, (\mathsf{lbl}', L')$)) $= \delta_{i,j}\delta_{L,L'}\delta_{\mathsf{lbl},\mathsf{lbl}'}$.[4]

The security properties are defined via games, see e.g. [14], and informally ensure: 1) **Existential Unforgeability:** Given a set of honestly generated public keys, EU ensures that even in the presence of a signing oracle that produces signatures for different, messages, rings and signers, no new verifiable signature can be constructed. 2) **Signer Anonymity:** Allows the adversary to adaptively corrupt and obtain oracle signatures. Then the adversary gets a challenge signature for a chosen ring and label, and has to guess better than random which of the non-corrupted users created it. 3) **Linkability:** Ensures a) that the adversary cannot frame a user by producing a new signature linkable to a signature from the honest user, other than by copying. b) That users cannot create extra unlinkable signatures for the same ring.

Given an LRS setup, the voting protocol in [13] is simple: Votes are cast in plaintext to a bulletin board BB via an *anonymous channel*, but signed with LRS, where the ring is over the public keys of all voters. The signatures prevent ballot stuffing from non-eligible parties. The signer anonymity of LRS means that the ballots are anonymous in the ring of all voters, and ensures ballot privacy. Finally, the linkability of LRS means that if someone submits multiple

---
[4] δ denotes the Kronecker delta function.

ballots these are linkable via the Link algorithm, and ensures one-vote-per-voter verifiability. Since the ballots have plaintext votes, the election is *self-tallying*, also with absentees, and anyone can confirm the result.

Conditional Linkable Ring Signatures. Our idea to prevent self-voting is to let voters publish public-verifiable signatures of their prohibited voting options, and change the LRS primitive to allow linking signatures across different rings and labels but only if the user signs the same message twice.[5] To be more general, this could also be a condition in terms of the messages, labels and rings of the two signatures – hence we name them Conditional Linkable Ring Signatures (CLRS).

We thus define a second algorithm for linking, denoted Link_R, for a given (symmetric) predicate R such that (here lbl, L, m are implicit in the signature) if $\sigma_i = \mathsf{Sign}(m, \mathsf{sk}_i, (\mathsf{lbl}, L))$ and $\sigma'_j = \mathsf{Sign}(m', \mathsf{sk}_j, (\mathsf{lbl}', L'))$

$$\mathsf{Link}_R(\sigma'_i, \sigma'_j) = \delta_{i,j} R\big((\mathsf{lbl}, L, m), (\mathsf{lbl}', L', m')\big)$$

In our case it is sufficient to consider the predicate defined to be true iff $m = m'$. We denote this by $R = id$.

The security properties of CLRS are straightforward generalisations of LRS, with a new linkability game for Link_R and anonymity needs to be updated since signatures fulfilling the relation are now linkable. When we only link same message signatures, users can ensure that anonymity is preserved by only signing messages including extra unique identifiers.

The idea is now as follows: In an initial round, each voter signs their disallowed voting options where the ring is their own public key. This is sent to BB and is publicly verifiable due to the ring being only the single voter. For the actual election round, all voters cast their plaintext votes with their ring signature, where the ring is now over all voters. If someone casts a self-vote it will be detectable since the plaintext vote is the same in the first and second round, making it linkable. We now make this precise.

The No-Self-voting Voting Protocol. Given a CLRS, the protocol preventing self-voting is a simple two-round protocol. Each of the n voters U_i generates a key pair $\mathsf{sk}_i, \mathsf{pk}_i$ for the chosen CLRS. Let C_k denote the voting options, and assume U_i is not allowed to vote for $\widehat{\mathsf{C}}_{U_i}$. In an initial round each voter U_i signs and publishes the prohibited option $\widehat{\mathsf{C}}_{U_i}$ signed under the ring consisting only of the user's own public key and label lbl_0 (this round is skipped for voters without candidate constraints):

$$U_i, \mathsf{Sign}\big(\widehat{\mathsf{C}}_{U_i}, \mathsf{sk}_i, (\mathsf{lbl}_0, \{\mathsf{pk}_i\})\big) \longrightarrow \mathsf{BB}$$

In the actual voting round, each voter U_i anonymously submits their candidate choice C_{U_i} signed under the ring of all voter public keys $L = \{\mathsf{pk}_i\}_{i=1,\ldots,n}$ and a second unique label lbl_1.

---

[5] The idea of tracing same message signatures goes back to the untraceable e-cash system [6] where it was used to avoid double spending.

$$\text{Sign}(C_{U_i}, \text{sk}_i, (\text{lbl}_1, L)) \stackrel{anom.}{\longmapsto} \text{BB}$$

Finally, everyone can verify all signatures, check that none of the second round signatures are linked with Link and check that none are linked to the initial round signatures using Link_{id}. Note that it is clear who signed each message in the initial round since the ring there is just the single public key of the signer.

$$\forall i \in \mathsf{C} \, \forall j = 1, \ldots, k : \text{Sign}(U_i || \text{lbl}_j, \text{sk}_i, (\text{elecID}, \{\text{pk}_i\})) \mapsto \text{BB}$$

$$\text{Sign}(U_{\pi(i,j)} || \text{lbl}_j, \text{sk}_i, (\text{lbl}_i, L)) \stackrel{anom.}{\longmapsto} \text{BB}$$

If we re-use keys for several elections or election rounds then each round needs a unique label lbl_j, and the candidate names in each round are appended with lbl_j to prevent linking between rounds. In the initial round, the voters sign all prohibited choices with the corresponding round labels. Alternatively, a CLRS with a different predicate can be used to ensure that there is no linkability between the voting rounds, but still between the voting round and the initial round for the same messages.

Verifiability: Each voter can check that their ballot appears on BB. Anyone can verify signatures (ensures no ballot stuffing from externals by existential unforgeability) and that they are not linked within the voting round using Link (ensures one-vote-per-voter) and not linkable to the initial round using Link_{id} (ensures no self-voting). Linkable ballots are simply removed.

Ballot-Privacy: Ballot privacy follows from the anonymity of the vote casting channels and the anonymity of the CLRS primitive. For multiple elections the unique labels ensure no linkability between rounds. It would be interesting to develop ballot privacy notions that also capture side-channels, e.g., if a voter always casts a vote fast and can be correlated between rounds.

Instantiating the Primitive. Until now we have only considered the CLRS as a primitive. We now demonstrate that when we have a given overall set of public keys L_{all}, we can instantiate CLRS for linking the same messages (or more generally if $f(\text{lbl}, L, m) = f(\text{lbl}', L', m')$ for a function f) by using two LRS signatures. This goes against the spontaneous nature of LRS which allows adding users ad hoc, but in the case of a voting protocol with a known set of public keys this is sufficient. The idea is that we sign as expected using the first signature and let the label of the second signature be the message itself. The message of the second signature is the first signature to bind them together[6] and the ring is L_{all}, i.e. the CLRS signature $\text{Sign}^{CLRS}(\text{sk}_i, m, (\text{lbl}, L))$ consists of the two LRS signatures

$$\sigma_1 = \text{Sign}^{LRS}(\text{sk}_i, 0||m, (0||\text{lbl}, L)), \sigma_2 = \text{Sign}^{LRS}(\text{sk}_i, 1||\sigma_1, (1||m, L_{all}))$$

---

[6] Using the first signature as the message in the second signature might not be strictly necessary but can provide stronger security e.g. strong unforgeability.

When the same message is signed twice, the second part becomes linkable since it has the same label, but otherwise when messages are different it is not linkable and anonymity is preserved since it is over the ring of all public keys. The security of the construction should be proven formally. However, intuitively existential unforgeability follows from the LRS primitive. We have appended 0 and 1 to the messages in σ_1 and σ_2 to prevent any malleability in reverting the order of signatures. For linkability, we define Link as the LRS link on the first signature and Link_{id} as the LRS link on the second signature. The anonymity of the CLRS follows intuitively like the anonymity of the underlying LRS. Even in the special case where a message should happen to collide with a label, there can be no cross-links between the first and the second part of the signatures because the labels have been appended with 0 resp. 1.

3 Conclusion

We have discussed how to prevent self-voting in many different voting contexts, from paper-based voting over centralised e-voting to decentralised voting. Especially, we designed a decentralised, robust scheme that allows public detection of self-votes using linkable ring signatures. Future work consists in proper definitions of security for the CLRS primitive and a detailed security analyses of the proposed decentralised scheme and its instantiation.

Acknowledgments. A special thanks goes to Peter Y A Ryan for comments and suggestions. This research was funded in part by the Luxembourg National Research Fund (FNR), grant reference C21/IS/16221219/ImPAKT. For the purpose of open access, and in fulfilment of the obligations arising from the grant agreement, the author has applied a Creative Commons Attribution 4.0 International (CC BY 4.0) license to any Author Accepted Manuscript version arising from this submission.

References

1. Ashur, T., Dunkelman, O., Talmon, N.: Breaching the privacy of Israel's paper ballot voting system. In: Electronic Voting: First International Joint Conference, E-Vote-ID 2016, Bregenz, Austria, October 18–21, 2016, Proceedings 1, pp. 108–124. Springer (2017)
2. Bernhard, D., Pereira, O., Warinschi, B.: How not to prove yourself: Pitfalls of the Fiat-Shamir heuristic and applications to Helios. In: Advances in Cryptology–ASIACRYPT 2012: Proceedings 18, pp. 626–643. Springer (2012)
3. Blazy, O., Bultel, X., Lafourcade, P., Kempner, O.P.: Generic plaintext equality and inequality proofs. In: International Conference on Financial Cryptography and Data Security, pp. 415–435. Springer (2021)
4. Blazy, O., Chevalier, C., Vergnaud, D.: Non-interactive zero-knowledge proofs of non-membership. In: Cryptographers' Track at the RSA Conference, pp. 145–164. Springer (2015)

5. Camenisch, J., Shoup, V.: Practical verifiable encryption and decryption of discrete logarithms. In: Annual International Cryptology Conference, pp. 126–144. Springer (2003)
6. Chaum, D., Fiat, A., Naor, M.: Untraceable electronic cash. In: Conference on the Theory and Application of Cryptography, pp. 319–327. Springer (1988)
7. Chaum, D., Pedersen, T.P.: Wallet databases with observers. In: Annual International Cryptology Conference, pp. 89–105. Springer (1992)
8. El Orche, F.E., et al.: Time, privacy, robustness, accuracy: trade-offs for the open vote network protocol. In: International Joint Conference on Electronic Voting, pp. 19–35. Springer (2022)
9. Giustolisi, R., Iovino, V., Rønne, P.B.: On the possibility of non-interactive e-voting in the public-key setting. In: International Conference on Financial Cryptography and Data Security. pp. 193–208. Springer (2016)
10. Hao, F., Ryan, P.Y., Zieliński, P.: Anonymous voting by two-round public discussion. IET Inf. Secur. 4(2), 62–67 (2010)
11. Juels, A., Catalano, D., Jakobsson, M.: Coercion-resistant electronic elections. In: Proceedings of the 2005 ACM Workshop on Privacy in the Electronic Society, pp. 61–70 (2005)
12. Liu, J.K., Au, M.H., Susilo, W., Zhou, J.: Linkable ring signature with unconditional anonymity. IEEE Trans. Knowl. Data Eng. **26**(1), 157–165 (2013)
13. Liu, J.K., Wei, V.K., Wong, D.S.: Linkable spontaneous anonymous group signature for Ad Hoc groups. In: Australasian Conference on Information Security and Privacy, pp. 325–335. Springer (2004)
14. Liu, J.K., Wong, D.S.: Linkable ring signatures: security models and new schemes. In: International Conference on Computational Science and Its Applications, pp. 614–623. Springer (2005)
15. McMurtry, E., Pereira, O., Teague, V.: When is a test not a proof? In: Computer Security–ESORICS 2020: Proceedings, Part II 25, pp. 23–41. Springer (2020)
16. Villar, J.: Zero-knowledge proofs notes. https://web.mat.upc.edu/jorge.villar/doc/notes/DataProt/zk.pdf. Accessed 29 Jan 2025

Anamorphic Voting: Ballot Freedom Against Dishonest Authorities

Rosario Giustolisi[1]([✉]), Mohammadamin Rakeei[2], and Gabriele Lenzini[2]

[1] IT University of Copenhagen, Copenhagen, Denmark
rosg@itu.dk
[2] SnT, University of Luxembourg, Esch-sur-Alzette, Luxembourg
{amin.rakeei,gabriele.lenzini}@uni.lu

Abstract. Electronic voting schemes typically ensure ballot privacy by assuming that the decryption key is distributed among tallying authorities, preventing any single authority from decrypting a voter's ballot. However, this assumption may fail in a fully dishonest environment where all tallying authorities collude to break ballot privacy.

In this work, we introduce the notion of *anamorphic voting*, which enables voters to convey their true voting intention to an auditor while casting an (apparently) regular ballot. We present new cryptographic techniques demonstrating that several existing voting schemes can support anamorphic voting.

1 Introduction

According to the Democracy Index published by the Economist Group [28] in 2024, 59 countries are classified as authoritarian regimes. To remain in power, such regimes need to demonstrate overwhelming support for the ruling party, often designing voting systems to ensure that the dictator decisively wins the election. Therefore, elections in these countries often lack transparency, raising concerns about the secrecy and integrity of the ballots.

An authoritarian regime that (falsely) seeks to address such concerns could still implement a voting scheme that is proven to be secure, while violating its trust assumptions. For example, ballot privacy is clearly compromised in most voting systems if an attacker controls all the election decryption keys and has access to the datasets containing the ballots cast at the voting phase. The absence of vote privacy intimidates voters, preventing them from freely expressing their true preferences. However, is it still possible for voters to communicate their real voting intentions without being detected by the authoritarian regime?

In this work, we introduce *anamorphic voting*, exploring how participants in an election might communicate covertly even when an authoritarian regime controls *all* communication channels and implements an *existing* voting scheme without satisfying the necessary trust assumptions. Anamorphic voting is inspired by the recent concept of anamorphic encryption [25] in the context

© International Financial Cryptography Association 2026
B. Haslhofer et al. (Eds.): FC 2025 Workshops, LNCS 15754, pp. 266–280, 2026.
https://doi.org/10.1007/978-3-032-00495-6_15

of electronic voting. While anamorphic encryption studies whether *a single* well-established public-key cryptosystem supports covert communication under stringent dictator conditions, anamorphic voting examines whether *a combination* of cryptographic primitives within a voting scheme can enable covert communication even in the presence of dishonest authorities.

We introduce the term *ballot freedom* to capture the most useful application of anamorphic voting. Ballot freedom is the ability of a voter to freely communicate their true voting intention to an auditor without the knowledge of the authoritarian regime.

At first glance, ballot freedom seems similar to receipt-freeness or coercion-resistance (by replacing the terms "auditor" with "tallier" and "coercer" with "authoritarian regime"). However, there are at least two key differences. First, receipt-freeness and coercion-resistance are properties that can be enforced by designing a new voting scheme, while ballot freedom is a property achieved through the combination of cryptographic primitives in an existing voting scheme. Second, receipt-free and coercion-resistant voting schemes need to assume the existence of anonymous and/or private channels at some point [9]. This very assumption is ruled out in the context of anamorphic voting, as authoritarian regimes often control all communication channels.

In this paper, we introduce the first constructions for anamorphic voting by investigating combinations of the most common cryptographic primitives in voting schemes. We show that anamorphic voting is possible in the Estonian Internet Voting System (IVXV) [22], CHVote [19], Helios [1] and Belenios [10] voting schemes. Additionally, we demonstrate that different levels of ballot freedom can be achieved depending on the available datasets. To the best of our knowledge, our constructions are the first to demonstrate anamorphism within the context of a combination of cryptographic primitives. Thus, these constructions may also prove useful in domain beyond voting.

2 Anamorphic Voting

We provide a primer of anamorphic encryption, from which we informally introduce anamorphic voting and ballot freedom, leaving a formal treatment for future work. We then discuss how to make CHVote [19] anamorphic, achieving ballot freedom using different cryptographic primitives.

2.1 From Anamorphic Encryption to Anamorphic Voting

Anamorphic encryption [25] enables entities to encrypt hidden messages evading the censorship imposed by a dictator within a well-established public-key cryptosystem. In its stronger formulation, the dictator owns the receiver's secret key (no receiver privacy) and can force the sender to send ciphertexts over a channel controlled by the dictator (no sender freedom), although sender and receiver might have previously exchanged keys over private channels.

In strongly secure anamorphic encryption, the dictator forces the sender to encrypt a message fm using a forced public key fpk for which the dictator knows the corresponding private key fsk. The sender can evade censorship by generating randomness for the encryption using a coin-toss faking algorithm fRandom, which takes as input fm, fpk, a double public key dpk (with the corresponding double private key dsk known only by the receiver) and a hidden message dm, and generates an anamorphic ciphertext that gives fm when decrypted with fsk, and dm when decrypted with dsk by the receiver.

In anamorphic voting, we extend the concept of anamorphic encryption to support the multiple cryptographic primitives that constitute a voting scheme, that is, we split anamorphic encryptions across multiple components, such as multiple ciphertexts, ciphertext and signature, or ciphertext and proof of knowledge. This approach allows entities to encrypt hidden messages, evading the censorship imposed by dishonest authorities within a well-established voting scheme.

Anamorphic voting is agnostic about the participants. It can apply to scenarios where, for instance, a voter wants to communicate with another voter or an honest authority with another honest authority. To address the specific case of voters conveying their true vote intentions to an auditor despite the presence of dishonest authority, we introduce the concept of ballot freedom.

Ballot freedom assumes the following strong threat model:

- The auditor double public key dpk is known to everyone, including voters and authority.
- The authority executes the voting scheme according to its prescribed specifications, including setup parameters.
- The authority knows at least the election decrypting key and may hold additional keys based on the roles in the voting scheme.
- The authority has access to all data generated within the voting scheme.
- The voter can only communicate through channels controlled by the authority (i.e. no anonymous, private, or untappable channels exist).

A notable distinction from anamorphic encryption is that ballot freedom does not assume the existence of private channels.

2.2 A Running Example: CHVote

CHVote [19] has been one of the two major e-voting system proposals in Switzerland. The system is universally verifiable, which means that independent verifiers can confirm the correctness of the election results. Verification ensures that only votes cast by eligible voters are included, that no voter casts more than one vote, and that every valid vote is tallied as recorded.

The election process in CHVote involves several key parties: Election Administrator, Election Authority, Printing Authority, Voter, and Verifier. CHVote is designed to support various election formats, including multiple elections and multiple answers. For simplicity, we focus on the case where voters cast a vote for a single candidate among n possible candidates. It relies on several cryptographic primitives, including ElGamal encryption [15], Schnorr signatures, and Schnorr identification proofs [26].

CHVote can be divided in three phases as follows:

Preparation Phase. The election administrator defines the election parameters, such as the number of candidates n, and works with the election authorities to generate a public encryption key pk. Each authority prepares partial verification codes for each voting option, which are hashed and combined into a single verification code v_c. The printing authority collectively generates and prints eligibility, confirmation, and validity data on the voter's election card.

Vote Casting Phase. To cast a vote, the voter provides their choice m to the voting client, which generates a ballot $\alpha = (\hat{x}, b, pk)$. Here, $\hat{x}$ is the voter's public credential derived from their private credential x, and $b = (b_1, b_2) = \mathsf{Enc}(pk, m; r) = (g^r, m \cdot pk^r)$ is an Oblivious Transfer (OT) query constructed using ElGamal encryption. The ballot also includes a non-interactive zero knowledge proof (NIZKP). The authorities, acting as OT senders, respond to this query, enabling the voting client to derive verification codes for the chosen candidate. Additionally, the ballot contains a Schnorr-like identification proof linking the public credential $\hat{x}$ and the encrypted vote. Let H be a secure hash function, and let $\hat{g}$ be the generator of $\mathbb{Z}_{\hat{p}}$, where $\hat{q} \mid \hat{p} - 1$, the NIZKP, consisting of three combined proofs, is generated as follows:

- pick $w_1 \xleftarrow{\$} \mathbb{Z}_{\hat{q}}$, $w_2 \xleftarrow{\$} \mathbb{Z}_p$, $w_3 \xleftarrow{\$} \mathbb{Z}_q$
- compute $t_1 = \hat{g}^{w_1} \bmod \hat{p}$, $\quad t_2 = w_2 \cdot pk^{w_3} \bmod p$, $\quad t_3 = g^{w_3} \bmod p$
- compute $s = H(\alpha, t_1, t_2, t_3)$
- compute $r_{v_1} = w_1 - s \cdot x \bmod \hat{q}$, $\quad r_{v_2} = w_2 \cdot m^{-s}$, $\quad r_{v_3} = w_3 - s \cdot r \bmod q$
- return $\pi = (r_v, s) = ((r_{v_1}, r_{v_2}, r_{v_3}), s)$

To verify the proofs, one computes $t'_1 = \hat{x}^s \cdot \hat{g}^{r_{v_1}}$, $t'_2 = b_2^s \cdot r_{v_2} \cdot pk^{r_{v_3}}$, and $t'_3 = b_1^s \cdot g^{r_{v_3}}$, and then checks if $s = H(\alpha, t'_1, t'_2, t'_3)$.

Tally Phase. After the election, authorities anonymize the ballots via a verifiable mixnet and collectively decrypt them using private key shares. The administrator finalizes the decryption and publishes the results, which independent verifiers validate for correctness and integrity. Several data sets, including encrypted votes and their proofs, are published for auditing purposes, as detailed in Table 7.2 of [19].

2.3 Ballot Freedom in CHVote

CHVote achieves ballot freedom thanks to an anamorphic construction that combines ElGamal and the Schnorr-like identification proof as follows.

Construction 1 (Combining ElGamal ans Schnorr). The voter chooses a random $w_1 \xleftarrow{\$} \mathbb{Z}_{\hat{q}}$ and then computes the ElGamal randomness as $r := \hat{H}(dpk^{w_1} \cdot g^{dm})$, where $\hat{H}$ is a hash function that maps group elements into the randomness space, $dpk = \hat{g}^{dsk}$ is the auditor double public key, and dm is the double (short) message or private vote chosen by the voter. Then, the voter computes the NIZKP and the ElGamal ciphertext $ct := \mathsf{Enc}(pk, m; r)$ accordingly to the CHVote protocol specifications outlined above.

Given the public available proof $\pi = ((r_{v_1}, r_{v_2}, r_{v_3}), s)$ and ballot $b = (b_1, b_2) = (g^r, m \cdot pk^r)$, the auditor can retrieve the double message dm using the procedure $\mathsf{dDecS}(dsk, (b, (r_{v_1}, s), \hat{x}))$ as detailed in Algorithm 1. This works because $b_1 = g^t = g^{\hat{H}(t_1^{dsk} \cdot g^{dm})} = g^{\hat{H}(\hat{g}^{w_1 \cdot dsk} \cdot g^{dm})} = g^{\hat{H}(dpk^{w_1} \cdot g^{dm})} = g^r$. Note that the authority knows all keys, including dpk, except dsk. The construction establishes a level of robustness, ensuring that the auditor, and only the auditor, can retrieve and understand if the encrypted message contains or not a double message.

This particular construction requires that the voter private credential x is not known to the authority. If so, given the ballot signature (r_v, s) the authority can compute $w_1 := s \cdot x + r_{v_1}$ and check whether $b_1 = g^{\hat{H}(dpk^{w_1} \cdot g^{dm})}$. To avoid this, the voter can instead link the randomness in the ElGamal encryption to the proof of knowledge of that very randomness, namely, r_{v_3}. The voter chooses a random $w_3 \xleftarrow{\$} \mathbb{Z}_q$ and computes $r = \hat{H}(dpk^{w_3} \cdot g^{dm})$. The proof $\pi = ((r_{v_1}, r_{v_2}, r_{v_3}), s)$ is generated as before, and the auditor retrieves the double message dm using $\mathsf{dDecS}(dsk, (b, (\mathbf{r_{v_3}}, s), \mathbf{b_1}))$.

Algorithm 1. $\mathsf{dDecS}(dsk, (b, (r_{v_1}, s), \hat{x}))$ // (Schnorr)

1: $b := \{b_1, b_2\}$
2: $t_1 := \hat{x}^s \cdot \hat{g}^{r_{v_1}}$
3: **for** $i \in \mathbb{M}$ **do**
4:     $t := \hat{H}(t_1^{dsk} \cdot g^i)$
5:     **if** $b_1 = g^t$ **then**
6:         **return** i
7:     **end if**
8: **end for**
9: **return** $\perp$

---

3 More Anamorphic Constructions

We provide a few more generic anamorphic constructions that can be used to achieve ballot freedom in other voting schemes.

Common to all the constructions are the forced message $fm \in \mathbb{M}$, the attacker key pair $(fpk, fsk) \leftarrow \mathsf{EKeyGen}()$, the receiver double key pair $(dpk, dsk) \leftarrow \mathsf{EKeyGen}()$, the double message $dm \in \mathbb{M}$, and a hash function $\hat{H}$ that maps group elements into the randomness space. $\mathsf{EKeyGen}()$ is the ElGamal key generation function that outputs a pair of keys $(sk, pk = g^{sk})$ where $sk \xleftarrow{\$} \mathbb{Z}_p$.

Algorithm 2. dDec($dsk, (ct_1, ct_2)$) (ElGamal)

1: $ct_1 := (c_{11}, c_{12})$
2: $ct_2 := (c_{21}, c_{22})$
3: $t := c_{11}^{dsk}$
4: **for** $i \in \mathbb{M}$ **do**
5: $\quad k := \hat{H}(t \cdot g^i)$
6: $\quad$ **if** $c_{21} = g^k$ **then**
7: $\quad\quad$ **return** i
8: $\quad$ **end if**
9: **end for**
10: **return** $\bot$

Algorithm 3. fRandom(dpk, dm) // (ℓ-bit message)

1: $dm := \mathsf{b}_1 \| \mathsf{b}_2 \| \cdots \| \mathsf{b}_\ell \in \{0,1\}^\ell$
2: **for** $i \in [\ell + 1]$ **do**
3: $\quad$ **if** $i = 1$ **then**
4: $\quad\quad r_i \xleftarrow{\$} \mathbb{Z}_q$
5: $\quad$ **else**
6: $\quad\quad r_i := \hat{H}(dpk^{r_{i-1}} \cdot g^{b_{i-1}})$
7: $\quad$ **end if**
8: **end for**
9: $R \leftarrow \{r_i\}_{i \in [\ell+1]}$
10: **return** R

Also here the attacker knows all keys except dsk and all constructions establish robustness, ensuring that decrypting anamorphic ciphertexts with the correct double key results in a valid message, otherwise an explicit abort signal is returned.

Construction 2 (Combining Two ElGamal Ciphertexts). The sender chooses a random $r_1 \xleftarrow{\$} \mathbb{Z}_q$ and computes $ct_1 = \mathsf{Enc}(fpk, fm; r_1)$. Given another forced message $fm' \in \mathbb{M}$, the sender computes $r_2 \leftarrow \hat{H}(g^{dm} \cdot dpk^{r_1})$ and ciphertext $ct_2 = \mathsf{Enc}(fpk, fm'; r_2)$, and sends (ct_1, ct_2). The receiver retrieves dm using the decryption function outlined in Algorithm 2. This works because $c_{21} = g^k = g^{\hat{H}(g^{dm} \cdot c_{11}^{dsk})} = g^{\hat{H}(g^{dm} \cdot dpk^{r_1})} = g^{r_2}$. Note that if $dm \in \mathbb{M} \setminus \{0\}$, r_2 can be computed as $r_2 \leftarrow \hat{H}(dm \cdot dpk^{r_1})$ and the receiver can avoid the exponentiations in step 5 in Algorithm 2.

Since the receiver must compute modular exponentiations to retrieve the message, the double message space is expected to be small, which is generally acceptable in voting, as the message space for the candidates is typically small.

Construction 3 (Combining $\ell+1$ ElGamal Ciphertexts). Alternatively, the sender can anamorphically send an l-bit long double message dm by casting $\ell+1$ ciphertexts. The sender selects the set of randomness $R := \{r_i\}_{i \in [1, \ell+1]}$ using the fake randomness generator as described in Algorithm 3, which is a simplified version of the sender-anamorphic extension for hybrid PKE with special KEM from [29]. Differently from [29], our fake randomness generator does not require key encapsulation. Algorithm 3 takes in dpk and dm, and outputs R to be used

Algorithm 4. dDecB(dsk, CT) // ℓ-bit message)
1: CT := $\{(c_{i1}, c_{i2})\}_{i \in [1, \ell+1]}$
2: **for** $i \in [2, \ell+1]$ **do**
3: $\quad b_i := \{c_{i1}, c_{i2}\}$
4: $\quad t_i^0 := \hat{H}(c_{1i-1}^{dsk})$
5: $\quad t_i^1 := \hat{H}(c_{1i-1}^{dsk} \cdot g)$
6: $\quad$ **if** $c_{1i} = g^{t_i^0}$ **then**
7: $\quad\quad b'_{i-1} := 0$
8: $\quad$ **else if** $c_{1i} = g^{t_i^1}$ **then**
9: $\quad\quad b'_{i-1} := 1$
10: $\quad$ **else**
11: $\quad\quad$ **return** $\perp$
12: $\quad$ **end if**
13: **end for**
14: **return** $b'_1 \| b'_2 \| \cdots \| b'_\ell$

in the ElGamal encryptions. In fact, it creates a link between the randomness used in the encryptions. This is only noticeable by the receiver owning the double secret key dsk. The receiver can decrypt dm using Algorithm 4.

Construction 4 (combining ElGamal and DSA). The last construction consider the DSA signature scheme, which we briefly discuss as follows.

DSA Signature. The DSA signature consists of three algorithms as:

- DKeyGen(1^λ): on input of a security parameter 1^λ, outputs a pair of keys ($vsk, vpk = g^{vsk}$) where $vsk \xleftarrow{\$} \mathbb{Z}_q$, with (p, q, g) satisfying $q \mid (p-1)$ and g being a generator of the subgroup of order q in $\mathbb{Z}_p^*$.
- DSign($vsk, m; w$): which, given a signing key vsk, a message $m \in \mathbb{M}$, and randomness $w \xleftarrow{\$} \mathbb{Z}_q$, and a hash function H, outputs a signature (r_v, s) where $r_v = (g^w \mod p) \mod q$, and $s = w^{-1}(H(m) + vsk \cdot r_v) \mod q$.
- DVerify($vpk, m, \sigma = (r_v, s)$): given a verification key vpk, a message m, and a signature σ, outputs $\top$ (valid) if $r, s \in \mathbb{Z}_q \setminus \{0\}$, $v = H(m)s^{-1} \mod q$, $u_1 = g^v \mod p$, $u_2 = vpk^{(r_v \mod q)} \mod p$, and $(u_1 \cdot u_2 \mod p) \mod q = r_v$. Otherwise, it outputs $\perp$.

The sender chooses a random $r \xleftarrow{\$} \mathbb{Z}_q$ and computes $ct := \mathsf{Enc}(fpk, fm; r)$. Given a (forced) message sm, the sender computes $w := \hat{H}(g^{dm} \cdot dpk^r)$, generates a DSA signature $(r_v, s) := \mathsf{DSign}(vsk, sm; w)$ and sends $(ct, (r_v, s))$. The receiver retrieves dm using the decryption function outlined in Algorithm 5. This works because $r_v = g^t = g^{\hat{H}(g^{dm} \cdot c_1^{dsk})} = g^{\hat{H}(g^{dm} \cdot dpk^r)} = g^w$.

All the constructions above are very efficient. For Construction 1, 2, and 4, the sender (voting device) just needs an extra exponentiation to send an anamorphic ciphertext. All the burden is on the receiver (auditor), who needs to perform a linear number of exponentiations in the size of the double message. Therefore, the double message space for this constructions is expected to be

Algorithm 5. dDecDSA$(dsk, ct, (r_v, s))$ (DSA)

1: $ct := \{c_1, c_2\}$
2: **for** $i \in \mathbb{M}$ **do**
3: $\quad t := \hat{H}(c_1^{dsk} \cdot g^i)$
4: $\quad$ **if** $r_v = g^t$ **then**
5: $\quad\quad$ **return** i
6: $\quad$ **end if**
7: **end for**
8: **return** $\bot$

---

small, like a vote preference. For Construction 3, the sender needs to perform $2 \times \ell$ extra exponentiations per bit-message. For example, to send a 32-bit long double message, the sender needs to perform only 64 extra exponentiations. However, it is different if we consider the burden on the voter rather than the voting device. In this case, it mainly depends on the specificities of the voting system, its implementation, and its user interface.

4 The Estonian Internet Voting System

The Estonian Internet Voting System, IVXV [22], allows voters to cast their vote online. To sign and encrypt a ballot, it uses a digital signature scheme and a homomorphic public-key encryption scheme, which is instantiated with ElGamal. Proof of shuffle and proof of correct decryption are also employed.

4.1 Protocol Description

IVXV is based essentially on the following participants: the election organizer, the registration service, the voter, the vote collector, the ballot box processor (IBBP), the mixing service, and the data auditor. The protocol can be divided into five distinct stages: initialization, voting, post-voting, tallying, and auditing.

Initialization. Before voting begins, the election organizer sets up and configures the IVXV system. In particular, this process includes generating cryptographic keys that will later be used to encrypt and decrypt votes as follows. On input of the security parameter 1^λ, electoral roll $\mathbb{V}$, and candidate list $\mathbb{C}$, the election organizer computes $(pkE_T, skE_T) \xleftarrow{\$} \mathsf{EKeyGen}(1^\lambda)$. Moreover, each voter v has access to their signing key pair spk_v, ssk_v, which were generated by governmental service by computing $(spk_v, ssk_v) \xleftarrow{\$} \mathsf{DKeyGen}(1^\lambda)$. In the IVXV implementation, the signature scheme is RSA-SHA256 (for authentication with ID card or digital ID) or ECDSA-SHA256 (for authentication with mobile ID). Here, we consider only the latter.

Voting. An eligible voter $v \in \mathbb{V}$ encrypts their choice $c_v \in \mathbb{C}$ using the election's public encryption key pkE_T and a randomly generated value r_v resulting in ballot $b = \mathsf{Enc}(pkE_T, c_v, r_v)$. The voter then signs the ballot b using their private signing key ssk_v and a random value rs_v. This creates $vote_v = \mathsf{Sign}(ssk_v, b, rs_v)$. The voter submits their identifier v, a certificate proving their voting eligibility, and $vote_v$ to the vote collector (VC).

Upon receipt, VC processes the submission and responds with a unique identifier vid, used for (individual) verification of the vote. Note that a voter can cast multiple votes. The set D_{VC} contains all cast votes during this phase, stored without removal.

Post-voting. After the voting phase concludes, IBBP checks the eligibility of each vote and cross-references the registration confirmations, which are stored in D_{RS}, with the data from D_{VC} to ensure consistency. Once this verification is complete, the IBBP compiles a new list of ballots, retaining only the most recent valid vote for each voter and removing those who also cast paper ballots. Then, the IBBP anonymizes the ballots by stripping any voter-identifying information (e.g. signatures) producing B_1. Optionally, the set B_1 can be mixed, producing an output set B_2 along with a proof of correct operation P_{mix} ensuring secure shuffling and re-encryption.

Tallying. The election organizer decrypts each choice c' and computes the voting result. Additionally, it provides a proof of correct decryption P_{dec} along with the plaintext.

Auditing. Different levels of auditing can be performed. Universal verifiability can be achieved by a *complete* audit, in which the auditor has access to all data sets D_{VC}, D_{RS}, B_1, B_2, P_{mix}, P_{dec}. As outlined in [22], a complete audit might leak a lot of information, such as whether a voter re-voted. This increases the risk of coercion, though the dictator already breaks ballot privacy, possibly allowing a complete audit. As an alternative, the auditor can perform a *partial* audit, in which only the data sets B_1, B_2, P_{mix}, P_{dec} are available.

4.2 Ballot Freedom in IVXV

We now explore how ballot freedom can be achieved in the IVXV system across three different scenarios as follows.

Case 1: Complete Audit with Revoting. In this scenario, the auditor has access to all data sets, including D_{VC} containing encrypted votes and their signatures. Revoting allows the voter to cast multiple votes, which the auditor can detect. Ballot freedom can be achieved using the constructions that combine ElGamal ciphertexts outlined in Sect. 3. According to Construction 2, the voter casts two ballots to communicate a message within a small message space. According to Construction 3, the voter casts $\ell + 1$ ballots to communicate an ℓ-bit-long double message. The auditor can identify all ballots cast by the same voter by examining the signatures.

Case 2: Complete Audit without Revoting. In this scenario, the voter casts only one vote. If the auditor has access to D_{VC}, the voter can link the randomness in the encryption and the randomness in the DSA signature using Construction

4. Interestingly, the IVXV architecture document suggests that the P-384 curve can be used for ElGamal encryption, which is the same curve commonly used in ECDSA. Therefore, they likely share the same parameters, including order and generator. Even if the parameters differ, the hash function in Construction 4 can maps elements between the groups. A practical challenge arises if the signature service is provided by an app that might not allow the voter to choose the randomness. Therefore, the voter would need to a modified version of the app that supports customized randomness input.

Case 3: Partial Audit. In this scenario, the auditor has access to anonymized ballots in B_1, therefore the previous approaches cannot straightforwardly signal the voter's real intention. However, if voters reveal their randomness to other voters, they could still signal their true vote intentions by using Construction 2 or Construction 3. The latter construction is more challenging because voters must reveal their randomness in sequence to form a link between them. In both cases, the decryption algorithms dDec and dDecB require the auditor to check all other ballots in B_1 for randomness links. Despite these challenges, ballot freedom remains feasible even in the partial audit scenario.

5 Helios

Helios [1] builds on Benaloh's Simple Verifiable Voting [4], separating ballot preparation and casting. Ballots can be prepared and viewed without authentication, while authentication is required only for casting, ensuring auditability by allowing anyone to verify the system's integrity. In this paper, we focus on Helios 2.0 [2], which, compared to the first protocol, replaces mixnet-based tallying with homomorphic tallying. In addition, voters now provide a NIZKP to demonstrate the validity of their encrypted votes without revealing their content.

The election process in Helios 2.0 is as follows, where the cryptographic descriptions are taken from [12]:

Ballot Casting. The voter selects their choice $m \in \{min, \ldots, max\}$ and forms the vote as $v = g^m$. Then, the voter encrypts v under the trustees' public key pk using ElGamal encryption yielding $ct = (c_1, c_2) = \text{Enc}(pk, v; r) = (g^r, g^m \cdot pk^r)$, and generates a NIZKP showing that ct is a valid encryption for a message m. The proof is generated as follows.

- For all invalid plaintexts $i \in \{m_{min}, \ldots, m_{m-1}, m_{m+1}, \ldots, m_{max}\}$: randomly generate a challenge $s_i \in \mathbb{Z}_q^*$ and a response $r_i \in \mathbb{Z}_q^*$. Compute the witnesses $c_{1i} = g^{r_i}/c_1^{s_i}$ and $c_{2i} = pk^{r_i}(c_2/g^i)^{s_i}$.
- For the valid plaintext m: select a random nonce $w \in \mathbb{Z}_q^*$. Compute the witnesses $c_{1m} = g^w$ and $c_{2m} = pk^w$. Derive the challenge s_m using the hash function H:

$$s_m = H(c_{1m_{min}}, c_{2m_{min}}, \ldots, c_{1m_{max}}, c_{2m_{max}}) - \sum_{i \neq m} c_i \mod q.$$

Compute the response $r_m = w + r \cdot s_m$. The proof for the vote is $\pi = (r_m, s_m)$

Before casting, the voter has the option to audit the ballot to confirm it accurately represents their intended vote. During this process, the randomness used in creating the ballot is revealed, allowing independent verification of its correctness.

Once satisfied, the voter submits their ballot to the election authority. The election authority authenticates the voter, verifies their eligibility, and checks the validity of the NIZKP. A valid ballot is published on the bulletin board along with the voter's identity.

After submission, the voter can verify that their ballot appears on the bulletin board. Observers can confirm that the proofs attached to each ballot are valid, ensuring all published ballots represent legitimate votes.

Tallying. After the voting period ends, the election authority homomorphically combines all the encrypted ballots to produce an encrypted tally. The encrypted tally is published on the bulletin board.

Each trustee publishes a partial decryption of the encrypted tally. Alongside the partial decryption, trustees include a signature of knowledge to prove its correctness. These proofs are publicly available for verification. The election authority decrypts the final tally and publishes the election result.

5.1 Ballot Freedom in Helios

Case 1: Audit with Revoting. In Helios, the voter can cast multiple ballots, all of which are published on a public bulletin board. Once they authenticate a ballot, that ballot is displayed on the bulletin board as their final choice, while all previously cast ballots are archived. Since the bulletin board data is auditable by anyone at any time, the voter can achieve ballot freedom by using any constructions that combine ElGamal ciphertexts. In Construction 2, the voter casts two ballots, whereas in Construction 3, the voter casts $\ell + 1$ ballots. Note that the voter must be able to freely select the randomness r in the encryption $\mathsf{Enc}(pk, v; r)$.

Case 2: Audit without Revoting. The voter can also use Construction 1 by using the ElGamal ciphertext and its corresponding proof. The voter selects $w \in \mathbb{Z}_q^*$ and computes the ElGamal randomness as $r = \hat{H}(dpk^r \cdot g^{dm})$. The voter generates the proof $\pi = (r_m, s_m)$, and when the auditor retrieves $ct = (c_1, c_2)$ and its corresponding proof π from the bulletin board, they can decrypt the double message dm using $\mathsf{dDecS}(dsk, (ct, (r_m, s_m)), c_1)$.

6 Belenios

Belenios [10] is an electronic voting system built upon Helios [1] that offers vote privacy and verifiability. Similar to Helios, it uses ElGamal and there is a public bulletin board that contains the accepted ballots and the result of the voting. Schnorr signatures are used to sign an encrypted ballot to avoid ballot stuffing.

6.1 Protocol Description

Due to space limitations, we refer the reader to the original paper [10] for a detailed description of the protocol. Here we provide a brief overview of the protocol that is instrumental to assess ballot freedom. We briefly recall the Schnorr signature scheme as follows.

Schnorr Signature. The Schnorr signature consists of three algorithms as:

- SKeyGen(1^λ): on input of a security parameter 1^λ, outputs a pair of keys ($vsk, vpk = g^{vsk}$) where $vsk \xleftarrow{\$} \mathbb{Z}_q$, with (p, q, g) satisfying $q \mid (p-1)$ and g being a generator of the subgroup of order q in $\mathbb{Z}_p^*$.
- SSign($vsk, m; w$): given a signing key vsk, a message $m \in \mathbb{M}$, and randomness $w \xleftarrow{\$} \mathbb{Z}_q$, and a hash function H, outputs a signature (r_v, s) where $s = H(m|g^w) \mod q$ and $r_v = w - vsk \cdot s \mod q$
- SVerify($vpk, m, \sigma = (r_v, s)$): given a verification key vpk, a message m, and a signature σ, outputs $\top$ if $s = H(m|A)$ where $A = vpk^s g^{r_v}$. Otherwise, it outputs $\bot$. Note that a variant of the Schnorr signature can be used to prove the knowledge of a discrete logarithm. For example, to prove knowledge of the randomness r used to generate an ElGamal ciphertext $ct = (c_1, c_2) = (g^r, m \cdot pk^r)$, set $vsk = r$ and $vpk = c_1$.

For each voter id, a unique signing key $sk_{id} \in \mathbb{Z}_q$ is generated. Then, the voter V encrypts the vote preference v as $ct = \text{Enc}(pk, v; r)$ and generate a signature $s = \text{SSign}(vsk, ct; w)$, where vsk is their signing key. The voter computes a hash $h = \text{hash}(b)$ to serve as a tracking number. The server appends b to the election data D. At any point, V can verify that h is included in the list of *pretty ballots* (P_B), which consists of the hashes of the final ballots submitted by voters. If the election includes non-homomorphic ciphertexts, the trustees shuffle the ballots. The server homomorphically combines the ciphertexts and sends the result to the trustees to compute the final election outcome.

An auditor can perform verifications during the voting phase and after the tally. During the voting phase, an auditor can retrieve the public board to verify its consistency. They check that for each ballot b, the proofs and signature of b are valid. After the tally, the auditor retrieves the public data D, including the list of ballots (B), shuffles (Σ), partial decryptions (Δ), and the result (res). They verify the consistency of B, ensure it matches previously monitored data, compute $\hat{B} = \text{last}(B)$ (the list of only the latest ballots for each voter), and confirm that the proofs in Σ, Δ, and the result res are valid with respect to $\hat{B}$.

6.2 Ballot Freedom in Belenios

In Belenios, the revoting policy allows voters to cast multiple ballots, with only the last ballot being considered for the tally. If all ballots are publicly available for auditing during the voting phase, a voter can use Construction 2 or Construction 3 as introduced in Sect. 3 to achieve ballot freedom.

If only the last ballots cast by each voter are available to the auditor, the voter can use Construction 1 to achieve ballot freedom. In doing so, the voter links the randomness in the ElGamal encryption to the Schnorr signature of the ballot. Similar to the case of ballot freedom in CHVote, this construction requires that the voter signing key sk_{id} is unknown to a dishonest authority. If the authority knows the key, given the ballot signature (r_v, s), it can compute $w := s \cdot sk_{id} + r_v$ and check whether the first element of the ElGamal encryption of the vote $ct := (c_1, c_2)$ is $c_1 = g^{\hat{H}(dpk^w \cdot g^{dm})}$. In this case, the voter can instead link the randomness in the ElGamal encryption to the proof of knowledge of that very randomness. The proof is generated as per the Schnorr signature by substituting sk_{id} with the ElGamal randomness r and vpk with c_1.

7 Related Work

Dishonest authorities can compromise the security of voting systems in various ways. Bernhard et al. [7] showed that weak Fiat-Shamir heuristics lead to security breaches in Helios when malicious trustees are present. Similarly, Cortier et al. [11] demonstrated that an attacker who corrupts both the voting server and trustees can break verifiability in Belenios if a variant of Fiat-Shamir heuristic is used. Haines et al. [20] showed that having honest trustees is sometimes insufficient to guarantee ballot privacy. Moreover, ensuring trustworthy trustees is not a trivial task. Benaloh et al. [5] examined the practical challenges that trustees face in preserving the privacy of votes.

There is a long stream of research on covert and subliminal channels in voting [3,16,23] but they all focus on the maliciousness of the channel rather than the ability of the voter to communicate their true intention.

Coercion, in general, requires that trust assumptions be carefully vetted. Finogina et al. [17] demonstrated that in coercion-resistant voting, a coercer can utilize new cryptographic tools to prevent voters from evading coercion. Tally-hiding [13,24] and cleansing-hiding [14] voting schemes typically rely on MPC to mitigate coercion even in the presence of dishonest trustees. All the schemes outlined above assume at least one honest trustee and/or a private or anonymous channel. Budurushi et al. [8] proposed a voting scheme in which the attacker controls all channels but not all tally servers. Similarly, Caveat coercitor [18] does not require a private channel but assumes the existence of at least one honest trustee. Solutions involving DRE machines without tallying servers have been proposed [21,27]. These schemes assume a private voting booth and that the machines do not reveal the voter's choice. The novel aspect of our work is to demonstrate that a voter can still achieve privacy in communicating with an auditor using an existing voting scheme, even when the attacker controls all communication channels and election keys.

8 Discussion and Future Work

In this work, we introduced the concept of anamorphic voting, which studies whether a combination of cryptographic primitives in a voting scheme can be used to send covert messages in the presence of dishonest authorities. We demonstrated that IVXV, CHVote, Belenios, and Helios each enable voters to freely communicate their true voting intention to an auditor without the knowledge of dishonest authorities, a property we refer to as ballot freedom.

Anamorphic voting is in its infancy, and several future research directions can be explored. One is to investigate ballot freedom in voting schemes recently implemented in real-world elections, such as ElectionGuard [6], or in schemes that rely on cryptographic primitives not covered in this work, such as commitment schemes and lattice-based cryptography. Another direction involves formalizing the concept of ballot freedom to enable proofs of whether a given voting scheme achieves of fails to achieve ballot freedom. Formalization can also help clarify the relationship between ballot freedom and other security properties, such as receipt-freeness. Intuitively, ballot freedom appears to be orthogonal to receipt-freeness: if a voting scheme supports anamorphic voting, a coerced voter could reveal their ballot to the coercer (auditor) as proof! However, our constructions might provide a form of coercion evidence such as in [18] but in a cleaner way.

Our constructions can be viewed as a form of strong anamorphic encryption instantiated across multiple cryptosystems. Exploring this independently of voting is worthwhile, as it may also prove useful for other secure applications.

Acknowledgment. Rakeei and Lenzini's research is supported by the ANR and FNR international project INTER/AN/20/14926102 - "Secure and Verifiable Electronic Testing and Assessment Systems" (SEVERITAS).

References

1. Adida, B.: Helios: web-based open-audit voting. In: USENIX Security Symposium (2008)
2. Adida, B., De Marneffe, O., Pereira, O., Quisquater, J.J., et al.: Electing a university president using open-audit voting: analysis of real-world use of Helios. EVT/WOTE 9(10), 10 (2009)
3. Adida, B., Neff, C.: Efficient receipt-free ballot casting resistant to covert channels. USENIX EVT/WOTE (2008)
4. Benaloh, J.: Simple verifiable elections. EVT 6, 5–5 (2006)
5. Benaloh, J., Naehrig, M., Pereira, O.: Reactive: rethinking effective approaches concerning trustees in verifiable elections. Cryptology ePrint Archive (2024)
6. Benaloh, J., Naehrig, M., Pereira, O., Wallach, D.S.: ElectionGuard: a cryptographic toolkit to enable verifiable elections. In: USENIX Security (2024)
7. Bernhard, D., Pereira, O., Warinschi, B.: How not to prove yourself: pitfalls of the Fiat-Shamir heuristic and applications to Helios. In: ASIACRYPT. Springer (2012)
8. Budurushi, J., Neumann, S., Olembo, M.M., Volkamer, M.: Pretty understandable democracy - a secure and understandable internet voting scheme. In: 2013 International Conference on Availability, Reliability and Security (2013)

9. Chevallier-Mames, B., Fouque, P.A., Pointcheval, D., Stern, J., Traoré, J.: On some incompatible properties of voting schemes. In: Towards Trustworthy Elections (2010)
10. Cortier, V., Galindo, D., Glondu, S., Izabachène, M.: Election verifiability for Helios under weaker trust assumptions. In: ESORICS, pp. 327–344. Springer (2014)
11. Cortier, V., Gaudry, P., Yang, Q.: How to fake zero-knowledge proofs, again. In: E-Vote-Id. Tal Tech Press (2020)
12. Cortier, V., Smyth, B.: Attacking and fixing Helios: an analysis of ballot secrecy. J. Comput. Secur. **21**(1), 89–148 (2013)
13. Cortier, V., Gaudry, P., Yang, Q.: A toolbox for verifiable tally-hiding e-voting systems. In:. ESORICS, pp. 631–652 (2022)
14. Cortier, V., Gaudry, P., Yang, Q.: Is the JCJ voting system really coercion-resistant? In: CSF, pp. 186–200 (2024)
15. Elgamal, T.: A public key cryptosystem and a signature scheme based on discrete logarithms. IEEE Trans. Inf. Theory **31**(4), 469–472 (1985). https://doi.org/10.1109/TIT.1985.1057074
16. Feldman, A.J., Benaloh, J.: On subliminal channels in encrypt-on-cast voting systems. EVT/WOTE **12**(40), 186 (2009)
17. Finogina, T., Herranz, J., Roenne, P.B.: Expanding the toolbox: coercion and vote-selling at vote-casting revisited. E-Vote-ID (2024)
18. Grewal, G.S., Ryan, M.D., Bursuc, S., Ryan, P.Y.: Caveat coercitor: coercion-evidence in electronic voting. In: 2013 IEEE Symposium on Security and Privacy (2013)
19. Haenni, R., Koenig, R.E., Locher, P., Dubuis, E.: Chvote protocol specification. Cryptology ePrint Archive (2017)
20. Haines, T., Mueller, J., Querejeta-Azurmendi, I.: Scalable coercion-resistant e-voting under weaker trust assumptions. In: SAC (2023)
21. Harrison, L., Bag, S., Hao, F.: Camel: E2E verifiable instant runoff voting without tallying authorities. In: Asia CCS, pp. 742–752 (2024)
22. Heiberg, S., Martens, T., Vinkel, P., Willemson, J.: Improving the verifiability of the Estonian internet voting scheme. In: E-Vote-ID (2016)
23. Karlof, C., Sastry, N., Wagner, D.: Cryptographic voting protocols: a systems perspective. In: USENIX Security Symposium (2005)
24. Liedtke, J., Küsters, R., Müller, J., Rausch, D., Vogt, A.: Ordinos: a verifiable tally-hiding electronic voting protocol. In: IEEE EuroS&P (2020)
25. Persiano, G., Phan, D.H., Yung, M.: Anamorphic encryption: private communication against a dictator. In: EUROCRYPT, pp. 34–63. Springer (2022)
26. Schnorr, C.P.: Efficient identification and signatures for smart cards, pp. 239–252. CRYPTO (1989)
27. Shahandashti, S., Hao, F.: DRE-ip: a verifiable e-voting scheme without tallying authorities. In: ESORICS, pp. 223–240 (2016)
28. The Economist Group: Democracy Index 2023 (2023). https://www.eiu.com/n/campaigns/democracy-index-2023
29. Wang, Y., Chen, R., Huang, X., Yung, M.: Sender-anamorphic encryption reformulated: achieving robust and generic constructions. In: ASIACRYPT (2023)

E2Easy: a Simple Lattice-Based in-Person End-to-End Voting Scheme

Eduardo L. Cominetti[1]([✉]), Marcos A. Simplicio[1], Diego F. Aranha[2], Paulo Matias[3], and Roberto Araújo[4]

[1] Escola Politécnica, São Paulo, Brazil
ecominetti@larc.usp.br
[2] Aarhus University, Aarhus, Denmark
[3] Universidade Federal de São Carlos, São Carlos, Brazil
[4] Universidade Federal do Pará, Belém, Brazil

Abstract. A voting system is responsible for collecting and recording voter intentions accurately to ensure the election outcome reflects the citizens' will. Unfortunately, mistrust in voting systems has increased in the last decade. Although most mistrust is caused by false claims, some doubts are legitimate, and questioning the correctness of an electronic voting procedure is fair. A solution to mitigate these doubts is the use of End-to-End (E2E) verifiable voting systems that produce proof, which is verifiable by each voter, that the intention of voters is correctly captured, recorded, and used to compute the election outcome. Our goal in this work is to create an in-person E2E verifiable voting system that is well-suited for scenarios where each voting machine produces its own verifiable tally and a central authority aggregates these results to produce the final election outcome. One example of this scenario is the Brazilian Election. In hardware similar to the Brazilian voting machine, our scheme can create and cast votes in milliseconds, causing a negligible overhead to voters in the machine's response time. Moreover, the most computationally heavy part of our protocol, the creation of Zero-Knowledge Proofs, requires approximately 6 min to be executed. However, this process is executed only once at the end of the voting period, and it does not require voters' participation.

Keywords: e-Voting · End-to-End Verifiability · Lattice cryptography

1 Introduction

In the election process, a voting system is responsible for collecting and recording voter intention, by accurately recording votes, tabulating them, and producing the correct tallying of the results. To reduce the election costs and speed up the tabulation of votes and tallying of results, electronic voting systems were created. Although the basic idea of a voting system is reasonably simple, a series of challenges need to be considered: the amount of data processed by the system; the large diversity of (lack of) technical knowledge the users of the system have; the requirement to guarantee that the system is suitably protected against external and internal actors; and the necessity for the system to be extremely accurate, even though it depends on fallible equipment. Moreover, it is important to emphasize that the peaceful transfer of power depends on public confidence in the election outcome. In recent years, this last observation has been a particularly complex challenge, as observed in recent demonstrations in the United States [3] and Brazil [9].

Two relevant public suspicions regarding electronic voting systems are (1) how they correctly collect the intentions of voters and accurately record them, and (2) how to guarantee that these votes are actually used for tabulation and tallying of the results. Providing a voter with the assurance that these procedures were properly executed presents a challenge due to ballot secrecy. Therefore, an electronic voting system has to ensure voters that their votes are correctly collected, recorded, and tallied without giving the voter any means to prove to a third party who they voted for. Among some methods proposed in the literature to tackle this issue, end-to-end verifiable voting systems (or E2E, for short) are prominent.

The main goal of E2E is to improve the system's integrity by giving voters the power to verify its various stages, such as vote casting, vote recording, and vote tallying. According to the U.S. Election Assistance Commission (EAC)[1], an E2E system allows individual voters to verify crucial elements of an election tally without requiring trust in voting software, hardware, employees chosen by the election authority, or even external observers.

To achieve this goal, an E2E-based system has to provide the properties of *cast as intended*, *recorded as cast*, and *tallied as recorded*. *Cast as intended* allows voters to verify that their votes were correctly interpreted by the voting system while in the polling place. *Recorded as cast* allows voters to verify that their votes were correctly recorded by the voting system and included in a public voting record. Finally, in *tallied as recorded*, the voting system provides a publicly verifiable tallying procedure from the public voting record. With these properties, voters can individually verify that their choices were correctly recorded by the system and subsequently used by the system to tally the election. Hence, an E2E provides assurances related to the *integrity* of an election and its systems.

The Brazilian Elections are a case of particular interest. Brazil began transitioning from paper voting to electronic voting in 1996 due to the large number of documented frauds in the process. In 2000, electronic voting was fully adopted, with 100% of voters using voting machines to cast their votes. However, the Brazilian uses a Direct-Recording Electronic machine, which does not ensure that votes are correctly cast, recorded, and tallied. Hence, the system relies on people believing in the electoral authority and in selected auditors that it was properly implemented. Although there is an interest from the electoral authority to improve the system, there are some requisites that a solution must have.

---

[1] https://www.eac.gov/voting-equipment/end-end-e2e-protocol-evaluation-process.

First, any solution has to be incremental to the system, without radical changes. This includes using the same hardware and maintaining the same procedure outside the voting machine, such as the global tally procedure that aggregates the partial results from each machine. Second, solutions have to support elections with a large number of candidates. It is not uncommon for some elections in Brazil to have more than 2000 candidates. Finally, it is a constitutional requirement to strongly protect vote secrecy, and the electoral authority requested that no (collusion of) entities in the system, not even the electoral authority, should be able to break vote secrecy. The only exception to this rule is the voting machine itself, as it is not possible to protect vote secrecy from it.

Contributions. We propose an in-person end-to-end verifiable voting system that fits the Brazilian Election model. Our system provides Tracking Codes that enable voters to: 1) check that their votes are correctly cast; and 2) verify that their votes are included in the already existing list of shuffled votes produced by the machine. Since it is already possible to check that the list of shuffled votes is used for the global election tally, this is enough to provide E2E verifiability. Moreover, our system uses lattice commitments to create the verification steps. As a result, only the machine that receives votes can link them to their commitments, and, since lattices offer post-quantum security, store-now-decrypt-later attacks via Tracking Codes are also mitigated. Also, our solution scales independently of the number of candidates in the election. Lastly, our system only adds a small time at the end of the process, which does not significantly change the global tally time of the election, which is important for our electoral authority.

This work is organized as follows. Section 2 presents the basic notation used throughout this paper and the main cryptographic algorithms used in our solution. Section 3 describes our solution and its principal aspects. Section 4 benchmarks our system on hardware similar to the current Brazilian voting machine, one of the target scenarios for our scheme. Section 5 concludes our work.

2 Notation and Cryptographic Blocks

Let $\mathbb{Z}$ be the set of integers. If Φ is a probability distribution, we write $a \xleftarrow{\$} \Phi$ to mean that a was sampled according to Φ. If $\mathcal{S}$ is a finite set, $b \xleftarrow{\$} \mathcal{S}$ means that b is sampled uniformly from set $\mathcal{S}$. We use bold lower-case letters like $\boldsymbol{x}$ to denote vectors, and bold upper-case letters like $\boldsymbol{A}$ to denote matrices.

2.1 Lattices

An integer lattice is a discrete set of points in $\mathbb{Z}^n$ closed under addition. If the matrix $\boldsymbol{B} = [\boldsymbol{b}_1, \ldots, \boldsymbol{b}_n] \in \mathbb{Z}^{n \times n}$ has full rank, the lattice $\mathcal{L}(\boldsymbol{B})$ is defined as:

$$\mathcal{L}(\boldsymbol{B}) = \left\{ \sum_{i=1}^{n} x_i \cdot \boldsymbol{b}_i \,:\, x_i \in \mathbb{Z} \right\} = \{ \boldsymbol{B}\boldsymbol{x} \,:\, \boldsymbol{x} \in \mathbb{Z}^n \}.$$

As $\mathcal{L}(\boldsymbol{B})$ is infinite, we use lattices defined in the ring of integers modulo q: $\mathcal{L}_q(\boldsymbol{B}) = \{\boldsymbol{Bx} \mod q : \boldsymbol{x} \in \mathbb{Z}_q^n\}$.

For this work, the relevant problems related to lattices are the Short Integer Solution (SIS) and the Learning With Errors (LWE). Let $\boldsymbol{A} \in \mathbb{Z}^{m \times n}$ be a random matrix. In SIS, the goal is to find a vector $\boldsymbol{z} \in \mathbb{Z}^n$ that is non-zero and whose coefficients are all lower or equal to $\beta, \beta < q$, such that $\boldsymbol{Az} = \boldsymbol{0} \in \mathbb{Z}_q^m$.

For the LWE problem, additionally let χ be an error distribution and $\boldsymbol{e} \xleftarrow{\$} \chi^m$, i.e., $e_i \xleftarrow{\$} \chi, \boldsymbol{e} = (e_1, \ldots, e_m)$. Let $\boldsymbol{s} \in \mathbb{Z}_q^n$ and $\boldsymbol{t} = \boldsymbol{As} + \boldsymbol{e} \mod q \in \mathbb{Z}_q^m$. Given $\boldsymbol{A}$, the goal in the (decision) LWE problem is to decide if a given vector $\boldsymbol{t'} \in \mathbb{Z}_q^m$ is generated as $\boldsymbol{t}$ or randomly.

These problems are considered computationally intractable by quantum computers if we choose adequate parameters. Indeed, the security of two NIST-standardized schemes for post-quantum schemes, ML-KEM and ML-DSA, relies on such mathematical problems[2].

In this work, we use a variant of these problems defined on Module Lattices. Additional information about lattices, module lattices, the SIS and LWE problem, and lattice-based algorithms can be found in [5,7,10].

2.2 The Rings R, R_q, and the Set of Elements S_β

Let q be a prime, $r \in \mathbb{N}^+$, and $N = 2^r$. We define the rings $R = \mathbb{Z}[X]/\langle X^N + 1 \rangle$, and $R_q = \mathbb{Z}_q[X]/\langle X^N + 1 \rangle$, i.e., the ring of polynomials modulo $X^N + 1$ with integer coefficients, and the same ring where all coefficients are reduced modulo q. We also define $\boldsymbol{I_k} \in R^{k \times k}$ to be an identity matrix of dimension k (over R).

For an element $f \in R$, so that $f = \sum_i f_i X^i$, we define the following norms:

$$\ell_1 : \|f\|_1 = \sum_i |f_i|, \quad \ell_2 : \|f\|_2 = \sqrt{\sum_i (f_i^2)}, \quad \ell_\infty : \|f\|_\infty = \max_{i:1..N} |f_i|.$$

For an element $g = \sum_i \overline{g}_i X^i \in R_q$, we associate each coefficient $\overline{g}_i$ with an element $g_i \in [-\frac{q-1}{2}, \frac{q-1}{2}]$, such that $\overline{g}_i = g_i \mod q$, and then compute the norms of g analogously, as if $g \in R$. Similarly, the above-defined norms also apply to any polynomial vector $\boldsymbol{a} \in R_q^k$, in which case those norms are computed simply by treating $\boldsymbol{a}$ as an $(N \cdot k)$-dimensional vector instead of an N-dimensional one.

Finally, for a small positive integer β, we denote by $S_\beta = \{x \in R_q : \|x\|_\infty \leq \beta\}$ the set of all elements in R with ℓ_∞-norm at most β.

2.3 BDLOP Commitment and ZKP of Linear Relation

BDLOP [2] is a commitment scheme based on structured lattice assumptions. The scheme can be instantiated to be statistically binding, statistically hiding, or computationally binding and hiding. The hiding property establishes that, given two different messages m_0 and m_1 and a commitment c to one of these

---
[2] https://csrc.nist.gov/Projects/Post-Quantum-Cryptography.

messages, an adversary $\mathcal{A}$ can only decide if c is the commitment of m_0 or m_1 with an advantage less than a selectable negligible value ϵ. Likewise, the binding property establishes that, given two different messages m_0, m_1, the probability that both these messages produce the same commitment c is less than ϵ.

The BDLOP commitment scheme comprises three algorithms:

- **KeyGen:** Creates public parameters to commit to messages $\boldsymbol{m} \in R_q^\ell$. This is accomplished by generating matrices $\boldsymbol{A_1} \in R_q^{n \times k}$ and $\boldsymbol{A_2} \in R_q^{\ell \times k}$:

$$\boldsymbol{A_1} = \begin{bmatrix} \boldsymbol{I_n} & \boldsymbol{A'_1} \end{bmatrix} \quad , \text{where } \boldsymbol{A'_1} \xleftarrow{\$} R_q^{n \times (k-n)}$$
$$\boldsymbol{A_2} = \begin{bmatrix} \boldsymbol{0}^{\ell \times n} & \boldsymbol{I_\ell} & \boldsymbol{A'_2} \end{bmatrix} , \text{where } \boldsymbol{A'_2} \xleftarrow{\$} R_q^{\ell \times (k-n-\ell)}$$

- **Commit:** Commit to message $\boldsymbol{m} \in R_q^\ell$ using the public parameters and a random polynomial vector $\boldsymbol{r} \xleftarrow{\$} S_\beta^k$:

$$\mathbf{Com}(\boldsymbol{m}; \boldsymbol{r}) := [\![\boldsymbol{m}]\!] = \begin{bmatrix} \boldsymbol{c_1} \\ \boldsymbol{c_2} \end{bmatrix} = \begin{bmatrix} \boldsymbol{A_1} \\ \boldsymbol{A_2} \end{bmatrix} \cdot \boldsymbol{r} + \begin{bmatrix} \boldsymbol{0}^n \\ \boldsymbol{m} \end{bmatrix}$$

The output is then the commitment $[\![\boldsymbol{m}]\!]$ together with $\boldsymbol{r}$.

- **Open:** Open commitment $[\![\boldsymbol{m}]\!]$ by revealing the 3-tuple $\boldsymbol{m} \in R_q^\ell, \boldsymbol{r} = \begin{bmatrix} r_1 \\ \dots \\ r_k \end{bmatrix} \in R_q^k$ and $f \in \overline{\mathcal{C}}$. The verifier can then verify the opening by checking that:

$$f \cdot \begin{bmatrix} \boldsymbol{c_1} \\ \boldsymbol{c_2} \end{bmatrix} = \begin{bmatrix} \boldsymbol{A_1} \\ \boldsymbol{A_2} \end{bmatrix} \cdot \boldsymbol{r} + f \cdot \begin{bmatrix} \boldsymbol{0}^n \\ \boldsymbol{m} \end{bmatrix}, \text{ and}$$
$$\|r_i\|_2 \leq 4\sigma\sqrt{N}, \text{ for all } 1 \leq i \leq k.$$

We note the presence of an extra polynomial $f \in \overline{\mathcal{C}}$ in the **Open** algorithm. In [2], the authors are unable to create efficient zero-knowledge proofs of knowledge for $\boldsymbol{r}$ and $\boldsymbol{m}$. However, they also declare that an honest committer can simply open the commitment by outputting $\boldsymbol{r}, \boldsymbol{m}$, and $f = 1$, without requiring a ZKP. In our voting system, the open protocol is used exactly to prove that the committer, the voting machine, is honest. Hence, in our scenario we use the setup of $f = 1$ because we are not required to prove knowledge of $\boldsymbol{r}$ and $\boldsymbol{m}$.

Zero-knowledge proofs for proving relations among committed values are also an integral part of BDLOP. In particular, we are interested in the ZKP of a Linear Relation, which is used in [1] to construct the ZKP of Correct Shuffle.

2.4 Zero-Knowledge Proofs of Correct Shuffle

The ZKP of Correct Shuffle presented in [1] is a public-coin $4+3\tau$-move protocol to prove the correct shuffle of τ messages by requiring the prover to solve a system of linear equations. The protocol uses the BDLOP commitment scheme and the ZKP of a Linear Relation introduced in Sect. 2.3. The main idea is to prove that the shuffled and the unshuffled messages can be used as roots of polynomials and that these polynomials evaluate to the same value in a certain point ρ. A description of this idea can be found in [1,8].

In summary, the Zero-Knowledge Proof of Correct Shuffle prove that there is a bijective relation between a group of plaintext messages and a group of commitments, without revealing the relation function.

3 E2Easy: a Lattice-Based E2E Verifiable Voting Scheme

E2Easy is a simplification of the scheme presented in [1], using a concept similar to a mixnet. In a mixnet E2E verifiable voting scheme, each vote is encrypted to be later shuffled by a mixnode and decrypted by one or more trustees. However, in E2Easy we simply store the plaintext vote and its commitment. After the election is over, we shuffle the plaintext votes and create a Zero-Knowledge Proof of Correct Shuffle. The Proof of Correct Shuffle proves that one of the stored commitments was created from one of the shuffled plaintext votes, without revealing which permutation was used. Thus, we establish a bijective relation between the commitment and the shuffled plaintext groups, but hide the relation.

3.1 Voting Scheme Overview

E2Easy is an E2E verifiable voting system for in-person voting, in which each machine produces its own tally and a central authority aggregates them. This model is used in the Brazilian elections. The voting machine executing the protocol is responsible for both creating votes and storing them. Hence, it does not require connection to any network and the resulting electoral data can be saved in local removable storage. Voter authentication, done externally to the voting machine, is outside the scope of our system.

The voting machine starts by creating an empty table for each contest to be held. Each table's entry stores a plaintext vote, its commitment, its opening, its Tracking Code, and its creation time. When the machine is enabled to create and cast a vote, voters input their choice for each contest. For each of these inputs, the voting machine creates a commitment and a Tracking Code of the vote and keeps the vote, the commitment, its opening, its Tracking Code, and its time in memory. After all votes are cast, the system provides the Tracking Codes for all contests to voters and starts the Benaloh Challenge. Here, voters can either: (1) cast the votes; or (2) challenge and discard the votes and all associated data. The system physically provides these Tracking Codes by printing them in a place visible by voters, but outside their reach until the end of the process. This prevents a (weak) coercion attack presented in Sect. 3.5.

If the vote is cast, the machine stores all the data in memory, using the proper tables. It also tags the previous Tracking Codes as "cast", signs them, and prints the signature to voters.

If a vote is challenged, the voting machine reveals the commitments' openings and the information required to compute the Tracking Codes by printing them.

Hence, voters can compute for themselves, using a device that they trust (e.g., their smartphones), the commitments and Tracking Codes, and then verify is they match those provided by the equipment. Because votes and commitments are discarded, voters have to reinitialize the voting process. As a result, new commitments, openings, and Tracking Codes are created for the new voting process. Because there are no relations between the old and new Tracking Codes, coercion attacks are mitigated. Figure 1 illustrates the voting procedure.

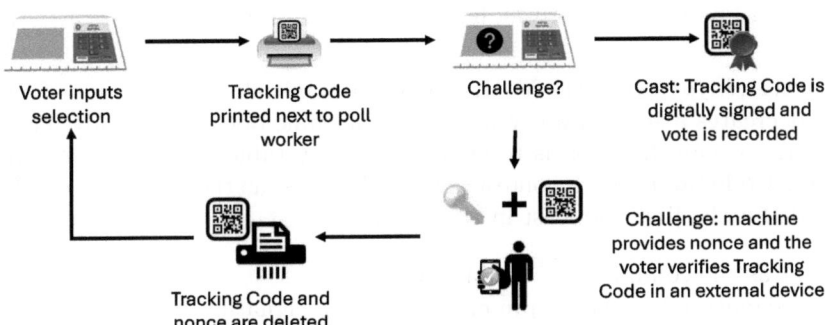

Fig. 1. Voting procedure from a voter's perspective.

Finally, at the end of the voting period, the machine receives a shutdown signal. When this happens, the equipment chooses a permutation function for each table, shuffles the votes, and computes the ZKP of Correct Shuffle. After that, the system outputs for each contest the commitments, their Tracking Codes, their associated time, the shuffled plaintext votes, and their ZKP data. All this data is digitally signed. The machine also deletes all the other contents previously stored in the contest tables, such as the commitments openings, the association between votes and commitments, and the permutation function used.

With the voting machine output data, any third party can (1) tally the plaintext votes, (2) prove that one of the commitments were created using one of the shuffled votes, and (3) check that there is an associated commitment to a Tracking Code. Moreover, any voters can check that their votes were used in the tally by checking all of the above and that their signed Tracking Codes were included in the output of the voting machine.

3.2 Detailed Description

The voting scheme is a tuple (**Setup, onStart, onVoterActive, onChallenge, onFinish, verifyVote, validateRDV, validateVoteOutput, validateZKPOutput**) of algorithms and protocols that are used by the Electoral Authority, voting equipment, voters, and election monitors.[3] Similar to

---

[3] The Brazilian voting system currently has a file named RDV that stores individually all the votes cast into the machine, after shuffling them. We simply reused the name.

the Brazilian election, we consider elections where a unique number ID represents each candidate. Additionally, multiple individual votes are created for a contest that allows more than a single choice to increase coercion protection. We also assume that the voters' identities are asserted by external means.

Setup(λ) - Electoral Authority: creates the commitment public key:

1. Create $A \leftarrow$ **KeyGen** from the BDLOP scheme.
2. Generate $infoContest$ for data related to the contests to be held in the election (e.g., number of contests, how many choices are allowed).

onStart(A, $InfoContest$) - Voting Machine: initializes the machine for operation. It creates a signature key pair if the machine does not already have one. However, its main function is to create an empty table of votes, and a unique Tracking Code tail for each contest. This tail is used as the previous vote Tracking Code for the first vote cast in the machine:

1. Set A as the commitment's public key.
2. If no signature key pair is present, generate a signature key pair.
3. Set Q as a configuration string, specifying used algorithms
4. Set $\overline{Q} = Hash(Q, A, PublicSignKey)$.
5. Create an empty table for each contest x.
   - Columns: **Commit**, **r**, **Vote**, **TrackingCode**, and **Time**.
   - For each table, set $H_{x,0} = Hash(\overline{Q}, x)$ as the tracking code tail.
6. Output Q and the public signature key.

onVoterActive($v_{x,i}$, contest x) - Voting Machine: receives a voter selection for each contest enabled in the election. It creates a random commit nonce and commits to this selection. Then, it creates the Tracking Code by hashing the previously cast Tracking Code, the current time, and the committed vote. It keeps all the data in memory and outputs the current time and Tracking Code:

1. For vote i in contest x:
   (a) Set T_i as the system's current time.
   (b) Create $r_{x,i} \xleftarrow{\$} S_\beta^k$.
   (c) Create $[\![v_{x,i}]\!] \leftarrow$ **Commit**$(v_{x,i}; r_{x,i})$.
   (d) Set $H_{x,i} = Hash(H_{x,i-1}, T_i, [\![v_{x,i}]\!])$ as the Tracking Code.
2. Output $H_{x,i}$, and T_i to the voter.
3. Keep $v_{x,i}$ and $r_{x,i}$ in memory.

onChallenge($Cast$) - Voting Machine: performs the Benaloh challenge. If the machine is challenged, it outputs the required material to verify the previously provided Tracking Code. It also deletes the data from the function **onVoterActive** that was kept in memory. If the vote is cast, it saves this data in the proper voting tables and digitally signs that Tracking Code:

- If $Cast = False$:
  1. Output $H_{x,i-1}$, $v_{x,i}$ and $r_{x,i}$ to the voter.
  2. Discard $H_{x,i}, T_i, [\![v_{x,i}]\!], v_{x,i}$, and $r_{x,i}$
- If $Cast = True$:
  1. Sign $H_{x,i}$ using sign key.
  2. Save $[\![v_{x,i}]\!], r_{x,i}, v_{x,i}, H_{x,i}$ and T_i in columns **Commit, r, Vote, TrackingCode** and **Time** of contest table x.
  3. Output the signature to the voter.

onFinish() Voting Machine: creates a Tracking Code head for each voting table, and is the last function the machine executes. Then, for each voting table, it shuffles the votes and creates a zero-knowledge proof of correct shuffle. It also creates three output files for each contest: RDV, a file that contains the shuffled votes; voteOuput, a file that contains the commitments, their Tracking Codes, creation times, and the Tracking Code head; and the ZKPOutput file, a file that contains the material produced by the zero-knowledge proof. All files are digitally signed. Finally, it deletes all voting tables, which deletes the commitments nonce and any association between a commitment and a plaintext vote:

1. For each contest table:
   (a) Set $\overline{H}_x = Hash(H_{x,last}, \text{``CLOSE''})$ as the tracking code head.
   (b) Choose permutation function π_x.
   (c) Shuffle votes in the table, creating $v'_{x,i}$.
   (d) Create ZKP of Correct Shuffle.
   (e) Create file RDV containing all $v'_{x,i}$.
   (f) Create file voteOutput containing all $[\![v_{x,i}]\!], H_{x,i}, T_i, \overline{H}_x$.
   (g) Create file ZKPOutput containing the ZKP of Correct Shuffle.
   (h) Sign all the files created.
2. Output RDV, voteOutput, ZKPOutput, and signatures.
3. Delete all contest tables.

verifyVote($H_{x,i}, H_{x,i-1}, T_i, v_{x,i}, r_{x,i}$) - Voter: uses the additional material provided by the Benaloh challenge with a target Tracking Code to check if this Tracking Code is correct:

1. Compute $[\![v_{x,i}]\!]' \leftarrow \textbf{Commit}(v_{x,i}; r_{x,i})$.
2. Compute $H'_{x,i} = Hash(H_{x,i-1}, T_i, [\![v_{x,i}]\!]')$.
3. Check the equality $H'_{x,i} = H_{x,i}$
4. Output *True* if equality holds, *False* otherwise.

validateRDV(RDV, signature of this file) Election Monitor: checks the digital signature of the RDV file:

1. Check the signature of the shuffled votes file.
2. Output *True* if signature is valid, *False* otherwise.

validateVoteOutput(voteOutput, signature of this file) Election Monitor: checks the voteOutput file. It validates the file's signature and then proceeds to check the Tracking Code hash chain using the Tracking Code tail, the commitments, their creation time, and the Tracking Code Head:

1. Check the signature of the voteOutput file.
2. Using $[\![v_{x,i}]\!], H_{x,0}$, and T_i, reconstruct the hash chain until $H'_{x,last}$ and then set $\overline{H}'_x = Hash(H'_{x,last}, \text{``CLOSE''})$.
3. Check if for every reconstructed $H'_{x,i}$ and file $H_{x,i}$, $H'_{x,i} = H_{x,i}$.
4. Check if $\overline{H}'_x = \overline{H}_x$.
5. Output *True* if all checks are valid, *False* otherwise.

ValidateZKPOutput(All Election Output) -Election Monitor: verifies the generated zero-knowledge proof. It first verifies the file signature and then proceeds to check the ZKP. This function should be used after executing both **validateRDV** and **validateVoteOutput**:

1. Check the signature of the ZKPOutput file.
2. Using all election public output, verify the ZKP of Correct Shuffle.
3. Output *True* if all checks are valid, *False* otherwise.

3.3 Election Integrity

To guarantee election integrity, it is necessary to ensure that voters' intentions are correctly recorded, the recorded votes are used during the tally, and that it is infeasible to undetectably change votes. For this, our scheme relies on the Benaloh challenge, and the security properties of the Tracking Code, the BDLOP commitment, and the Zero-Knowledge Proofs.

We use the Benaloh challenge to ensure correct vote casting. After voters input their choices, the voting machine prints the Tracking Codes and asks voters if they want to challenge or cast the votes. Because the machine does not know if votes will be cast or challenged, if it acts maliciously, there is a probability that it will be caught. Related work has shown that the Benaloh challenge is not ideal for a voter population that does not consist of security experts [6]. However, methods to mitigate these issues are outside the scope of this paper.

If voters choose to challenge the machine, it provides them with the nonce used to create the commitment. The nonce allows voters to verify that the Tracking Codes were created accordingly and that the voting machine used the correct vote in the computation. For this, voters simply repeat the steps to create a Tracking Code: they use their votes and the provided nonces as input to create a commitment, concatenate the results with the provided public data, and finally hash the result. Then, voters compare the newly computed and the previously provided Tracking Codes. If they match, the voting machine behaved honestly and used the provided vote. This statement is possible because it is infeasible for the machine to provide a nonce that generates the same commitment (and by extension, the same Tracking Codes) for different votes. To do this, the machine would have to break the hardness assumption associated with the BDLOP commitment or be able to find the second pre-image of the cryptographic hash used. It is important to note that, as voters are provided with all the required data for computing new Tracking Codes, as well as the original one, this procedure can be done on *any* device. Therefore, voters can use any hardware and software they trust, such as their smartphones running software provided by their candidates, or even their own code, to perform the verification. Hence, they are not required to trust in any equipment provided by the electoral authority or any other entity in regards to the *integrity* of the cast vote.

Because it is infeasible to find a second pre-image of a cryptographic hash, an attacker cannot change a vote commitment with a different commitment for a different vote without changing the signed Tracking Code hash chain. However, an attacker may try to create a commitment from a second vote that results in the same committed value. This attack is also invalid because of the binding property of the BDLOP commitment.

The binding property of a commitment states that the probability of producing two different messages that result in the same commitment is negligible. In the BDLOP commitment, the binding property relies on the hardness of solving the Module-SIS problem, a problem which is considered to be intractable by classical or quantum computers. Therefore, an attacker cannot create two equal commitments for different votes and this attack is mitigated.

Because of the soundness property of the ZKP of Correct Shuffle, an attacker cannot replace a plaintext vote with a different one and produce a correct proof. As stated previously, an attacker cannot change the vote commitments or alter the vote they are associated with, but they could replace plaintext votes in the output file. However, to replace a plaintext vote with a false one, the attacker has also to produce a valid zero-knowledge proof for the false statement. Since the soundness property of the zero-knowledge proof also relies on the hardness of solving the Module SIS problem, this is considered to be infeasible. Hence, an attacker cannot produce a valid proof for a false statement.

3.4 Vote Secrecy

Vote secrecy relies on the security proof of the commitment scheme, the ZKP, and on the trust that the voting machine is honest and error-free.

The Tracking Code of our proposal is considered to be public. Therefore, even if an attacker has access to the Tracking Code of voters, their secrecy has to be guaranteed. Because of the hiding property of the commitment, it is possible to guarantee that votes cannot be revealed by the Tracking Code.

According to the hiding property definition, given only the commitment c, created from a vote in A or B, it is infeasible to decide if c is a commitment to vote A or vote B. In the BDLOP commitment, the hiding property relies on the hardness of solving the Module LWE problem, which is also a problem considered to be intractable by classical or quantum computers. Thus, an attacker cannot break the hiding property and reveal the committed vote.

The Zero-Knowledge Proof of Correct Shuffle is used at the end of the voting process to prove to voters that votes represented by their commitments are used in the election tally. This proof, as the name zero-knowledge implies, is designed to prove the existence of a bijective relation between a group of commitments and a group of plaintext messages without providing any other knowledge.

The zero-knowledge property of the protocol is demonstrated in [1, Appendix A]. In summary, the zero-knowledge property of the proof relies on the hiding property of the BDLOP commitment. As previously discussed, breaking this property of the commitment is considered to be infeasible. Thus, the relation between the commitment and plaintext vote groups is concealed and voters cannot use the proof to break vote secrecy.

Finally, it is necessary to place (some) trust that voting machines are correctly executing their algorithms and protocols to guarantee vote secrecy. For instance, a voting machine can keep the contest tables in its internal memory, instead of deleting them at its shutdown phase. This would allow a technician to later collect this data and break vote secrecy for all the votes in this machine. We observe that this malicious behavior only attacks vote secrecy because vote integrity is guaranteed through cryptographic means. We also note that trust in the machine is also required in any electronic voting system since voting machines can always keep information that breaks secrecy. For instance, any voting machine can maliciously keep the order the votes were cast, and an observer can later associate this order with the vote precinct queue order.

3.5 Some Attacks and Their Mitigations

In Sect. 3.1, we mentioned that Tracking Codes are printed in a place outside the reach but visible to voters. Although printing Tracking Codes near voting machines seems the best solution, as voters have immediate access to them, there is a minor coercion attack using this method. This attack was presented in [4].

When voters have direct access to their Tracking Code and its contents before challenging the machine, it is possible to coerce voters. An attacker asks a voter to select a specific candidate. Additionally, if the resulting Tracking Code is even, for example, the voter should challenge it, and if it is odd, the voter should allow the machine to record it. Because the voter cannot predict if a Tracking Code will be even or odd, the voter is forced to follow the attacker's coercion. It is a minor attack because the attacker has to monitor voters until they cast a final vote. Otherwise, voters can cast any vote they want and keep challenging the machine until the attacker's conditions are met, discarding any challenged Tracking Codes that do not meet the requirements. Therefore, this attack does not scale well for elections with many voters.

However, a simple mitigation technique is to print Tracking Codes in an out-of-reach but visible place. Using this method, voters know that Tracking Codes were provided to them and at the same time cannot access their contents. The method also does not negatively impact vote secrecy, because Tracking Codes are considered public data and do not reveal candidate selection as long as the cryptographic function and hash are considered secure.

We prevent machine ballot stuffing attacks by checking the number of voters who turned up and the number of votes in the machine output when it shuts down. This check is currently carried out in the Brazilian elections.

Additionally, because voter identification is performed through biometry in Brazil, it is possible to detect ballot stuffing by poll workers. Although poll workers can manually authorize voters if the biometric check fails, poll workers have to submit their fingerprints in this case. Because it is a law that voters have to declare when they did not vote, if their names appear on their precinct voters' list, it is possible to see which fingerprint was used to authorize the vote.

4 Experimental Results

We evaluate the viability of our proposed scheme considering one of its use case scenarios, the Brazilian Election. For this, we performed our benchmark using hardware similar to the current Brazilian voting machine. The benchmark was performed in a machine running Ubuntu 22.04.1 LTS, with an Intel Atom J6412/X6413E at 1.50GHz, 2×8GB SODIMM DDR4 3200Mhz RAM, and a Crucial P2 500GB 3D NAND NVMe PCIe M.2 SSD harddrive.

The test code is available at https://github.com/ecominetti/E2Easy. For the commitments and ZKPs, we use the code provided at https://github.com/dfaranha/lattice-voting-ctrsa21 with adaptations.

Additionally, the goal of our scheme is to offer post-quantum security. For this, to compute the Tracking Code we select the SHA2-512 as the cryptographic hash function and we use the IETF RFC 4634 implementation. For the digital signature scheme, we use the Dilithium-2-AES reference implementation.

For this benchmark, we only considered the protocols that are executed in the voting machine: **onStart**, **onVoterActive**, **onChallenge** (always casting the vote), and **onFinish**. For each of these functionalities of our voting scheme, we performed 1000 independent executions using random keys to evaluate variations in execution time. For each execution, we considered an election with 6 contests and we varied the number of voters from 100 to 500, with a step of 100 voters. Thus, our system receives 600 to 3000 total votes, divided into 6 groups. This approach was chosen because each voting machine in Brazil serves at most 500 voters, so we used this ceiling as the worst-case scenario.

The results are shown in cycles of CPU and whenever the results are converted to time we consider the CPU frequency as 1.5GHz.

4.1 Benchmark Results

First, we present the results for the **onStart** function. This protocol is executed when the voting machine is turned on. As expected, this function is not dependent on how many voters the machine serves, and its time varies from approximately 3.33ms to 3.5ms. The results are presented in Fig. 2.

Next, we proceed with the **onVoterActive** function. This function creates the commitment and Tracking Code for a candidate selection. For this function, we present the cycles required to create one vote for a contest. Thus, this is the time voters have to wait for the machine to allow selection confirmation and go to the next contest. As illustrated in Fig. 3, the average time the machine requires to create one vote is around 6ms. We additionally observe that the worst-case performance for this protocol is 6.128ms.

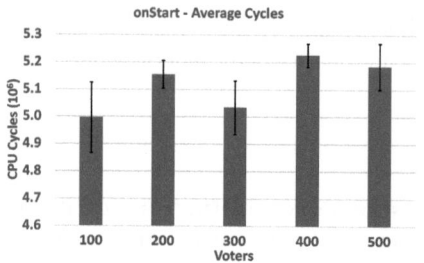

Fig. 2. Average CPU cycles (10^6) for protocol **onStart**.

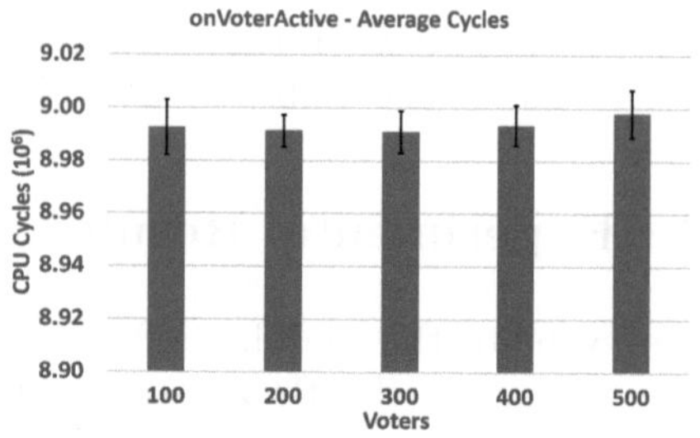

Fig. 3. Average CPU cycles (10^6) for protocol **onVoterActive**.

The protocol **onChallenge** in the benchmark is set to measure how many cycles the voting machine requires to record the vote data in its execution memory, insert the plaintext vote in the RDV file, and digitally sign the Tracking Codes. Because the **onChallenge** is executed once for the 6 contests each voter votes, we present the performance of this protocol for each voter. We observe that the performance of the **onChallenge** protocol for each voter does not vary significantly with how many voters a voting machine serves during its operation. On average, a voting machine requires around 1.167ms to record and digitally sign the 6 votes when a voter chooses to cast them (Fig. 4). We similarly analyzed the worst-case performance for this protocol, which is 7.133ms.

Finally, the protocol **onFinish** creates the zero-knowledge proof of correct shuffle, signs all the voting machine public output files, and deletes the voting tables for all contests. As expected, this is the most computationally intensive protocol of our scheme. It is possible to see that the computational cost of the protocol increases almost linearly with the number of voters the machine serves. For 100 voters, the **onFinish** requires 68.277 s, and for 500 voters, it requires 342.218 s. Fortunately, this protocol has to be executed only once and its execution is at the shutdown of the voting machine. Hence, its performance does not affect voters' experience with the system, and although 6 min is a long delay for a voter, it is negligible for the computation of an election outcome. The results of the protocol **onFinish** are presented in Fig. 5.

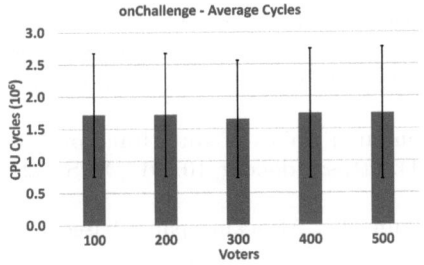
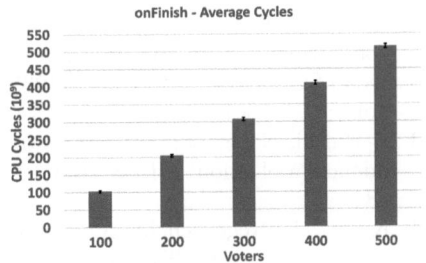

Fig. 4. Average CPU cycles (10^6) for protocol **onChallenge**.

Fig. 5. Average CPU cycles (10^9) for protocol **onFinish**.

4.2 Size of Output Files

Lastly, we present the output size for the public files created by our voting scheme. We note that to tally an election, only the RDV file is required. The other two files, voteOuput and ZKPOutput, are used for integrity verification.

As expected, the RDV file is the smallest, ranging from 17.0 to 27.0 kB. The voteOutput file, which has the Tracking Codes and commitments, ranges from 5.0 to 24.8 MB. Finally, the ZKPOutput file ranges from 29.5 to 147.5 MB.

5 Conclusion

In this work, we presented an in-person lattice-based end-to-end verifiable voting scheme. Our voting scheme achieves satisfactory results when it is executed on one of its use case scenarios, the Brazilian Election. In particular, vote and Tracking Code creation takes around 6ms, and casting the vote and signing the Tracking Code takes around 1.2ms. Both these results accomplish the goal of providing a fast response time (below 1 s) to voters. Although the Zero-Knowledge Proof generation takes around 6 min, this process is executed only once and it does not require or affect voters. The most challenging aspect of our system is the proof size, which can reach about 150 MB, and its transmission.

Acknowledgments. This work was in part supported by the Brazilian CNPq (Research productivity grant 307732/2023-1), and CAPES (Finance Code 001).

References

1. Aranha, D.F., Baum, C., Gjøsteen, K., Silde, T., Tunge, T.: Lattice-based proof of shuffle and applications to electronic voting. In: Paterson, K.G. (ed.) CT-RSA 2021. LNCS, vol. 12704, pp. 227–251. Springer, Cham (2021). https://doi.org/10.1007/978-3-030-75539-3_10

2. Baum, C., Damgård, I., Lyubashevsky, V., Oechsner, S., Peikert, C.: More efficient commitments from structured lattice assumptions. In: Catalano, D., De Prisco, R. (eds.) SCN 2018. LNCS, vol. 11035, pp. 368–385. Springer, Cham (2018). https://doi.org/10.1007/978-3-319-98113-0_20
3. Berlinski, N., et al.: The effects of unsubstantiated claims of voter fraud on confidence in elections. JEPS **10**(1), 1–16 (2021). https://doi.org/10.1017/XPS.2021.18
4. Kelsey, J., Regenscheid, A., Moran, T., Chaum, D.: Attacking paper-based E2E voting systems. In: Towards Trustworthy Elections. LNCS, vol. 6000, pp. 370–387. Springer (2010)
5. Langlois, A., Stehlé, D.: Worst-case to average-case reductions for module lattices. Des. Codes Cryptogr. **75**(3), 565–599 (2015)
6. Marky, K., Zollinger, M.L., Roenne, P., Ryan, P.Y.A., Grube, T., Kunze, K.: Investigating usability and user experience of individually verifiable internet voting schemes. ACM Trans. Comput. Hum. Interact. **28**(5), 1–36 (2021). https://doi.org/10.1145/3459604
7. Micciancio, D.: Introduction to lattices (2010). https://cseweb.ucsd.edu/classes/wi10/cse206a/lec1.pdf
8. Neff, C.A.: A verifiable secret shuffle and its application to e-voting. In: CCS, pp. 116–125. ACM (2001)
9. Nicas, J., Milhorance, F., Ionova, A.: How Bolsonaro built the myth of stolen elections in Brazil (2022). https://www.nytimes.com/interactive/2022/10/25/world/americas/brazil-bolsonaro-misinformation.html
10. Peikert, C.: A decade of lattice cryptography. Found. Trends Theor. Comput. Sci. **10**(4), 283–424 (2016)

Security Analysis of the Australian Capital Territory's eVACS 2020/2024 Paperless Direct Recording Electronic Voting System

Chris Culnane[1], Andrew Conway[1,2], Vanessa Teague[2(✉)], and Ty Wilson-Brown[1,2]

[1] Castellate Consulting Ltd., London, UK
chris@castellate.com, andrew@andrewconway.org, twb@riseup.net
[2] Thinking Cybersecurity Pty. Ltd., Melbourne, Australia
vanessa.teague@anu.edu.au

Abstract. Electronic voting is a *wicked problem*: voters must only vote once, voting must be auditable, and votes must be permanently preserved—but they must also be anonymous. We examine the source code of a paperless Direct Recording Electronic voting system and find serious integrity and privacy issues. Those issues were reported to the relevant authorities and patched, but the underlying design issues remain.

1 Introduction

Paperless Direct Recording Electronic (DRE) Voting machines are uncontroversial in most democracies because they are forbidden. Independent studies across at least 4 continents have shown serious problems with both the integrity and privacy of their votes [1,4,6,7], but it is the inherently unverifiable design— rather than specific vulnerabilities— that has lead many legislators and electoral authorities to conclude that they should not be used. One holdout is the Australian Capital Territory (ACT), which maintains (and has recently reimplemented) its paperless DRE system, known as eVACS.

This report describes the impact on eVACS of two cryptographic errors in the Ada Web Services Library. We identified these errors in the course of examining and testing the 2024 eVACS code, which was made publicly available in April 2024. We disclosed the problems to AdaCore and explained the implications to the relevant electoral authority, Elections ACT. After a 90-day disclosure period, the two errors were published as CVE-2024-41708 and CVE-2024-37015. Although both issues are quite general, and may have implications for other software systems, this paper concentrates on the implications for eVACS.

Ada Web Services released updated library functions and documentation, which Elections ACT have incorporated into an updated version of the eVACS software, released in September 2024. We will refer to this version as eVACS-Sep-24.[1] This is the version that (we assume) ran in the October 2024 election. We did not test this thoroughly—indeed, thorough testing is not possible because the published code does not include everything necessary to get the system running.

Most of this report deals with the insecure version released in April 2024, which we refer to as eVACS-Apr-24. Section 2 describes the implications of CVE-2024-41708, in which a non-cryptographic pseudorandom number generator (PRNG) was used for shuffling votes. We demonstrate reversing the shuffle and hence recovering the order in which the votes were cast, which allows for identifying individual voters' choices if information on voting order is known. Section 3 describes a different implication of the way the PRNG was used: the randomised column selection for candidates was also slightly biased.

Section 4 examines the TLS implementation, intended to maintain the integrity and confidentiality of votes as they were transmitted from the voting client to the server on the local network in a polling place. We found empirically that no TLS certificate validation was occurring in eVACS-Apr-24. The underlying issue in the Ada Web Services Library was published as SEC.AWS-0031.

Nothing about this report is intended to suggest that the system was adequate for public elections once these specific vulnerabilities were patched. eVACS suffers from fundamental design flaws, particularly the absence of any opportunity for voters and scrutineers to verify the results, that remain unresolved. It is a step forward that the code has been made available in advance of the election, and this openness allowed for the amelioration of the cryptographic errors described in this report. However, there is no way to verify that that code is properly installed on the voting devices or the voting server, nor that it functions properly on election day. The design does not produce evidence that the votes that determine the result are the accurately-recorded intentions of voters.

Related Work. Similarly insecure shuffling of votes has been observed in Brazilian electronic voting machines [4] and some US vote-scanning machines [5].

About eVACS and Voting in the Australian Capital Territory.

The ACT is an internal territory of Australia. It hosts the Australian federal government in Canberra, and (like the US District of Columbia) is not part of any state. Since 1989 the territory has also elected its own Legislative Assembly, responsible for local government within the territory. The ACT is divided into five electorates (Brindabella, Ginninderra, Kurrajong, Murrumbidgee and Yerrabi), each of which elects five members to the Assembly using the Single Transferable Vote (STV) algorithm.[2] For each electorate, candidates are arranged into political groups (parties) in columns—Fig. 1 shows a sample ballot.

---

[1] https://www.elections.act.gov.au/__data/assets/file/0009/2571975/eVACS-Source-Code-15-Sept-2024.zip.

[2] https://www.elections.act.gov.au/elections/our-electoral-system/education/fact-sheets/fact-sheet-hare-clark.

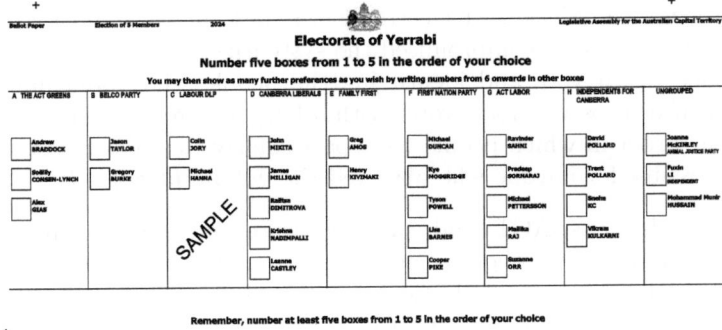

Fig. 1. Yerrabi Sample ballot, from Elections ACT https://www.elections.act.gov.au/ _data/assets/pdf_file/0010/2578789/Yerrabi-SAMPLE.pdf.

eVACS is a pollsite paperless DRE, implemented by a private company and used for ACT elections since 2001. In most years since then (2020 being a notable exception), much of the source code (though generally not enough to configure and run the system) has been openly available for public scrutiny. Voters who visit a polling place may choose between a paper ballot and eVACS. In 2020, more than 70% of the 273,143 voters opted for eVACS [2]; in 2024, the fraction had reduced to 55% of the total of 279,370 [3]. eVACS is usually accessed via a touchscreen, but is also available by audio to voters with disabilities, who can also access it remotely by telephone—this is relevant for Sect. 3. An unrelated system was briefly used for remote Internet voting, but is not considered here.

2 Linking Voting Order to Votes in eVACS 2020 and Apr-24

Main Finding (Privacy). The pseudorandom value (called pindex) attached to each published vote can be used to recover the voting order. An attacker who learns individual voting order can therefore learn some individuals' votes.

The ACT *Electoral Act 1992* requires e-voting systems to protect the secret ballot. Section 118A(2) states "The commissioner may approve a program under subsection (1) (a) only if the program will– ... (d) not allow a person to find out how a particular elector cast their vote."

In 2018 Ty Wilson-Brown identified a risk to the secret ballot for eVACS voters: because electronic votes were stored sequentially, information about voting *order* could be used to identify the individual's vote in the database.[3] The publicly-released vote data also maintained this order, listing each batch of votes in the order they were cast. Wilson-Brown listed several example attacks:

---

[3] https://github.com/teor2345/Elections2018/blob/master/ElectionsACTDisclosure.md.

- linking the vote database with electronic roll mark-off data (possible for insiders or an attacker who compromised the system);
- finding one's own vote and identifying the people who voted immediately before or after (possible for a voter with a long preference list);
- noting the order in which people vote, particularly the first or last groups of voters (possible for anyone who observed the polling place).

Although Elections ACT and their software provider did not publicly acknowledge the problem, they nevertheless attempted to ameliorate it. Public documents about the 2020 election stated that "the vote order within the votes database will be shuffled as part of the daily export process."[4] However, the source code for the 2020 version of eVACS was not openly available, so we could not independently assess the security of the new solution at the time.

When Elections ACT published eVACS-Apr-24, it was immediately clear that the shuffling algorithm was not secure—voting order was easily recovered, again allowing voters to be linked to their votes in the database or the published votes, using the attacks described in 2018. As described below, we successfully recovered voting order on almost all votes cast via eVACS in 2020.

The GNAT (GNU Ada library) random number generator (used by eVACS-Apr-24 and eVACS-20) was not suitable for this purpose, for three reasons:

Small Seed the random number generator was seeded using a 32 bit value, where approximately 3 of the bits were guaranteed to be zero;
Predictable Sequence the "Mersenne Twister" random number generator produced a sequence that could be predicted after seeing around 600 outputs;
Predictable Seed the seed was the clock time when the system started up.

2.1 How eVACS Shuffles Votes

Detailed vote data are published for each ACT election, including individual preferences and significant metadata about each ballot such as the location where it was cast, whether it was a paper or electronic vote, and a random-looking number called pindex. Figure 2a shows two votes cast in Gininderra in 2020.

Within each batch, votes are sorted by pindex. A document published on the Elections ACT website[5] stated that it is a requirement to "Ensure that an elector and their preferences cannot be matched through the use of timestamp data." This was addressed by "shuffling the vote," though the exact mechanism was not described. It seems to have been achieved by generating the pindex value, then sorting according to that value. The eVACS Voting_server.Random module used Ada's Numerics.Discrete_Random package to generate a value in the range from 0 to 999,999. eVACS used its implicit initialisation (Reset) option, which

---

[4] https://www.elections.act.gov.au/__data/assets/pdf_file/0009/1659798/Security-and-eVACS-v1.1.pdf.
[5] https://www.elections.act.gov.au/__data/assets/pdf_file/0009/1659798/Security-and-eVACS-v1.1.pdf.

with the GNAT library initialised the seed to a time-based value. The series of pseudorandom values were then generated via successive calls to get the next value. This process was not cryptographically secure— the initialisation value had only 32 bits, so all 2^{32} possible seeds could be enumerated easily.

2.2 Algorithm for Un-shuffling Ballots

The simple generation structure suggested a simple un-shuffling algorithm, which could be applied to each batch in turn: try each possible seed and, for each seed, generate as many random values as there are ballots in the batch, then check whether the *set* of generated values (in any order) matches the set of published pindex values for the batch. If the sequence of generated values perfectly matched a (reasonably long) set of published pindex values, we could be confident that seed was used to generate those values, and that the order of voting matched the generation order in the algorithm.[6]

When we tried this, we found that the generated values occasionally miss— that is, a sequence that otherwise completely matches a set of public values occasionally produces a value that is not present in the published list. We speculate that these correspond to test votes, or perhaps to voters who commenced a voting session but did not complete it, or to previously encountered pindex values produced a second time and declared ineligible. We therefore allowed a threshold MISS_THRESHOLD of size comparable to the number of ballots (in practice it is significantly smaller). eVACS votes are identifiable in the published vote data by their 000-terminated batch numbers—recovery obviously does not work for paper ballot batches.

Figure 2b describes an idealised version of the final algorithm, which simply takes a black-box approach to the PRNG and iterates through all possible seeds. Once one has the seed, one can replay the order in which the pindex values were found to order the votes by time of casting. We implemented two optimizations to this idealised algorithm: only seeds divisible by 8 need checking, due to details of GNAT library seeding, and also we can check on a smaller number of ballots and give up on a seed when the number of misses gets too large (just trying the most successful seeds after ten ballots works). The data is also not quite perfect: some files had combined groups due to using a new seed on each day for early voting or bunching together multiple polling places. This required looking for a run hitting a large number (about half), but not all, of the known pindex values. The resulting algorithm tests all seeds in a few minutes on a commodity laptop.

2.3 Results

We were able to recover voting order for all batches of votes cast via eVACS in the 2020 ACT election, except the 327 votes in the Central Scrutiny, which seem to include a mix of smaller collections of votes cast elsewhere. This represents 99.8% of the 153,180 votes cast electronically, and 54.7% of all votes cast.

---

[6] False-positives are possible but highly improbable, especially for long sequences.

	A	B	C	D	E	F
1	batch	pindex	pref	pcode	ccode	rcand
2	2022001	19778032	1	10	1	3
3	2022001	19778032	2	10	3	2
4	2022001	19778032	3	10	2	5
5	2022001	19778032	4	10	4	1
6	2022001	19778032	5	10	5	4
7	2022001	19778032	6	9	2	5
8	2022001	19778032	7	9	1	3
9	2022001	19778032	8	9	3	2
10	2022001	51129330	1	10	1	4
11	2022001	51129330	2	10	4	1
12	2022001	51129330	3	10	2	3
13	2022001	51129330	4	9	2	3
14	2022001	51129330	5	9	1	4
15	2022001	51129330	6	5	2	3
16	2022001	51129330	7	5	1	4
17	2022001	51129330	8	4	2	3
18	2022001	51129330	9	4	1	4
19	2022001	51129330	10	3	1	4

(a) Two published votes from Ginninderra 2020. Each vote has several different preferences, all with the same pindex

Algorithm 1 Seed recovery algorithm. U is the set of unseen **pindex** values.

for $seed = 0$ to $2^{32} - 1$ do
  Random_Id.Reset(seed)
  U ← { set of known **pindex** values}
  Misses ← 0
  while U is not empty and Misses¡MISS_THRESHOLD do
    r ← Random_Id.Random
    if $r \in U$ then
      U ← U-$\{r\}$.
    else
      Misses ← Misses+1
    end if
  end while
  if U is empty then
    return seed.
  end if
end for

(b) Seed recovery algorithm

Fig. 2. The pindex listed with each vote, and the algorithm for using them to recover the seed and hence the voting order.

For the eVACS votes cast on polling day, for each location (other than Central Scrutiny), one seed could generate all the pindex values. The number of missed pindex values tended to be very small. For eVACS votes cast through the early voting period (19 days), every location required 19 seeds to generate all pindex values, except Dickson and Kippax, which both required 20. This is consistent with the server being restarted daily, and once more in those two locations.

3 Bias in the Generation of Random Column Selections

Main Finding (Party Bias). The column initially selected by the UI is slightly biased, for audio voting at polling booths and by phone.

The ballot order of the columns given to political groups (parties) is randomised using a physical process (typically, drawing a ball from a container).

At the start of electronic voting, one of these columns is selected by eVACS at random. For audio voting, this column is read out first. Unfortunately, the eVACS-Apr-24 (and, we assume, eVACS-20) implementations were slightly biased towards the parties on the left side of the ballot. Audio voting is used for telephone voting, and for visually disabled people at polling booths. It is unclear whether this bias also happens for touch screen voting.

eVACS-Apr-24 takes a large pseudorandom number, converts it to a small number r between 0 and 255, then takes r modulo the number of parties p on the ballot. For example, if there were 10 parties ($p = 10$), then if r were 0, 10, 20,...,

250, the first party would be chosen; if r were 1, 11, 21,..., 251, the second party would be chosen. However r will never be 256, so the seventh and subsequent parties will each get one fewer opportunity to be chosen than the first six parties. The impact depends on the number of columns. For 2020, the biases were:[7]

Brindabella *(8 columns, divides evenly into 256)* no bias
Ginninderra *(11 columns)* 1.2% bias (3/256) towards 3 unelected parties
Kurrajong *(9 columns)* 1.6% bias (4/256) towards Grn, Lib, 2 unelected parties
Murrumbidgee *(9 columns)* 1.6% bias towards Grn and 3 unelected parties
Yerrabi *(9 columns)* 1.6% bias towards Grn, Lib, 2 unelected parties

This is a small source of bias, which impacts a small portion of voters. It is difficult to estimate its impact because margins in ACT elections are very small.

Correction. eVACS-Sep-24 has been corrected to produce unbiased initial columns, by calling the PRNG using the exact range of columns on the ballot paper.

4 TLS Security

Main Finding (Network Security). Polling place voting booth clients used a software library which did not check it was talking to the correct server. This meant network intruders could easily collect or modify votes.

eVACS conveys vote selections from voting clients to a server via the polling station's local area network (LAN). Earlier versions of eVACS used an unencrypted http connection, trusting that the network was perfectly secure, but from 2020 the TLS protocol was added to protect these transmissions.

When we examined the publicly-available code of eVACS-Apr-24 we noted that the TLS certificate was not correctly formed to allow hostname validation, specifically, it did not contain a hostname in any of the applicable attributes. This provided a strong indicator that the certificate validation was either not functioning correctly or was incorrectly configured.

eVACS-Apr-24 was using the default configuration for the Ada Web Server (AWS) Client component. We discovered that the default configuration did not correctly handle certificate validation. More specifically, validation errors returned from OpenSSL were silently ignored. This included expired certificates, untrusted certificates, and hostname validation errors.

Whilst there was an esoteric way of configuring the AWS Client to capture some validation errors, it required including a superfluous client TLS certificate to trigger the necessary certificate checking configuration option. Furthermore, there was no way of triggering hostname validation as the necessary functionality was not implemented within AWS. Thus eVACS-Apr-24 (and probably also eVACS-20) was operating without any TLS certificate validation. This implies that any attacker present on the network, if they could intercept the unencrypted TLS handshake, could spoof the server and collect, read and alter votes.

---

[7] Source: https://www.elections.act.gov.au/elections_and_voting/2020_legislative_assembly_election/list-of-candidates.

5 Conclusion, Implications and Recommendations

Disclosure and AdaCore Patches. We disclosed our discoveries to AdaCore, which confirmed the issues described in Sects. 2 and 4, then published CVEs and corresponding patches for both the PRNG (CVE-2024-41708) and the TLS certificate check (CVE-2024-37015). [8] These were incorporated into eVACS-Sep-24.

The Importance of Openly Available Election Source Code and the Inadequacy of Certification-Based Testing. Openly releasing the eVACS source code early in 2024 gave us time to discover and report these vulnerabilities, thus getting the relevant libraries patched before the 2024 election. Unfortunately, in 2020 there was a strict NDA, which prevented us from doing a similar analysis. This delayed the discovery of counting bugs until the open release of the full preference data, and the column bias, vote privacy problems and TLS security issues until 2024.

The internal testing and certification conducted by the electoral commission and its contractors in 2020 was clearly inadequate. Whilst the underlying TLS issue was in the Ada Web Server Client component, this does not explain why the lack of certificate validation was not picked up during testing or auditing. It was obvious to us that the certificate validation was not functioning correctly, or at least conventionally, because the contents of the TLS certificate lacked the necessary attributes. Test cases should have included invalid TLS certificates.

Privacy. Unfortunately, there is no straightforward fix to the privacy problem (Sect. 2). Although secure shuffling (which seems to be implemented now, though we have not checked thoroughly) may protect *future* elections, the votes exposed in the past cannot be un-exposed. It may also still be possible in future to derive timing information from the raw database log files, which may still be accessible to insiders. This is important as a large portion of the purpose of a secret ballot is keeping people's votes secret from the authorities. Insiders are also the people who have the easiest time linking individuals to vote order.

Verifiability. The system's design is also fundamentally insecure. Even ignoring the TLS issues described above, the system suffers from a fundamental design flaw: it is not designed to produce evidence that the published votes are the accurately recorded and properly processed intentions of the voters. Undetectable failures could be due to bugs, hardware errors, operator errors, deliberate manipulation, insiders or supply chain attacks. Voters must be able to verify a human-readable paper record of their vote, which must be included in a transparent counting process.

---

[8] AdaCore security updates are at https://www.adacore.com/cybersecuritycenter.

References

1. California top-to-bottom review of voting (2007). https://www.sos.ca.gov/elections/ovsta/frequently-requested-information/top-bottom-review
2. ACT Electoral Commission: Report on the ACT legislative assembly election 2020 (2021). https://www.elections.act.gov.au/__data/assets/pdf_file/0009/2472453/2020-Election-report.pdf
3. ACT Electoral Commission: Election statistics 2024 (2024). https://www.elections.act.gov.au/__data/assets/excel_doc/0006/2799717/Stats-Book-2024.XLSX
4. Aranha, D.F., Barbosa, P.Y., Cardoso, T.N., Araújo, C.L., Matias, P.: The return of software vulnerabilities in the Brazilian voting machine. Comput. Secur. **86**, 335–349 (2019)
5. Crimmins, B.L., Narayanan, D.Y., Springall, D., Halderman, J.A.: DVSorder: ballot randomization flaws threaten voter privacy. In: 33rd USENIX Security Symposium (USENIX Security 24), pp. 6525–6541 (2024). https://dvsorder.org/
6. Gongrijp, R., Hengeveld, W.J.: Studying the Nedap/Groenendaal ES3B voting computer (2007). https://www.usenix.org/legacy/event/evt07/tech/full_papers/gonggrijp/gonggrijp.pdf
7. Wolchok, S., et al.: Security analysis of India's electronic voting machines. In: Proceedings of the 17th ACM Conference on Computer and Communications Security, pp. 1–14 (2010)

opn.vote: A Publicly Verifiable Blockchain-Based eVoting System

Felix Maduakor[1(✉)], Thi Van Thao Doan[2], and Joerg Mitzlaff[1]

[1] openPetition gGmbH, Berlin, Germany
`maduakor.research@gmail.com, joerg@openpetition.net`
[2] UCLouvain, 1348 Louvain-la-Neuve, Belgium
`thi.doan@uclouvain.be`

Abstract. opn.vote is a publicly verifiable e-voting system that mitigates the single point of failure in traditional bulletin board architectures by moving critical processes to a public blockchain. Using Ethereum's Account Abstraction, it lets voters cast and re-cast ballots without wallets or cryptocurrency. The protocol combines Schnorr blind signatures with ElGamal encryption to ensure anonymity and auditability. opn.vote pilots in Germany's ABSTIMMUNG21 referendum in September 2025, aiming to shift 50% of votes online while reducing per-vote transaction costs from €2 to under €0.01. Compared to MACI, Ethereum's leading voting system, it achieves approximately two times lower on-chain costs.

Keywords: Electronic voting · Ethereum · Blind signatures · Blockchain · Public verifiability · Account Abstraction

1 Introduction

Verifiability in e-voting is often realized via a public bulletin board [1,5,12], typically maintained by a centralized server [4]. Such centralization introduces a single point of failure (e.g., DoS/data breaches) that can undermine security guarantees, like privacy, correctness, and resistance to voter suppression. Public blockchains offer a decentralized alternative that strengthens protocol integrity without relying on a trusted party. Yet, many blockchain-based voting systems overlook constraints like computational limits and transaction costs: they often require users to install wallets and manage cryptocurrency to pay fees [8], which impairs accessibility and deployability.

Contributions. We present opn.vote, a decentralized e-voting system designed to address these challenges. Unlike existing blockchain-based schemes, opn.vote eliminates the need for voters to install wallets or pay transaction fees by leveraging Ethereum's EIP-4337 (Account Abstraction) [3], thus removing usability barriers. Our voting system is inspired by FOO [7], where voters derive anonymous credentials via authority interaction and cast an anonymous vote. For privacy, we formalize and achieve *voter anonymity,* based on indistinguishability, against colluding authorities (assuming an anonymous channel), using Schnorr blind signatures. Post-tally, the decryption key is published, enabling public verification and ensuring both individual and universal verifiability. Unlike FOO, opn.vote supports vote recasting without re-registration. Furthermore, opn.vote reduces on-chain costs by $\approx 51\%$ compared to MACI [9], making it the selected voting system for Germany's ABSTIMMUNG21 referendum in September 2025.

2 System Design

In opn.vote, the public bulletin board is realized through the Ethereum blockchain (see Fig. 1). Each voter V holds a key pair (sk_V, vk_V), where sk_V is a randomly generated signing key that remains private to V, and vk_V is the verification key. Each ballot submission is represented as an ERC-4337 UserOperation (UserOp), which is digitally signed using sk_V. vk_V is unique to each voter and also serves as their smart wallet address. Together, (sk_V, vk_V) form the voter's smart wallet.

Election Setup. The Election Coordinator CO generates an ElGamal key pair (ek, dk) [6] and publishes the encryption key ek within the Voting Smart Contract VSC. The Registrar R creates a signing key pair (sk_R, vk_R) and publishes vk_R in the VSC. Election metadata is stored in the VSC and on IPFS [2].

Registration Phase. After eligibility verification by CO, each V interacts with R to obtain a valid signature cred, which is R's signature on vk_V. In opn.vote, this process employs the Schnorr blind signature scheme [10,11]. The pair $(vk_V, cred)$ forms the voter's anonymous credential. R publishes all successful registrations, and CO publishes all successful eligibility checks within the VSC.

Voting Phase. V creates a ballot $b = (cred, c)$, where c is the encryption of their vote v using CO's ek. Since vk_V matches V's wallet address, VSC extracts it directly from the transaction, eliminating the need for inclusion in the ballot. b is signed by sk_V and sent as a UserOp to the decentralized Bundler Network BN. Nodes in BN validate the UserOp against CO's sponsorship rules and submit an on-chain transaction invoking the VSC's vote casting function. Transaction fees are sponsored by the CO through a Sponsor Smart Contract. To recast a vote, V generates a new ballot $b' = (\varnothing, c')$, where $\varnothing$ is an empty credential. After the initial ballot, authentication uses the public key vk_V, removing the need for cred in recasts. Only the most recent vote cast by each voter is counted.

Tallying Phase. After the election deadline, everyone can check whether the ballot is signed properly using vk_V and whether cred is a valid credential under vk_R. Invalid ballots are discarded. CO then publishes the decryption key dk and the election results. Voters can verify that their ballot was correctly recorded and counted, and confirm the election results by running the tally process locally.

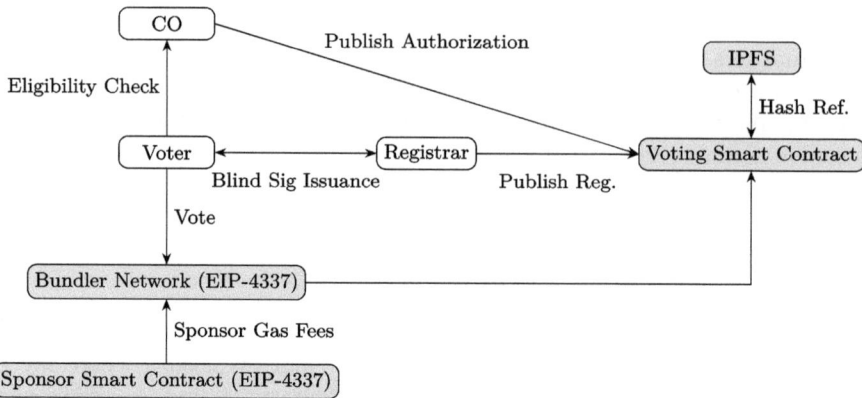

Fig. 1. High-level architecture of opn.vote, highlighting decentralized components.

References

1. Adida, B.: Helios: web-based open-audit voting. In: Proceedings of the 17th USENIX Security Symposium, pp. 335–348. USENIX Association (2008)
2. Benet, J.: IPFS-content addressed, versioned, p2p file system. arXiv preprint arXiv:1407.3561 (2014)
3. Buterin, V., et al.: ERC-4337: Account abstraction using alt mempool. Technical report, Ethereum Improvement Proposals (2021)
4. Cortier, V., Lallemand, J., Warinschi, B.: Fifty shades of ballot privacy: privacy against a malicious board. In: 2020 IEEE 33rd Computer Security Foundations Symposium (CSF), pp. 17–32. IEEE (2020)
5. Culnane, C., Ryan, P.Y.A., Schneider, S.A., Teague, V.: vvote: A verifiable voting system. ACM Trans. Inf. Syst. Secur. **18**(1), 3:1–3:30 (2015)
6. ElGamal, T.: A public key cryptosystem and a signature scheme based on discrete logarithms. IEEE Trans. Inf. Theory **31**(4), 469–472 (1985)
7. Fujioka, A., Okamoto, T., Ohta, K.: A practical secret voting scheme for large scale elections. In: Seberry, J., Zheng, Y. (eds.) AUSCRYPT 1992. LNCS, vol. 718, pp. 244–251. Springer, Heidelberg (1993). https://doi.org/10.1007/3-540-57220-1_66
8. Kharman, A.M., Smyth, B.: Perils of current dao governance. arXiv preprint arXiv:2406.08605 (2024)
9. MACI: Maci github page (2022). https://github.com/privacy-scaling-explorations/maci. Accessed 17 Nov 2023
10. Pointcheval, D., Stern, J.: Provably secure blind signature schemes. In: Kim, K., Matsumoto, T. (eds.) ASIACRYPT 1996. LNCS, vol. 1163, pp. 252–265. Springer, Heidelberg (1996). https://doi.org/10.1007/BFb0034852
11. Pointcheval, D., Stern, J.: Security arguments for digital signatures and blind signatures. J. Cryptol. **13**, 361–396 (2000)
12. Ryan, P.Y.A., Rønne, P.B., Iovino, V.: Selene: voting with transparent verifiability and coercion-mitigation. In: Clark, J., Meiklejohn, S., Ryan, P.Y.A., Wallach, D., Brenner, M., Rohloff, K. (eds.) FC 2016. LNCS, vol. 9604, pp. 176–192. Springer, Heidelberg (2016). https://doi.org/10.1007/978-3-662-53357-4_12

Enhancing Helios for Elections at Qatar University

Jurlind Budurushi[1(✉)], Khalid Abdallah[2], Farhan Al Sadi[2], Hosam Zarouk[2], Abdelwahab Almasri[2], and Armstrong Nhlabatsi[2]

[1] Baden-Württemberg Cooperative State University Karlsruhe, Karlsruhe, Germany
jurlind.budurushi@dhbw-karlsruhe.de
[2] Qatar University, Doha, Qatar

Abstract. At Qatar University, campus elections are held regularly, including those for the Qatar University Student Representative Board (QUSRB). These elections enable students to elect representatives from each college to serve as their voice in university decision-making. Currently, voting takes place via the myBanner Self-Service System. This platform lacks robust security measures and does not offer verifiability, raising concerns about the integrity and transparency of the process. Helios, an end-to-end verifiable voting system widely studied and used in academic settings, presents a promising alternative. However, its current implementation suffers from several security and usability limitations. Drawing on previous literature, this article identifies key shortcomings, such as weak voter authentication and compromised privacy due to ballot tracker exposure, and proposes concrete enhancements. With these improvements, Helios can serve as a secure and feasible alternative to the voting system currently used in the QUSRB elections.

Keywords: Internet voting · Biometric authentication · Verifiability

1 Background on Helios and Its Limitations

Helios [1] is an open-source, end-to-end verifiable internet voting system. It has been used in several real-world elections, including the UC Louvain presidential election [2], the ACM general elections [16], and the IACR elections, which have relied on Helios since 2010[1]. Its transparency, auditability, and ease of deployment have supported its adoption in academic and organizational settings.

Despite its strengths and widespread use, previous research has highlighted several security and usability issues in the current Helios implementation. For example, from a security perspective, its dependency on a single factor for voter authentication makes it vulnerable to impersonation attacks [4]. Moreover, displaying voters' identities alongside their respective ballot trackers on the bulletin board violates voter participation privacy [9]. Concerning usability, a significant issue lies in the complexity of the vote verification process [8], particularly challenging for non-technical voters dealing with large encrypted datasets [13].

---

[1] https://www.iacr.org/elections/.

2 Towards a More Secure and Usable Helios Implementation

This section presents an overview of the proposed improvements[2] to Helios, focusing on enhancing its security and usability.

Building on the concept of *verifiable eligibility* introduced in [6,15], we improve the voter registration and authentication process by integrating biometric authentication as a second factor. Although previous approaches enforce eligibility through mechanisms such as ballot signing or token-based encryption, our enhancement focuses on binding voter identity to the voting process in a verifiable manner using biometrics. To preserve voter privacy, the biometric authentication mechanism is implemented using secret sharing techniques [12], ensuring that biometric data is never stored or exposed in its entirety.

Similarly to the approaches proposed in [3,9], our enhancement achieves *private eligibility verifiability* by disassociating voter identities from their ballots (i.e., ballot trackers). Specifically, voter names are removed from the public bulletin board, thereby protecting voter privacy while mitigating the risks of ballot copying [14] and clash attacks [10]. However, unlike the solutions in [3,9], our method also addresses the challenge of overcrowding the bulletin board. Furthermore, we extend the notion of *strong receipt-freeness* as introduced in [5] by adopting *practical coercion-resistance*. This is achieved by allowing voters to update their vote under the assumption that they are free from coercion at some point during the election period.

Finally, based on the proposals by Karayumak et al. [7] and Neumann et al. [13], and the findings of Marky et al. [11], we improve the process of *individual verifiability* by introducing *HelioScan*, a mobile application that encodes ballot trackers as QR codes. During the voting phase, voters can scan and store the QR code of their ballot tracker at each step, allowing them to verify its integrity throughout the process. Any tampering before the final vote casting can be detected, as alterations would result in a mismatch with the stored tracker. In addition, *HelioScan* allows voters to automatically verify *stored-as-cast* by confirming the presence of their ballot tracker on the election bulletin board. By simplifying the verification steps and reducing technical barriers, *HelioScan* improves both the transparency and usability of the voting process.

References

1. Adida, B.: Helios: web-based open-audit voting. In: USENIX Security Symposium, vol. 17, pp. 335–348 (2008)
2. Adida, B., De Marneffe, O., Pereira, O., Quisquater, J.J., et al.: Electing a university president using open-audit voting: analysis of real-world use of Helios. EVT/WOTE **9**(10), 10 (2009)

---

[2] Our improvements can be accessed on GitHub: https://github.com/Jurlind/Enhanced_Helios_QatarUniversity.

3. Bernhard, D., Kulyk, O., Volkamer, M.: Security Proofs for Participation Privacy and Stronger Verifiability for Helios. CRISP-Center for Research in Security and Privacy (2016)
4. Bonneau, J., Herley, C., Oorschot, P.C.v., Stajano, F.: The quest to replace passwords: a framework for comparative evaluation of web authentication schemes. In: 2012 IEEE Symposium on Security and Privacy, pp. 553–567 (2012). https://doi.org/10.1109/SP.2012.44
5. Cortier, V., Fuchsbauer, G., Galindo, D.: BeleniosRF: a strongly receipt-free electronic voting scheme. IACR Cryptol. ePrint Arch. **2015**, 629 (2015)
6. Cortier, V., Galindo, D., Glondu, S., Izabachène, M.: Election verifiability for Helios under weaker trust assumptions. In: Kutyłowski, M., Vaidya, J. (eds.) ESORICS 2014. LNCS, vol. 8713, pp. 327–344. Springer, Cham (2014). https://doi.org/10.1007/978-3-319-11212-1_19
7. Karayumak, F., Kauer, M., Olembo, M.M., Volk, T., Volkamer, M.: User study of the improved Helios voting system interfaces. In: 2011 1st Workshop on Socio-Technical Aspects in Security and Trust (STAST), pp. 37–44. IEEE (2011)
8. Kulyk, O., Henzel, J., Renaud, K., Volkamer, M.: Comparing "challenge-based" and "code-based" internet voting verification implementations. In: Lamas, D., Loizides, F., Nacke, L., Petrie, H., Winckler, M., Zaphiris, P. (eds.) Human-Computer Interaction - INTERACT 2019, pp. 519–538. Springer, Cham (2019)
9. Kulyk, O., Teague, V., Volkamer, M.: Extending Helios towards private eligibility verifiability. In: E-Voting and Identity: 5th International Conference, VoteID 2015, Bern, Switzerland, September 2–4, 2015, Proceedings 5, pp. 57–73. Springer (2015)
10. Kusters, R., Truderung, T., Vogt, A.: Clash attacks on the verifiability of e-voting systems. In: 2012 IEEE Symposium on Security and Privacy, pp. 395–409. IEEE (2012)
11. Marky, K., Kulyk, O., Renaud, K., Volkamer, M.: What did I really vote for? On the usability of verifiable e-voting schemes. In: Proceedings of the 2018 CHI Conference on Human Factors in Computing Systems, pp. 1–13. CHI '18, Association for Computing Machinery, New York, NY, USA (2018). https://doi.org/10.1145/3173574.3173750
12. Naor, M., Shamir, A.: Visual cryptography. In: Advances in Cryptology—EUROCRYPT'94: Workshop on the Theory and Application of Cryptographic Techniques Perugia, Italy, May 9–12, 1994 Proceedings 13, pp. 1–12. Springer (1995)
13. Neumann, S., Olembo, M.M., Renaud, K., Volkamer, M.: Helios verification: to alleviate, or to nominate: is that the question, or shall we have both? In: Kő, A., Francesconi, E. (eds.) EGOVIS 2014. LNCS, vol. 8650, pp. 246–260. Springer, Cham (2014). https://doi.org/10.1007/978-3-319-10178-1_20
14. Smyth, B., Bernhard, D.: Ballot secrecy and ballot independence coincide. In: Crampton, J., Jajodia, S., Mayes, K. (eds.) ESORICS 2013. LNCS, vol. 8134, pp. 463–480. Springer, Heidelberg (2013). https://doi.org/10.1007/978-3-642-40203-6_26
15. Srinivasan, S., Culnane, C., Heather, J., Schneider, S., Xia, Z.: Countering ballot stuffing and incorporating eligibility verifiability in Helios. In: Au, M.H., Carminati, B., Kuo, C.-C.J. (eds.) NSS 2014. LNCS, vol. 8792, pp. 335–348. Springer, Cham (2014). https://doi.org/10.1007/978-3-319-11698-3_26
16. Staff, C.: ACM's 2014 general election: please take this opportunity to vote. Commun. ACM **57**(5), 9–17 (2014). https://doi.org/10.1145/2597769

Author Index

A
Ababneh, Mohammed II-69
Abdallah, Khalid II-309
Al Sadi, Farhan II-309
Al-Chami, Joseph II-196
Almasri, Abdelwahab II-309
Angel, James II-50
Aranha, Diego F. II-281
Araújo, Roberto II-281

B
Bachu, Brad I-78, I-111
Bar-On, Yogev I-137
Bartoletti, Massimo I-147
Ben Aoun, Hichem I-32
Blom, Michelle II-226, II-241
Broby, Daniel II-212
Brunetta, Carlo I-263
Budurushi, Jurlind II-309

C
Clark, Jeremy II-196
Cominetti, Eduardo L. II-281
Conway, Andrew II-297
Culnane, Chris II-297

D
Derka, Martin I-63
Diaconescu, Denisa II-162
Doan, Thi Van Thao II-306
Droll, Jan I-32

E
Ek, Alexander II-226, II-241

F
Friolo, Daniele II-100

G
Gansäuer, Robin I-32
Giustolisi, Rosario II-266
Gogol, Krzysztof M. I-94

Gogol, Krzysztof I-17
Goodell, Geoffrey II-100
Gorzny, Jan I-63
Grötschla, Florian I-1

H
Hartenstein, Hannes I-32
Heimbach, Lioba I-1
Hioki, Leona II-162
Huang, Maozhou II-1

I
Inés Silva, Maria I-17

K
Kemper, Phillip I-63
Kolachala, Kartick II-69
Kopyciok, Yannik I-200
Kraner, Benjamin II-50
Kuehlkamp, Andrey II-138

L
Larangeira, Mario II-1
Lee, Suhyeon I-164
Lenzini, Gabriele II-266
Liao, Gordon I-78
Liu, Dingyue I-78
Livshits, Benjamin I-17, I-47, I-94, I-127

M
Maduakor, Felix II-306
Matias, Paulo II-281
Matsuo, Shin'ichiro II-50
Messias, Johnnatan I-17, I-47
Mitzlaff, Joerg II-306
Moallemi, Ciamac C. I-111
Moallemi, Ciamac I-78

N
Nabi, Mahmudun I-216
Nabrzyski, Jarek II-138
Nakib, Hazem Danny II-100

Ndiaye, Abdoulaye I-245
Nhlabatsi, Armstrong II-309

P

Paruchuri, Rohil II-50
Pekel, Umut II-29
Priyadarshini, Emily I-147

R

Rakeei, Mohammadamin II-266
Richner, Severin I-1
Rønne, Peter B. II-256
Rybakken, Erik II-162

S

Safavi-Naini, Reihaneh I-216
Sala, Massimiliano I-263
Schmid, Stefan I-200
Schneider, Manvir I-94
Silva, Maria Inês I-47, I-127
Silváši, František II-162
Simplicio, Marcos A. II-281
Spoto, Fausto I-180
Stark, Philip B. II-241
Stuckey, Peter J. II-226, II-241
Su, Xiangyu II-1
Sugino, Takaya II-50
Sutherland, Julian II-162

T

Tanaka, Keisuke II-1
Teague, Vanessa J. II-241
Teague, Vanessa II-226, II-297
Tessone, Claudio J. I-94
Toliver, D. R. II-100

V

Valencia Jr., Eduardo T. II-212
Vaughan, Owen II-84
Victor, Friedhelm I-200
Vishwanathan, Roopa II-69
Vukcevic, Damjan II-226, II-241

W

Wan, Xin I-78, I-111
Wattenhofer, Roger I-1
Wilson-Brown, Ty II-297

X

Xu, Jiayu II-122

Y

Yaksetig, Mario II-122, II-162
Yayla, Oğuz II-29
You, Shengwei II-138

Z

Zarouk, Hosam II-309
Zhu, Brian I-78

MIX
Papier aus verantwortungsvollen Quellen
Paper from responsible sources
FSC® C105338

If you have any concerns about our products,
you can contact us on
ProductSafety@springernature.com

In case Publisher is established outside the EU,
the EU authorized representative is:
**Springer Nature Customer Service Center GmbH
Europaplatz 3, 69115 Heidelberg, Germany**

Printed by Libri Plureos GmbH
in Hamburg, Germany